The History of Poland

THE

CABINET CYCLOPÆDIA.

LONDON :
Printed by A. SPOTTISWOODE,
New-Street-Square.

THE

CABINET CYCLOPÆDIA.

CONDUCTED BY THE

REV. DIONYSIUS LARDNER, LL.D. F.R.S. L.&E.

M.R.I.A. F.R.A.S. F.L.S. F.Z.S. Hon. F.C.P.S. &c. &c.

ASSISTED BY

EMINENT LITERARY AND SCIENTIFIC MEN.

𝔥𝔦𝔰𝔱𝔬𝔯𝔶.

POLAND.

A NEW EDITION.

LONDON:

PRINTED FOR

LONGMAN, ORME, BROWN, GREEN, & LONGMANS,

PATERNOSTER-ROW;

AND JOHN TAYLOR,

UPPER GOWER STREET.

1840.

THE
HISTORY OF POLAND.

BY

S. A. DUNHAM, LL.D. &c.

H. Corbould del.   E. Finden sculp.

Murder of St. Stanislas, p. 41.

London.
PRINTED FOR LONGMAN, ORME, BROWN & LONGMANS, PATERNOSTER ROW
AND JOHN TAYLOR, UPPER GOWER STREET.

PREFACE.

In submitting the following compendium to his readers, the author hopes, in justice both to them and himself, that he may not be charged with presumption for saying that it is no *compilation*. Its parts have been carefully derived from about sixty original sources — Polish, Bohemian, Hungarian, German, French, &c., of which some are very scarce in this country. His honesty in this respect must be apparent to any one who will be at the trouble of verifying his references.

A consideration no less important is, whether he has shown the same honesty in relating facts as in ascending to their sources: in other words, is he impartial?

To that numerous, to that all indeed but universal, class of politicians, who at present praise every thing that is Polish, and decry every thing that is Muscovite, — who with one voice predict the inevitable if not speedy triumph of the Poles, — his wish to do justice to the Russians may be construed into approbation of their cause. He protests against such an interpretation of his feelings. If he has a prejudice for either

party it is for the weaker. While he expresses
his impression that, unless some extraordinary
circumstance intervene, the Poles, almost super-
human as is their valour, must eventually fall,'
he deeply and sincerely laments the probability
of that catastrophe. He cannot, however, shut
his eyes to the force of facts: he cannot be made
to believe that the contest is to be conducted on
equal terms: he cannot but see that great phy-
sical superiority and immense resources are on
the side of Russia: he cannot therefore join in
the general anticipation as to the result. Popular
opinion is as contagious as it is veering: though
inconstant as the wind, its empire is not the less
secure. Whoever recollects how its current
ran during the late war between Russia and
Turkey, — now in favour of the former, now as
strongly directed towards the latter, and how it
reverted to its original channel, will pardon
those who hesitate to sail with it.

But, whether victors or vanquished, the Poles
must have the respect of humanity. During the
present struggle they have exhibited, not only a
heroism far surpassing any thing to be found in
modern history, but a forbearance and a liberality even, towards their prisoners, which covers
them with a glory immeasurably above it. Though
their cause has been sullied by some excesses,
they have, at length, abandoned their ferocious

habit of refusing quarter; and towards " disarmed guests," now so numerous, in Warsaw
especially, they use, not only all the courtesy of
the most polished, but all the generosity of the
most warm-hearted nation. Not less to be ad-
mired is their unbending constancy in resisting
their giant antagonist, — a constancy worthy the
best age of Rome. In this there is something
infinitely more valuable than the brute courage
which defies, or the mechanical discipline which
coolly faces, danger: there is all the moral elevation of a great and holy purpose, acting alike
on the understandings and hearts of the most
high-minded people in Europe. The present
struggle, indeed, exhibits throughout a moral
picture of greatness and interest, perhaps unparalleled in the historical annals of Europe.

Nor, while advocating the Polish cause — the
cause of justice, of humanity, and of policy —
must the author withhold the meed of praise to
some acts of the Russian emperor, who in the
strictest manner enjoined his troops, " not merely
to refrain from the slightest wanton ravage, but
to show themselves the protectors, the friends,
of the peasantry."

There is no evidence to prove that these orders
have been in the main disobeyed, whatever
isolated instances of their infraction — possibly

exaggerated by a partial press — have been adduced. However strange the assertion may sound
in most English ears, nothing is more certain than
that Europe does not contain a sovereign more
averse to oppression or cruelty than the tsar
Nicholas, — not one more disposed to better the
condition of all his people. Throughout his connection with Poland (and the case is equally true
of his predecessor) he has omitted no opportunity
of confirming the prosperity of the country, —
often by considerable grants from his treasury
both to national and individual objects, — nor can
he be reproached with having exhibited more
favour to his hereditary than to his newly-ac-
quired subjects. Of the just complaints brought
against his government by the Poles, he has since
said, — and there is no reason to doubt his sincerity
— that he was ignorant. Nor will this circumstance surprise any one acquainted with the extreme difficulty of complaints ever meeting the
imperial notice. They have to pass through such
an army of underlings scattered over so immense
a line of communication, — all suspicious of their
misdeeds being exposed, and consequently vigilant to prevent the exposure — that their arrival
at their destination is little less than miraculous.
The Poles, however, had channels enough for
bringing their grievances before the tsar. Though

memorials or petitions would probably have failed,
any Polish noble might have proceeded to St.
Petersburgh, and might have obtained an audience
of his sovereign. That Nicholas would have redressed the wrongs of his people, and that the
necessity of appealing to arms would have been
averted, is firmly believed by those best acquainted with his sentiments and character.
Among those who think they have grounds for
this opinion, is the writer of the present volume.

Conjecture, however, as to what might have
been is now vain: the two parties hold each
other in the deadly grasp, and neither can draw
back with policy. If the emperor were now to
recognise the independence of his revolted subjects, the step would be attributed, not to magnanimity, but to weakness: if the Poles submitted without further struggle, that submission
might only invite to renewed oppression. They
are fighting for a mighty stake—for independence,
or for utter, if not helpless, degradation : the alternative is fearful. But alas! could even the acquisition of independence atone for the horrors sustained by the Poles during the present contest —
for the total exhaustion which those horrors must
leave behind? However valuable liberal institutions be, we may reasonably doubt whether
they are not too dearly purchased by the sacri-

fices sometimes made for them ; whether plenty,
under the most absolute of governments, be not
preferable to want with the utmost limit of
human liberty.   The peasant of Spain or of the
Tyrol does not appear less happy that he lives
under an arbitrary ruler ; neither certainly would
exchange conditions with the English labourer.

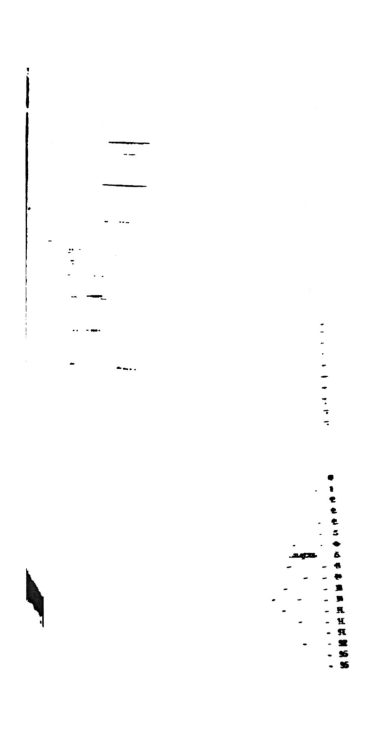

A. D.		Page
	BOLESLAS I.	20
	His Character	20
1001.	Poland made a Kingdom	20
1002—1018.	Wars of Boleslas : — 1. With Bohemia and the Empire	21
1008—1019.	2. With Muscovy	22
	Labours for the Good of his People	24
1025.	His Death	24
	MIECISLAS II.	25
1026—1034.	His inglorious Wars	25
	Death	27
1034—1041.	*Interregnum*	28
1041.	CASIMIR I.	32
	His Prudence	32
1042, 1043.	War with Masos	33
1043—1058.	Wise Government	33
	Death	34
1058.	BOLESLAS II.	34
1062—1076.	Wars with the Bohemians, Hungarians, and Muscovites	35
1076.	His Dissipation at Kiow	38
	Extraordinary Relation	39
1077—1079.	His Excesses at Home	41
	Murder of St. Stanislas	42
	Punishment, Death, and Character of Boleslas	43
1082.	ULADISLAS I.	44
	Not recognised as King	44
1083—1086.	Birth of Boleslas	45
1089.	Recall and Death of his Nephew	45
1090—1096.	His Wars	45
	His bastard Son rebels	48
1098.	Conduct of both Sons	49
1102.	His Death and Character	50
	BOLESLAS III.	51
1102—1106.	Perversity of Sbigniew	51
1107.	Intrepidity of Boleslas	52
1109.	Siege of Glogaw	54
1116.	Sbigniew assassinated	56
1116—1129.	Remorse of Boleslas	56
1135—1138.	Boleslas is defeated	57
1139.	His Death	58

CHAP. II.

1139.	Poland divided into Governments	59
1140.	ULADISLAS II.	60
1141—1146.	Invades the Rights of his Brothers	60
	Is resisted and expelled	61
	BOLESLAS IV.	62
1149—1163.	His Transactions with the Empire	62
1164—1173.	His Disasters and Death	63

A. D.		Page
1174.	MIECISLAS III.	64
1177.	His Vices and Expulsion	65
1178.	CASIMIR THE JUST	65
1180.	Reforms Abuses	65
1181—1191.	Restlessness of Miecislas	66
	Wars of Casimir	67
1194.	His Death and Character	68
	LESKO THE WHITE	68
1200.	Opposed by Miecislas, who obtains the Government	69
1202.	Death of Miecislas	69
	ULADISLAS III.	69
1205.	Resigns	70
1206.	LESKO THE WHITE restored	70
1227.	Is assassinated	72
	Corruption of Morals at this Period	72
1228.	BOLESLAS V.	72
	The Teutonic Knights	73
1233.	Settled in Poland	74
1233—1240.	Disasters of the Duchy	74
1241.	Invasion of the Tatars	75
	Unworthy Conduct of Boleslas	75
1247—1260.	New Disasters	76
1264.	The Jadvingi subdued	76
1279.	Death and Character of Boleslas	77
	LESKO THE BLACK	78
1279—1289.	Internal Troubles	78
	Death of Lesko	79
1289—1295.	Horrid Anarchy	79

CHAP. III.

1295.	PRZEMISLAS, King of Poland	80
	His wise Government	81
1296.	His Murder	82
	Troubles	82
1300.	WENCESLAS	82
	Is unpopular, and abandons Poland	83
1306.	ULADISLAS IV. *the Short*	84
1307—1331.	His Transactions and Wars with the Teutonic Knights	85
1322.	Loss of Silesia	88
1325.	Alliance with the Lithuanians	89
1333.	Death and Character	90
	The Dulcean Heretics	90
	CASIMIR III. or *the Great*	91
	Makes Peace with the Knights	91
	Reforms Abuses	91
1347.	Mends the Laws. Code of Wisliza	92
	Encourages Industry and the Arts	95
	Chooses Lewis of Hungary to succeed him	95

A. D.		Page
1349.	His Success in War	96
1356.	His Vices	97
1370.	Death and Character	98
	The Flagellants	98
	Lewis	99
	Is unpopular	100
1376.	Abandons Poland	100
1382.	Death and Character	101
	Interregnum	102
1383.	Troubles	102
1384.	Hedwig	103
1385.	Her Suitors, and romantic Attachment to William Duke of Austria	103
1386.	Consents to marry Jagello	104
	Uladislas V. (Jagello)	105
1387.	Converts the Lithuanians	105
1387, &c.	His Transactions with them	106
1404, &c.	With the Teutonic Knights	108
	His Generosity towards the Emperor Sigismund	109
	His Jealousy of his Wives	110
1430.	His Son declared his Successor	111
1434.	His Death and Character	112
	Uladislas VI.	112
1435, &c.	Troubles during his Minority	112
1439.	He is called to the Throne of Hungary	113
1443.	His Wars with the Turks	114
1444.	Peace made, and shamefully broken by the Christians	114
	Indignation of the Sultan Amurath	115
	Defeat and Death of Uladislas	116
1445.	Casimir IV.	117
1447, &c.	His Repugnance to take the Oaths	117
1454, &c.	His Transactions with the Knights	118
1459, &c.	With the Lithuanians	119
1479, &c.	With the Russians and Tatars	119
1471, &c.	With the Bohemians and Hungarians	120
	Progress of Aristocracy under Casimir IV. Origin of Aristocratical Representation	121
1492.	Death and Character of Casimir	123
	John I. (Albert)	124
1496.	He penetrates into Wallachia	125
1498.	Invasion of the Turks, &c.	125
1499.	Of the Muscovites	126
1500.	Perfidy as well as Weakness of John Albert	126
1501.	His Death and Character	127
	Selfishness of the Aristocracy	127
	Alexander	127
1502, &c.	His Baseness to Achmet. Noble Behaviour of that Prince	128
1506.	Defeat of the Tatars	129
	Death of Alexander, and Character of his Reign	129

A. D.		Page
1506.	SIGISMUND I.	- 130
1508, &c.	His Transactions with Muscovy	- 130
1509, &c.	With the Wallachians	- 132
1510, &c.	With the Knights	- 132
1525.	Abolition of the Teutonic Order. Origin of the Greatness	
	of the House of Brandenburg	- 134
	Moderation (and Embarrassments) of Sigismund	- 135
	Yet he persecutes the Lutherans	- 136
1548.	His Death and Character	- 136
	SIGISMUND II. (Augustus)	- 137
1549.	Opposition to his clandestine Marriage	- 138
1552.	Religious Dissensions. Progress of the Reformation	- 139
	Appeal of a married Priest against the Infliction of the	
	Ecclesiastical Penance	- 141
1553, &c.	Strange Policy of the King	- 142
1556, &c.	His Transactions with Livonia and the Russians	- 144
	With Lithuania	- 146
1572.	His Death and Character	- 146

BOOK II.

CHAP. I.

1572.	*Interregnum*	- 148
	Preliminary Proceedings	- 148
	Opening of the Diet of Election	- 150
	Candidates	- 150
1573.	Election of Henry de Valois	- 151
	Pacta Conventa, afterwards called "Articles of Henry"	152
1574.	HENRY	- 154
	His Unpopularity	- 154
	Incident	- 155
	His inglorious Flight	- 156
1575.	STEPHEN	- 158
1576.	Troubles consequent on his Election	- 158
1577, &c.	His Wars with Muscovy	- 160
	The Cossacks	- 162
1585.	Judicial Reforms, &c.	- 164
	Licentiousness of the Nobles	- 165
1586.	Death and Character of Batory	- 166
	SIGISMUND III.	- 167
1587.	Troubles consequent on his Election	- 168
1588.	He triumphs over his Rival	- 168
	His Unpopularity	- 169
1593, &c.	He loses the Swedish Crown	- 171
1609, &c.	His Wars in Livonia	- 171
1605—1618.	His Transactions with Muscovy	- 172
1620—1623.	With the Turks. Heroism of the Poles	- 175

A. D.		Page
1620—1629.	His Wars with the Swedes	177
1632.	His Death and Character	178
	ULADISLAS VII.	179
1634, &c.	His Wars with the Muscovites	180
1635.	His Transactions with the Turks	181
	His Transactions with Sweden	181
1638.	Insurrection of the Cossacks	182
1648.	Bogdan, their Chief	183
	Death and Character of Uladislas	184
	Interregnum	185
	Ravages of Bogdan	185
1649.	Election of a new King	186
	JOHN II. (Casimir)	187
1649—1653.	His Wars with the Cossacks, &c.	187
	The Veto	189
1654.	Invasion of the Russians	190
1655—1660.	Of the Swedes. Subjugation of Poland	191
1660.	Its Emancipation	192
1658.	Death and Character of Bogdan	194
1660—1667.	Other Wars of John Casimir	195
1658.	Civil Dissensions	196
1668.	Abdication of the King	197
	Character of his Reign	198
	Extraordinary Election of Prince Michael Koributh	199
	MICHAEL, his Character	200
1669, &c.	His disastrous Reign	200
1670—1673.	War with the Cossacks and Turks. Triumphs of Sobieski	201
	Death and Character of Michael	204
1673, 1674.	*Interregnum.* Election of Sobieski	205
1676.	JOHN III. Wars with the Turks, &c.	207
	His splendid Success	208
1678.	His imprudent Truce with Muscovy	209
1678—1682.	Internal Disorders	209
	His Alliance with the Empire	210
1683.	Campaign of Vienna	211
1684—1691.	Imprudent Policy of the King	212
	His Weakness	213
1696.	His Death and Character	215
1696—1697.	*Interregnum*	216
	Election of FREDERIC AUGUSTUS I.	218
1699.	The King recovers Kaminiec	219
1700—1705.	His Alliance with Peter the Great, and his War with Sweden	219
	He is deposed by Charles XII.	220
	Elevation of Stanislas	221
1710.	Restoration of Frederic Augustus	221
1710—1718.	Civil Dissensions	222
1726.	Loss of Courland	222
1724.	Religious Intolerance. Affair of Thorn	223

A. D.		Page
	Horrid Cruelty - - - - -	- 224
1733.	Death of the King - - - -	- 225
	Troubles of the Interregnum - - -	- 225
	FREDERIC AUGUSTUS II. forced on the Poles -	- 227
1736, &c.	His Idleness and Dissipation - -	- 227
	Influence of Russia - - - -	- 228
	Factions - - - - -	- 230
	Russian Influence increases - -	- 230
1763.	Death of the King - - - -	- 232
	Disasters of his Reign - - -	- 232
	Interregnum - - - -	- 232
	Policy of the Empress Catherine -	- 233
	State of Parties. Manœuvres of Russia and Prussia	- 233
1764.	Tumultuous Diet. Patriotism of two noble Poles -	- 234
	Illegal Election of STANISLAS AUGUSTUS -	- 237
1765, &c.	His good Intentions frustrated by Russia - -	- 237
1768, &c.	Violence of that Power - - -	- 238
	The Poles vainly endeavour to throw off the Yoke	- 238
1772.	*First Partition* of Poland - - -	- 239
	Impudent Pretensions of the Three Powers -	- 239
1773.	Diet of this Year. Intrepidity of Reyten -	- 240
1775, &c.	Selfishness of the Polish Nobles - -	- 242
1778—1792.	Remarkable Diet. New Constitution - -	- 242
	Violence of Catherine, and Weakness of Stanislas	- 243
1793.	*Second Partition* - - -	- 244
	The Poles rise. Exploits of Kosciusko -	- 244
	They are reduced by Suwarof and the Prussians -	- 245
1795.	*Third Partition.* Annihilation of the Republic -	- 245
	Reflections - - - -	- 246

CHAP. III.

1796.	Sympathy for the Poles - - -	- 247
1797.	Polish Nobles enter the French Service -	- 248
	They are deceived by Bonaparte - -	- 249
1801.	Their Exploits in Italy - - -	- 249
	Condition of their Countrymen at home -	- 250
1806.	Bonaparte draws them to his Standard - -	- 252
1807.	Grand Duchy of Warsaw formed - -	- 253
	Its Constitution - - -	- 253
1809.	Its Condition, and its Services to France -	- 254
1812.	Bonaparte again draws them to his Standard -	- 255
	His insulting Duplicity - - -	- 256
1813.	Fall of the Grand Duchy - - -	- 257
1814.	Attention of the Allied Sovereigns directed to Poland	- 257
1815.	Policy of Alexander - - - -	- 258
	Bases of the Treaty of Vienna. Kingdom of Poland restored - - - -	- 259

a

THE
HISTORY OF POLAND.

BY

S. A. DUNHAM, L.L.D. &c.

H.Corbould del.   E.Finden sculp.

Murder of S.ͭ Stanislas. p.41.

London,

PRINTED FOR LONGMAN, ORME, BROWN & LONGMANS, PATERNOSTER ROW
AND JOHN TAYLOR, UPPER GOWER STREET.

HISTORY OF POLAND.

INTRODUCTION.

AMIDST the incessant influx of the Asiatic nations into Europe, during the slow decline of the Roman empire, and the migrations occasioned by their arrival, we should vainly attempt to trace the descent of the Poles. Whether they are derived from the Sarmatians, who, though likewise of Asiatic origin, were located on both sides of the Vistula long before the irruptions of the kindred barbarians, or from some horde of the latter, or, a still more probable hypothesis, from an amalgamation of the natives and new comers, must for ever remain doubtful. All that we can know with certainty is, that they formed part of the great Slavonic family which stretched from the Baltic to the Adriatic, and from the Elbe to the mouth of the Borysthenes. As vainly should we endeavour, from historic testimony *alone*, to ascertain the origin of this generic term *slave*, and the universality of its application. Conjecture may tell us, that as some of the more powerful tribes adopted it to denote their success in arms (its signification is *glorious*), other tribes, conceiving that their bravery entitled them to the same enviable appellation, assumed it likewise. It might thus become the common denomination of the old and new inhabitants, of the victors and the vanquished; the more readily, as most of the tribes comprehended under it well knew that the same cradle had once contained them. Other people, indeed, as the Huns or the Avars, subsequently arrived from more remote re-

gions of Asia *, and in the places where they forcibly
settled, introduced a considerable modification of customs
and of language: hence the diversity in both among the
Slavonic nations — a diversity which has induced some
writers to deny the identity of their common origin.
But as, in the silence of history, affinity of language will
best explain the kindred of nations, and will best assist
us to trace their migrations, no fact can be more indisputable than that most of the tribes included in the
generic term *slavi* were derived from the same common
source, however various the respective periods of their
arrival, and whatever changes were in consequence produced by struggles with the nations, by intestine wars,
and by the irruption of other hordes dissimilar in manners
and in speech.   Between the Pole and the Russian is
this kindred relation striking; and though it is fainter
among the Hungarians from their incorporation with
the followers of Attila, and among the Bohemians, from
their long intercourse with the Teutonic nations, it is
yet easily discernible.†

Of these Slavonic tribes, those which occupied the
country bounded by Prussia and the Carpathian mountains, by the Bug and the Oder — those especially who
were located on both banks of the Vistula — were the
progenitors of the present *Poles*.   The word *Pole* is not
older than the tenth century, and seems to have been
originally applied, not so much to the people as to the
region they inhabited; *polska* in the Slavonic tongue
signifying a level field or plain.

* I have little doubt that the Huns and Avars were one and the same
people, or that the latter were of the same descent as the former : — " Fue-
runt autem Avares Unnorum gens, et exercitûs Attilæ reliquiæ. — Unni
vero qui cladi superfuerant (by the Gepidæ), Unnorum nomen exosi, ab
Avario, qui Zeliorbi successit in regno, sese *Avares* noncupavere, relictisque
Pannoniis in Noricum recesserunt, à quibus ea regio *Bavaria* dicta est."
Bonfinii Rerum Ungaricarum Decades, lib. viii. p. 82.   This is more probable than the assertion of Strabo, that Bavaria was named from the *Boii*,
who passed thither from Italy.

† The Lithuanians, though their history is so closely connected with that
of the Muscovites and Poles, are not originally Slavonic ; a fact sufficiently
clear from their language.   By some of the learned they have been deemed
of Gothic, by others of Alanic, descent.   Many Gothic words, indeed, are
to be found in their language, but more Latin and Greek : the basis, however, is none of the three, but something perhaps resembling the Finnish.

The Poles as a nation are not of ancient date.[*] Prior to the ninth century they were split into a multitude of tribes, independent of each other, and governed by their respective chiefs : no general head was known except in case of invasion, when combination alone could save the country from the yoke. Like all other people, however, they lay claim to an antiquity sufficiently respectable : their old writers assure us that one of the immediate descendants of Noah colonised this part of ancient Sarmatia.[†] But the absurdity of the claim was too apparent to be long supported, and less extravagant historians were satisfied with assigning the period of their incorporation as a people to Lech or Lesko I., who reigned, say they, about the middle of the sixth century.[‡] As the laws of evidence became better understood, even this era was modestly abandoned, and the authentic opening of Polish history was brought down three centuries; namely, to the accession of Ziemowit (Semovitus), A. D. 860.[§] Finally, it was reserved for the Polish writers of our own day to abstract another century from the national existence, and hail Miecislas I. as the true founder of the monarchy.[‖]

In the present compendium, the history of Poland will be divided into two parts, in regard to the two distinct classes of its rulers : — I. The crown hereditary ; II. The crown elective. The first will comprise the dynasty of the Piasts and the Jagellos [¶] ; the second,

---

[*] "La nation Polonaise est à la fois la plus nouvelle de l'Europe, si on s'arrête au temps où elle se constitua, et la plus ancienne, si on remonte jusqu'à son origine." — *Salvandy, Histoire de Pologne avant et sous le Roi Jean Sobieski,* i. 19. What carelessness is this ? Both assertions are utterly and miserably unfounded.

[†] Vincentii Kadlubek Episcopi Cracoviensis Historia Polonica. Boguphali Episcopi Posnaniensis Chronicon Poloniæ. Stanislai Sarnicii Annalium Polonorum,lib viii.

[‡] Joannis Dlugossi Historia Polonica. Cromeri de Origine et Rebus Gestis Polonorum lib. xxx. Neugebaver, Historia Rerum Polonorum, &c., cum multis aliis.

[§] Bandtkia, Solignac, Narnszewits, Waga, Salvandy, &c.

[‖] Lelewel, Niemcewitz, Golembiowski, Zielinski, with many others.

[¶] I am aware that during the reign of the Jagellos the kings were elected, but the election was *always* confined to one family, which was indisputably hereditary : the eldest son was elected if at a suitable age ; if too young, one of the uncles was chosen. The laws of succession seem not very clearly defined in any country during the middle ages.

What confirms still more strongly the propriety of the above division is

the reigns of the various princes, natives or foreigners, whom the suffrages of the nobles raised to the dignity.

But though the severity of historical criticism has rejected as fabulous, or at least doubtful, the period antecedent to Miecislas I., many transactions of that period are admitted as credible. Tradition, indeed, is the only authority for the existence of preceding rulers, but it cannot be wholly disregarded: its first beams are visible through the darkness of time, and enable us to perceive that *some* of those rulers *were*, whatever we may think of the events recorded concerning them. For this reason, they may properly occupy a place in the present Introduction.

According to ancient chroniclers, one of the most famous dukes of the Poles was

LECH I., who lived about the middle of the sixth century. One day as he was clearing away the ground which he had marked out for the site of a residence, he found an eagle's nest: hence he called the place Gnesna, from the Slavonic word *gniazda*, a nest: hence, too, the representation of that bird on the banners of the nation. A multitude of huts soon surrounded the ducal abode: a city arose, destined for some centuries to be the capital of the country, and eventually the archiepiscopal see of the primate. From this prince Poland was sometimes called *Lechia.*

Of the immediate descendants of Lech nothing is known. We are only told that their sceptre was one of iron; and that the indignant natives at length abolished the ducal authority, and established that of voivods, or palatins, whose functions appear to have been chiefly, if not wholly, military. Experience, however, taught that one tyrant was preferable to twelve: they accordingly invested with the supreme power one of the palatins and deposed the rest; one whose virtues and genius rendered

---

the fact, that, previous to the time of Henry de Valois, the Polish monarchs styled themselves *hæredes* regni Poloniæ; and that, from the accession of the French prince, the nobles in the pacta conventa insisted on the disuse of the hereditary title.

him worthy of the choice. CRACUS repressed the licentious, encouraged the peaceable, established tribunals for the administration of justice, and triumphed over all his enemies, domestic and foreign. He founded Cracow, whither he transferred the seat of his government.

LECH II.—His son, Lech II., ascended the ducal throne by a fratricide: he assassinated his elder brother in a wood; but he had the address to conceal for a time his share in that dark deed. But divine justice slumbered not — his crime was discovered, and he was deposed and banished by his indignant subjects. The tender affection, however, which they bore to the memory of Cracus induced them to elevate his daughter Wenda to the throne.

WENDA. [750.] — This princess was of surprising beauty, of great talents, and of still greater ambition. Power she deemed too sweet to be divided with another, and she therefore resolutely refused all offers of marriage. Incensed at her haughtiness, or in the hope of accomplishing by force what persuasion had attempted in vain, Rudiger, one of her lovers, who was a German prince, adopted a novel mode of courtship. At the head of an army he invaded her dominions. She marched against him. When the two armies met, Rudiger again besought her to listen to his suit, and thereby spare the effusion of blood. The maiden was inexorable: she declared that no man should ever share her throne; that she would never become the slave of a husband, since, whoever he might be, he would assuredly love her person much less than her power. Her answer being spread among the officers of Rudiger, produced an effect which he little foresaw. Filled with admiration at the courage of the princess, whom they perceived hurrying from rank to rank in the act of stimulating her followers to the combat, and convinced that all opposition to her will would be worse than useless, they surrounded their chief, and asked him what advantage he hoped to gain from such an expedition. " If thou shouldst defeat the princess, will she pardon thee the loss of her troops? If thou art subdued, will she be more disposed to love thee?" The passion of Rudiger blinded him to the rational remonstrances of his followers: he persisted in his resolution of fighting; they refused to advance: in utter despair he laid hands on himself, and turned his dying looks towards the camp of the Poles. Wenda, we are told, showed no sign of sympathy at the tragical news, but returned triumphant to Cracow. Her own end was not less violent. Whether, as is asserted, to escape similar persecution, or, as is equally probable, from remorse at her own cruelty, having one day sacrificed to the gods, she threw herself into the waters of the Vistula and there perished.

With this princess expired the race of Cracus. Again, it is said, the fickle multitude divided the sovereign power, and subjected themselves to the yoke of twelve palatins. The two periods have evidently been confounded; either the power never existed, or — an hypothesis, however, not very probable — as this form of government was common to the Slavonic tribes, it may have been the only one admitted in Poland prior to the domination of the Piasts. Anarchy, we are told, was the immediate effect of this partition of power. The new chiefs were weak, indolent, and wicked; the tyrants of their subjects, and enemies of each other. In vain did the people groan; their groans were disregarded, and their efforts to shake off the bondage they had imposed on themselves were rendered abortive by the power of their rulers, who always exhibited considerable energy when their privileges were threatened. The general wretchedness was increased by an invasion of the Hungarians, who had sprung from the same origin as the Poles, and who were inclined to profit by the dissensions between the chiefs and people. The palatins, whose duty it was to defend the country which they oppressed, were too conscious of their own weakness, and still more of their unpopularity, to risk an action with the enemy. Nothing but subjugation and ruin appeared to the dismayed natives, when both were averted by the genius of one man.

Fable. — Though but a simple soldier, Prezemislas aspired to the glory of liberating his country. One dark night he adopted an expedient which had the merit of novelty at least to recommend it, and which has never since been imitated by any other general. With the branches and barks of trees he formed images of men with lances, swords, and bucklers: these he smeared with certain substances proper to reflect the rays of the sun, and render the illusion more striking. He placed these on a hill on the border of a forest directly opposite to the Hungarian camp. The stratagem succeeded: the following morning some troops of the enemy were despatched to dislodge the audacious few who appeared to confide in the excellence of their position. As the assailants approached the plain, the reflection ceased, and they were surprised to find nothing but fantastic forms of trees. The same appearance, however, of armed soldiers was discovered at a distance; and it was universally believed that the Poles had fallen back to occupy a more tenable post. The Hungarians pursued until, artfully drawn into an ambuscade, they were enveloped and massacred. How to ensure the destruction of the rest was now the object of Prezemislas: it was attained by another stratagem scarcely less extraordinary. He clothed some of his followers in the garb and armour of the slain Hungarians, and marched them boldly towards the enemy's camp, while another body of Poles, by circuitous paths, hastened towards the same destination. Having thus reached the outposts, the former suddenly fell on the astonished Pannonians; while the latter, rushing forwards from another direction, added to the bloody horrors of the scene. In vain did the invaders attempt a combined defence: before they could be formed into any thing like systematic order they were cut off almost to a man, notwithstanding individual acts of bravery which called forth the admiration of the assailants.*

The victor was rewarded with a sceptre ; the twelve palatins were deposed: and he was thus confirmed in an authority undivided and absolute. Under the name of Lesko I., which he assumed from reverence to the celebrated founder of Gnesna, he reigned with equal glory and happiness. Unfortunately, however, for the natives, he left no children ; the palatins armed, some to enforce the restitution of their alleged rights, others to seize on the supreme power. But the voice of the country, to which experience had at length taught a good lesson, declared so loudly against a partition of sovereignty, that the chiefs ceased to pursue a common interest ; each laboured for himself. According to ancient usage, the people were assembled to fill the vacant throne by their suffrages. But to choose where the pretensions of the candidates were, to outward appearance, nearly balanced, and yet where the consequences of an improper choice might be for ever fatal to liberty, was difficult. Where the risk was so great, they piously concluded that it was safer to leave the event to the will of the gods than to human foresight.

A horse-race was decreed, in which the crown was to be the prize of victory. One of the candidates had recourse to artifice : the course, which lay along a vast plain on the banks of the Pradnik, he planted with sharp iron points, and covered them with sand. In the centre, however, he left a space over which he might pass without danger ; but lest he should accidentally diverge from it, he caused his horse to be shod with iron plates, against which the points would be harmless. Every thing seemed to promise success to his roguish ingenuity, when the secret was discovered by two young men, as they were one day amusing themselves on the destined course. One of them was silent through fear ; the other through cunning. On the appointed day the candidates

* Of this expedition no mention is made by the Hungarian writers : it is probably fabulous.

arrived, the race was opened, and the innumerable spectators waited the result with intense anxiety. The inventor of the stratagem left all the rest far behind him except the youth last mentioned, who kept close to his horse's heels; and who, just as the victor was about to claim the prize, exposed the unworthy trick to the multitude. The former was immediately sacrificed to their fury; and the latter, as the reward of his courageous conduct, notwithstanding the meanness of his birth, was invested with the ensigns of sovereignty.*

LESKO II. [804—810.] — The new duke was humble enough to remember, and rational enough to acknowledge, his low extraction. He preserved, with religious care, the garments which he had worn in his lowly fortunes, and on which he often gazed with greater satisfaction than on his regal vestments. His temperance, his love of justice, his zeal for the good of his people, are favourite themes of the old chroniclers.

LESKO III. [810—815.] — Lesko III. inherited the virtues no less than the name of his father; for though of his twenty-one sons one only was legitimate, incontinency would scarcely be considered a blemish in a pagan and a Slave. After a short but brilliant reign, ennobled by success in war and wisdom in peace, he divided his dominions among his sons, subjecting all, however, to the authority of his lawful successor Popiel I.

POPIEL I. [815.] — Of this prince little is known beyond his jealousy of his brothers, and his addiction to debauchery. After a base and ignoble life he was succeeded by his son, Popiel II., while yet a child.

POPIEL II. — The fostering care of the uncles, whose fidelity appears to have been as rare as it was honourable, preserved the throne to the chief of their house. But the prince showed them no gratitude; he was, in-

* Kadlubek, Histor. Polon. lib. i. Epist. 12. Dlugoss, Hist. Polon. lib. i. col. 62. Cromer, *De Rebus Gestis Pol.*, lib. i. p. 61. Sarnicki, Annal. Pol. lib. v. c. 1. Though I am inclined to consider the above relation fabulous, I am aware that there was precedent enough for the course adopted. Antiquity exhibits it to us in the sons of Endymion for Elis, and in Pelops for Pisa (Diod. Sicul. lib. xv.). Pindar (Pyth. Od. ix.) tells us that Anteas, a Libyan king, promised his daughter to the lover who should triumph in the course. — See Solignac, Histoire de Pologne, tom. i. p. 44.

deed, incapable of such a sentiment : every day exhibited to his anxious guardians some new feature of depravity, which, with a commendable prudence, they endeavoured to conceal from the nation, in the hope that increasing years would bring reformation. Their pious exhortations were in vain : he proceeded from bad to worse ; he associated with none but the dissipated, — " with drunkards, spendthrifts, and fornicators,"—or with mimics and jesters. To correct one of his vices at least, a wife was procured for him : the expedient failed ; it had even a mischievous effect, since his consort was avaricious and malignant, and was but too successful in making him the instrument of her designs. On reaching his majority, his passions burst forth with fury : no woman was safe from his lust, no man from his revenge. His extortions, his debaucheries, his cruelty, at length exhausted the patience of his people, who resolved to set bounds to his excesses. The formidable confederacy was headed by his uncles, who sacrificed the ties of blood to their patriotism or their ambition. To dissolve it, and at the same time to gratify his revenge, he was stimulated alike by his own malignity and by the counsels of his wife. He feigned sickness, sent for his uncles, as if to make his peace with them, and poisoned them in the wine which was produced for their entertainment. He even carried his wickedness so far as to refuse the rites of sepulture to his victims.

Fable. — But, say the chroniclers, divine justice prepared a fit punishment for this Sardanapalus and Jezebel. From the unburied corpses sprung a countless multitude of rats, of an enormous size *, which immediately filled the palace, and sought out the guilty pair, and their two children. In vain were great numbers destroyed, greater swarms advanced. In vain did the ducal family enclose themselves within a circle of fire ; the boundary was soon passed by the ferocious animals, which, with unrelenting constancy, aimed at them and them alone. They fled to another element, which

* The larger *mures* or rats, not *mice*, as we find in some historians

availed them as little. The rats followed them to a neighbouring lake, plunged into the water, and fixed their teeth in the sides of the vessel, in which they would soon have gnawed holes sufficient to let in the water and sink it, had not Popiel commanded the sailors to land him on an island near at hand. In vain; his inveterate enemies were on shore as soon as he. His attendants now recognised the finger of Heaven, and left him to his fate. Accompanied by his wife and children, he now fled to a neighbouring tower; he ascended the highest pinnacle: still they followed; neither doors nor bars could resist them. His two sons were first devoured, then the duchess, then himself, and so completely that not a bone remained of the four.*

With Popiel was extinguished the legitimate race of royalty; but the sons of the murdered uncles remained, the eldest of whom, with the aid of his brother, aspired to the throne. Again the palatins stepped forth to vindicate the ancient form of government. The two parties disputed, quarrelled, and, lastly, armed their adherents to decide the question by force; but the more enlightened portion of the nation was not convinced that a problem affecting the happiness or misery of millions ought to be resolved in such a way. Two assemblies were successively consulted at Kruswick, to discuss the respective claims of monarchy and oligarchy: but the forces, if not the arguments, of the two parties were so nearly equal that nothing was decided. Both were preparing to try the efficacy of arms, when Heaven, in pity to the people, again interfered, and miraculously filled the vacant throne.

Fable. — There dwelt in Kruswick a poor but vir-

* " Ex cadaveribus putrefactis enati mures inusitatæ magnitudinis, impium parricidam cum scelerata conjuge atque liberis fugientem cum horrendis sibilis quoque versus per aquam flammamque persequuntur: nam ter injecto igne propellere eos volebant aulæ servi, sed non poterant: nec claustra prosunt aut abigentium satellitum præsidia. Ad extremum diffugientibus omnibus, absumptis prius filiis, deinde uxore, postremus ipse infelix miserabiliter lenta morte consumitur." — *Stan. Sarn. Annal. Pol.* lib. v. cap. 4.
Dlugoss (lib. i. col. 76.) has a much more copious and rhetorical account of this prodigy. — See Extract B in the Appendix.

tuous man, named Piast ; so poor indeed that his wants
were but scantily supplied by a small piece of ground
which he cultivated with his own hands, and so virtuous that the blessings of thousands accompanied his
steps.   He had a wife and a son, both worthy of
him.   He lived contented in his poverty, which he had
no wish to remove, since he had wisdom enough to perceive that the state most exempt from artificial wants is
the most favourable to virtue, and consequently to happiness.   When the time arrived that his son should be
first shorn of his locks of hair and receive a name, — a
custom of great antiquity among the pagan Slavi *,—he
invited, as was usual on such occasions, his neighbours
to the ceremony.   On the day appointed, two strangers
arrived with the rest, and were admitted with the hospitality so honourable to the people.   Piast laid before his
guests all he could furnish for their entertainment : that
all, he observed, was little; but he hoped the spirit with
which it was offered would compensate for the lack of
good cheer.   They fell to the scanty stock of viands and
meal, when, lo ! a miracle ! both were multiplied prodigiously ! the more they ate and drank, the more the
tables groaned under the weight of the viands ! The por-
tent was spread abroad with rapidity.   Numbers daily
flocked to the peasant's house to share his hospitality, and
to witness the miraculous increase of his provisions.   A
scarcity of these good things at that time afflicted the
place, through the influx of so many thousands who met
for the choice of a government.   All hastened to Piast,
who entertained them with princely liberality during
several successive weeks.   " Who so fit to rule," was
the universal cry, " as this holy man, this favourite of
the gods !" Prince and palatin desisted from their
respective pretensions, and joined their suffrages to that

* The shaven crowns of the Polish nobles who visited Paris to offer Henry
of Anjou the sceptre of Poland, were an extraordinary spectacle to the Parisians. " Ils admiraient surtout," says De Thou, " les têtes rasées, n'of-
rant qu'une touffe de cheveux au-dessus."
The origin of this custom might be connected with religion, but convenience perpetuated it. Long hair, which could be seized by the hands of
an enemy in the heat of battle, often occasioned the destruction of the
wearer.

of the people. Piast was unanimously elected, in the year 842, to the vacant dignity; but so great was his reluctance to accept the glittering honour, that he would have remained for ever in his then humble condition, had not the two identical strangers, whom he found to be gods, and whom later Christian writers consider two angels, or at least two blessed martyrs, again favoured him with a visit, and prevailed on him to sacrifice his own ease to the good of the nation.*

PIAST. — The reign of Piast was the golden age of Poland. No foreign wars, no domestic commotions, but respect from without, abundance and contentment within, signalised his wise, firm, and paternal administration. The horror with which he regarded the scene of Popiel's guilt and punishment, made him abandon the place of his birth and transfer his court to Gnesna, which thus became a second time the capital of the country.

ZIEMOWIT. — Ziemowit's was no less glorious. He was the first chief who introduced regular discipline into the armies of Poland. Before his time they had fought without order or system: their onset had been impetuous, and their retreat as sudden. He marshalled them in due array; taught them to surrender their own will to that of their officers; to move as one vast machine obedient to the force which rules it; and whenever fortune was adverse, to consult their safety, not in flight, but in a closer and more determined union, in a vigorous concentrated resistance. The Hungarians, the Moravians, the Russians, who had insulted the country under the feeble sway of Popiel, and who had despised the inexperience of the son of Piast, were soon taught to fear him and to sue for peace: Ziemowit was satisfied with the terror produced by his arms; he thirsted not after conquest; he loved his subjects too well to waste their blood in gratification of a selfish ambition. Their welfare was his only care, their gratitude and affection his only reward.

* Kadlubek, lib. ii. epist. 111. Dlugoss, i. 80. Cromer, ii. 40. The celestial visitants, says the second of these veracious authorities, deigned to cut the boy's hair, and called him Ziemowit (*Semovitus*).

An able captain, an enlightened statesman, an affable patriotic sovereign, his person was adored during life, and his memory long revered after death.

LESKO IV. [892—921.] — His son and successor, LESKO IV., successfully imitated all his virtues but one. This prince refrained from war, making all his glory to consist in promoting the internal happiness of the people. His moderation, his justice, his active zeal, his enlightened care, were qualities, however, not very acceptable to a martial and ferocious people, who longed for war, and who placed all greatness in conquest.

ZEMOMYSL. [921—962.] — Of the same pacific disposition, and of the same estimable virtues, was ZEMOMYSL, the son and successor of Lesko.   For the same honourable reason, the reign of this prince furnishes no materials for history.   The tranquil unobtrusive virtues must be satisfied with self-approbation, and a consciousness of the divine favour ; the more splendid and mischievous qualities only attain immortality.   That men's evil deeds are written in brass, their good ones in water, is more than poetically just.*

Zemomysl, however, has one claim to remembrance, which posterity has not failed to recognise : he was the father of Miecislas, the first Christian duke of Poland, with whom opens the authentic history of the country.

* Solignac (Histoire de Pologne), i. 70., has totally misrepresented the character of these two princes.   He represents them as weak and useless; as fallen and slothful: on the contrary, that their administration was vigorous, active, and beneficial in a very high degree, is confirmed by every ancient chronicler of the country.   I am at a loss to account for this perversion of truth, perhaps I might say carelessness, in a writer justly held in esteem.—See Kadlubek, lib. ii. epist. 10.   Dlugoss, i. 86. Cromer, xi. 43., cum multis aliis.

BOOK I.

CHAPTER I.

MONARCHS OF THE HOUSE OF PIAST, 962—1139.

MIECISLAS I.

962—999.

THIS fifth prince of the house of Piast is entitled to the remembrance of posterity; not merely from his being the first Christian ruler of Poland, but from the success with which he abolished paganism, and enforced the observance of the new faith throughout his dominions. He who could effect so important a revolution without bloodshed, must have been no common character.

When the duke assumed the reins of sovereignty, both he and his subjects were strangers to Christianity, even by name. At that time almost all the kingdoms of the North were shrouded in idolatry: a small portion of Saxons, indeed, had just received the light of the Gospel, and so had some of the Hungarians; but its beams were as yet feeble, even in those countries, and were scarcely distinguishable amidst the Egyptian darkness around. Accident, if that term can be applied to an event in which Christian philosophers at least can recognise the hand of Heaven, is said to have occasioned his conversion. By the persuasion of his nobles, he demanded the hand of Dombrowka, daughter of Boleslas, king of Hungary. Both father and daughter refused to favour so near a connection with a pagan; but both de-

clared, that if he would consent to embrace the faith of
Christ his proposal would be accepted. After some deliberation he consented: he procured instructors, and
was soon made acquainted with the doctrines which he
was required to believe, and the duties he was bound to
practise. The royal maiden was accordingly conducted
to his capital [965]; and the day which witnessed his
regeneration by the waters of baptism, also beheld him
receive another sacrament, that of marriage.*

The zeal with which Miecislas laboured for the conversion of his subjects, left no doubt of the sincerity of
his own. Having dismissed his seven concubines, he
issued an order for the destruction of the idols throughout the country. He appears to have been obeyed without much opposition. Some of the nobles, indeed, would
have preserved their ancient altars from violation; but
they dreaded the power of their duke, who, in his administration, exhibited a promptitude and vigour previously unknown, and who held an almost boundless sway
over the bulk of the people. His measures seem at first
to have been regarded with disapprobation; but the
influence of his personal character secured the submission of the people, especially when they found that their
deities were too weak to avenge themselves. The extir-
pation, however, of an idolatrous worship was not sufficient; the propagation of a pure one was the great
task, — a task which required the union of moderation
with firmness, of patience with zeal. Happily they were
found in the royal convert, and still more in his consort.
Instructions were obtained from pope John XIII.; seven
bishoprics, and two archbishoprics, all well endowed,
attested the ardour and liberality of the duke.† He
even accompanied the harbingers of the Gospel into several parts of his dominions, aiding them by his authority,

---

* Kadlubek, lib. xi. epist. 98. Stanis. Sarn. lib. vi. col. 1043. Dlugoss,
lib. xi. col. 91—104. Cromer, lib. iii. p. 44—47. See also the Chronicle of
Dithmar, who was contemporary with Miecislas, lib. xi. (in Scriptor. Rerum
Brunsvic. tom i.)

† Posnania Smogorzow (afterwards transferred to Wratislaw), Kruswick
(transferred to Wladislaw, now Cuyavia), Plocsko, Culm, Lebuff, and Ca-
menitz, were the saffragan sees; Gnesna and Cracow the metropolitan.

and inspiriting them by his example. By condescending to the use of persuasion, reasoning, remonstrance, the royal missionary effected more with his barbarous subjects than priest or prelate, though neither showed any lack of zeal, or paused in the good work. The duchess imitated his example; her sweetness of manner, her affability, her patience of contradiction, prevailed where an imperious behaviour would have failed.

The nobles, being the fewest in number, and the most easily swayed, were the first gained over. To prove their sincerity, when present at public worship, and just before the priest commenced reading the Gospel for the day, at the intonation by the choir of the *Gloria tibi, Domine!* they half drew their sabres, thereby showing that they were ready to defend their new creed with their blood.* Their example, the preaching of the missionaries, and, above all, the entire co-operation of their duke, at length prepared the minds of the people for the universal reception of Christianity; so that when he issued his edict in 980, that every Pole, who had not already submitted to the rite, should immediately repair to the waters of baptism, he was obeyed without murmuring. They were subsequently confirmed in the faith by the preaching of St. Adalbert, whose labours in Bohemia, Hungary, Poland, and Prussia, and whose martyrdom in the last-named country, then covered with the darkest paganism, have procured him a veneration in the north little less than apostolic.†

When we consider the difficulties with which the new faith had to contend, among a people so deeply plunged in the vices inherent in their ancient superstitions, we shall not be surprised that fourteen years of assiduous exertions were required for so great a change; we shall rather be at a loss to account, on human grounds at least, for the comparative facility with which it was ef-

* This whimsical custom was perpetuated in Poland full seven centuries.
† Kadlubek, Dlugoss, Cromer, Sarnicki, Dithmar, ubi supra. See also Pontanus, Bohemia Pia, Cosmæ Pragensis Chronica Bohemorum, and the Vita Sancti Adalberti (all three in Rerum Bohemicarum Antiqui Scriptores) Bonfinius, Historia Pannonica, decad. ii. lib. i. p. 115.

fected. Drunkenness, sensuality, rapes, plunder, bloodshed even at their entertainments, were things to which
they had been addicted from time immemorial; and to
be compelled to relinquish such enjoyments as these
they naturally considered as a tyrannical interference
with their liberties. The severe morality of the Gospel,
and the still severer laws which the new prelates, or
rather the duke, decreed to enforce it, must have been
peculiarly obnoxious to men of strong passions, rendered
stronger by long indulgence, and fiercely swayed by that
impatience which is so characteristic of the Slavonic
nations. If Miecislas was persuaded to dismiss his concubines, and thereby overcome his strongest propensity
at the mere call of duty, more powerful motives were
necessary with his subjects, if any faith is to be had in
the statement of a contemporary writer.* And, after
all, the reformation in manners was very imperfect. It
was probably on account of their vices that pope Benedict refused to erect Poland into a kingdom, though the
honour was eagerly sought by the duke, and though it
was granted at the same time to the Hungarians.† There
are not wanting writers to assert that the royal convert
himself forfeited the grace of his baptism, and relapsed
into his old enormities; but there appears little foundation for the statement.‡

* Si quis in hoc (regno) alienis abuti uxoribus, vel fornicari, præsumit,
hanc vindictæ subsequentis pœnam protinus senset. In pontem mercatu
ductus, per follem testiculi clavo affigitur, et novacula prope posita, his mo-
riendi, sive de his absolvendi, dura electio sibi datur." *Dithmar.* This is
bad enough, but the punishment of the women was still worse; it is too
indelicate to be transcribed. The same author adds, that the teeth of those
who eat flesh meat in Lent were drawn. " Il n'est presque pas concevable,"
says Solignac, with much simplicity (Histoire de Pologne, tom. L. liv. i.
p. 76.), " que des payens ayent eu le courage de se convertir à ce prix."

† "The pope," says Dlugoss, " *did* intend to honour in this way the zeal
of the duke, but he was deterred from his purpose by a curious vision, in
which an angel informed him that the Poles were not yet worthy of having
a king; that they were " magis sanguini, cædi, et venationibus, quam de-
votioni et misericordiæ operibus; magis oppressioni subditorum et rapinis,
magis mendacio et dolis quam veritati, deditos esse; majorem illos agere
belluarum et canum quam hominum curam, in effusionemque sanguinis
humani procllves," &c. (lib. ii. col. 122.) This is candid from a native.

‡ Baronius (as quoted by Solignac) charges the duke with marrying a
nun after the death of Dombrowka, and that he had three children by her.
Dithmar affirms that her name was Oda, daughter of the marquis Thiedric;
and that her zeal for religion, her works of mercy, silenced the clergy,
though the marriage greatly displeased them. But when he afterwards

While Miecislas was thus occupied in forwarding the conversion of the nation, he was not unfrequently called to defend it against the ambition or the jealousy of his neighbours. In 968 he was victorious over the Saxons, but desisted from hostilities at the imperial command of Otho I., whose feudatory he acknowledged himself. Against the son of that emperor, Otho II., he leagued himself with other princes who espoused the interests of Henry of Bavaria; but, like them, he was compelled to submit, and own not only the title but the supremacy of Otho, in 973. He encountered a more formidable competitor in the Russian grand duke, Uladimir the Great, who, after triumphing over the Greeks, invaded Poland in 986, and reduced several towns. The Bug now bounded the western conquests of the descendants of Ruric, whose object henceforth was to push them to the very confines of Germany. But Miecislas arrested, though he could not destroy, the torrent of invasion : if he procured no advantage over the Russian, he opposed a barrier which induced Uladimir to turn aside to enterprises which promised greater facility of success. His last expedition (989—991) was against Boleslas, duke of Bohemia. In this contest he was assisted with auxiliaries furnished by the emperor Otho III., whose favour he had won, and by other princes of the empire. After a short but destructive war, the Bohemian, unable to oppose the genius of Miecislas, sued for peace; but this triumph was fatal to the peace of the two countries. Hence the origin of lasting strife between two nations, whose descent, manners, and language were the same, and between whom, consequently, less animosity might have been expected.*

But contiguity of situation is seldom, perhaps never, favourable to the harmony of nations. Silesia, which

mentions another daughter of that nobleman, also a nun, and married to a Slavonian, it is impossible not to suspect that he has mistaken one for the other.

* Dlugoss, ii. col. 126. Cromer, iii. 51, &c. Stanis. Sarn. lib. vi. Dithmar, iv. 340, &c. Æneas Sylvius, Historia Bohemica, cap. xvii. This last writer is very severe on Miecislas, whom he accuses of perfidy and cruelty. So also Dubravius, Historia Bohemica, lib. vi. p. 44.

was the frontier province of Poland, was thenceforth
exposed to the incursions of the Bohemians, and doomed
to experience the curse of its limitrophic position.

Miecislas died in 999, universally regretted by his
subjects.

BOLESLAS I.

999—1025.

BOLESLAS I., surnamed Chrobri, or the Lion-hearted,
son of Miecislas and Dombrowka, ascended the ducal
throne A.D. 999, in his thirty-second year, amidst the
acclamations of his people.

From his infancy this prince had exhibited qualities
of a high order,—great capacity of mind, undaunted
courage, and an ardent zeal for his country's glory.
Humane, affable, generous, he was early the favourite
of the Poles, whose affection he still further gained by
innumerable acts of kindness to individuals. Unfortunately, however, his most splendid qualities were neutralised by his immodérate ambition, which, in the
pursuit of its own gratification, too often disregarded
the miseries it occasioned.

The fame of Boleslas having reached the ears of
Otho III., that emperor, who was then in Italy, resolved,
on his return to Germany, to take a route somewhat
circuitous, and pay the prince a visit. He had before
vowed a pilgrimage to the shrine of St. Adalbert, whose
hallowed remains had just been transported from Prussia to Gnesna. He was received by Boleslas with a
magnificence which surprised him, and a respect which
won his esteem. No sooner were his devotions performed, than he testified his gratitude, or perhaps consulted his policy, by elevating the duchy into a kingdom,
which he doubtless intended should for ever remain a
fief of the empire. Boleslas was solemnly anointed by
the archbishop of Gnesna; but the royal crown, it is
said, was placed on his head by imperial hands. To

bind still closer the alliance between the two princes, Rixa, a niece of Otho, was affianced to the son of the new king. The emperor returned home with an arm of St. Adalbert, which he probably considered as cheaply procured in exchange for a woman and a title.[*]

The king was not long allowed to wear his new honours unmolested: he soon proved that they could not have been placed on a worthier brow. His first and most inveterate enemies were the Bohemians, who longed to grasp Silesia. Two easy triumphs disconcerted the duke of that country, who began to look around him for allies. The same disgrace still attended his arms; his fields were laid waste; his towns pillaged; his capital taken, with himself and his eldest son; the loss of sovereignty, of liberty, and soon of his eyes, convinced him, when too late, how terrific an enemy he had provoked. For a time his country remained the prey of the victor; but the generosity or policy of Boleslas at length restored the ducal throne to Ulric, the second son of the fallen chief. All Germany was alarmed at the progress of the Polish arms. Even the emperor, Henry of Bavaria, joined the confederacy now formed to humble the pride of Boleslas. Superior numbers chased him from Bohemia, dethroned Ulric, and elevated the elder brother, the lawful heir, to the vacant dignity. The king returned to espouse the interests of Ulric; but, though he was often successful, he was as often, not indeed defeated, but constrained to elude the combined force of the empire. Ulric did at length obtain the throne, not through Boleslas but through Henry, whose cause he strengthened by his adhesion. Peace was frequently made during these obscure contests, and the king was thereby enabled

* Kadlubek, lib. ii. epist. xi. Dlugoss, lib. ii. col. 129. Cromer, lib. iii. p. 53. Sarnicki, lib. vi. cap. 5. Dithmar (in Script. Rerum Brunsvicarum, tom. i.). The old Polish writers dwell with much complacency on the splendid reception of the emperor by the duke: the gold and precious stones displayed on the occasion exceed all belief. Then the seven miles which Otho traversed on foot, before arriving at the shrine of St. Adalbert, were carpeted, as we are gravely assured, with cloths of various colours. " Omne iter a Posnania usque Gnesnam, variorum pannorum coloribus, per quod imperator Otho transiturus erat, consterni disposuit; ut, in gradiendo, imperator cum militibus nullibi terram contingeret."—*Dlugoss*, ubi supra.

to repress the incursions of his enemies on other parts of
his frontier; but none could be of long continuance,
where, on both sides, the love of war was a passion
scarcely equalled in intensity even by ambition.   In one
of his expeditions, Boleslas penetrated as far as Holstein,
reducing the towns and fortresses in his way, and filling
all Germany with the deepest consternation.   His conquests, however, were but transiently held; if he found
it easy to make them, to retain them in opposition to the
united efforts of the princes of the empire required far
more numerous armies than he could raise.   He fell
back on Silesia to repair the disasters sustained by the
arms of his son Miecislas, whose talents were inadequate
to the command of a separate force.

To recount the endless alternations of victory and
failure during these obscure contests would exhibit a dry
record — dry as the most lifeless chronicle of the times.
It must be sufficient to observe, that what little advantage was gained fell to the lot of Boleslas, until the peace
of Bautzen, in 1018, restored peace to the lacerated
empire.*

But the most famous of the wars of Boleslas were
with the dukes of Russia.   After the death of Uladimir
the Great, who had imprudently divided his estates
among his sons, the eldest, Swiatopelk, prince of Twer,
endeavouring to unite the other principalities under his
sceptre, was expelled the country by the combined forces
of his enraged brothers.   He took refuge in Poland, and
implored the assistance of the king.   Boleslas immediately armed, not so much to avenge the cause of Swiatopelk as to regain possession of the provinces which
Uladimir had wrested from Miecislas.   He marched
against Yaroslaf, who had seized on the dominions of
the fugitive brother, and whom he encountered on the

* Kadlubek, lib. ii. epist. 11. Cronica Polonorum, and Cronica Principum
Poloniæ (in Script. Rerum Siles. tom. i.). Dlugoss, ii. 137—163. Cromer, iii.
160. Sarnicki, vi. cap. 6. Dithmar (in Script. Rerum Brunsvic. tom. i.
p. 376—416.). Æneas Sylvius, Historia Bohemica, cap. xviii. Dubravius,
Hist. Bohem. lib. vi. vii. Between the Polish and Bohemian authorities
national animosity is to be found. in all its perfection: it is difficult to reconcile their conflicting accounts.

banks of the Bug.   For some time he hesitated to pass
the river in the face of a powerful.enemy ; but a Russian
soldier from the opposite bank one day deriding his cor-
pulency, he plunged into the water with the most intrepid
of his followers, and the action commenced.   It .was
obstinately contested, but victory in the end declared
for the king.   He pursued the fugitives to the walls
of Kiow, which he immediately invested and took.
Swiatopelk was restored, but he made an unworthy
return to his benefactor ; he secretly instigated the Kiovians to massacre the Poles, whose-superiority he envied,
and whose presence annihilated his authority.   His treachery was discovered, and his capital nearly destroyed,
by his incensed allies, who returned home laden with immense plunder.   The Russians pursued in a formidable
body, and the Bug was again destined to behold the strife
of the two armies : again did victory shine on the banners of Boleslas, who, on this occasion, almost annihilated the assailants.   Thus ended this first expedition :
the second was not less decisive.   Yaroslaf had reduced
the Polish garrison left by the king in Kiow, had seiĥed
on that important city, and penetrated into the Polish
provinces, which submitted at his approach.   A third
time was the same river to witness the same sanguinary
scenes.   As usual, after a sharp contest, the Russians
yielded the honour of the day to their able and brave
antagonist, who hurried forward in the career of conquest : but his name now rendered further victories unnecessary ; it struck terror in the hearts of the Russians,
who hastened to acknowledge his supremacy.   On this
occasion he appears to have conducted himself with a
moderation which does the highest honour to his heart :
he restored the prisoners he had taken, and after leaving
garrisons in the more important places, returned to his
capital to end his days in peace.*

Towards the close of life, Boleslas is said to have
looked back on his ambitious undertakings with sorrow :

* To the Polish authorities before quoted, add Karamsin, Histoire de
Russie, tom. iii. et iv.

they had added nothing to his prosperity, but had
exhausted his people. He now began to regret that
he had not devoted his time, and talents, and means,
'to objects which would have secured for them happiness—for himself, a glory far more substantial than
his brilliant deeds could bestow. Perhaps, too, he
began to be apprehensive of the account which a greater
potentate than himself might exact from him. Certain it is, that the last six years of his reign were
passed in the most laborious efforts to repair the evils he
had occasioned,—to improve alike the temporal and
moral condition of his people. He administered justice
with impartiality. Delinquents he punished with inflexible severity; the meritorious he honoured and en-
riched. Knowing the infirmity of his own judgments,
he associated with him twelve of his wisest nobles. With
their aid he redressed the wrongs of his subjects, not
only in his capital but in various parts of his kingdom,
which he traversed from time to time to enquire into the
way justice was administered by the local magistrates.
Nothing escaped his activity; it destroyed oppression,
and ensured triumph to innocence. Perhaps the severity of his labours, which allowed of no intermission by
day, and which were often continued during the silence
of night, hastened his end. Having convoked an assembly at Gnesna, in which his son was nominated his
successor, he prepared for the approaching change. With
his dying breath he exhorted that prince to favour the
deserving, by conferring on them the distinction of wealth
and honours; to love his God; to reverence the ministers of religion; to cherish virtue; to flee from pleasure;
to reign by justice, and to inspire his subjects with love
rather than fear. He died shortly afterwards, in 1025,
leaving behind him the reputation of the greatest sovereign of his age; and, what is far more estimable, the
universal lamentations of his subjects proved that he had
nobly deserved their affectionate appellation of Father.
Poland had never seen such a king as the last six years

of his life exhibited: he was the true founder of his country's greatness.*

MIECISLAS II.

1025—1034

MIECISLAS II. ascended the throne of his father, in 1025, in his thirty-fifth year; an age when the judgment is reasonably expected to be ripened, and the character formed. But this prince had neither; and he soon showed how incapable he was of governing so turbulent a people as the Poles, or of repressing his ambitious neighbours. Absorbed in sloth, or in . pleasures still more shameful, he scarcely deigned to waste a glance on the serious duties of royalty; and it was soon discovered that his temperament fitted him rather for the luxurious courts of southern Asia than for the iron region of Sarmatia.

Yaroslaf, the restless duke of Kiow, was the first to prove to the world how Poland had suffered by a chan of rulers. He rapidly reduced some fortresses, desolated the eastern provinces, and would doubtless have carried his ferocious arms to the capital, had not the Poles without a signal from their king, who quietly watched the progress of the invasion, flocked to the national standard, and compelled this second Sardanapalus to march against the enemy. The duke, however, had no wish to run the risk of an action: with immense spoil, and a multitude of prisoners, he returned to his dominions in the consciousness of perfect impunity. Miecislas, thinking that by his appearance in the field he had done enough for glory, led back his murmuring troops to his capital; nor did the sacrifice of his father's conquests

---

* Kadlubek, Dlugoss, Cromer, Sarnicki. The second of these writers is most lavish in his praises of Boleslas the Great. He is evidently fond of any object which will afford him an opportunity of declamation, though even declamation cannot do much more than justice to the virtues of this monarch's last years. His cruelty, however, to the Bohemians (see Æneas Sylvius, Dubravius, ubi supra, and Pontanus, Bohemia Pia, lib. ii.) is a dark stain on his memory.

draw one sigh, not even one serious thought, from the confirmed voluptuary, who esteemed every moment abstracted from his sensual enjoyments as a lamentable loss of time and life; a loss, however, that he was resolved to repair by more than usual devotion to the only deities he worshipped. For the mead of Odin, the purple juice of Bacchus, and the delights of the Cytherean goddess, he deemed no praise too exalted, no incensè too precious. From this dream of sensuality he was at length rudely awakened, not by the revolt of the Bohemians, or that of the Moravians, whose countries his father had rendered, for a short time, tributary to Poland; not by the reduction of his strongest fortresses, nor even by the escape of whole provinces from his feeble grasp, but by the menaces of his people, who displayed their martial lines in front of his palace, and insisted on his accompanying them to crush the wide-spread spirit of insurrection. He reluctantly marched, not to subdue, but to make an idle display of force which he knew not how to wield. The Bohemians were too formidable to be assailed; the Moravians easily escaped his unwilling pursuit, and suffered him to wreak his vengeance — if, indeed, he was capable of such a sentiment — on a few miserable villages, or on such straggling parties of their body as accident threw in his way. As the enemy no longer appeared openly, he naturally wished it to be believed that none existed; and his discontented troops were again led back from the inglorious scene. He now hoped to pass his days in unmolested enjoyment; but — vexation on vexation! — the Pomeranians revolted. His first impulse was to treat with his rebellious subjects, and grant them a part at least of their demands, as the price of the ease he courted; but this disgraceful expedient was furiously rejected by his nobles, who a third time forced him to the field. In this expedition he was accompanied by three Hungarian princes, who had sought a refuge in his dominions from the violence of an ambitious kinsman. Through their ability, and the valour of the Poles, victory declared for him. With

all his faults he was not, it appears, incapable of gratitude, since he conferred both the hand of his daughter
and the government of Pomerania on Bela, the most
valiant of the three princes. *Now*, he had surely done
enough to satisfy the pugnacious clamours of his people.
The Bohemians, the Moravians, and the Saxons, whom
Boleslas the Great had subjugated, were, indeed, in open
and successful revolt ; but he could safely ask the most
martial of his nobles what chance did there exist of
again reducing those fierce rebels ? And though his
cowardice might be apparent enough, no wise man would
blame the prudence which declined to enter on a contest
where success could scarcely be considered possible.
But Miecislas was indifferent to popular opinion : to
avoid the grim visages of his nobles, which he hated no
less than he feared, he retreated wholly from society,
and, surrounded by a few companions in debauchery,
abandoned himself without restraint to his favourite excesses. The consequences were such as might be expected. He at length experienced the fatal truth, that
whatever sullies the heart also saddens it ; that, however closely connected vice and pleasure may appear at
a distance, the near observer finds " a gulf between
them which cannot be passed." He fell into a languor
— the inevitable effect of his incontinency — which excluded enjoyment, and which rendered him insensible
to every thing but the touch of pain. Already enfeebled
in the prime of life, this wretched voluptuary found his
body incapable of sustaining the maladies produced by
continued intemperance, his exhausted mind still less
able to bear the heavy load of remorse which oppressed
it. Madness ensued, which soon terminated in death.[*]

[*] Kadlubek, lib. ii. epist. 15. Dlugoss, lib. ii. col. 180—188. Cromer,
lib. iii. p. 66—69. Sarnicki, however, speaks only of the *weakness*, entirely
omitting all mention of the *vices*, of this prince. They are reprobated suc-
cinctly by the first of these authorities, more rhetorically by the second,
and most rationally by the third. See also Æneas Sylvius, Dubravius, ubi
supra, Bonfinius, Historia Pannonica, dec. ii. lib. i. p. 134, and Karamsin,
t. iv. Bonfinius ascribes the subjugation of Pomerania to the valour of
Bela, the Hungarian prince, who, in a single combat, overcame the barbarian general : — " Dicto celerius Bela hostem equo deturbat, mox gladio
confossum prostravit humi." Miecislas *should* have met the barbarian ; but
it is needless to say that he had little relish for steel, and that he joyfully
accepted the proposal of Bela to enter the lists for him.

Fortunately for humanity, there are few evils without some intermixture of good. If Miecislas the Idle was cowardly, dissipated, and despicable, there were moments when he appeared sensible of the duties obligatory on his station. To him Poland was indebted for the distribution of the country into palatinates, each presided over by a local judge, and consequently for the more speedy and effectual administration of justice. He is also said to have founded a new bishopric.

INTERREGNUM.

1034—1041.

POLAND was now doomed to experience the fatal truth, that any permanent government, no matter how tyrannical, weak, or contemptible, is beyond all measure superior to anarchy. Miecislas the Idle left a son of an age too tender to be intrusted with the reins of the monarchy; and his widow Rixa was accordingly declared regent of the kingdom, and guardian of the prince. But that queen was unable to control the haughtiness of chiefs who despised the sway of a woman, and who detested her as a German; of all Germans, too, the most hated, as belonging to the archducal house of Austria. She added to their discontent by the evident partiality she showed towards her own countrymen, of whom it is said numbers flocked to share in the spoils of Poland. Complaints followed on the one side, without redress on the other; these were succeeded by remonstrances, then by menaces, until a confederacy was formed by the discontented nobles, whose ostensible object was to procure the dismissal of foreigners, but whose real one was to seize on the supreme authority. They succeeded in both: all foreigners were expelled the kingdom, and with them the regent. Whether Casimir, her son, shared her flight, or immediately followed her, is uncertain; but Europe soon beheld both in Saxony,

claiming the protection of their kinsman, the emperor
Conrad II.

The picture, drawn even by native historians, of the
miseries sustained by the country after the expulsion of
the queen and prince, is in the highest degree revolting.
There was, say they, no authority, no law, and consequently no obedience. Innumerable parties contended
for the supreme power; and the strongest naturally
triumphed, but not until numbers were exterminated.
As there was no tribunal to which the disputants could
appeal, no chief, no council, no house of legislature, the
sword only could decide their pretensions. The triumph
was brief : a combination still more powerful arose to hurl
the successful party from its blood-stained pre-eminence;
and this latter, in turn, became the victim of a new
association, as guilty and as short-lived as itself. Then
the palatins or governors of provinces asserted their independence of the self-constituted authority at Gnesna.
The whole country, indeed, was cursed by the lawless
rule of petty local sovereigns, who made an exterminating
war on each other, and ravaged each other's territories
with as much impunity as greater potentates. One Masos, who had been cup-bearer to the late king, seized by
force on the country between the Vistula, the Narew,
and the Bug, which he governed despotically, and which
to this day is named from him, *Masovia.*

But a still greater evil was the general rising of the
peasants, whose first object was to revenge themselves
of the petty tyrants that oppressed them, but who,
through the very success of the attempt, were, as must
in all times and in all places be the case, only the more
incited to greater undertakings. However beautiful the
gradation of ranks which law and custom have established
in society, the lowest class will not admire it, but will
assuredly endeavour to rise higher in the scale, whenever
opportunity holds out a prospect of success. Hence the
necessity of laws backed by competent authority to curb
this everlasting tendency of the multitude : let the barrier which separates the mob from the more favoured

orders be once weakened, and it will soon be thrown down to make way for the most tremendous of inundations, one that will sweep away the landmarks of society, level all that is noble or valuable, and leave nothing but a vast waste, where the evil passions of men may find a fit theatre for further conflict. Such, we are told, was the state of Poland during the universal reign of anarchy. The peasants, from ministers of righteous justice, became plunderers and murderers, and were infected with all the vices of human nature. Armed bands scoured the country, seizing on all that was valuable, consuming all that could not be carried away, violating the women, massacring old and young; priests and bishops were slain at the altar; nuns ravished in the depths of the cloisters. To add to horrors which had never before, perhaps, been parallèled among Christian nations, came the scourge of foreign invasion, and that too in the most revolting forms. On one side Predislas duke of Bohemia sacked Breslaw, Posnania, and Gnesna, consuming every thing with fire and sword [*]; on another advanced the savage Yaroslaf, who made a desert as he passed along. Had not the former been recalled by preparations of war against his own dominions, and had not the latter thought proper to return home when he had amassed as much plunder as could be carried away, and made as many captives (to be sold as slaves) as his followers could guard, Poland had no longer been a nation. Even now she was little better than a desert. Instead of the cheerful hum of men, her cities exhibited smoking ruins, and her fields nothing but the furrows left by "the plough of desolation." Countless thousands had been massacred; thousands more had fled from the destroying scene. Those who remained had little hope that the present calm would continue; the evil power was

---

[*] This prince, with all his atrocities, made great pretences to devotion. Though he plundered the churches, and afterwards consumed them, he wished to remove the relics of St. Adalbert to his capital, and to make that martyr the protector of his own dominions. He was afterwards cited to Rome to answer for his conduct, and, on failing to appear, was excommunicated. He is very tenderly treated by Æneas Sylvius, Dubravius, Pontanus, and other writers of Bohemian history; and savagely, perhaps also a little unjustly, by those of Poland.

rather exhausted than spent. But the terrific lesson had not been lost on them ; they now looked forward to the restoration of the monarchy as the only means of averting foreign invasion, and the heavier curse of anarchy. An assembly was convoked by the archbishop at Gnesna. All, except a few lawless chiefs who hoped to perpetuate a state of things where force only was recognised, voted for a king ; and, after some deliberation, an overwhelming majority decreed the recal of prince Casimir.

But where was the prince to be found ! No one knew the place of his retreat. A deputation waited on queen Rixa, who was at length persuaded to reveal it. But here, too, an unexpected difficulty intervened : Casimir had actually taken the cowl in the abbey of Clugni. The deputies were not dismayed ; they proceeded to his cloister, threw themselves at his feet, and besought him with tears to have pity on his country. "We come unto thee, dearest prince, in the name of all the bishops, barons, and nobles of the Polish kingdom, since thou alone canst restore our country and thy rightful heritage." They prayed him to return them good for evil, and drew so pathetic a picture of the woes of his native land, that he acceded to their wishes. He allowed an application to be made to Benedict IX. to disengage him from his monastic engagements, who, after exacting some concessions from the Polish nobles and clergy, absolved him from his vows. He accordingly bade adieu to his cell, and set out to gratify the expectations of his subjects, by whom he was received with the most enthusiastic demonstrations of joy, and justly hailed as their saviour.*

* For the groundwork of this melancholy picture of Polish anarchy (which I suspect to be somewhat overcharged), I am indebted to the authorities last quoted, and also to Albert Crantz Vandal, lib. ii. cap. 37., to Solignac, Histoire Générale de Pologne, tom. i. p. 157—181., and to Zielinski, Histoire de Pologne, tom. i. p. 66—71. It is a pity the last-named writer is so meagre ; he is particularly useful as a faithful, though not always judicious, condenser of the modern Polish historians, whose works, however, would not bear translation. A history of Poland, on a plan at once comprehensive and critical, I expect not to see. Even such a one would be dry — dry at least to English readers in these days.

CASIMIR I.

1041—1058.

CASIMIR, surnamed *the Restorer*, proved himself worthy of the confidence reposed in him by his people ; no higher praise can be given him than that he was equal to the difficulties of his situation. His first care was to repair the evils which had so long afflicted the country. The great he reduced to obedience,— some by persuasion, others by firm but mild acts of authority ; and, what was more difficult, he reconciled them to each other. The affection borne towards his person, and the need which all had of him, rendered his task not indeed easy, but certainly practicable. The submission of the nobles occasioned that of the people, whose interests were no less involved in the restoration of tranquillity and happiness. Where there was so good a disposition for a basis, the superstructure could not fail to correspond. The towns were rebuilt and repeopled ; industry began to flourish ; the laws to resume their empire over brute force ; and hope to animate those whom despair had driven to recklessness.

Nor was this politic prince less successful in his foreign relations. To conciliate the power of Yaroslaf, the fiercest and most formidable of his enemies, he proposed an alliance to be still more closely cemented by his marriage with a sister of the duke.* His offer was accepted, and he was also promised a considerable body of Prussian auxiliaries to assist him in reconquering Silesia, Pomerania, and the province of Masovia, which still recognised the rebel Masos.

This adventurer gave him more trouble than would have been anticipated. Though signally defeated. by the

* This princess, whose mother was the daughter of a Greek emperor, had no scruple to abjure the Greek religion, and embrace that of the Latin church. Her original name was *Maria*, but on her re-baptism she received that of *Dobrogneva*.

king, he had yet address enough to assemble another
army, chiefly of pagan Prussians, much more numerous
than any he had previously commanded.   Casimir was
for a moment discouraged ; his forces had been weakened
even by his successes ; and he apprehended that, even
should victory again declare for him, he would be left
without troops to make head against his other enemies.
At this time he is said to have looked back with sincere
regret to the peaceful cloister he had abandoned.* But
this weakness soon gave way to thoughts more worthy
of him : he met the enemy on the banks of the Vistula,
when a sanguinary contest afforded him an occasion of
displaying his valour no less than his ability. He fought
like the meanest soldier, was severely wounded, and was
saved from destruction by the devotion of a follower.
But in the end his arms were victorious ; 15,000 of the
rebels lay on the field ; Masos was glad to take refuge
in Prussia, by the fierce inhabitants of which he was
publicly executed, as the author of their calamities.

The rest of the reign of Casimir exhibits little to
strike the attention.   Bohemia was restrained from disquieting him, rather through the interference of his ally
the emperor Henry III., than his own valour.   Silesia
was surrendered to him ; Prussia acknowledged his superiority, and paid him tribute ; Pomerania was tran-
quillised, and Hungary sought his alliance. But signal as
were these advantages, they were inferior to those which
his personal character and influence procured for his
country.   Convinced that no state can be happy, however wise the laws that govern it, where morality is not
still more powerful, he laboured indefatigably to purify

* He is said by Dlugoss (lib. iiL col. 225.) to have actually resolved on
leaving his wife, his crown, and the world, again to seek the tranquillity of
his monastery. By a vision, however, his courage was renewed. Having
raised that of his followers by the prospect of victory, he led them eagerly
to the field, where an angel clothed in white, and mounted on a white horse,
animated them by his exhortations. " Visus enim est tunc a Polonis signa
infesta in hostes inferentibus et prælium capessentibus, vir quidam niveo
amictus vestitu, alboque equo insidens, vexillum quoque candidum gestans,
in aëre consistere et continua adhortatione Polonos, usque certamen du-
rabat, ad dimicandum animare." It is strange that the legend of the old
Castilians should have found its way into Poland. The Spaniards would
not be well pleased to hear that Santiago had favoured other people besides
themselves.

the manners of his people, by teaching them their duties, by a more extended religious education, and by his own example, as well as that of his friends and coun- sellors. For the twelve monks whom he persuaded to leave their retirements at Clugni, to assist him in the moral reformation of his subjects, he founded two mon- asteries, one near Cracow, the other on the Oder, in Silesia. Both establishments zealously promoted his views; instruction was more widely diffused; and the de- cent splendour of the public worship made on the minds of the rude inhabitants, not yet fully reclaimed from paganism, an impression which could never have been produced by mere preaching.

Before his death this excellent prince could congratu- late himself that he had saved millions, and injured no one individual; that he had laid the foundation of a purer system of manners; that he was the regenerator no less than the restorer of his country. His memory is still dear to the Poles.*

BOLESLAS II.

1058—1081.

Boleslas II., surnamed the Bold, was only sixteen when he assumed the reins of government. But long before that period he had exhibited proofs of extraor- dinary capacity, and of that generosity of sentiment in- separable from elevation of mind. Unfortunately, how- ever, he wanted the more useful qualities of his deceased father: those which he possessed were splendid indeed, but among them the sparks of an insatiable ambition lay concealed, which required only the breath of opportunity to burst forth in flames.

* The reign of Casimir is extracted from Kadlubek, lib. ii. epist. 16 ; from Dlugoss, lib. iii. col. 201—247. ; from Sarnicki, lib. vi. cap. 8. ; from Cromer, lib. iii. p. 74—79. ; from Krantz, Vandal., lib. ii. cap. 37. ; and from Narus- zewitz (as condensed by Zielinski), ii. 216, &c. See also the Bohemian autho- rities before quoted, and the two chronicles in the collection of the Sile- sian historians.

That opportunity was not long wanting. A few years after his accession, three fugitive princes arrived at his court, to implore his aid in recovering their lost honours. None indeed of the three had any well grounded claim to sympathy, since all had forfeited the privileges of their birth by misconduct of their own; but the protector of unfortunate princes was a title which he most coveted, and all were favourably received.

The first of these, Jaromir, brother of Wratislas duke of Bohemia, had early entered the church, allured by the prospect of the episcopal throne of Prague: but he soon became disgusted with a profession which set a restraint on his worst passions; and ambitious of temporal distinctions he left his cloister, plunged into the dissipations of the world, but was soon compelled by his brother to return to it. He escaped a second time, and endeavoured to gain supporters in his wild attempts to subvert the authority of Wratislas; but finding his freedom, if not his existence, perilled in Bohemia, he threw himself into the arms of Boleslas. The result was a war between the two countries, which was disastrous to the Bohemians, but to which an end was at length brought by the interference of the Germanic princes. Jaromir was persuaded to resume his former vocation, and to bound his ambition within the limits of a mitre; the marriage of Wratislas with the sister of the Polish king secured for a time the blessings of peace to these martial people.*

The second expedition in favour of Bela, prince of Hungary, who aspired to the throne of his brother Andrew, was no less successful. Andrew was defeated, and slain in a wood, probably by his own domestics, and Bela was crowned by the conquering Boleslas. This was not all. Seven years afterwards he again invaded Hungary, to espouse the interests of Geysa the son of Bela, who had been killed in a hut which the violence of

* Dubravius, lib. viii. p. 618. Pontanus, lib. ii (in Scriptor. Rerum Bohemicarum, collected by Freher) Cosma of Prague, Chronica, lib. i. et ii. (in eadem collectione.)

a storm had tumbled on the royal guest. Salomon the son of Andrew had been crowned by the influence of the emperor Henry III. Again was he joined by numerous partisans of the exiled prince. Salomon fled into Lower Hungary; but he there occupied a position so strong by nature as to defy the force of his enemies. In consternation at the evils which impended over the kingdom, some prelates undertook the appropriate task of effecting an accommodation between the contending princes. Through their influence an assembly was held at Mofo, which was attended by the rival claimants; and it was at length agreed that Salomon should retain the title of king; that Geysa and his brothers should be put into possession of one third of the country, to be governed as a duchy; and that the Polish monarch should be indemnified by both for the expenses he ·had incurred in the expedition. The reigning king was to be crowned anew, and to receive the ensigns of his dignity from the hands of Geysa.[*]

But the most splendid of the warlike undertakings of Boleslas was his expeditions into Russia. His ostensible object was to espouse the cause of Isislaf. " I am obliged to succour that prince," said he, " by the blood which unites us, and by the pity so justly due to his misfortunes. Unfortunate princes are more to be commiserated than ordinary mortals. If calamities must necessarily exist on earth, they should not be allowed to affect such as are exalted for the happiness of others." This show of generosity, however, though it had its due weight with him, was not the only cause of his arming. The recovery of the possessions which his predecessors had held in Russia, and of the domains which he conceived he had a right to inherit through his mother and his queen (like his father he had married a Russian princess), was the aim he avowed to his followers. He accordingly marched against Ucheslaf, who had expelled

Sviatoslar

* Bonfinius (dec. ii. lib. ii. et iii.) is unwilling to allow Boleslas much honour in the Hungarian war; he scarcely, indeed, condescends to mention him: I suspect that the Poles have here exaggerated the exploits and influence of their monarch.

Isislaf from Kiovia: both were sons of Yaroslaf, who
had committed the fatal, but in that period common,
error of dividing his dominions among his children, and
thereby opening the door to the most unnatural of
contests.

The two armies met within a few leagues of Kiow.
The martial appearance and undaunted mien of the Poles
struck terror into Ucheslaf, who secretly fled from his
tent. He had not gone far before his pusillanimity made
him despicable even in his own eyes; he blushed and
returned. Again was he seized with the same panic
fear; he fled with all haste towards Polotsk, and his
army, deprived of its natural head, disbanded. Kiow
was invested; it surrendered to the authority of Isislaf;
Polotsk followed the example, but Ucheslaf first contrived to escape. Boleslas remained some time at Kiow,
plunged in the dissipation to which his temperament
and the loose morals of the inhabitants alike inclined
him. He was not, however, wholly unmindful of his
military fame, since he forsook the luxurious vices of
that city for the subjugation of Prezemysl, an ancient
dependency of Poland. Probably he would at the same
time have amplified his territories by other conquests,
had he not been summoned into Hungary to succour, as
before related, the son of the deceased Bela.

On the pacification of that kingdom he returned to
Russia, to inflict vengeance on the brothers of Isislaf,
whom they had again expelled from Kiow. Though he
was resolved to restore that prince, he was no less so to
make him tributary to Poland. He speedily subjugated
the whole of Volhynia, with the design of having a retreat in case fortune proved inconstant. Such precau-
tions, however, were useless: in a decisive battle fought
in the duchy of Kiovia, he almost annihilated the forces
of the reigning duke Usevolod. Kiow was again invested;
but as it was well supplied with provisions, and still
better defended by the inhabitants, it long set his power
at defiance. Perhaps Boleslas, who was impetuous in
every thing, and with whom patience was an unknown

word, would soon have raised the siege, and proceeded
to less tedious conquests, had not a contagious fever suddenly broke out among the besieged, and driven the
greater portion of them from the city.   Those who remained were too few to dream of defending it any longer;
they capitulated, and admitted the victor just as the fury
of the plague had exhausted itself. Isislaf was restored,
and the other provinces of the dukes given to his children. Boleslas might have held them by the right of
conquest, but. he preferred leaving friends rather than
enemies behind him ; he preferred having these territories tributary to him, and dependent on him as sovereign paramount, rather than incorporating them at
once with his dominions, and thereby subjecting himself
and successors to the necessity of perpetually flying to
their protection against the inevitable struggles of the
Russians for freedom.   Even this advantage he must
either have perceived would be transient, or he must
have had little sagacity. Ambition, however, seldom
reasons ; and Boleslas, from his great success, might
almost be justified in believing that for him was reserved
a fortune peculiar to himself.

The generosity with which he behaved to the Kiovians, the affability of his manner, and a mien truly
royal, soon rendered him a favourite with them.   He
plunged into dissipation with even more·than his former
ardour : his days and nights were passed in feasting,
drinking, and the company of the frail beauties of the
place. Ere long his officers, then his meanest followers,
so successfully imitated his example, that, according to
the statements of both Russian and Polish historians, all
.serious business seemed suspended, and pleasure was the
only object of old and young, of Pole and Muscovite.
Isislaf, from gratitude no less than policy, endeavoured
to make the residence of his benefactor as agreeable as
he could. On one occasion, when desirous of a visit
from Boleslas, he offered to the king as many marks of
gold as the royal horse should take steps from the palace
of the king to that of the duke ; a distance, we are told,

considerable enough to enrich the monarch. Sunk in such unworthy sensuality, both Boleslas and his followers forgot their country, when both were reminded of it by a circumstance too extraordinary to be related, were it not unanimously attested by ancient, and received as indubitable by all modern, authors.

Boleslas and his followers, say they, had now been seven years absent from home (in Hungary and Russia), and during the whole of that period had never seen their wives and children. Of these ladies many, doubtless, were widows, but none could be sure of the fact; many more wished to be considered such: year after year had passed away, and in all weakened, in many destroyed, their attachments to their absent lords. Weary at length of their cheerless condition in this worse than widowhood, they sought, or submitted to, the embraces of their slaves,—whether as mistresses, or actually married to their gallants, is doubtful. This prostitution, or bigamy, is said to have been all but universal, since one lady only is mentioned who had the virtue to resist the torrent. Her name (which histories have been careful to preserve, as if the observance of a common duty were a species of prodigy,) was Margaret, the wife of count Nicholas de Zembosin. Whether through distrust of her own resolution, or from apprehension of violence, she shut herself up, some say in the dungeon of a fortress, others in the steeple of a neighbouring church, where she remained in secrecy until the return of her husband. No sooner did the news of this unexpected depravity reach the husbands, than in a transport of shame and fury they begged permission to return. For a time Boleslas, who had perhaps more confidence in his queen, or more pleasure in the arms of his new connections, amused them with the prospect of departure; but as he made no preparations for it, numbers of them at length lost all patience, and returned without his permission. On their arrival they found their slaves comfortably presiding at their boards, and in possession of all their privileges. What followed is related as vari-

D 4

ously as any other point of this strange history. That
the culprit paramours were punished is natural to be
believed; but, if any faith is to be had in one historian,
the injured husbands had great difficulty in dispossessing
them of the places they had usurped. By some of the
ladies they are said to have been preferred to their lawful partners, whom they even encouraged their paramours
to resist to the last extremity. Despair of pardon might,
indeed, unite great numbers of both; but it is more probable that the far greater portion consulted their safety
by flight. A few of the women were sacrificed by their
enraged lords; the rest contrived to elude chastisement,
by what means we are left to guess: many, no doubt,
would vociferously attest their innocence, which might
be difficult to disprove in cases where the positive guilt
had not been witnessed by the injured party himself.*
However this be, all seems to have become tranquil on
the arrival of Boleslas, who was soon compelled to follow them, breathing vengeance against them for deserting
him. And vengeance, it is said, he inflicted, both on
his disobedient soldiers and their guilty wives.†

Much of this is fabulous; yet, from the concurrent
testimony of tradition and history, it is impossible not
to believe that the foundation of the story is true. If
one hundred women only, — and surely that number
would be found in any country, and at any time, under
similar circumstances, — were really guilty of such infidelity, fame would multiply them at least tenfold.
Though the dishonour of the reputed thousand would
not be the dishonour of every married man, yet every
one might think it his own. Hence the anxiety of each

* " Les femmes eurent recours aux armes ordinaires de leur sexe, à des
larmes feintes, à des protestations de repentir, et quelques unes peut-être à
uu desaveu formel de leurs désordres."—*Solignac*, i. 270. This writer never
loses sight of the raillery for which his countrymen are so unrivalled.
† The men, we are told, were put to death; but a singular punishment
awaited the women. " Mulieribus, quibus mariti pepercerant, fœtu quem
ex servis suo ceperant, abjecto, catulos ad mamillas in ultionem admis-
sorum stuprorum, applicari mandat, indignas agens eas prolem humanam,
sed caninam, idoneas lactare, quæ humanitatis oblitæ, viris militam agen-
tibus, toro violato, servis se miscuerant, denique exterminium, et quælibet
probra, non vitam, promeruisse."—*Dlugoss*, iii. 282. The gravity with which
such things are related is edifying.

husband to return home to ascertain whether *he* was one of the injured: hence, too, we may account for the general desertion of Boleslas.

The cruelty of the king is said to have sunk deep into the hearts of his subjects. There is more reason for believing that the excesses to which he abandoned himself after his return produced that effect. His character — outwardly at least — had changed: his industry, his love of justice, his regal qualities, had fled, and he was become the veriest debauchee in his dominions. No man was safe from his anger, no woman from his lust: his virtuous counsellors were dismissed, and none were retained near his person but such as consented to share his orgies. To increase the general discontent, impositions, equally arbitrary and enormous, were laid on an already burdened people.

Had conduct such as this been practised by almost any other sovereign of Poland, the popular indignation would have been appeased only by his deposition. But the son of Casimir, independently of his former merit, and of his splendid deeds in war, required to be treated with greater indulgence. His reformation, not his ruin, was the prayer of his subjects. Such was the impetuosity of his disposition, and such the cruelties he had practised since his fatal residence at Kiow, that Stanislas, bishop of Cracow, was the only man whom history mentions courageous enough to expostulate with him on his excesses, and to urge the necessity of amendment. Mild, and even affectionate, as was the manner of this excellent prelate, the only effect which it had was to draw on him the persecution of the king. But persecution could not influence a man so conscious of his good purposes, and so strong in his sense of duty. He returned to his exhortations; but finding that leniency had no good result, he excommunicated the royal delinquent. Rage took possession of the soul of Boleslas; but instead of " turning from the evil of his ways," he became the more shameless in his iniquities. Stanislas had now recourse to one of the last bolts which the church held

in the storehouse of her thunders: he placed an interdict on all the churches of Cracow; a measure at all
times more violent than just, and in the present case not
likely to have any other effect than to harden impeni-
tence.   Now no longer master of his fury, the king
swore the destruction of the prelate, whose steps he
caused to be watched by his creatures.   Hearing one
day that Stanislas was to celebrate mass in a chapel
situated on a hill beyond the Vistula, he took with him
a few determined followers, and on reaching the extensive plain in the centre of which the hill lay, he perceived from afar his destined victim ascending to the
chapel.   He was at the doors of the sacred edifice before
the conclusion of the office; but eager as was his thirst
for instant vengeance, he forbore to interrupt the solemn
act of worship in which Stanislas and the attendant
clergy were engaged.   When all was over, he ordered
some of his guards to enter and assassinate the prelate.
They were restrained, say the chroniclers, by the hand
of heaven; for in endeavouring to strike him with their
swords, as he calmly stood before the altar, they were
miraculously thrown backwards on the ground.   They
retreated from the place, but were again forced to return
by Boleslas.   A second and a third time, we are told,
was the miracle repeated, until the king, losing all patience, and fearless alike of divine and human punishment, entered the chapel himself; and, with one blow of
his ponderous weapon, dashed out the brains of the
churchman.   If the miracle be fabulous, the tragedy at
least was true.

    Neither Boleslas of Poland nor Henry of England
could murder an ecclesiastic with impunity; and enemies
as we must all be to the extravagant pretensions of the
church in these ages, we can scarcely censure the power
which was formidable enough to avenge so dark a deed.
Gregory VII., who then filled the chair of St. Peter,
hurled his anathemas against the murderer, whom he
deposed from the royal dignity, absolving his subjects
from their oaths of allegiance, and at the same time

placing an interdict on the whole kingdom.   The proud
soul of Boleslas disdained submission to the church : he
endeavoured to resist the execution of its mandates ;
but he speedily found, that in an age when the haugh-
tiest and most powerful monarchs were made to bend
before the spiritual throne, such resistance could only
seal the fate denounced against him.   He was now regarded with horror by clergy and people.   In daily fear
of assassination by his own people, who universally
avoided him, he fled into Hungary, accompanied by his
son Miecislas, in the hope of interesting in his behalf
the reigning king of that country.   But Uladislas, the
brother of Geysa, who had succeeded Salomon, though
he pitied the fugitive, had no wish to bring down on
his own head the thunders of Gregory ; and Boleslas,
after a short stay, was compelled to seek another asylum.
His end is wrapt in great obscurity.   One account says
that he retired to a monastery in Carinthia, to expiate
his crime by penance ; another, that his senses forsook
him, and that in one of his deranged fits he destroyed
himself ; a third, that he was torn to pieces by his own
dogs when hunting ; and a fourth, that being compelled
to occupy a mean situation, he preserved his incognito
until the hour of death, when he astonished his confessor
by the disclosure of his birth and crimes.   Of these
versions of the story it need scarcely be added, that the
first is the only one probable.*

Had Boleslas known how to conquer his own passions
with as much ease as he conquered his enemies †, he
would have been one of the greatest princes that ever filled
a throne.   His character differed at different periods.
Before his expedition to Russia he was the model of
sovereigns ; active, vigilant, just, prudent, liberal, the
father of his subjects, the protector of the unfortunate,
the conqueror and bestower of kingdoms.   *Afterwards*

* None of the old Hungarian writers — as far at least as I can gather
— mention this flight of Boleslas into their country. Their silence, however, does not invalidate the fact
† In the intervals between the expeditions into Bohemia and Hungary,
he reduced the Prussians who had revolted.

his elevation of mind gave way to meanness, his valour to cowardice, his justice to tyranny, his boundless generosity to a pitiful selfishness, which valued no person or thing except in so much as its own gratification was concerned. At one time he was the pride, at another the disgrace, of human nature.*

ULADISLAS I.

SURNAMED THE CARELESS.

1082—1102.

AFTER the disappearance of Boleslas and his son, the state remained without a head almost a year: perhaps it would have remained so much longer but for the incursions of two neighbouring powers, the Russians and the Hungarians, the latter of whom reduced Cracow. In great consternation the nobles then raised to the throne Uladislas Herman, son of Casimir, and brother of the unfortunate Boleslas.

The first act of Uladislas was to despatch a deputation to Rome to procure a reversal of the interdict. The churches were in consequence opened, and permission given that Poland should again be ranked among Christian nations ; but the royal dignity was withheld : Uladislas was allowed to reign as *duke ;* but no prelate in Poland dared to anoint him as *king.* It cannot but surprise us, in these times, that the chief of a great people should have incurred the humiliation of submitting to the papal pretensions ; but perhaps Uladislas expected the

---

* Authorities for the reign of Boleslas II., besides those already quoted, Kadlubek, lib. ii. epist. 20, 21. Dlugoss, lib. iii. col. 247—298. Cromer, lib. iii. 79—91. Sarnicki, lib. vi. cap. ix. Albert Krantz, Vandal, lib. iii. cap. xii. Naruszewitz (as quoted by Zielinski), ii. 254—275., and the two chronicles (in the collection of Silesian historians). Some aid has also been derived from Solignac, tom. i. p. 213—288. This last-named writer is by far the best *narrative* historian of Poland in any language, but he is not always faithful, — the fault of negligence rather than of design. A much greater defect is, that he takes little notice of the laws, institutions, and manners of the people whose history he writes : besides, his work is left unfinished.

return of his brother, over whose fate a deep mystery was believed to hang, and had no very strong wish to assume a title which he might hereafter be compelled to resign. The example, however, was disastrous for the country : during more than 200 years the regal title was disused; nor could the rulers of Poland, as dukes, either repress anarchy at home, or cómmand respect abroad, so vigorously as had been done by the kings their predecessors.

But whether Boleslas should return or not, Uladislas, sensible that he had a powerful party in his interests, resolved to marry, and perpetuate his authority in his offspring. Judith, daughter of Andrew, king of Hungary, was selected as the duchess of Poland. As, however, in two years from her arrival this princess exhibited no signs of pregnancy, both Uladislas and his clergy were apprehensive that she was cursed with barrenness, and no less so of the consequences which such a misfortune might produce. Recourse was had to the interference of heaven ; prayers, alms, pilgrimages, were employed in vain, until the bishop of Cracow advised her to implore the intercession of St. Giles, who had done wonderful things in this way. Pilgrims with rich presents were accordingly sent to a monastery in Lower Languedoc, where that saint had spent and ended his days. Her prayers were heard ; for who could doubt that the son which she afterwards brought forth was miraculously vouchsafed to her ? Her child was christened *Boleslas ;* but the mother did not long live to enjoy her happiness.

Soon after his marriage Uladislas surprised his subjects by the recall of his nephew, Miecislas. By some this step was imputed to magnanimity, by others to policy. Certain it is that the young prince was very popular in Hungary, and the duke might have reason to fear for the prospects of his infant son should the interests of the exile be espoused by that country. However this be, he received Miecislas with much apparent cordiality, and, in four years from his arrival, procured him

the hand of Eudoxia, a Russian princess; but the prince
became a greater idol in Poland than he had ever been
in Hungary, and the apprehensions of the duke naturally
acquired threefold strength.   Things were in this state
when the sudden death of Miecislas was spread over the
country, and caused a sincerer national grief than had
ever been felt since the loss of Casimir.   That his death
had been violent was the general impression; and suspicion pointed to the duke as the murderer, merely because
no other man was supposed to be so deeply interested in
his removal.   Uladislas, however, was not a man of
blood; on the contrary, he was remarkable beyond any
prince of his age for the milder virtues of humanity;
and some better foundation than suspicion must be found
before impartial history will allow his memory to be
stained with so dark a crime.*

It was the misfortune of Uladislas that, during the
greater part of his reign, his dominions were exposed to
the incursions of his fierce neighbours; and a still heavier one that he had neither the vigour nor the talents
to repress them.   The Russians were the first to revolt;
the conquests made by Boleslas the Bold were lost with
greater rapidity than they had been gained.   Before the
duke could think of recovering them (if such, indeed, was
ever his intention), the Prussians, a people more savage,
though much less stupid perhaps, than the ancient Muscovites, prepared to invade his dominions.   With great
reluctance he marched against them.   The steady valour
of his followers enabled him, or rather his general,
Sieciech, to triumph over the undisciplined bravery of

---

* I have my doubts that the death of Miecislas was violent.   Dlugoss
(lib, iv. col. 314.) is, as far as I can gather, the first Polish historian who
adverts to the rumour of violence; but even rumour throws the blame on
a portion of nobles hostile to the prince and his father, not on Uladislas.
Neither Kadlubek nor Boguphal (in Script. Rer. Siles. tom. ii.), both anterior by two centuries to Dlugoss, make any mention of the circumstance.
It is, indeed, darkly alluded to by the *anonymous* authors of two meagre
chronicles (in Script. Rer. Siles. tom. i.), of whom both were very little prior
to Dlugoss; and whose authority, on a point three centuries preceding their
times, is worth absolutely nothing.   It is strange that Solignac (i. 300.)
should appear to credit this vulgar rumour.   Modern native historians
'Naruszewitz, Bandkia, Zielinski,) follow Dlugoss, and throw the blame on
the nobles; but they have no ancient authority for the statement.

these pagan barbarians. But no sooner did the victors retire from the forests of Prussia, than the natives again rose, massacred the garrisons which had been left in their fortresses, and joined in pursuit of the Poles. An obstinate and a bloody battle ensued on the banks of the Notez (Netz), which arrested the advance of the enemy, but so weakened the invaders that they were compelled to return in search of fresh reinforcements. Having gained these (chiefly Bohemian mercenaries), they again directed their march to the Notez, and assailed the strong fort of Nackel on the bank of that river; but on this occasion, we are told, they were seized with an unaccountable dread: they stood so much in fear of an irruption into their tents by the wild defenders of the fort, that they could scarcely be persuaded to snatch a few moments of repose. Every bush, every tree, every rocky height, to their alarmed imaginations seemed peopled with the terrific enemy; and one night, when it had covered the plain before them with these visionary beings, they left their tents to run the risk of an action. The besieged, in the mean time, penetrated to their tents, which they plundered and set on fire, and massacred all whom the light attracted to the place. The loss of the Poles in this most inglorious scene was so severe that they were compelled to retreat. To veil their cowardice, they averred that they had been driven back by supernatural means; that armies of spectres had arisen to oppose them. Absurd as was their plea, it was generally believed: the pagans were thought to be in league with the powers of darkness; so that in the following year when Uladislas returned to vindicate the honour of his arms, not a few wondered at his temerity.* This time he was more successful; Prussia and Pomerania submitted, but with the intention of revolting whenever fortune presented them with the opportunity.

The wars of the duke with Bohemia were less decisive.

* That demons are always favourable to idolaters, we have no less a testimony than that of the sage Kadlubek. " Dæmones suos idololatras ab inimicis suis protegunt, et circa hos miracula faciunt."

Bretislas, duke of that country, resolved to claim the
rights which the emperor Henry, in a fit of displeasure
with Uladislas, had, a few years before, pretended to
bestow on his father, — rights involving even the possession of the Polish crown, which Henry, as lord paramount, claimed the power of transferring, — invaded
Silesia, and wrapt every thing in flames.   By the duke's
command reprisals were made in Moravia, a dependency
of the Bohemian crown.   The Pomeranians advanced
to the assistance of Bretislas, and threw themselves into
the strongest fortress in Silesia.   They were reduced by
Boleslas, son of Uladislas, who, though only in his tenth
year, began to give indications of his future greatness.
The army indeed was commanded by Sieciech, the Polish
general; but the glory of the exploit belonged only to
the prince.   It is certain that from this time jealousy
took possession of the general's heart, and that he did all
he could to injure the prince in the mind of Uladislas,
over whom his influence was without a rival, — an influence which he exerted solely for his own advantage,
and very often to the detriment of the people.   Hence
the dissensions which began to trouble the peace of the
duke; dissensions too in which another individual was
destined to act not the least prominent part.

Before his marriage with the princess Judith, the
duke had a natural son named Sbigniew, whose depravity is represented as in the highest degree revolting,
and who became a dreadful scourge to the kingdom.
The youth, indeed, owed little gratitude to a parent by
whom he had been grossly neglected.   From a peasant's
hut, in a mean village, he had been sent to a monastery
in Saxony, where it was intended he should assume the
cowl.   During his seclusion in the cloister, the tyrannical conduct of Sieciech, to whom the duke abandoned
the cares and the rewards of sovereignty, forced a considerable number of Poles to expatriate themselves and
seek a more tranquil settlement in Bohemia.   With the
view of disquieting Poland, Bretislas persuaded these
emigrants to espouse the cause of Sbigniew, whom he

drew from the monastery to procure for him the sovereignty of Silesia. The hope of crushing the haughty favourite, and of living in peace under the sway of one of their native princes, made them readily join the standard of the new chief.

At the head of these men, Sbigniew boldly advanced to the gates of Breslaw, the governor of which he knew to be unfriendly to the favourite. As his avowed object was merely to effect the removal of an obnoxious minister, the city at length received him. Uladislas advanced to support his authority: Sbigniew fled, collected an army of Prussians, and again took the field. The father conquered; the rebellious prince fell into the hands of Sieciech, his greatest enemy, by whom he was thrown into a dreary dungeon: but the advantage was counterbalanced by the incursions of the Bohemians, who ravaged Silesia, and whom the duke was too timid or too indolent to repress; and ere long the bishops procured the liberation of Sbigniew, whose influence they well saw would soon annihilate that of the detested favourite. The youth, indeed, was more than pardoned; he was raised to the highest honours, and associated with his brother Boleslas in the command of an army which was despatched against those inveterate rebels, the Pomeranians. The two brothers, however, disputed and effected nothing; when Uladislas, alarmed at the prospect of the civil wars which might arise after his decease, took the fatal resolution of announcing the intended division of his states between his two sons: to Boleslas he promised Silesia, the provinces of Cracow, Sendomir, and Siradia, with the title of duke of Poland; to Sbigniew, Pomerania, with the palatinates of Lenszysa, Cujavia, and Masovia. This expedient, which he adopted in the belief that it would prevent all further contention between the princes, became the source of the worst troubles; the example, as we shall hereafter perceive, proved fatal to the prosperity, and even threatened the existence, of Poland.

For a time, indeed, the two youths were united. Both

burned for the destruction of Sieciech, and each had
need of the other to secure the common object. With
the troops which they had obtained to oppose a pretended invasion of the Bohemians, they forced the
feeble and infirm Uladislas to exile his favourite to a distant fortress. But even this did not satisfy them ; they
besieged the place : Uladislas, by means of a disguise,
threw himself into it, resolved to share the fate of his
favourite. His unnatural sons had the army, and, what
was more, the hearts of the Poles in their favour ; nor
would they lay down their arms until the odious minister was banished the country : they then submitted to
their parent.

During the few remaining months of this feeble duke's
life, Poland was governed by the two princes. Its frontiers were frequently a prey to the Pomeranians and
Prussians : the valour of Boleslas chastised their presumption. As for Sbigniew, his ambition indeed was
boundless, and his disposition restless; but his abilities
were slender, and his weakness betrayed him into situations from which he found it hard to escape. There is
reason to believe he was meditating the means of weakening, if not of supplanting, his brother, when the death
of the aged duke suspended for a moment his criminal
designs. By some writers, indeed, that event is said to
have been hastened by a dose of poison, administered by
this precious limb of illegitimacy ; but as Boleslas affectionately took his station by the bed of the dying prince,
which he left not until the last sigh had been breathed,
it is impossible to believe that he should not have known
the crime were it really committed, and that knowing it
he should not have punished it.

Uladislas deserved a better fate. He appears to have
been a Christian and a patriot ; a mild and benevolent
monarch. That his weakness of mind rendered him
the instrument of others, and his infirmity of body prevented him from long enduring the iron labours of war,
can scarcely be attributed to him as a fault, however
disastrous both proved to his subjects. Even for the

fatal division of his dominions between his children,—
fatal more as an example to others than for the positive evil it produced in this case, though that evil was
great,—he had precedents enough, not only in the early
history of Poland, but in the neighbouring country of
Russia.*

BOLESLAS III.

SURNAMED WRYMOUTH.

1102—1139.

SCARCELY were the last rites paid to the deceased duke,
than Sbigniew began to show what the nation had to
expect from his perversity, and from the imprudence
which had left him any means of mischief. He forcibly
seized on the ducal treasures at Plotsko, which, however, the authority of the archbishop of Gnesna compelled him to divide with his brother Boleslas. He
hoped, too, to usurp the provinces and title of that prince,
whose assassination he had probably planned; and his
rage may be conceived on learning that Boleslas was
about to marry a Russian princess, to perpetuate the
hereditary dignity in the legitimate branch of the family.
Instead of attending the nuptials, he proceeded into Bohemia, and at the head of some troops, furnished him
by the duke of that country, he invaded Silesia. But
his followers, who neither respected nor feared him, soon
abandoned him, and returned to their homes, before
Boleslas could march to the defence of that province.
The latter despatched one of his generals to make reprisals in Moravia; and, after the conclusion of his marriage feasts, he himself hastened to humble the presump-

* For the reign of Uladislas I., my Polish authorities are Kadlubek, lib. ii.
epist. 23. Boguphal, the Chronica Polonorum, and the Chronica Principum
Poloniæ (all three contained in the collection of Silesian historians, tom. i.
et ii. Lipsiæ, 1729.). Dlugoss, lib. iv. col. 301—348. Cromer, iii. 100—
104. Sarnicki, lib. vi. cap. 10. Narnszewitz (as quoted by Zielinaki), iii.
57—74. See also Æneas Sylvius, cap. 22—27. Dubravius, lib. ix. et x., and
the Chronicle of Cosma of Prague, lib. iii. Cosma lived in the twelfth century.

tion of the Bohemians. But they fled before him, and
left him nothing but the satisfaction of laying every
thing waste with fire and sword.

Though Sbigniew had thus signally failed, his disposition was too restless, and his breast too depraved, to
suffer him to remain long at peace either with his country or his brother. In the Pomeranians, whose spirit
was in many respects kindred to his own, he found ready
instruments. They armed with the intention of re-
treating to their forests whenever a large Polish force
appeared on their frontiers, and of emerging from their
recesses on its departure. Boleslas, however, took a circuitous route, and fell by surprise on their town of Colberg. The place was valiantly defended, and the duke
was obliged to raise the siege.

A second expedition was not more decisive : the barbarians fled before him. Soon he was constrained to
make head a third time against not only them and his
rebellious brother, but the Bohemians, the cause of
whose exiled duke he had espoused. The latter retreated ; their cowardice ashamed him, since it rendered
his success too easy. He now marched into Pomerania,
and furiously assailed Belgard. The place was defended
with great obstinacy : even women and children appeared on the walls to roll stones or boiling pitch on the
heads of the Poles. The duke was undaunted ; with a
buckler in one hand, and a battle-axe in the other, he
hastened to one of the gates, passed over the ditch by
means of long planks, and assailed the ponderous barrier with the fury of a demon. Boiling water, pitch,
stones, missiles, fell on him in vain : he forced the door,
admitted his soldiers, and with them made a terrible
slaughter of the people, sparing neither age nor sex, and
desisting only from the carnage when their hands were
tired with the murderous work. No people in Europe,
not even excepting the Russians, have shown themselves
so vindictive in war as the Poles. The fall of this town
was followed by that of four others no less considerable, and by the submission of the whole country.

In this expedition Boleslas exhibited another proof of his fearless intrepidity. He had been invited to pass a few days at the house of a noble in the country, to be present at the consecration of a new church. While there he set out early one morning for the chase, accompanied by eighty horse. He was suddenly enveloped by 3000 Pomeranians. He tranquilly drew his sabre, and, followed by his heroic little band, speedily fought his way through the dense mass which encompassed him. This was not all: disdaining to flee, he turned round on the enemy, and again passed through them. His followers were now reduced to five; yet he was foolhardy enough to plunge a third time into the middle of the Pomeranians. This time, however, he was well nigh paying dear for his temerity: his horse was killed; he fought on foot, and was on the point of falling, when one of his officers arrived with thirty horse, and extricated him from his desperate situation.— Is this history or romance?

Sbigniew, disconcerted at the success of his brother, now sued for pardon through the duke of Kiow, father-in-law of Boleslas. He readily procured it on engaging to have no other interests, no other friends or enemies, than those of his brother. Yet at this very moment he was in league with the Bohemians to harass the frontiers of Poland. He had scarcely reached his own territories when, on Boleslas requesting the aid of his troops, he refused it with expressions of insult and defiance: he knew that both Bohemia and Pomerania were arming in his cause. The patience of Boleslas was worn out: with a considerable body of auxiliaries from Hungary and Kiow he invaded the territories of his brother, whose strongest places he reduced with rapidity: all were ready to forsake the iron yoke of a capricious, sanguinary, and cowardly tyrant. Sbigniew implored the protection of the bishop of Cracow, and by the influence of that prelate obtained peace, but with the sacrifice of all his possessions except Masovia. He was too restless, however, to remain long quiet; so that, in the following year, an

assembly of nobles was convoked to deliberate on the
best means of dealing with one who violated the most
solemn oaths with impunity. It was resolved that he
should be deprived of Masovia, and for ever banished
from Poland.

At this time Boleslas was engaged in a serious war
not only with the Bohemians, but with Henry V., emperor of Germany, who espoused their interests. He
was victorious; but, like the enemy, having occasion to
recruit his forces, he abandoned the field. Hearing that
the town of Wollin in Pomerania had revolted, he
marched to reduce it. He had invested the place, when
he was suddenly assailed in his rear by a troop of the
natives, whom he soon put to flight, several prisoners
remaining in his hands. One of these refused to raise
the vizor of his helmet; it was forcibly unlaced, and
then was discovered Sbigniew! A council of war was
assembled, and the traitor was condemned to death: but
he was merely driven from the country by Boleslas, who
warned him, however, that his next delinquency,—nay,
his next appearance in Poland,—should be visited with
the last punishment. But Gnievomir, one of the most
powerful Pomeranian chiefs, who had some time before
embraced Christianity, had sworn fealty to Boleslas, and
had now both abjured his new religion and joined the
party of Sbigniew, was not so fortunate as that outlaw:
he was hewn to pieces in presence of the Polish army—
a barbarous act, but one which had for a time a salutary
effect on the fierce pagans.

In the war which followed with the imperialists, who
were always ready to harass a power which refused to
acknowledge the supremacy of the empire, which they
hated and dreaded at the same time, nothing is more
deserving of remembrance than the heroic defence made
by the city of Glogaw against the power of Henry. The
women and children shared in the toils and the glory of
the men. The emperor was often driven from the walls,
his works demolished, the breaches repaired; but he as
often returned, and vowed he would never leave the place

until it fell into his power. At length both sides agreed
to a suspension of hostilities, on the condition that if
Boleslas did not relieve the place within five days, it
should be surrendered to Henry, to whom hostages were
delivered. The Polish duke was not far distant; but he
was waiting for the arrival of his reinforcements from
Russia and Hungary, without whose aid he durst not
attack the combined force of the empire: he exhorted
the inhabitants to hold out at the expiration of the period
limited, assuring them that he would hang them if they
surrendered. The time expired; the citizens refused to
fulfil their engagements. The indignant Henry moved
his legions to the walls, placing in front the hostages he
held. Not even the sentiments of nature affected them
so powerfully as their hatred of the German yoke, and
their apprehensions of Boleslas: they threw their missiles, beheld with indifference the deaths of their children
transfixed by their own hands, and again forced the
imperialists to retire from the walls. Boleslas now approached: he enclosed the Germans between himself and
the ramparts, and held them as much besieged in the
plain as were his subjects in the city. For several succeeding days his cavalry harassed them in their entrenchments, but no general engagement took place.

Irritated at the delay, he had then recourse to a diabolical expedient: he procured the assassination of the
Bohemian chief for whose cause Henry had armed, and
in the very tent of that emperor. The Bohemians, as
he had foreseen, now insisted on returning to their homes;
Henry, weakened by their desertion, slowly retreated:
the Poles pursued until both armies arrived on the vast
plain before Breslaw, where the emperor risked a battle.
It was stoutly contested; but in the end the Germans
gave way; and the Poles, true to the ferocity of their
character in all ages, committed a horrible carnage on
such as were unable to flee. Peace was soon after made
between the emperor and duke; the latter, who was a
widower, receiving the hand of Adelaide, and his son

Uladislas that of Christina (or Agnes), the one sister, the other daughter of Henry.

During the following four years Boleslas was perpetually engaged in war, either with the Bohemians or the Pomeranians, or, as was more frequently the case, with both at the same time. His own ambition was as often the cause of these wars as the restlessness of the enemy. He appears, indeed, to have been so far elated with his successes as to adopt a haughty domineering tone towards his neighbours; a tone to which they were never willing to submit. Yet he had many great traits of character: he often behaved nobly to the vanquished Bohemian duke; and he even so far mastered his aversion as to recal his exiled brother, who never ceased either to importune for his return, or to plot against his peace.

Sbigniew made a triumphal entry into Poland; the very reverse of one that became a pardoned criminal. Every man who considered his ungrateful character, his insolence, his incorrigible depravity, and the irascible disposition of the duke, foresaw the fatal termination of his career. In a few short months Boleslas yielded to the incessant arguments of his courtiers, and Sbigniew was assassinated.

During the succeeding years of his life Boleslas endeavoured to stifle his remorse, by such works as he hoped would propitiate the favour of Heaven. Having quelled repeated insurrections in Pomerania, he undertook to convert it to the true faith. His efforts were to a certain extent successful; not, perhaps, so much through the preaching of his ecclesiastics, especially of Otho, bishop of Bamberg, as through the sums which he expended in disposing the minds of the rude but avaricious chiefs to the doctrines of Christianity. Many towns publicly embraced the new religion. For a time Stettin stood out; but the golden argument, or at least the promise of an exemption from imposts, brought about its conversion. Idols were in most places demolished, churches erected, priests ordained, and bishops consecrated. Still the voice of inward conscience spoke out too loud to be silenced, and the unhappy duke had recourse to the usual expedient of the times. He built churches and monasteries; fasted; subjected himself to rigorous acts of penance; and visited, in the garb and with the staff of a pilgrim, the shrines of several saints. Not only did he thus honour the relics of St. Adalbert at Gnesna, and the tomb of St. Stephen of Hungary, but, it is said, he ventured on a long and painful pilgrimage to the shrine of St. Giles in Languedoc, the efficacy of whose intercession had been so signally experienced by his mother. On his way he relaxed not from the severe austerities he had imposed: with naked feet he daily stood in the churches, joining with the utmost fervency in the canonical hours, in the penitential psalms, and all other offices of devotion; at every chapel or oratory he turned aside to repeat his prayers, or offer gifts; he relieved all the poor he approached; and wasted himself with vigils. On reaching the end of his journey he practised still greater austerities; during fifteen successive days he lay prostrate before the tomb of St. Giles: such, indeed, was his abstinence, his contrition, his humility, that the monks were as edified by his visit as he himself. He returned safely to his country, lightened, in his own mind at least, of no small burden of his guilt, and purified completely in the eyes of his subjects. If his reformation was in some respects mistaken, it was certainly sincere, and charity may hope availing.

But a mortification more bitter than any which religious penance could inflict awaited him. Until within four years of his death his arms were almost invariably successful. He had repeatedly discomfited the Bohemians and Pomeranians; he had humbled the pride of emperors; had twice dictated laws to Hungary, and gained signal triumphs over the Russians.* It was now his turn to meet with a reverse of fortune: he was sur-

* The old Polish histories lead Boleslas into Denmark. This is a fable arising probably from an alliance (obscurely hinted at) between him and Nicholas, the usurper of that kingdom, in which both engaged to act in concert in subduing the wild inhabitants on the southern coast of the Baltic.

prised and defeated on the banks of the Niester by a
vastly superior force of Hungarians and Russians: the
Polish historians throw the blame on the palatin of Cracow, who retired from the field in the heat of the action.
After a precipitate retreat, Boleslas deliberated what
vengeance should be inflicted on a man through whose
cowardice his arms had been thus fatally dishonoured.
His first impulse was to execute the recreant; but vengeance gave way to a disdainful pity. The palatin was left
with life and liberty; but the reception of a hare skin,
a spindle, and distaff, from the hands of the duke, was
an insult too intolerable to be borne, and he hanged
himself.

One of the last acts of Boleslas was to redeem as
many of the prisoners made on this occasion as could be
mustered. The blow fell heavily on his heart. The
victor in forty-seven battles, the bravest prince of the
age, could not review his disgrace at an age when his
bodily strength had departed, and when no one was to
be found on whom he could devolve the task of repairing
it. After a year's indisposition — more of the mind than
of the body — in which he followed the fatal precedent
of his father, by dividing his dominions among his sons,
death put a period to his temporal sufferings. With
him was buried the glory of Poland until the restoration
of the monarchy. His character must be sufficiently
known from his actions.[*]

---

[*] Kadlubek, lib. ii. epist. 27—30., and lib. iii. epist. 1—28. Dlugoss, lib. iv.
col. 349—452. Boguphal, Chronica Poloniæ. Chronica Polonorum, nec-
non Chronica Principum Poloniæ (in Script. Rer. Siles. tom. i. et ii.).
Cromer, lib. iii. p. 135, &c. Sarnicki, lib. vi. cap. xi. Naruszewitz (as
quoted by Zielinski), iii. 86—172. See also Dubravius, ubi supra, and Bonfinius, dec. ii. lib. v.

CHAP. II.

HOUSE OF PIAST CONTINUED. — ARISTOCRATIC RULERS.

1139—1295.

THE period from the death of Boleslas Wrymouth to the restoration of the monarchy is one of little interest; it exhibits nothing but the lamentable dissensions of the rival princes, and the progressive decay of a once powerful kingdom.

By the will of the late duke, Poland was thus divided among his sons: —

The provinces of Cracow, Lentsysa, Sieradz, Silesia, and Pomerania fell to the eldest, *Uladislas*, who, to preserve something like the unity of power, was also invested with supreme authority over the rest.

Those of Masovia, Kujavia, with the territories of Dobrezyn and Culm, were assigned to the second brother, *Boleslas*.

Those of Gnesna, Posen, and Halitz were subjected to *Miecislas*, the third brother.

Those of Lublin and Sendomir were left to *Henry*, the fourth in order of birth.

There remained a fifth and youngest son, *Casimir*, to whom nothing was bequeathed. When the late duke was asked the reason why this best beloved of his children was thus neglected, he is said to have replied by a homely proverb; " The four-wheeled chariot must have a driver:" a reply prophetic of the future superiority of one whose talents were already beginning to open with remarkable promise. It is more probable that his tender years alone were the cause of his present exclusion; and that, as the provinces before enumerated were intended to be held not as hereditary, but as moveable fiefs, reversible to the eldest son, as lord paramount, on the death of the possessors, he was secure of one in case such an event should happen during his life.

The fatal effects of this division were soon apparent. The younger princes were willing, indeed, to consider their elder brother as superior lord ; but they disdained to yield him other than a feudal obedience, and denied his authority in their respective appanages.   In an assembly at Kruswick, however, they were constrained not only to own themselves his vassals but to recognise his sovereignty, and leave to his sole decision the important questions of peace and war.

But such discordant materials could not be made to combine in one harmonious frame of goverment.   Uladislas naturally considered every appearance of authority independent of his will as affecting his rights of primogeniture.   His discontent was powerfully fomented by the arts of his German consort, who incessantly urged him to unite under his sceptre the dissevered portions of the monarchy.   Her address prevailed.   To veil his ambition under the cloak of justice and policy, he convoked an assembly of his nobles at Cracow.   To them he exposed, with greater truth than eloquence, the evils which had been occasioned in former periods of the national history from the division of the sovereign power ; and he urged the restoration of its union as the only measure capable of saving the country either from domestic treason or from foreign aggression.   But they were not convinced by the arguments of one whose ambition they justly deemed superior to his patriotism : those arguments, indeed, they could not answer ; but they modestly urged the sanctity of his late father's will, and the obligation under which he lay of observing its provisions. Disappointed in this quarter, he had recourse to more decisive measures.   He first exacted a heavy contribution from each of the princes : his demand excited their astonishment, but they offered no resistance to it.   With the money thus summarily acquired, he not only raised troops, but hired Russian auxiliaries to aid him in his design of expelling his brethren from their appanages.

Their territories were soon entered, and, as no defence had been organised, were soon reduced; and these unfortunate victims of fraternal violence fled to Posmania, the only place which still held for Henry. In vain did they appeal to his justice no less than his affection: in vain did they endeavour to bend the heart of the haughty Agnes, whom they well knew to be the chief author of their woes. A deaf ear was offered to their supplications; and they were even given to understand that their banishment from the country would follow their expulsion from their possessions.

This arbitrary violence made a deep impression on the Poles. The archbishop of Gnesna espoused the cause of the deprived princes. Uszebor, palatin of Sendomir, raised troops in their behalf. The views of both were aided far beyond their expectation by a tragic incident. Count Peter, a nobleman of great riches and influence, who had been the confidential friend of Boleslas Wrymouth, and who lived in the court of Uladislas, inveighed both in public and private against the measures of the duke. But as his opposition was confined to speaking, it did not wholly destroy his favour with the latter. One day both being engaged in hunting, they alighted to take refreshment. As they afterwards reclined on the hard, cold ground (it was the winter season), Uladislas observed: — " We are not so comfortably situated here, Peter, as thy wife now is, on a bed of down with her fat abbot Skrezepiski!"—" No," replied the other; " nor as yours in the arms of your page Dobiesz!" Whether either intended more than as a jest is doubtful; but the count paid dear for his freedom. The incensed Agnes, to whom the duke communicated the repartee, contrived to vindicate herself in his eyes; but she vowed the destruction of the count. She had him seized at an entertainment, thrown into prison, and deprived both of his tongue and eyes.[*] The popular indignation now

* Kadlubek (iii. ep. 28.) quaintly assures us : — " Mulieris truculentiam sæviorem esse omni severitate." Even the placidity of the sex is destruction. " Est enim omnis mansuetudo fœminæ omnium (beasts) severitate truculentior, omnium truculentiâ severior."

burst forth in every direction. Uszebor defeated the
Russian auxiliaries; the Pomeranians poured their wild
hordes into Great Poland; the pope excommunicated the
princess, because through her he was disappointed of
the aids he solicited against the infidels; and the same
dreaded doom was hurled at the head of the duke by the
archbishop of Gnesna, the staunch advocate of the exiled
princes. Uladislas himself was defeated, and forced to
take refuge in Cracow. Thither he was pursued by his
indignant subjects, who would probably have served him
as he had done count Peter, had he not precipitately
abandoned both sceptre and consort, and fled into Germany to implore the aid of his brother-in-law, the emperor Conrad. Cracow fell; Agnes became the captive
of the princes whose ruin she had all but effected. Her
mean supplications moved their contempt as much as
her ambition and cruelty had provoked their hatred.
She was, however, respectfully conducted over the frontiers of the duchy, and told to rejoin her kindred.*

By the princes and nobles BOLESLAS, the eldest of
the remaining brothers, was unanimously elected to the
vacant dignity.

The new duke had need of all his talents and courage
— and he possessed both in no ordinary degree — to
meet the difficulties of his situation. By confirming
his brothers in their respective appanages, and even increasing their territories, he effectually gained their support; but he had to defend his rights against the whole
force of the empire, which espoused the cause of the
exiles. In a personal interview, indeed, he disarmed
the hostility of Conrad, who was too honest to oppose
a man whose conduct he could not fail to approve; but
Frederick Barbarossa, the successor of that emperor, was
less scrupulous, or more ambitious. A resolution of the

* Authorities for the reign of Uladislas II. Kadlubek, lib. iii. epist. 28.
and 29. Dlugoss, lib. v. col. 453—473. Chronica Principum Poloniæ, nec-
non Chronica Polonorum (in Script. Rerum Siles. tom. i.). Boguphali
Chronica (in eadem collectione; t. ii.). Cromer, 136—146. Stanislai Sarnicii Annalium Polon. lib. vi. cap. 12. Narussewits (as quoted by Zielinski),
tom. iii. p. 201—219. The last of these writers is sometimes, on points of
chronology, strangely at variance with the old authorities.

diet having summoned the Polish duke to surrender his throne to Uladislas, or acknowledge his country tributary to the empire, he prepared to defend his own dignity and the national independence. Aided by his brothers, whose privileges he had so religiously respected, and by his subjects, whose welfare he had constantly endeavoured to promote, he feared not the result, though an overwhelming force of imperialists and Bohemians rapidly approached Silesia. Had he ventured, however, to measure arms with the formidable Barbarossa, neither the valour of his troops nor the goodness of his cause would have much availed him; but by hovering about the flanks of the enemy, by harassing them with repeated skirmishes, and, above all, by laying waste the country through which they marched, he constrained them to sue for peace. The conditions were, that Uladislas should have Silesia, and that Barbarossa should be furnished with three hundred Polish lances in his approaching expedition into Italy. The former died before he could take possession of the province; but through the interference of the latter it was divided among his three sons, who held it as a fief of Poland, and did homage for it to duke Boleslas.*

The subsequent exploits of Boleslas were less successful. In one expedition, indeed, he reduced the Prussians, who, not content with revolting ever since the death of Boleslas Wrymouth, had abolished Christianity and returned to their ancient idolatry; but, in a second, his troops were drawn into a marshy country, were there surprised, and almost annihilated. This was a severe blow to Poland: among the number of the slain was Henry, the duke's brother, whose provinces of Sendomir and Lublin now became the appanage of Casimir.

---

* From the latter of these conditions, and the concurrent testimony of the German histories, I am not sure that Poland was altogether so independent of the empire as the national writers pretend. It is certain that the former unanimously term the country as tributary as Bohemia itself. Servit et ipsa (Polonia) sicut Boëmia, sub tributo imperatoriæ majestatis, are the words of Helmotd, who wrote in the time of Barbarossa. Another authority adds, that Boleslas, before he could obtain peace, was obliged to approach the emperor with naked feet, and a sword held over his head. This is incredible.

To add to the general consternation, the sons of Uladislas demanded the inheritance of their father ; the whole
nation, indeed, began to despise a ruler who had suffered himself to be so signally defeated by the barbarians : by a powerful faction of nobles Casimir was
invited to wrest the sceptre from the hands which held
it. Fortunately for Boleslas his brother had the virtue
to reject with indignation the alluring offer ; and he
himself, with his characteristic address, succeeded in
pacifying the Silesian princes. His reverses, however,
and the little consideration shown him by his subjects,
sunk deep into his heart, and hastened his death. To
his surviving son, Lesko, he left the duchies of Masovia and Cujavia ; but, in conformity with the order of
settlement, the government of Poland devolved on Miecislas (1174.)*

This prince, from his outward gravity, and his affect-
ation of prudence, had been surnamed *the Old ;* and the
nation, on his accession, believed it had reason to hope
a wise and happy administration. But appearances are
proverbially deceitful ; and gravity more so than any
other. He had scarcely seized the reins of government
before his natural character, which it had been his policy
to cover, unfolded itself to the universal dismay of his
people. His cruelty, his avarice, his distrust, his tyranny, made him the object alike of their fear and
hatred. They were beset with spies ; were dragged
before his inexorable tribunal for fancied offences ; were
oppressed by unheard-of imposts, which were collected
with unsparing rigour ; and were subjected to sanguinary laws, emanating from his caprice alone. Confiscation, imprisonment, and death, were the instruments
of his government. The people groaned ; the nobles,
whose privileges had increased inversely with the decline
of the monarchy, and whose pride made them impatient
of a superior, openly murmured ; the clergy execrated
one whose exactions weighed even on *them.* At length

* The authorities for the reign of Boleslas IV. are the same as those last
quoted.

Gedeon, archbishop of Cracow, after vainly endeavouring to effect his reformation, and employing, like the prophet of old, a striking parable to convict him of his injustice from his own lips, joined a conspiracy formed against him. Cracow was the first to throw off its allegiance; the example was followed by the greater part of the kingdom, and with such rapidity, that before he could dream of defending his rights, his brother CASIMIR was proclaimed duke of Poland. This event was soon followed by his expulsion.

It was not without considerable difficulty that this youngest of the sons of Boleslas Wrymouth was prevailed on to accept the ducal crown. With philosophic indifference he had twice declined the brilliant offer: his sense of justice too made him averse to receive what he regarded as belonging to another; and he was still more loth to profit by the errors of a brother. But the same philosophy which taught him to prefer a humble station, would not long permit him to sacrifice to his own ease, or to a mistaken delicacy, the happiness of millions who looked up to him alone for security and enjoyment.

One of the first acts of Casimir was to procure the abolition of an abuse which had long oppressed the poorer portion of the landed proprietors. From the accession of the Piasts, the Polish monarchs, in their progress through the country for the administration of justice, had been furnished with horses, food, lodging, and every other necessary, both for themselves and their numerous suites, by the inhabitants of the districts through which they passed. Very soon, whatever the occasion of the journey, the same aid was demanded. This evil was sufficiently great; but it became intolerable when the powerful barons imitated the state of kings, and insisted on the same supplies in their never ceasing migrations, and in their perpetually recurring feuds with each other. Then the insolent rapacity of the claimants; their frequent violations of the most sacred rites of hospitality; their lewd conversation, and dissolute habits, had gene-

rated a deeply-rooted feeling of aversion towards them.
In an assembly of nobles and clergy, convoked at
Lenszysa, which is regarded as the first effort towards
Polish legislation, the suppression of this obnoxious
privilege, as far as regarded the nobles, was solemnly
decreed ; the peasants were declared exempt from claims
which had reduced them to wretchedness; and a
dreadful anathema was pronounced against prince or
noble ˙ who should disturb them in their possessions.
At the same time the nobles were relieved from some
heavy compositions sanctioned by the canon law ;
and the goods of the clergy, which, on the death of the
possessors, had long been subject to the usurpations
of the barons, were declared thenceforth inviolable.
These, and several other laws equally salutary, were solemnly approved by Casimir, by Otho (son of the exiled
Miecislas) duke of Posnania, by Boleslas duke of Breslaw (son of Uladislas and Agnes), by Lesko duke of
Mazovia, and by all the nobles and prelates. They were
confirmed by pope Alexander III., who, at the entreaty
of Casimir, abolished the law of Boleslas Wrymouth,
and declared the sovereignty of Poland hereditary in the
descendants of the reigning grand duke. Still the great
grievance remained untouched ; though the dukes of
Posuania, Masovia, Breslaw, &c. were rendered incapable of aspiring to the throne of Casimir so long as a
legitimate offspring existed to claim it, yet were they
all confirmed in their respective appanages, and the
succession vested in *their* descendants, in the order of
primogeniture. Thus the existence of four or five
hereditary, and almost independent, governments was
acknowledged.

The peculiar mildness of Casimir's administration, his
known aversion to punish, his neglect of his own interests, emboldened Miecislas, who had sought a refuge
in Silesia, to request from him the restitution of the
throne. Posterity will have some difficulty in believing
— what we are yet assured is the fact — that he seriously
proposed his own abdication to make way for this hope-

ful and modest exile; a proposal, however, which his nobles received with so much indignation that he was compelled to desist from his design. Disappointed in this appeal to fraternal generosity, Miecislas had recourse to arms. At the head of some Pomeranian allies he advanced into Great Poland, which he wrested from the feeble hands of Otho, without any opposition from Casimir. His success led the way to bolder attempts. During the absence of his brother, whose military talents he had not yet learned to appreciate, on an expedition against the Russians, by corrupting the minister of Lesko, duke of Mazovia and Cujavia, he procured himself to be declared heir of that duchy, and even obtained its administration. The return of Casimir, whose arms had been victorious, was followed by the restoration of the rightful possessor, and by the declaration of Lesko that the duke of Poland himself should inherit the two provinces. The third attempt was still more audacious, but equally unsuccessful. While the grand duke was occupied in another expedition, Miecislas had the address to persuade the people that he was dead, and to procure his recall to the supreme government. His authority was not recognised by all the nobles; and while he was endeavouring to reduce them Casimir arrived, and the insurrection was instantly crushed. From this time he desisted from disturbing the tranquillity of one whom success invariably attended, and by whose generosity his offences were so readily pardoned.

The foreign wars of Casimir, however decisive in his favour, merit little attention. He triumphed over the Hungarians * and the Russians, and reduced the revolted Prussians. His fame as a captain was not inferior to his reputation for justice. His last days were tranquil. By his nephews, the Silesian princes, he was respected; by Miecislas he was feared; by the neighbouring powers his valour had been too often felt to be provoked with impunity; by his own subjects he was idolised. He

* So say the Polish writers, but no mention is made of such a circumstance by the Hungarians.

now hoped long to enjoy the blessings which he had so nobly earned : his days were passed in redressing the complaints of his people, in the exercise of an hospitality truly princely, or in disquisitions with his prelates on the nature and end of man.   One day, however, after drinking a small cup of wine he fell backwards and ex- pired.   Apoplexy was probably the cause of his death ; though poison was also hinted at.

In clemency and justice Casimir was unrivalled, in many other virtues he was eminent.   That clemency, however, sometimes degenerated to a culpable weakness, especially as by his facility of pardoning he invited to new commotions among his people ; and those virtues were sullied by frequent adultery.   His piety has been praised — his prayers, his fastings, his alms-giving, and above all, his zeal in the foundation of churches and monasteries ; but the piety which can subsist with con- jugal infidelity has little claim to our respect.

In his reign the crusade against Saladin was preached. in Poland, and a provincial council held at Cracow, the capital, for the reformation of ecclesiastical abuses.[*]

Casimir left two sons ; but as both were of tender age, and unequal to the defence of the kingdom and the repression of rebellion, Miecislas again offered himself to the electors at Cracow.   He was, however, set aside, and. LESKO, surnamed *The White,* from his fair complexion, the elder of the two princes, was declared duke of Poland.

The enraged Miecislas having engaged the Silesians in his interests invaded the realm. He was met by the pa_ latine of Cracow within seven leagues of that capital, — a battle was fought, which, though of the most sanguinary description, was indecisive.   By it, however, both par- ties were so much weakened that neither could for some time continue hostilities.   But what the cunning old man had failed to obtain by force, he at length secured by stratagem.   He had the address to persuade the prin-

---

Kadlubek, lib. iv. cap. 6—19.   Boguphal, Chronica Polonorum.   Chro. nica Principum Poloniæ (all three in Script. Rerum Silesiæ, i. ii.).   Dlu- goss, vi. 534—567.   Cromer, 163—174.   Sarnicki, vi. cap. 14.   Narussewitz (as abridged by Zielinski), tom. iv. pp. 34—70.

cess Helen, mother and guardian of Lesko, that in aiming at the government of the state he had only in view .he welfare of her two sons—of what use, he asked, was power to one on the brink of the grave? Though he had sons of his own, the credulous princess was made to believe that on his death, an event not far distant, Lesko would be restored. Through her influence the young prince abdicated; the civil war ceased, and Miecislas seized on the administration of Poland.

No sooner had this wily prince obtained the object of all his hopes than the princess Helen had reason to lament her credulity. She had been promised the palatinate of Cujavia, for the investiture of which she now sued in vain, and as unsuccessful were her efforts to procure the recognition of her son as heir to the crown. She had still credit enough to frame a formidable conspiracy, which, for a moment, deprived him of his usurped powers; but he acquired them a third time. He did not, however, long live to enjoy a dignity for which he had sacrificed every tie of nature, and every obligation of morality.

In the death of Miecislas the nation regarded the restoration of Lesko the White as inevitable. The intrigues, however, of the palatine of Cracow, whom the mother of that prince had once offended, favoured the election of ULADISLAS III. son of the deceased duke. The sovereign power had lamentably diminished, and that of the aristocracy as fatally increased, when one of the great nobles could thus, by influencing his own order, procure the election or rejection of any candidate. Even now the nobles of Cracow began to consider the throne as no longer subject to the claims of either testamentary bequest or hereditary descent; but as something which they were at liberty to confer on whatever prince of the house of Piast they chose to invest with the honour.

Their early assumption of such a dangerous privilege was ominous enough of their future preponderancy, and of the endless evils that awaited the country. On the present occasion, however, it must not be concealed, that

Lesko would again have obtained the throne had he
consented to sacrifice a virtuous minister to, the personal
enmity of the palatine; but he scorned to purchase even
a throne by an act of injustice, and he had the magnanimity to behold the elevation of Uladislas, not merely
without mortification, but, as we are assured, with satisfaction. This, indeed, seems to have been the age of
magnanimity, no less than of domestic anarchy; for the
new duke refused to accept the dignity until it was peremptorily declined by Lesko.

But in the absence of the unity of power, and of a
well defined law of succession, and still more, in the
fondness of change so characteristic of a fierce and all-
powerful aristocracy, the ruler who could long enjoy his
authority undisturbed must have been more than man.
Lesko having gained a splendid victory over the Russians,
became in the opinion of the nation the only prince fit
to be intrusted with their destinies.   Uladislas was accordingly deposed — or rather he abdicated the moment
he found that his deposition was contemplated — and
Lesko the White was again raised to a precarious dignity.   The former returned to the tranquillity of private
life with more joy than he had abandoned it.   Such instances of moral heroism, such unparalleled self-sacri-
fices, would be incredible, were they not too well attested
to be doubted.   But our admiration must be somewhat
qualified by the inferior temptations held out to ambition
in an unsettled throne, — a throne, too, which had long
ceased to inspire reverence, and which the nobles had
learned rather to protect than to obey.*

Great as were the virtues of Lesko, his reign was not
fortunate: if he was admirably adapted for a private

* Kadlubek, iv. cap. 21—26. Boguphal, Chronica Polonorum. Chronica
Princip. Polon. (in Script. Rer. Siles. tom. i. ii.). Dlugoss, vi. 569 — 600.
Cromer, 174—188. Sarnicki, vi. cap. 15—18. Solignac, ii. 186—211. Naruszewitz (as condensed by Zielinski), iv. 72—103.
I must here take leave of Kadlubek, the father of Polish historians, from
whose meagre chronicle little indeed can be gathered, yet that little is
sometimes amusing from its conceited pedantry, nay, even from its stu-
pidity. His work, which ends in 1204, was undertaken at the command of
Casimir the just. If that prince could always understand it, he must have
been a better Latinist than I am : it is one of the most obscure books I ever
consulted.

station, or even for a crown in times of peace, he had not sufficient vigour to curb the ambition either of his fierce neighbours or of his powerful barons. If he had once triumphed over the Russians, who contended for th• possession of Halitz — a province rendered dependent on Poland by Casimir I. — very different was his success in a subsequent expedition. Halitz was wrested from his grasp; and he had some difficulty in defending his more immediate territories against the Russian invaders. On another side the Prussians ravaged the provinces of Mazovia and Cujavia, the government of which he had confided to his brother Conrad. These barbarians had long been kept in check by a valiant palatine, the faithful counsellor and friend of Conrad; but on the death of this " God of Poland," as they termed him, who fell a sacrifice to the tyranny of his master, they resumed their ancient ravages. They burned two hundred churches and oratories; penetrated to Plotsk, the capital of Mazovia, and compelled the now trembling Conrad to purchase his security by the most humiliating concessions. But the most fatal enemy of Lesko was one Swantopelk, whom he had placed over eastern Pomerania. From his first investiture this man had aimed at independence of his liege lord; an object which, considering the weakness of Poland, and the pacific disposition of her ruler, he regarded as easy of acquirement. He refused at length to pay the customary tribute: as he was powerful, stratagem and not force was employed to destroy him. He was invited to a diet where affairs of importance were to be discussed. He had sagacity enough to penetrate the design, yet he resolved to attend. With a strong body of armed men he approached the place, — the village of Gansaw, in Great Poland, — where many members of the diet, with Lesko himself, had already assembled. These followers he concealed in a wood, prior to the execution of the purpose he had formed, which was neither more nor less than to cut off at one blow the Polish nobles and their duke. Hearing one day that Lesko was in the bath, he led them to the vil-

lage, slew all whom he encountered, and eagerly rode
forward in quest of his victim.   On hearing the tumult,
the duke had precipitately left the bath, had mounted a
horse and fled.   He was soon overtaken, surrounded,
and after a gallant defence was assassinated by his ruthless pursuers.

Thus fell Lesko the White, whose virtues, however
shining, were useless to his country, since they were
unsupported by the energy necessary to give them effect.
The promise of his early years was woefully belied by
the weakness of his mature age.   It has been truly observed of him, that had he never reigned he would have
been thought eminently worthy of reigning.

The corruption of morals seems to have reached a
fearful height in this reign.   Feeble were the re-
straints either of law or conscience over a licentious
and independent nobility, who recognised no authority
but brute force.   With respect to the clergy the case
was no better.   Ignorance, luxury, incontinence, not
merely existed but abounded.   Some were openly married, others had concubines, and in both cases their
children were admitted to the rights of inheritance.
Among the laity marriage had ceased to be considered
indissoluble, or at least pretexts were found for evading
its obligations.   These abuses cried aloud for reformation ; they reached the ears of pope Celestine III., who
despatched cardinal Peter, with legatine authority, to
enquire into their extent, and to apply the canonical
remedies.   The cardinal acquitted himself of his task
with unbending rigour.   Terrible punishments were
decreed against every priest who married or maintained
a concubine ; and to render lay marriages less disputable
they were thenceforth to be solemnised in presence of
the congregation.*

BOLESLAS V., surnamed the Chaste, was but seven
years old on the murder of his father : no wonder that
new disasters should arise.   The first was a struggle
between Conrad, uncle of the prince, and Henry duke

* Authorities, the same as those last quoted.

of Breslaw, his cousin, for the guardianship of his person. After a bloody battle Conrad prevailed. The second was the irruption of the Prussians into the very heart of Poland, who on this occasion exceeded, if possible, their former ferocity. A third, and eventually a greater, was the calling in the aid of the ambitious Teutonic knights against these saguinary pagans.

In its origin this order was distinguished for humility. In the siege of Acre eight Germans, seeing the number of wounded Christians who daily perished for lack of assistance, formed themselves into a voluntary association for the purpose of mitigating, by their personal attendance, the agonies of which they were the spectators. For the victims left to expire under a burning sun, or amidst the deadly dews of night, they constructed tents made of the sails of ships : their next acts of mercy were to wash the wounds and to relieve the wants of the sufferers. Their zeal, so honourable to humanity, and their valour, which it exalted, drew on them the admiration of their generals. On the reduction of Acre, an hospital and a church were built for them in that town, and subsequently at Jerusalem. Their numbers were soon increased ; their time was divided between the field and the bed of sickness ; and their services were of such acknowledged utility, that the king of Jerusalem formed them into an order, to be called Knights of our Lady of Mount Sion. It was approved in 1191, by the emperor Henry VI., and pope Celestine III. By the statutes the knights were to be of noble descent, bound by their vows to celibacy, to the defence of the Christian church and the Holy Land, and to the exercise of hospitality towards pilgrims of their own nation ; their habit was a black cross on a white mantle ; their rule that of Saint Augustine. Their original number, besides their first grand master Henry of Waelfort, was twenty-four laymen, and seven priests : the latter had permission to celebrate mass clothed in complete armour, with swords at their sides. They were soon raised to forty, exclusive of numerous attendants. For some time their discipline was sufficiently rigorous; among other things they suffered their beards to grow, and slept on the ground. Under their fourth grand master, Herman of Salsa, when their revenues had prodigiously increased, they relaxed from their austerities. On their expulsion from the Holy Land, Herman, with his knights, retired to Venice, ignorant in what country they might obtain a settlement, but resolved to oppose the enemies of the cross,—and northern Europe had yet many,—wherever their services might be required. The application of Conrad, regent of Poland, was readily embraced. Seven knights proceeded to that country to receive his instructions. On condition of their subjugating Prussia, and effecting its final conversion to Christianity, they were offered in perpetuity the fortress and territory of Dobrzyn. Their exploits were so successful that the grateful Conrad surrendered to them the territory of Culm, and all the country between the Vistula, the Mokra, and the Druentsa. This cession, we are told, of so considerable a portion of the state, was designed to be but temporary; that on the successful termination of the war it was to be restored to the Poles, with one half the conquests the order might wrest from the pagans; and it was accompanied by another condition,—that of assisting the Poles against the Lithuanians, the Livonians, or any other enemies of the cross. One or two of these conditions have been disputed: that none were observed will be but too apparent from the sequel of this history.

More pressing evils left no room for even just anticipation of such as were distant. The aim of Conrad was evidently directed at the life and throne of his ward. Boleslas, though a close prisoner, contrived to escape, and claim the aid of Henry of Breslaw. That duke, at the head of a powerful army, entered Poland, and seized on the regency. At the end of a two years' civil war, his authority was recognised by Conrad: but his wise administration was short lived. His death left the feeble Boleslas a prey to the arts of the ambitious uncle. To fortify himself, the young prince espoused Cunegund,.

daughter of Bela king of Hungary; but their alliance could little avail him with a new and more dreaded enemy, who now arrived to lay waste his dominions.

The Tatars, whom Ghengis Khan had so often led to victory and plunder, after subduing Russia and making it a desert, carried their terrific depredations into more western countries. Poland, torn by internal faction, and weakened by rival contests, became their easy prey. Its towns they took by assault; its fields they wasted; its rivers they dyed with the blood of the inhabitants; its temples they plundered and destroyed; the conflagration of the whole kingdom evinced their work of destruction. Some of the Polish nobles, true to the gallantry of their nation and order, endeavoured to make a stand, but they were speedily overwhelmed. The tide of destruction at length rolled on to Silesia and Moravia, or diverged to Hungary, whence it quietly subsided; but it left effects behind which a century could not repair.

During these horrors where was Boleslas? His first step was to flee into Hungary: when danger approached that country, he retreated to a monastery in the heart of Moravia. His example was followed by many thousands of his subjects, whom, had he remained, he might have disposed to resistance. His pusillanimous desertion of the most sacred of duties,—that of defending his people or of perishing with them,—drew on him the execration of those who survived. During his abode in Moravia they resolved to elect another chief, and they actually invested a prince of the blood of Piast with the dignity. Again the restless Conrad, incensed at his rejection, kindled the flames of civil war, and triumphed. His capricious iron yoke was more odious than the imbecile one of the absent Boleslas, whom they hastened to recall. But his restoration could not be effected without the effusion of more blood. In one battle he was victorious; in a second he was defeated; and he would probably have been expelled the kingdom, had not his inveterate enemy been removed by death.

While these disasters were afflicting the very heart of the country, others, not less ruinous, were harassing the frontier provinces. Swantopelk, the assassin of Lesko the White, taking advantage of the heavy losses sustained by the Teutonic knights in the recent struggle with the Tatars, and of the hatred borne towards them by the Prussians, persuaded the latter to join him in hostilities against that enterprising order. Prezemislas, duke of Great Poland, aided the knights. A most destructive war followed, in which Eastern Pomerania, Culm, and Cujavia, were frequently ravaged with fire and sword. Silesia was no less unfortunate. The ambition of one of its princes gave rise to a succession of destructive contests, by which its resources were exhausted, its plains deluged with blood ; and the same scourge fell on several interior provinces. Of the twenty-four vassal princes among whom Poland was shared, scarcely one obeyed the feeble Boleslas ; many openly derided his authority. The cup of his disgrace was not yet full. To this picture of horrors must be added the destroying fury of the Tatars, whose re-appearance was characterised by the same excesses as on the preceding occasion. Boleslas again fled into Hungary, whence he did not dare to return until he was satisfied that the formidable hordes had departed.

Impartial history, however, must not conceal the fact, that Boleslas sometimes remembered the martial virtues of his ancestors. Four years after the retreat of the Tatars he made head against the Jadvingi, a most warlike people who inhabited Podlasia, a country lying between Lithuania and Mazovia, and extending northward as far as the palatinate of Lublin. They had often harassed the eastern provinces of Poland, sometimes alone, sometimes in concert with the Lithuanians : they had supported the rebellion of Mazos ; and though they had owned the conquering arm of Casimir the Just, they were ever ready to act on the offensive. They were still pagans ; for though, with the view of subduing their savage ferocity, the Franciscans and other missionaries had entered their country, and partially converted them, they had abjured their new faith, and joined their heathen neighbours, the Lithuanians, in menacing the very existence of Poland. They were the most formidable of northern barbarians. Of extraordinary strength and still greater courage, they avoided not the combat with an enemy ten times their superior in number. In vain did the Teutonic knights labour to effect what the Franciscans had left incomplete. The haughtiness of these military monks, and their cruelties towards apostates, exasperated this ferocious people, who renewed their incursions on the eastern frontiers of Poland. Boleslas triumphed, doubtless through an immense preponderance of force. He not merely subdued, but almost annihilated, these sons of the forest, and compelled the few who survived to receive baptism. Their overthrow was followed by that of the Russians; but to this success the only share which he contributed was to hold up his hands, and pray at a distance, in modest imitation of the Jew of old, while the brave palatine of Cracow routed and pursued the enemy.

The last years of this prince's life were happily free from the troubles which had so long agitated it. At peace within and without, he occupied himself in ecclesiastical erections, and in works of charity. His devotion was fervent, but often mistaken. With a monastic admiration of chastity, he observed it when to do so was no virtue, but a crime. It was his boast that throughout the period of his marriage he had taken no other freedom with his beautiful and excellent consort than a brother might lawfully take with a sister. Hence his surname *The Chaste*. It is as singular as it is true, that princes of this extraordinary temperament have seldom been otherwise distinguished; they may have preserved the milder, but history shows us they were strangers to the higher, virtues; that they were alike unfit to rule in peace or lead in war.[*]

[*] Dlugoss, lib. vi. col. 638. to lib. vii. col. 818. Cromer, pp. 191—238. Boguphal, Cronica Poloniæ (in Script. Rer. Siles. tom. ii.). Sarnicki, lib. vi. cap. 20. Naruszewitz (as quoted by Zielinski), tom. iv. p. 168. to tom. v p. 150. Dubravius, lib. xvi. Bonfinius, lib. ii. 8.

By the will of the late ruler, LESKO THE BLACK, duke of Sieradz and Cujavia, succeeded to the throne.* The union of his provinces with the crown·caused his accession to be regarded with hope. His reign, however, was destined to prove as disastrous as that of his predecessor.

The new duke, immediately after his elevation, had to contend with one of his own subjects, the bishop of Cracow, whose hatred he had incurred at a former period, and who was resolved to dethrone him. This prelate was fitter to head banditti, of whom he had actually many in his interests, than to edify the church. He had no scruple to seize nuns in their cloisters, to convey them to his tower, and keep them openly as mistresses. He offered the crown to a Silesian prince, whom he induced to take the field against Lesko, and whom he joined at the head of his creatures and retainers. Lesko triumphed. The bishop had subsequently recourse to the Lithuanians, whom he persuaded to ravage Poland. They too yielded to the valour of the duke. The restless rebel was now imprisoned: he contrived soon to escape, and to incite several discontented chiefs against their sovereign. Cracow, the capital, was besieged: it made, however, a gallant defence until it was relieved by Lesko, who had previously vanquished the rebels on the banks of the Raba. Not less signal was his success over the Muscovites, whom internal treachery, not less than their own ambition, had armed against him. To the Tatars, however, who a third time arrived to inundate the country, he offered no resistance. Like his predecessor Boleslas, he precipitately fled into Hungary, whence he did not dare to return until the enemy, after laying waste several provinces, had retired into Russia. Despised for his cowardice, harassed by Conrad duke

---

* Did this choice of Lesko arise from a kindred feeling? Some years before, Consors Leskonis Nigri, Ducissa Griphina, filia Roscislai Russiæ Ducis, quamvis prope sex annis in viri sui Leskonis Nigri contubernio degeret, virginem tamen se gessit in eam diem, nec a viro suo cognitam, impotentiam et fragilitatem illi objiciens, baronum et militarium *matronarumque* concione advocata, agente etiam Leskone duce coram, et accusationem silentio profitente, deduxit The lady very naturally retired to a convent, Leskonis ducis consortia evitare, *conjugii hujusmodi* divortiam quæsitura. — *Dlugoss,* 794.

of Mazovia, his cousin, who had long aimed at his crown,
and whom he had persecuted with singular animosity,
his life became a burden, and he died of a broken heart.

The death of Lesko the Black, who left no posterity,
was followed by disasters greater, perhaps, than any
which had previously existed even in this land of lawless
violence. The numerous princes of the blood of Piast
simultaneously arose to procure by force their elevation
to the vacant dignity. Boleslas duke of Masovia was
the first who obtained it : he was speedily deprived of
it by Henry duke of Breslaw : Henry in his turn was
driven away by Uladislas, brother to Lesko the Black.
Uladislas was compelled to yield to that duke, who a
second time seized the reins of government, but did not
long live to hold them. The number of claimants was
now increased by the pretensions of Wenceslas, king of
Bohemia, in whose favour his aunt Griffina, widow of
Lesko the Black, forged a will.* By this pretended
document indeed she constituted herself heiress of the
realm, of which she at the same time made a donation
to that prince. He sent an army to support his claims :
it was defeated by Uladislas. The success of the victor
urged the disappointed claimants to call in the aid of
the Lithuanians. He retreated before these new enemies,
but only to measure his arms with Wenceslas, who arrived in person to defend the validity of the forged will.
The Bohemians made some conquests, which he gar-

---

* The Bohemian writers mention the will, but not the forgery. I am
not sure it was not a perfectly legal instrument, though *every* Polish authority loudly denounces it as a forgery : but what authority had Lesko the
Black, still less what authority had his widow, to confer absolutely what
belonged to neither, but to the nobles and clergy of the realm ? " Monstro
persimile foret, matronam Bulgariæ ortam, Polonorum principatus do-
nandi et conferendi potestatem nactam esse, quam falso sibi in Leskone
Nigro Duce, viro suo, ementiebatur, literis, si quæ extabant, vitiatis, et
præter mariti voluntatem false signatis, attributam."— *Dlugoss*, vii. 858.
Now let us hear Dubravius : — " Nam Lesko Niger cognominatus, Griffinæ
uxori suæ moriens testamento Cracoviam et Sandomitiam cum amplis di-
tionibus legavit. Eaque Griffina jus suum Venceslao nepoti suo ex sorore
delegavit, quippe Cunegundis mater Venceslai, et ipsa Griffina sorores ger-
manæ, ambæque filiæ regis Bulgariæ erant "— *Hist. Bohem.* lib. xviii.
p. 148. Whether the will was genuine or not, I am persuaded Wenceslas
thought it so : he was too honourable a man to participate in deception, he
has been canonised for his virtues. He cannot so easily be defended from
his eagerness to grasp a sceptre which he well knew no individual could
bequeath him, — which the magnates of the state only could confer.

risoned with his own troops; but seeing no hope of
finally securing his election, he returned to his own
kingdom, leaving Uladislas to struggle with a host of
foreign and domestic enemies. This beautiful state of
things was not all: the Tatars came a fourth time; the
Prussians and Bohemians invaded another frontier. Poland was about to be erased from the list of nations —
we may well be surprised how such a catastrophe had
been hitherto averted — but the very imminency of the
danger proved its salvation. The nobles and clergy, in
consternation at the prospect before them, felt that without an approach to something like a monarchy, without
a union of the petty independent chiefs, the ruin of the
country was inevitable. They looked round for a prince
of martial reputation, and of superior possessions. They
found one in Prezemislas duke of Great Poland and of
Pomerania, and heir of Cracow and Sandomir. The
propriety of the choice was so evident that the other
candidates desisted from their pretensions; even Uladislas retired without murmuring to his hereditary states,
confessing that a better one could not have been made. *

CHAP. III.

HOUSE OF PIAST CONCLUDED. — MONARCHY RESTORED.

1295—1386.

PREZEMISLAS.

1295—1300.

WITH the authority this prince assumed the title of
king. Without stooping to the humiliation of soliciting

* Boguphal, Chronica Polonorum. Chronica Principum Poloniæ (in
Script. Rer. Siles. tom. i. ii.). Dlugoss, vii. 818 — 874. Cromer, 247 — 269.
Sarnicki, vi. cap. 20—22. Solignac, iii. 309—347. Naruszewitz (as followed
by Zielinski), tom. v. p. 160—200. Æneas Sylvius, cap. xxviii. p. 136. (in
Script. Rer. Bohem.). Dubravius, ubi supra.

the crown from the hands of the pope, he received it from his nobles and clergy, amidst the acclamations of a whole people. The important ceremony was performed at Gnesna by the archbishop of that see.

The new monarch fully justified the confidence of the nation. Combining firmness with moderation, a clear vigorous understanding with promptitude of decision, undaunted courage with great prudence, and exhibiting astonishing activity without the least precipitation, he was admirably fitted to allay the animosities, and quell the turbulence, of his nobles. Some he reasoned, others he forced into submission : on all he successfully inculcated the necessity of union among themselves, and of obedience to the laws. But the evils of two centuries were not to be cured in a day; and he could do no more than lay the foundation of future prosperity : time alone could raise the structure.

Having restored peace within, the king endeavoured to cultivate it with his neighbours, to whom he despatched embassies worthy of his new title. He fortified Dantzic, and established his authority throughout the greater part of Pomerania. In memory of his success he caused a seal to be engraved, on one side of which might be read, "*Sigillum Premislai Polonorum Regis et Ducis Pomeraniæ;*" on the other, "*Reddidit ipse suis victricia signa Polonis;*" a boast which he was fully entitled to make.

Unfortunately for Poland, she had scarcely begun to enjoy the sweets of a settled government when the smiling prospect was again obscured. The elevation and success of Prezemislas awakened the fears no less than the jealousy of his neighbours. To unbend his mind from his arduous duties he had retired to Rogozno, to celebrate with feasts and tourneys one of the high festivals of the church. One night, when the diversions were over, and the numerous guests were wrapped in sleep, when even his guards were overcome by the strength of their potations, his cousin, the margrave of Anhalt, accompanied by a few ruffians, entered his apartment. He

G

awoke in time, indeed, to make a resolute defence, but not to avert his fate. He fell beneath their redoubled blows, before any member of his household could hasten to his assistance.[*]

His crime, say the national historians, went not unpunished: in twenty years the house of Anhalt, which then consisted of twelve nobles, ceased to exist.

As the murdered king left no offspring but a female child, and as the Bohemians, the Silesians, and the Brandenburgers were preparing to profit by this melancholy event, the suffrages of the Poles fell on the same Uladislas who had relinquished his pretensions in favour of Prezemislas. He triumphed over his enemies; but success corrupted him: he became severe and tyrannical. Detested by his people, excommunicated by the church, an assembly at Posen pronounced his deposition, and proclaimed Wenceslas of Bohemia king of Poland. In selecting this prince, less regard was had to the will forged by Griffina than to his connection with the royal family of the nation, and to the transforming a powerful enemy into a friend: besides, submission to a foreigner and a sovereign was less galling than to a native and an equal. Wenceslas, too, was a widower, and at liberty to marry the daughter of the deceased Prezemislas.[†]

WENCESLAS.

1300—1306.

HAVING espoused Rixa, daughter of Prezemislas, this king was crowned at Gnesna amidst the silence rather than the acclamations of the Poles. They regretted

---

[*] Another account says — perhaps with equal probability of truth — that the attendants of the king flew to his succour, and that many of the margrave's followers were slain before the royal victim was laid low. In this case John of Brandenburgh must have been accompanied by a numerous party, and fallen on the royal residence while the king and his nobles were unprepared for resistance. The account in the text is generally received by modern Polish writers.

[†] Dlugoss, vii. 875—892. Cromer, xi. 270—274. Sarnicki, vi. cap. 23. and 24. Naruszewitz, v. 200—220. Æneas Sylvius, Dubravius, ubi supra; and Pontanus, Bohemia Pia, lib. ii.

their expulsion of Uladislas, and their subjection to one whose ancestors had been the most bitter foes to their country.

The first acts of the new monarch were not of a nature to allay the national animosity. He filled the fortresses with Bohemian soldiers; none, it is said, but Bohemians shared his confidence or his favours: Bohemians, in short, had his whole affection. First jealousy, next discontent seized on his new subjects, who began to regard their deposed prince with compassion and loyalty. By Wenceslas he had been deprived of his patrimonial estates and driven into exile. He sought a refuge with his friend the king of Hungary, who promised to assist him in regaining his throne.

In the mean time the events which happened in Poland cheered the hopes of the exile. On one side the Lithuanians, on another the dukes of Eusi and Rugen, ravaged the kingdom: to these evils was added the plague, which raged with destructive fury. To escape it, and troubles which he knew not how to appease, — apprehensive, too, lest the emperor, his personal enemy, should raise disturbances in his hereditary states, — Wenceslas confided the administration of Poland to the Bohemian garrisons, and with his consort departed for Prague. The sway of these foreigners is said to have been tyrannical and rapacious: we must remember, however, that the account is given us by enemies. That they defended the country with vigour and success, is evident from the victory which they gained over the combined Russians, Tatars, and Lithuanians, near Lublin. Wenceslas could interfere little with the Poles; more pressing interests absorbed him. He had been called to the throne of Hungary, in right of his mother Cunegund; but three kingdoms exceeded alike his ambition and his ability to govern. That of Hungary he abandoned to his son; but the young prince became so unpopular, that a Bohemian army was sent to support him, but in vain. Then the wars of the emperor Albert in Moravia, and the opposition of the pope, for both envied his increased possessions, left him no time to consult the interests of a people that feared and disliked him.

In the mean time Uladislas was not idle. He journeyed to Rome, where, by his penitence for his past errors, he procured the favour of the pontiff; he made irruptions into the duchy of Cracow, at the head of some troops furnished him by the duke of Transylvania. On the first occasion the Poles wept and pitied him, but durst not espouse his cause; on the second, perceiving that Wenceslas was too much occupied in Moravia to return immediately, many eagerly flocked to his standard. Several easy victories gave new vigour to their efforts, especially after news arrived of the death of Wenceslas. Though the Bohemian governors and their new prince, who laid claim to the throne, made some show of resistance, the affection of a people for one whom they believed purified by exile and suffering bore down all opposition. The assassination of his presumptuous and unfortunate rival, by the hands of those who were suspected to have deprived the father of life[*], put an end to his struggles and his fears.[†]

ULADISLAS IV.

1306—1333.

ULADISLAS IV., surnamed *Loketek*, or the Short, was immediately acknowledged by Little Poland and Pomerania; but Great Poland, which could not soon forget

[*] Albert was suspected of the murder, to settle his son Rodolph on the throne of Bohemia. With Wenceslas III., who left no posterity, expired the race of Premislas, which is said by the ancient chroniclers to have governed Bohemia 584 years. From this period the kingdom has obeyed foreign princes.

[†] Chronica Princip. Polon. (in Script. Rer. Siles. t. i.). Dlugoss, ix. 893 —911. Cromer, Sarnicki, Narussewitz, ubi supra. I do not think the death of St. Wenceslas, the father, was violent; that event was more likely to have been occasioned by anxiety or disease. "Valetudo adversa, sive ex morbo, sive ex senio, sive ut quorundam habuit assertio ex *veneno*, illunc cœpit impetere," is too indefinite to fix the charge of murder on Albert. Disease seems to have been the cause of his death: it is the cause assigned by Æneas Sylvius and Dubravius.

his former tyranny, refused to submit, and placed itself under another prince of the house of Piast. On the death, however, of that prince, which took place about four years after his accession, an assembly convoked at Gnesna unanimously proclaimed him king of all Poland; but he did not assume the title until the fourteenth year of his reign: he was superstitious enough to fear that without the papal sanction, which neither Prezemislas nor Wenceslas had been able to obtain, the royal dignity would not be considered sufficiently sacred; and even then its assumption was the effect of the implied permission rather than the sanction of Clement V.*

The long reign of Uladislas was chiefly one continued struggle with the Teutonic knights, whom, fatally for the kingdom, Lesko the Black had located in Culm. Dantzic, the chief city of Pomerania, being closely invested by the marquis of Brandenburg, who had rapidly reduced that province, the king, considering the urgency of the danger, and the impossibility of his marching in time to relieve it, summoned the knights, in virtue of their original compact with his predecessor, to succour it. They readily complied; they threw supplies into the place, and forced the Brandenburgers to raise the siege: but no sooner had they performed this duty than, by their superior numbers, they disarmed the Polish garrison, and declared the city a possession of the order. In vain did Uladislas expostulate with these unscrupulous monks; in vain did he remind them of the generosity of his ancestor, who had received them when Europe was closed against them; in vain did he tax them with their treachery, and menace them with his vengeance if the place were not immediately restored: they derided

* It must not, however, be concealed, that the situation of the pontiff was rather delicate. At the time Uladislas urged his claim, a similar one was pressed by John king of Bohemia, whose pretensions rested on the right of his wife, daughter of the elder Wenceslas, and grand-daughter of Prese-mislas. As there was no law to exclude females from the succession, the rights of the princess, hereditarily considered, were superior to those of Uladislas; but neither hereditary descent nor actual possession were much regarded by the Poles.

alike his remonstrances and threats, and proceeded to
reduce other fortified towns of the province; besides, they
knew that he had enough to do in Great Poland, which
was then ravaged by the Germans, whom a Piast had
called in to oppose him.   To colour their usurpation,
they had recourse to an extraordinary expedient. Under
the pretext that the marquis of Brandenburg was the
lawful sovereign of Pomerania, they offered him 10,000
marks for that province.   An emperor of Germany,
indeed, had once promised to an ancestor of that prince
the investiture of this maritime region, provided he
could conquer it from the Prussians and Poles, the actual
possessors : the marquis was surprised; but the money
was too tempting to be refused in exchange for an imaginary title, and the bargain was effected.   The bare-
faced impudence of this transaction was more provoking
to Uladislas than even the loss of the province.   He
burned to inflict vengeance on these audacious, unprincipled monks; but whenever he prepared to put
his troops in motion, some disturbance or other within
his kingdom, raised up no doubt by the knights, prevented his departure.   Compelled from time to time
to defer his long-meditated expedition, he applied to
pope Julius XXVI., who had many heavy grounds of
complaint against the order, as well for its condemnation
as for the restoration of the province.   Commissioners
were accordingly appointed, who, after observing the pre-
scribed formalities, gave judgment against the knights,
and condemned them besides to pay a heavy sum to the
king by way of indemnification.   This was not all: sentence of excommunication was pronounced against them,
and an interdict laid on their territories until they made
satisfaction for their injustice.   It appears, however,
either that the thunders of the church passed harmless
over their heads, or that the presents they distributed
among the confidential advisers of the pope purchased
their impunity: they restored nothing; they proposed
nothing.   In 1328, Uladislas resolved to chastise them

with a considerable force of Poles and of Hungarian and Lithuanian auxiliaries: he laid waste their palatinate of Culm, and thereby ruined the innocent peasantry for the iniquities of their oppressive masters.   Here ended his first expedition.   In a second, he penetrated into the heart of their territory, where he committed horrible excesses.   He strictly enjoined his plunderers, who were of themselves sufficiently inclined to ferocity, to spare neither age nor sex, to disregard alike pity or remorse, and to perpetrate every imaginable excess.   The knights were not strong enough to meet him in the field, but from their fortresses they safely defied his arms.   A truce concluded this second expedition, in which the barbarous conduct of Uladislas must consign his name to everlasting infamy.   In a third, the success was more varied. He had made his son Casimír governor of Great Poland; and, to make way for him, had displaced Samatulski, a noble of great wealth and influence.   Indignant at what he conceived an injustice, the latter passed over to the knights, whom he offered to aid against his country.   By his advice they crossed the Vistula at Thorn, and by circuitous, though rapid marches, pushed their bands into Great Poland, which they ravaged without mercy, and with perfect impunity.   In a second irruption they wasted Cujavia and Kalisch : even Gnesna was taken and pillaged.   They were, indeed, at this time resistless, from the number of their allies and their own valour — they were always the bravest of the brave : they were joined by the troops of John of Bohemia, who openly aspired in right of his wife to the Polish crown.   It is probable that Uladislas, notwithstanding his experience and valour, would have been compelled to bend before the storm, had he not succeeded in allaying it by a hazardous expedient.   He knew that Samatulski was the soul of the hostile manœuvres : the monarch sued to the rebel, whom he secretly won over by promises of pardon, and even of favour.   Remorse had long torn the heart of Samatulski : he threw himself at the feet of his king, whom he engaged to aid by a second treachery. He kept his word. In a battle which took place two days after his nocturnal visit to the Polish tents, and in which he commanded a considerable body of men entirely devoted to him, he turned round on the knights his allies, in the very heat of the action, and by this unexpected manœuvre decided the fortune of the day.* As usual, no quarter was shown by the victors; 20,000 of the vanquished were massacred on the field. In the utmost consternation, the knights despatched messengers to their ally, the Bohemian king, to make a diversion in their favour on the western frontiers of Poland. Accordingly John advanced, and laid siege to Posen. Uladislas hastened to its succour, leaving the monks to retreat unmolested, and to combine their plans for the ensuing campaign; but, though they did not fail to resume their operations, and to reduce several important places, their further career was checked by the valour of the king, who, though at an advanced age, carried on the war with the spirit of youth. This was the last expedition he undertook against an enemy whose arms had done more to harass his kingdom than the efforts of all his other enemies combined. In spite of all his successes, of all the money he had expended, and the blood he had spilt, Pomerania, Cujavia, and other possessions, remained in the hands of the knights.

But this province was not the only one lost during this reign. By address rather than open force, John king of Bohemia procured his recognition as lord paramount over Silesia from the independent princes of that country. Ever since the establishment of a separate, though nominally subordinate, government in that province, by the immediate heirs of Boleslas Wrymouth, Poland had lost her hold over it; the last feeble link which bound it to her was now for ever broken: Silesia became an appendage of the Bohemian crown.

The other warlike actions of Uladislas do not merit

* Samatulski was afterwards torn in pieces by the enraged nobility of Great Poland.

particular attention. He obtained some partial successes
over the Bohemians and Brandenburgers; but his murderous expeditions procured him no solid advantage, while
they tarnished the lustre of his exploits. He made warlike a captain of banditti, rather than as a Christian
knight.*

If the wars of Uladislas led to unfavourable results, it
was not so with his policy. The Lithuanians had always
been the most formidable enemies to Poland; their incursions had never ceased; their valour had almost always rendered those incursions successful; their activity
enabled them to elude pursuit whenever a powerful army
of Poles approached to defend the eastern provinces. In
the inaccessible recesses of their forests they enjoyed the
plunder they had amassed, and devolved on their numerous prisoners the servile employments of life. To procure the alliance of these warlike pagans, was the anxious
object of Uladislas. He sent a deputation to Gedymin,
duke of Lithuania, to solicit the hand of that prince's
daughter for Casimir his son: this proposal was accepted;
the princess was brought to Poland, and with her 24,000
captives who had long groaned in the most rigorous
bondage. The restoration of these wretches to their
country was more gratifying to the monarch's heart than
the most brilliant portion could have been. The gratitude of their kindred, the disarming of a fierce enemy,
the acquisition of auxiliary troops in his wars with the
Bohemians and Teutonic knights, were the present advantages of this happy alliance; the future ones, as we
shall hereafter see, were still more valuable.

The last words of Uladislas to his son Casimir urged
him to an exterminating war with the perfidious knights
of Pomerania. " Rather bury yourself," said the dying

---

* During one of these expeditions the nuns were not spared. The way
in which one of these intended victims of brutality escaped violation, is
related with applause by all ancient historians (the *modern* writers of Poland are not always honest enough to notice the evil deeds of their ancestors). She was a Prussian nun. " She told a soldier that if he would spare
her, she would communicate to him an important secret which would render
him invulnerable; and, to convince him of its efficacy, she bade him strike
her with his sword. He believed her; and, by cutting off her head, preserved her chastity."—*Dlugoss,* 990.

king, "under the ruins of your throne, than suffer them
to possess the territories they have invaded. Punish the
traitors; drive them out of the kingdom if you can!"

The qualities of this prince have been overrated. That,
after his restoration to the throne, he exhibited the salutary effects of adversity; that he was temperate, active,
just, clement towards his people, whom his abilities, no
less than his valour, often preserved from foreign subjugation and domestic anarchy, are indisputable facts;
but his reign was one series of disasters, a great portion
of which seems to have been imputable to himself. His
talents as a general were not of a high order, and his
cruelty towards the innocent vassals of his enemies, as
we have before seen, strongly urged by himself, proves
him to have been destitute of that generosity, that chi-
valric clemency, inseparable from true greatness of mind.

Under this monarch the Dulceans (so called from their
leader, an Italian heretic,) made many proselytes. Dul-
cean contended that he was the apostle of religious reform; that the pope and cardinals knew nothing of the
gospels; that in the communion of Christians every thing
should be common, even wives and children. In two
years he was quartered and burnt. Another sect, the
Fratricelli, openly attacked all existing authority, temporal or spiritual: their monsttous doctrines occasioned
the establishment of the inquisition, which continued in
force until the time of Sigismund I. *

* Chronica Principum Poloniæ (in Script. Rer. Siles. tom. i. p. 13.). Dlugoss, ix. 914—1030. Cromer, 277—305. Sarnicki, vi. cap. 26. and 27.
Neugebaver, Historia Rerum Poloniarum, lib. iii. 177—197. Narussewitz
(abridged by Zielinski), v. 238—277. Dubravius, lib. xx. et xxi. Bonfinius, ii. lib. ix.

CASIMIR III. THE GREAT.

1333—1370.

NOTWITHSTANDING the dying injunctions of his father, Casimir made no attempts to expel the Teutonic knights from his dominions. The reason doubtless was his inability to carry on the war with any prospect of success. His situation was not without its difficulties: the Bohemian king still aspired to the Polish throne; two of his own palatins were in the interests of that monarch; and the internal state of the kingdom, the nullity of the laws, the insecurity of property and persons, were evils which loudly called for reparation. Peace with these enterprising monks was indispensable to the reforms he meditated: it was at length concluded through the mediation of the Hungarian king, but on conditions deeply mortifying to the nation. Cujavia, and the territory of Dobrzyn, were restored; but Casimir, renounced for himself and successors, Culm, Michalow, and Pomerania. The clergy, the barons, the equestrian order, long refused to sanction so unexpected a concession; but the arguments of the king convinced them that no better terms could be procured, and they reluctantly concurred.

In his proposed reformation of abuses, Casimir first applied his attention to one which threatened to dissolve the frame of society. The highways were infested by numerous parties of robbers, chiefly disbanded soldiers, who plundered alike travellers and peasantry, and long defied punishment. Many of them were doubtless protected by certain nobles, whose interests in return they zealously espoused. They were now pursued to their last hiding-places, were brought before the tribunals of the country, and punished with inflexible severity. The scaffolds of Cracow and the provincial towns continually smoked with the blood of the guilty. His severity not only struck a salutary terror into the hearts of the law-less, but impressed the whole nation with a high idea of his vigour.

Casimir at length aspired to the noble ambition of be-coming the legislator of his people. He found the laws barbarous, but so sanctioned by time and custom that their abrogation or improvement was a work of great delicacy. Nor were the judges who administered them a less evil: their sentences were not according to equity, but capricious or venal; corruption had seized on all, from the princely palatine to the lowest link in the ju-dicial chain. To frame a body of laws uniform in their character, and of universal application, he convoked at Wisliza a diet of bishops, palatins, castellans, and other magistrates; and, in concert with the best-informed of these, he digested a code which was thenceforth to be received as obligatory and perpetual. It was comprised in two books, one for Little, the other for Great Poland. Their provisions were on the whole as good as could be expected in an age when feudality reigned undisputed, and when civil rights were little understood. They se-cured to the peasant, no less than to the nobles, the pos-session and the rights of property; and subjected both, in an equal manner, to the same penalties and tribunals. In other respects, the distinction between the two orders was strongly marked. Hitherto the peasants had been adscripti glebæ, slaves to their masters, who had power of life and death over them, and were not allowed to change owners. Servage was now abolished; every serf employed in cultivating the ground, or in colonisation, was declared entitled to the privileges of the peasant: but the peasants were still chained by a personal, though not a territorial dependence. Of this order there were two descriptions: those who, as serfs previously, could do nothing without their master's permission; and those who, as born free, or made so, could offer their industry to whatever master they pleased. Yet even one of the latter class — free as he would be thought — who, by his agreement with his feudal superior, could migrate to another estate with or without that superior's permission, was affected by the system.   If he sued another at the law, and sentence was pronounced in his favour, his lord shared the compensation awarded.   The murderer of a peasant paid ten marks : five went to the lord, the other five to the family of the deceased.   The reason of these regulations, apparently so arbitrary, was, that as the time of the peasant, so long as he remained on his lord's estate, belonged to that lord, so any injury inflicted on him which interfered with his labour, or diminished in any way the profits of his industry, must be felt by the other : by his death he left his family chargeable to the owner of the estate ; the lord then, as he participated in the injury, had a claim to share also the compensation. The peasants not free — those who could not migrate as they pleased, and whose families were subject to the same dependence — were yet entitled to a share of the profits arising from their industry, and with these were qualified to purchase their freedom.   On their decease their effects devolved, not as heretofore, to their lords, but to their surviving kindred.   If ill-treated themselves, or if their wives and daughters were persecuted by their masters, they could remove as free peasants to another estate: the freed peasant could even aspire to the dignity of a noble. Money, or long service in the martial retinue of the great barons, or success in war, or royal favour, could procure that distinction.   The importance of the several orders was carefully graduated by the code under consideration. The murder of a free peasant was redeemed by ten marks ; of a peasant recently ennobled, or, in more correct language, recently admitted to the privileges of a gentleman, fifteen marks ; of a common noble (Anglicè, gentleman) thirty marks ; of a baron or count, sixty marks.   These distinctions in time gradually disappeared ; all were merged in the common designation of *noble;* every noble was thenceforth equal: but the more the order was confounded in itself, the more it laboured to deepen the line of demarcation between itself and the inferior order of peasants.   In the following reigns, indeed, the salutary regulations made in favour of the latter by this prince were disregarded. The nobles again assumed over them a despotic authority, and arrogated to themselves a jurisdiction which rightly belonged to the local magistrates. Until within a very modern period, this judicial vassalage subsisted in Poland. The lord of the soil held his court for the trial of his peasantry, as confidently as any judge in the realm : in capital cases, however, the culprit lay within the jurisdiction of the palatinal courts.

Poland had two description of laws,—the German, or Teutonic, which was obligatory on the *citizens ;* and the *national,* which bound the *nobles* and the *peasants :* they may be more correctly denominated the *burger* and the *feudal.* As the latter was not favourable to foreigners, - whom policy, however, required to settle in the towns and villages, Casimir retained so much of the former, for the encouragement of industry and the arts, and the establishment of communities, as agreed with the improved circumstances of his people. The tribunals in the cities, towns, and villages, over which the feudal system had no control, and which were consequently subject to the Teutonic law, were still composed of advocates, bailiffs, and syndics ; but appeals to Magdeburg were prohibited. A Teutonic tribunal was established at Cracow, consisting of a judge duly conversant with the foreign law, and of seven respectable householders nominated by the starost.* Its jurisdiction extended over the subordinate tribunals of other towns. Its decisions were not final : an appeal lay open to a court extraordinary of twelve counsellors, nominated by the king, (two from each of the towns,—Cracow, Sandecz, Bochnia, Wielitzka, Kazimierz, and Ilkusz,) whose sentence was irrevocable.

Hence it appears, that the Poles were divided into three great classes,—the nobles, the peasants, and the burgers. The clergy were taken from all three, and constituted a fourth body, but subject to the same laws, except where the discipline of the church was concerned. The dignified clergy and the barons were generally the

* See the last chapter of this work.

only members of the national diet; but sometimes Casimir admitted the inferior clergy, the magistrates, many of the nobles, and the burger deputies. By submitting to their decisions questions so important as the cession of provinces; the abrogation, change, or enacting of laws; the control, if not the assessment of taxes; and even the power of electing kings, and of departing from the strict line of hereditary descent (as will be soon shown), he impressed the members with a new confidence in their own powers, and laid the foundation of that aristocratic domination, and that monarchical feebleness, which occasioned first the decay, and next the destruction, of the nation.

But Casimir was the great patron of industry, no less than a legislator. Through his encouragement numbers flocked into his kingdom from various parts of Germany, and by their means commerce and the useful arts of life were taught to flourish. He fortified many of his chief towns, which had previously been unprotected by walls and open to the ravages of every enemy. He did more,— he embellished them : rude edifices of wood gave way to erections of brick, which astonished the eye by their architectural proportions. Colleges, hospitals, churches, and other public buildings, attested alike his genius, his magnificence, and his patriotism.

As from his union with the princess Anne of Lithuania Casimir had only a daughter *, his attention was anxiously directed towards the choice of a successor. Though several princes remained of the house of Piast, he did not consider any one of them sufficiently powerful either to repress the insurrectionary disposition of his nobles, or to make head against the military monks, whose ambition he so justly dreaded. He proposed Lewis king of Hungary, the son of his sister, and therefore a Piast, to the diet he had convoked at Cracow. He thus recognised in that body a right to which they had never dared to make a claim. They felt their im-

* Cunegund, afterwards married to Romulus, son of the emperor Charles IV. By a third marriage he had two other daughters.

portance, and resolved to avail themselves of it.   He encountered great opposition.   One party would have him to
nominate the duke of Mazovia ; another, the duke of Oppelen: both reproached him for his partiality to a foreigner,
in prejudice of the male descendants of his house.   Fortunately for his views, they opposed each other with so
much animosity, that, in the end, both adopted his proposition as a means of avoiding the shame of a defeat.
But though they thus united in the election of Lewis, they
resolved to draw their own advantage from it.   The
sceptre of Casimir, though never swayed more rigorously
than justice permitted, they felt to be one of iron, after
the long impunity they had enjoyed during two centuries.
Some years afterwards they sent deputies to Breda, to
inform Lewis that, though in compliance with the wishes
of their king they had concurred in his election, they
should yet consider themselves free to make choice of
any other prince if he refused them certain concessions.
He was not to invest Hungarians or any other foreigners
with the offices of the state ; he was to declare the
Polish equestrian order exempt from contributions, to
confirm them in their utmost privileges, and even to
support their retinues in his warlike expeditions.   The
Hungarian king had the weakness to comply with these
and other demands (all unreasonable, except the first),
and thereby to forge chains for his successors.   Hence
the origin of the *pacta conventa*, or the covenants between the nobles and the candidate they proposed to
elect, — covenants exclusively framed for their own benefit, and for the detriment alike of king and peasantry.

Casimir was a man of peace.   War he desired not, yet
he never shunned it when it was forced upon him, or
when the voice of his nobles demanded it.   Both he and
they, perhaps, feared the knights too much to engage with
them ; but he triumphed over the Silesians (now subject to the Bohemians), the Russians, the Lithuanians,
and Tatars : he subdued Volhinia and Podolia, with the
palatinates of Brescia and Beltz.   These successes,
with the alliance of two princes so powerful as Lewis

and the emperor, rendered him formidable to his neighbours, and deterred his enemies of Pomerania from their cruel aggressions.

But the great qualities of this prince were sullied by some excesses. He was much addicted to drunkenness, and immoderately so to women. Long before his father's death he had dishonoured the daughter of an Hungarian noble, and fled from the vengeance of her friends. To none of his wives (and he had three) did he dream of fidelity. After the death of the princess Anne, he married Adelaide, a German princess ; but her jealousy, and still more her reproaches, incensed him so much that he exiled her to a fortress. His career of intemperance was thenceforth the more headstrong. He soon became enamoured of a Bohemian lady, whom all his arts, however, failed to seduce, and who declared she would yield only to marriage. (How his engagement with Adelaide was to be set aside, we are not informed ; perhaps he had the art to convince her that he had obtained a divorce.) He feigned to comply ; but instead of the bishop of Cracow, whom she wished to perform the ceremony, and whose authority she conceived would sanction the act, he substituted a monk (the abbot of Tynieck), who assumed the pontifical robes, and thus became a participator in the most detestable of deceptions. Her he soon discarded, to make way for a Jewess named Esther, by whom he had two sons. During this concubine's favour, Poland was the paradise of the Israelites : the privileges, indeed, which at her entreaties he granted to them, remained in force long after his reign; and, no doubt, was the cause why they have continued for so many ages to regard this kingdom with peculiar affection, and to select it as their chief residence. After Esther, or perhaps contemporary with her, we find a multitude of favourites. His licentiousness knew no bounds: he established a regular seraglio, which he filled with frail beauties. The bishops murmured, but dared not openly reproach him : the pope expostulated, but in vain. A priest of Cracow, at length, had

H

the courage to reprove him; but, as he was quickly
thrown into the Vistula, his fate deterred others from
imitating his temerity. Age effected what reason and
religion had attempted in vain. After his union with
a third wife (a Piast), he became less notorious for his
amours; and as the fire of lust expired before the chilling
influence of age, his subjects had the consolation of finding that their wives, sisters, and daughters were safe
from pollution.

Casimir's death was occasioned by a fall from his
horse while hunting. The accident might not have been
fatal, had he not turned a deaf ear to the advice of his
physicians. To this day his memory is cherished by
his country, which justly regards him as the greatest
prince of a great line. Of his genius, his patriotism,
his love of justice, his success in improving the condition
of his people, his acts are the best comment; but his
splendid qualities must not blind us to his vices, — vices
which not only sully the lustre of his character, but must
have had a pernicious influence on the minds of a people
with whom the obligations of religion and morality were
not in that age usually strong.*

During the reign of this last male prince of the house
of Piast, the Flagellants, a numerous sect of enthusiasts,
so called from the rigour of their self-inflictions, entered
Poland from Hungary : they went naked to the waist,
wore crosses on their lower garments, and entered every
town two by two, with caps descending to their eyes, and
exhibiting on their breasts and backs the wounds caused by
their merciless whippings. Twice a day, and once during
the night, did they inflict upon themselves this horrible
penance, — sometimes in the churches, sometimes in the
public cemeteries, vociferating the whole time, *mercy!*
After which, joining in a song alluding to our Saviour's

* After reckoning the virtues and vices of the great Casimir, Dlugoss
adds, " Redimens vitia virtutibus, plura habebat quæ merito laudari de-
buerant, quam quibus debebat ignosci." If this excellent canon alludes to
the *public* character of the monarch, he is right; if to the *private* one, he
is notoriously wrong. No private virtues can redeem gluttony, drunkenness, ill usage of a wife, continued adultery, treachery, and murder.

passion, they would suddenly throw themselves on the
ground, regardless of stones, flint, or mud : one of their
lay preachers would then pass from one to another, saying, " *God forgives thee thy sins !* " Thirty days' continued suffering they considered a full atonement for sin :
hence they dispensed with the sacraments, which they
taught were abrogated, grace being obtained, and guilt
removed, by this penance alone. They took in a strange
sense that most Christian of truths, " without shedding
of blood there can be no remission."   The success of
these madmen in making proselytes would appear incredible, had we not instances enough in our times how
easily heresy and fanaticism — and those too of the
worst kind — may be propagated among the vulgar.
Hungary, Poland, Germany, Italy, France, and even
England, were overrun by the Flagellants.   They were
long treated with respect even by those who considered
them as displaying more zeal than knowledge; but, in
the end, it was found that their vices were superior to
both.   Men and women roamed together from kingdom
to kingdom; and while thus publicly enduring so severe
a discipline, made ample amends for it in secret: they
lived in the worst species of fornication.   Until their
knavery was discovered, and they were scouted by the
very populace, pope and prince vainly endeavoured to
repress them.*

LEWIS.

1370—1382.

SCARCELY had this king arrived at Cracow when his
unpopularity commenced. One of his first acts was
to confer two of the best fiefs of the crown on strangers,
whose only merit consisted in being his relations.   In
the fear that the two youngest daughters of Casimir

* Dlugoss, 1029—1116. Cromer, 304—329. Sarnicki, vii. cap. 1. Neugebaver, 195—209.   Krantz, viii. cap. 28. Solignac, iii. 104—181. Zielinski, l. 241—278. Dubravius, cap. xxii. Bonfinius, lib. x.

might contract royal alliances, and thereby endanger the
stability of a throne which he wished to remain in his
own family, he removed them into Hungary. Both measures called forth the indignation of the Poles. But what
most dissatisfied his new subjects was his ignorance of
their language : whenever favours were solicited, or
complaints laid before him, an interpreter was necessarily present, who, it may be reasonably supposed, did
not always faithfully render the wants of the one party,
or reply of the other. Distrust, discontent, dislike soon
arose on both sides. Finding that there was little happiness or glory to be reaped in this country, he confided
the regency to his mother Elizabeth, and returned to his
Hungarian subjects, whose prosperity he had constantly
at heart, and by whom he was beloved.

This queen was more disliked than even himself.
Capricious, arrogant, avaricious, distrusting the fierce
people she was called to govern, and fond of lavishing
entertainments on her Hungarian visitants alone, she
raised herself a host of enemies, but did not secure a native
friend. She was soon despised ; her authority was defied ; 160 Hungarians were massacred in an insurrection
of the populace ; bands of robbers scoured the country ;
and a numerous army of Lithuanians ravaged the palatinates of Lublin and Sendomir. The terrified old lady
fled to her son, who, perceiving that if he did not return
Poland would be lost to himself and successors, hastened
to remedy the evils which his absence had occasioned.

Lewis had the good sense to overlook what he could
not punish. He spoke not of the Hungarian massacre ;
he showed no sign of discontent : on the contrary, he
behaved to his Polish subjects with the greatest kindness, and with them he speedily triumphed over the
Lithuanians. His object was to procure the election of
his daughter, Maria, to the throne after his decease (he
had no male offspring). With much difficulty he
attained it, but not without making new concessions to
the nobles, the true tyrants of the country. He then
returned to his Hungarians, leaving the duke of Oppelen

regent of the kingdom. The Poles refused to obey the new governor : the regency was then put in commission, and intrusted to three natives. Their administration was any thing but a benefit; the Poles obeyed no authority with willingness, much less that of equals.

This prince died in 1382. His memory is unjustly treated by the Poles. He had great qualities and great virtues. That he favoured his Hungarian in preference to his Polish subjects, is natural enough : the former idolised, the latter hated him ; the former served him with alacrity and constancy, the latter disobeyed him in every thing. As he could not reside in both kingdoms, he preferred his native country to a foreign land. To the Poles, however, he was a mild, but a weak ruler. By yielding to the exorbitant demands of the turbulent and interested nobles ; by increasing their privileges, and exempting them from the necessary contributions, he threw a disproportionate burden on the other orders of the state, and promoted that aristocratic ascendancy before which monarch and throne were soon to bow. There is another and a better founded charge brought against him by the national writers. He relinquished all claims of sovereignty over Silesia, and annexed Red Russia, a dependency of Poland, to the Hungarian crown. For the former act it may be urged in his defence, that, as the re-conquest of Silesia was impossible, he only abandoned a vain title ; and for the latter, that he surrendered two or three provinces in exchange for the country thus annexed,—a country, too, which his Hungarian troops had assisted to subdue. Still, the one was impolitic, the other unjust. Had he, on finding his inability to govern two nations, resigned the crown of Poland to one of his daughters, his fame would have been amplified, and his real powers undiminished ; but the *shadow* of power is not willingly abandoned, even by good princes.[*]

* Authorities the same as last quoted. According to Bonfinius (lib. x.) the Hungarians mourned three whole years after the death of Lewis. " Quantum ejus mors et Ungaris et sociis moeroris attulerit, hinc facile considerari potest, quod annos tres universa Ungaria pulla veste incessit,

HEDWIG.

1382—1386.

THE death of Lewis was speedily followed by troubles
raised chiefly by the turbulent nobles.   Notwithstanding
their oaths in favour of Mary and her husband Sigismund, —oaths in return for which they had extorted such
great concessions, — they excluded both, with the design
of extorting still greater from a new candidate.   Sigismund advanced to claim his rights.   Ziemovit, duke
of Mazovia, and a Piast, also aspired to the throne; a
civil war desolated several provinces.   The latter prince
might have united the suffrages in his favour had he not
exhibited great ferocity, rashness, impatience, and other
qualities sufficient to disgust the Poles with his pretensions.   The factions at length agreed that the crown
should be offered to Hedwig, youngest daughter of the
late king, and grand-daughter of Casimir the Great, on
condition that she should accept as husband any one of
the princes whom her subjects might propose to her.

As this princess was only in her fourteenth year,
the deputies treated with her mother Elizabeth.   That
queen, however, being bent on the succession of her
eldest daughter Maria, to whom the Poles had sworn
obedience *, had recourse to policy.   She accepted the
throne, indeed, for Hedwig; but, on the plea that the
princess was too young to undertake the onerous duties of government, she despatched Sigismund to act
as regent, in the view that he would be able to reconcile
the people to his authority.   Her stratagem failed ; he
was not even allowed to enter the country ; and a mes-

---

totidem annis luctum regionatim celebravit. Nusquam risus, jocus, sonus,
chorea, aliquodve festivitatis genus spectatum est." It is a pity that exaggeration is made to spoil every thing.
* The fate of mother and daughter was a hard one. Elisabeth was
drowned in the troubles which followed in Hungary; Maria narrowly escaped the same end, was long confined a prisoner, and treated with rigour.
In the sequel she was restored, when her husband Sigismund had gained
possession of the throne.

senger was sent to inform her, that if Hedwig was not given to the nation in two months, a new election would be made. This menace had the desired effect; Hedwig arrived in Poland, and was immediately crowned at Cracow.

HEDWIG.—The beauty of this princess, her affability, her virtues, discernible even at that tender age, and above all her crown, soon brought her many suitors. Among them was the duke of Mazovia; but the evils his ambition had brought on the country (his ravages had never ceased since the death of Lewis) caused his rejection. The most powerful was Jagello, son of Gedymin, duke of Lithuania, and his proposals most advantageous to the nation. He offered not only to abjure paganism, and to introduce the Christian faith into his hereditary dominions,—Lithuania, Samogitia, and a portion of Russia,—but to incorporate these dominions with the Polish crown, and even to reconquer Silesia, Pomerania, and the other territories formerly dependent on it. His pretensions were instantly supported by the whole nation; but a difficulty intervened which threatened to blast its fairest hopes.

Young as was the queen, she had long loved, and been affianced to, William duke of Austria. In a virtuous heart such a passion could not be readily sacrificed. She remembered his elegant form, his pleasing manners, and, above all, the tender affection he had shown her in her childhood; and she could not avoid contrasting him with the rude, savage, uncomely pagan. Her subjects well knew what passed in her mind; they knew too that she had written to hasten the arrival of duke William; they watched her day and night, intercepted her letters, and kept her like a prisoner within her own palace. When her lover arrived he was not permitted to approach her. She wished to see him once — but once — to bid him a last adieu; in vain. Irritated, or perhaps desperate at the refusal, she one day seized a hatchet, with which she threatened to break open her iron gates to admit the duke; and it was not without

difficulty that she was forced to desist from her purpose.
This was a paroxysm of the passion scarcely to be wondered at in one of her strong feelings. But she was
blessed with an understanding remarkably clear for her
years : in her cooler moments she perceived the advantages that must accrue to her people from her acceptance
of Jagello ; and, after a few violent struggles with nature,
she resolved to see the formidable barbarian, and, if
possible, to subdue the repugnance she felt for him. He
arrived, and did not displease her.* His baptism, by
the name of *Uladislas*,— a name dear to the Poles,—his
marriage, and coronation, followed. The disappointed
duke of Austria long concealed himself in Cracow, in
the hope that a first love would eventually plead for
him. On one occasion he hid himself in a chimney, to
escape the pursuit of men who were anxious to remove
him from the city and country; and when, from the
success of his rival, he indignantly left Cracow, he left
his treasures behind him,—treasures which had doubtless lost all value in his eyes. There is something exceedingly romantic in the attachment of these royal
lovers. By sacrificing the heart's best and purest affections, Hedwig attained the dignity of heroism ; but she
might be excused if, after her union with a jealous
though fond husband, she looked back with a sigh to the
destruction of her earthly hopes.†

---

* " Petit, laid, cruel, toujours vêtu de peaux de bêtes fauves, ce barbare
épouvantait la tendre Hedvige." — *Salvandy, Histoire de Pologne, &c.* i. 93.
Romance.

† Dlugoss, lib. x. 1. 102. Cromer, 348—368. Sarnicki, vii. cap. 2. et 3.
Petr. de Rewa, Rerum Hungaricarum, cent. iv. et v. Solignac, iii. 185—
245. Zielinski, i. 278—296. Bonfinius, dec. iii. lib. i. Michaëlis Ritii de
Regibus Ungariæ, lib. ii.

CHAP. IV.

DYNASTY OF THE JAGELLOS. *

1386—1572.

ULADISLAS IV. (JAGELLO.)
1386—1434.

FAITHFUL to his engagements, one of the first acts of
the new monarch was to effect the conversion of the
Lithuanians. A diet, assembled at Wilna, declared that
idolatry should be destroyed. Hedwig had the consolation to see her husband zealously assist the priests in
this great work. He accompanied them in their visits
of instructions, often translated their meaning into the
Lithuanian language, and, though but a novice himself
in such matters, enforced the leading doctrines and duties
of Christianity in a way creditable alike to his sincerity
and ability. These rude people were, very wisely, not
burdened with much theological knowledge. A moderate acquaintance with the Lord's Prayer and the
Creed, both which they carefully committed to memory,
and were taught to understand, was the only preparation
required for the first and the greatest of the sacraments.
This change was effected with much less difficulty than
might have been reasonably expected. Some were seduced by the condescension, others by the gifts, of Uladislas; and few were inclined to respect their ancient
faith, when they saw the sacred fire at Wilna extinguished,
the deified reptiles slain, and the consecrated woods cut
down with perfect impunity.† The establishment of a

* During this period the monarchy was as much elective as hereditary.
† The first grand duke of Lithuania was Ringold, who assumed that title
in 1235. Gedymin was the fourth hereditary ruler; he was slain on the
field of battle by a Teutonic knight. Olgerd, his brother, succeeded, and
greatly extended the limits of the grand duchy. Uladislas was one of the
thirteen sons of this fierce pagan.

bishopric at Wilna, and of seven parishes in its vicinity, all well endowed, laid the foundation of future success.

On his accession to the Polish crown, Uladislas confided the government of Lithuania to Skirgello, one of his brothers. This was a fatal error: he might have known that the pride of barbarians would not long brook even the suspicion of dependence on a country which they had so often ravaged with fire and sword. Had he crowned himself king of Lithuania as well as of Poland, and occasionally honoured the former country with his residence, the disasters which followed would probably have been averted. Skirgello was a tyrant; his rule, consequently, became odious to the people: their discontent was fomented by Witold, another brother, who aspired to his place, and who, in his blind ambition, had recourse to the Teutonic knights, the inveterate enemies of Poland, to assist him in deposing Skirgello. Their armies suddenly attacked the frontier places of Lithuania: Uladislas hastened to oppose them. Though defeated, they returned to renew the war in greater numbers than before. Wilna, however, was invested in vain during two or three successive campaigns. But the war was troublesome to Uladislas, who had the weakness at length to sue for peace with Witold, and even to invest him with the government of the country. Indignant that rebellion should be rewarded while fidelity was openly neglected, Skirgello now took up arms: he was pacified by concessions from the king. A third brother naturally imitated their example: the same policy, if such weakness deserves the name, was employed with respect to him. Whenever any of the three wished to extort more concessions from their royal brother, they had only to league themselves with the knights, the German emperor, or some other enemy of Poland. It was now evident that Witold aspired to royalty and to independence. His courage was of the first order, and was exceeded only by his ambition: had his policy been equal to either, his object would not have been difficult of attainment. By plunging into a war with the Tatars, commanded

by a lieutenant of Timur, his forces were annihilated,
and he was, for a time, too much weakened to measure
arms with his brother. Yet, though he preserved the
appearance of peace, though he even rendered important
services to Uladislas against the knights and other foes,
he never lost sight of the one great purpose. To counter-
act his designs, the Polish king at length adopted an
expedient which, for a time, disconcerted his aims. The
Lithuanian nobles were admitted to the same privileges
as those of the crown; were qualified to vote at the
election of a king; and were required, in return, to admit the Polish nobles to vote with them at the election
of a grand duke. This was an important step towards
an incorporation of the two countries; but ages were
required to extinguish the animosity which ages had
cherished. As Uladislas advanced in years he became
more pacific, and the measures of Witold less disguised.
Being refused by the Polish senate the title of king, he
prepared to usurp it. His alliance with the knights and
the emperor Sigismund, of whom both constantly urged
him to establish an independent regal dignity, rendered
him so formidable, that Uladislas, to avert the separation
of the two kingdoms, proposed to resign to him the
Polish crown. This was opposed by the senate, to whom
the ambition of Witold gave just umbrage, and who were
successful enough to frustrate his designs. He died
from pure vexation.* Swidrigal, another brother, of
equal ambition but inferior abilities, was appointed to
succeed. Uladislas was one of those whose fate it was
to learn no wisdom from experience. One of the first
acts of the new grand duke was to arrest and imprison
him immediately after the funeral of Witold, to attend
which he had left Poland accompanied by a slender retinue. Through the efforts of pope Martin V., and still

* " Avec cette diversité de penchans, *les deux branches de la race Slavonne*
(the Lithuanians and Poles) eurent de la peine à se conjoindre. La Lithuanie lutta *long-temps à main* armée contre la réunion. Un prince du
sang de Gedemin, le célèbre Vitold, la tint *près de quarante ans* en re-
volte contre son *cousin* Jagellon."— *Salvandy, Histoire de Pologne*, &c. i. 95.
Here are three consecutive sentences, containing more than as many gross
errors.

more through dread of the Polish nobles, the grand duke now released his prisoner ; on condition, however, of his being confined in his government. But peace was of short continuance: he aspired to the incorporation of Podolia and Volhynia with Lithuania. This insolent demand incensed the Poles ; a destructive war followed, in which the knights and the allies of Swidrigal exhibited even more than their usual ferocity. At length the Lithuanians themselves became tired of the war, and still more of their duke, whom they expelled from the country. His nephew, Starodubski, succeeded, who promised to hold Lithuania as a fief reversible to the crown on his decease, and never to make war or peace without the sanction of the Polish kings, his liege lords — a compact solemnly ratified by the Lithuanian senate. The sequel will show how this compact was observed.

Nor was the policy of Uladislas more successful in his transactions with the Teutonic knights.* He had promised to recover Pomerania, Culm, Dobrzyn, and the other possessions usurped by the order. It was a promise, as he soon found, not quite so easy to perform as to make. By a treaty with them he recovered Dobrzyn; but it was only by paying 50,000 florins, and by the sacrifice of Samogitia. Five years afterwards they again took that territory, and insisted that Uladislas should abandon the title of duke of Pomerania. The monarch unwillingly armed for the defence of his people's rights and his own. After some unimportant operations on both sides, a great battle took place between Tannenberg and Grunnervaldt, in which 50,000 men, we are told, were slain on the part of the knights, with their grand master.† This was by far the greatest and most deci-

* " Grace à lui (Jagello), les Polonais après tant de siècles revirent les ravages de la mer Baltique : on raconte qu'ils dansoient de joie à l'aspect de ses flots d'azur. L'ordre Teutonique..... rendit hommage dans les diètes à la nation Polonaise." *Salvandy, Histoire de Pologne,* &c. Utterly without foundation.

† It seems doubtful that the number of the slain, or even that of the Teutonics *previous* to the action, reached so high. Where could a few monks raise such an army? This is not the twentieth instance in which the national writers, who never lose sight of the national glory, are at variance with those of Germany. The truth is seldom to be got from either when

sive victory Poland had ever gained : it placed the order at her mercy ; but, by his want of decision, Uladislas lost the benefits of this splendid action. Instead of hastening to improve it by the reduction of the Pomeranian fortresses,. he allowed the knights time to repair their losses : he refused even to accept their proposals of peace,— proposals that went so far as to surrender three fourths of their possessions to the victors ; he seemed resolved to extirpate the order, yet neglected to take any measures for doing so at the only moment success could be expected from such a resolution. Witold, to whose valour the victory was chiefly owing, was seduced by the emissaries of the knights, who promised to aid him in his long-meditated views of ambition : he drew off his troops in opposition to the prayers and menaces of the king, and returned into Lithuania. Weakened by his desertion, the Poles, after some unimportant operations, consented to a peace, as the price of which they again received Dobrzyn, with 200,000 florins, but agreed to restore Samogitia on the death of Witold. In another expedition, Witold no less fatally crossed the designs of the king. Just as the Poles, who had penetrated into Prussia, were sanguine of success, at the instigation of the knights he again weakened them by his desertion. They were persuaded to submit their cause to the pope and the council of Constance, then assembled to condemn the doctrines of Huss ; but nothing was decided in their favour. Their interests were perpetually crossed by the emperor Sigismund, the inveterate enemy of Poland, who supported the knights or Witold whenever either felt disposed to harass them.

Uladislas, indeed, had it frequently in his power to be revenged of that selfish emperor. Dissatisfied with the sway of Sigismund, at one time the Hungarians, at another the Bohemians (he possessed the throne of both in addition to that of the empire), offered to accept the

---

their respective interest or fame is concerned. Dlugoss is more honest than the *modern* historians of his country. "Quamvis difficile credam quanti ex hostibus ceciderunt, exacta supputatione asserere."

Polish monarch as their ruler. To the throne of Hungary Uladislas had a good claim; since, on the accession of Hedwig, it had been agreed, that if Maria, the wife of Sigismund, should die without issue, that throne should devolve on the Polish queen. But he had no ambition; or, if he had, it was inferior to his moderation or his love of ease: perhaps, too, he found one sceptre too much for his grasp. He declined both, on the ground that, as Sigismund was the lawful ruler, he would not usurp the rights of that emperor. Besides, he was at no pains to conceal his aversion to the Bohemian *heretics*, as he termed the disciples of Huss, whose opinions were then prevalent in that kingdom. This generosity had no effect on Sigismund, whose hostility he continued to experience to the very close of life.*

In his domestic character, Uladislas exhibited the same melancholy weakness that attended his foreign policy. To the magnanimous Hedwig he proved a disagreeable consort. Exceedingly jealous by nature, conscious of his own inability to please, and, above all, convinced of the admiration which her personal attractions, no less than her sweetness of disposition, produced, his suspicions of her fidelity allowed her little peace. Duke William perpetually haunted his thoughts. One of those court reptiles who, to crawl a little longer in the sunshine of royal favour, would commit any baseness, endeavoured to destroy her reputation. The credulous king was made to believe that the Austrian's visits were neither few nor innocent. In the pride of injured virtue, she demanded a rigid inquisition into her conduct: she was triumphantly absolved, and her accuser compelled, in the singular fashion of the country, to lie prostrate under a table, and declare that he had " lied like a dog," and at the same time to imitate

* It may be doubted whether Sigismund deserves the hard names bestowed on him by Polish authorities. Of course they are not warranted by any thing to be found in the Bohemian or Hungarian writers. By Bonfinius (Dec. iii. lib. iii.), by Dubravius (p. 128.), he is extravagantly lauded; but the very extravagance proves that he had many regal qualities. His persecution of the Hussites is a stain on his memory.

the barking of that animal.*   She was thus restored
to the confidence of her husband, but a confidence which
would assuredly be interrupted by the first unreasonable
whim.   The death of this princess (in 1399) afflicted
him severely; her memory dwelt continually in his heart,
as it did in that of the whole nation.†   Whether through
indifference to a world no longer pleasing to him, or from
a fear that, as he had derived the throne in her right, he
should no longer be allowed to fill it, immediately after
her funeral he retired into Russia.   He was soon prevailed on to return, and to marry the princess Anne, a
niece of Casimir the Great, through whom his claim to
the throne of the Piasts was rendered still stronger.   Of
this queen we know little, and as little of her successor,
Elizabeth; but his fourth and last wife, a Lithuanian
princess, was destined to suffer the same injustice as the
first.   The accuser of this queen was her own uncle,
Witold, who could not pardon her for refusing to promote his interests with the aged monarch.   She too was
justified, according to the usage of the times, by her own
oath, and that of seven matrons of high rank and unble-
mished virtue.‡   But though she was speedily restored
to his favour, her tranquillity was but of short duration:
his outrageous suspicions embittered her life, as they had
embittered that of her predecessors.

At the diet of Jedlin his son Uladislas was declared
his successor.   As usual, this honour was by no means
gratuitously conferred, not till several important con-

* " Decretum autem sententiæ hujusmodi, Gnievossius (the false ac-
cuser) implere extemplo compulsus, subter bancum corpore curvato intravit.
Et revocatione factâ, in qua se profitebatur falso et mendaci probro, reginam
Hedwigim insimulasse, publicum etiam latratum edidit."—*Dlugoss*, x. 123.
The barking was to be repeated three times.   This singular punishment for
defamation continued in force in Poland unto the last century.

† The affecting observation of this queen on the restoration by Uladislas
of some cattle, unjustly seized by his authority, does her infinite honor.
" Though the cattle is restored, who will restore the tears ? " Dlugoss
(x. 161.) calls her the Star of Poland, and says that miracles were wrought
at her intercession.   She might have been canonised with much more reason
than many other Polish saints.

‡ This odd mode of justification was resorted to in other countries.   Some
doubts having been cast on the legitimacy of Clothaire, infant son of Chil-
peric, three bishops, and three hundred persons of distinction, swore that
the child was in reality son of that king.   The same course was adopted
with regard to Judith, wife of Lewis le Débonnaire.

cessions had been extorted from him : besides an exemption from every species of contribution, and an allowance
of five marks for every horseman whenever occupied in
war beyond the frontiers, the nobles insisted that none
of the higher offices, either in the army or state, should
be conferred on any member of the royal family, or on
any person other than the landed aristocracy of the
country.

Uladislas died in 1434. The most prominent parts
of his character were, honour, sincerity, generosity, and
justice, an ardent zeal for religion and for the happiness
of his people. His chief defects were profusion, incon-
stancy, credulity, idleness: his addiction to the pleasures
of the table rendered early rising impossible, and, consequently, abstracted considerably from the hours which
he owed to the administration of justice.*

ULADISLAS V.

1434—1445.

THOUGH the Poles owed much to the memory of Jagello,
and had extorted from him such important privileges as
the price of their election of his son, they now showed
that neither gratitude nor their own oaths had much influence over them. They were preparing to set aside
the young prince, then only in his eleventh year, when
the address, even more than the influence, of the virtuous Olesnicki, bishop of Cracow, made them, for a moment, ashamed of their criminal design, and raised prince
Uladislas to the throne.

The minority of the young king was inevitably a season of troubles. Lithuania was a prey to the ferocity of
the Russians and Teutonic knights, whom Swidrigal
armed in his support. The defeat of this rebel only

---

* Dlugoss, x, xi. 106—660. Cromer, 368—471. Sarnicki, vii. cap. 4, 5.
Neugebaver, 230—297. Solignac, iii. 245—378. Zielinski (the abbreviator
of Naruszewitz, &c.), i. 296—321. Æneas Sylvius, cap. 51—54. Dubravius,
cap. 25—27. Pontanus, Bohemia Pia, lib. ii. p 28. Bonfinius, ubi suprà, et
Ritius (Rizzio) de Regibus Ungariæ, lib. ii.

made way for the ambition of Starodubski, the grand duke, who, like Witold, aspired to royalty and independence. A sect of the rebellious Hussites * having elected Casimir, brother of Uladislas, to be king of Bohemia, troops were sent to support the pretensions of the prince; in the end legitimacy triumphed in the establishment of Albert, formerly Sigismund. Casimir, on the assassination of Starodubski, was nominated grand duke of Lithuania: he, too, openly aspired to sovereignty. But an event soon occurred which, more than all these, influenced the destiny of Uladislas.

Albert, king of Bohemia and Hungary, dying without male issue, and the latter country lying open to the ravages of the Turks, whose formidable empire now began to threaten the neighbouring powers, the Hungarian nobles were anxious to appoint a successor capable of defending their liberty. The promising talents of Uladislas; the military reputation of the people whose resources he wielded; and his affinity with the blood of their kings (he was the grandson of their favourite king Lewis), pointed him out as by far the most proper person to fill the vacant throne. The widow of Albert was, indeed, pregnant, and might be delivered of a son; but the danger was considered too pressing to wait the possible birth of a prince who would himself require the protection which the kingdom expected from its ruler. At the suggestion of John Corvinus, then an inferior officer, but afterwards the famous Huniades, it was agreed that the crown and widow of Albert should be offered to the Polish king. The glory of being constituted the bulwark of Christendom raised the ambition of Uladislas, who, after appointing a regency, accompanied the Hungarian deputies to Buda. He was immediately acknowledged by most of the kingdom; but Elizabeth, who, in the interim, had brought forth a male child,

---

* Their rebellion will surprise no one acquainted with the persecutions they had endured; but what can justify it? . If unable to obtain toleration by peaceful means, they ought, to use their own scriptural expression, to have girded up their loins, and tabernacled with their brethren of some freer region. In no state can harmony long subsist where the will of the minority is allowed to disturb that of the greater number.

naturally espoused its interests, and prevailed on a considerable party to oppose his coronation. In the end she
sued for peace, acknowledged him as king, and affianced to him her eldest daughter, with a valuable portion.

Monarch of two powerful states, Uladislas now turned
his undivided attention to the long-meditated war with
the Turks. The sultan Amurath II. was pressing the
siege of Belgrade ; he offered to raise it, on condition that
Hungary would become tributary ; or, if surrendered
into his hands, he would in future abstain from disturbing the kingdom.   The insulting alternative was indignantly rejected by Uladislas, who, at the head of a
combined army of Hungarians and Poles, crossed the
Danube, and advanced into Bulgaria.   Success attended
his arms : Sophia, the capital, he took and destroyed ;
his general, Huniades, whom he had made voivode of
Transylvania, killed 30,000 in a nocturnal sally of the
Moslems.   In the mountains of northern Macedonia
he defeated the army of the pacha of Natolia, and took
that general prisoner.   All Europe resounded with his
praises ; and the states which had hitherto taken little
interest in the war, showed a disposition to aid him.
Amurath was alarmed ; he offered as the price of peace
to restore Servia, and all conquests, except Bulgaria,
which had been subdued by his predecessor Bajazet.
The proposal was too advantageous to be declined ; a
ten years' suspension of hostilities was agreed upon, and
ratified by solemn oaths, — by the Christians on the gospel, by the Turks on the koran.

Glorious as was the peace, it was disapproved by the
pope, and by several Christian princes, who at this time
appeared to have adopted the preposterous notion that
the Turks might be expelled from Europe.   How
powers proverbial for their disunion, and a thousand
times more jealous of each other than fearful of the
Moslems, could hope to subvert a compact united empire, and one, too, *then* the most military under heaven,
is difficult to conceive.   Perhaps it was believed that

Europe would, at length, lay aside its dissensions, and join in one general crusade against the misbelievers. Charles VII. of France, Philip of Burgundy, the republics of Venice and Genoa, Scanderbeg of Epirus, and the emperor of Constantinople, loudly expressed their determination to join heart and hand in it. Cardinal Cesarini undertook to incline Uladislas to renew the war. That monarch had the weakness to believe that he could be righteously absolved from the oaths he had taken: besides, his own ardour responded to the spirit which was said to shake Europe to its extremities. Again he passed the Danube—this time at Orsova, and descended into the plains of Bulgaria.

No sooner was the sultan acquainted with the perfidy of the Christians, than he returned with a mighty force to the theatre of war. He found Uladislas at the head of about 15,000 horse and the same number of infantry, drawn up to receive him in the vicinity of Varna. Huniades led the attack, and charged with such fury that the Moslems gave way. At this critical moment, Amurath is said to have drawn from his bosom the treaty he had recently concluded, and to have exclaimed, while looking up to heaven, " Christ, if thou art the true God, avenge thyself and me of the perfidy of thy disciples !"* He then rallied his followers, and attacked with confidence the right wing of the Christians, which fell back. Uladislas now advanced with the reserve to support his heroic general. His ardour led him to push one division of the Turks to their very camp: in vain did Huniades caution him to beware lest they should suddenly extend their line, and envelope him. He penetrated to the janizaries, who formed the body-guard of

---

* This invocation of Christ by Amurath seems apocryphal. It is very differently related by Cantemir and Leunclavius (of whom both follow, or rather transcribe, Turkish authorities), and still more so by subsequent Christian writers. Some will have it that the sultan produced *the host* on the field,—not the treaty. Cantemir (i. 284.) says, " *There is a tradition* that Amurath did so and so." Sarnicki, Bonfinius, and Peter de Rewa also allude to it, professedly following the Turkish annals. They have no other annals of that people than what is contained in the two authors already mentioned. Bonfinius, however, imputes the loss of the battle to the imprecations of the Turks:—" Tales igitur poenas, exauditis Turcæ imprecationibus, Deus justus à Christianis exegit." P. 334.

the sultan; but here his triumphs ceased: he was instantly surrounded by overwhelming numbers, and furiously assailed. The conviction of his danger only served to heighten his courage. His horse fell under him: he maintained the combat on foot, and slew Karam Beg, one of Amurath's lieutenants, who advanced to take him. He astonished the Turks by his fearless intrepidity; but the contest was too unequal to continue long: the valiant band which accompanied the king was destroyed, and he himself fell among a heap of slain, most of whom his own hand had laid low. With great difficulty Huniades saved the wreck of the army.

Thus fell Uladislas VI. ere he had reached his twentieth year. His great capacity of mind, his magnanimity, his virtues, rendered him the most promising prince of his age. His fate was not immediately known: Huniades could give no information respecting it; both Hungarians and Poles were loth to believe that their beloved monarch was no more. It was not until many months had elapsed that either abandoned the hope of his return. Their grief and that of Christendom was his noblest monument. The powers which had driven him to the renewal of hostilities by their promise to support him, and which were selfish or cowardly enough to abandon him when exposed to the vengeance of the mighty Amurath, will not be forgotten by posterity.*

* Dlugoss, 662—812. Cromer, 472—501. Sarnicki, vii. cap. 6. Neugebaver, 298—318. Bonfinius, Rerum Ungaricarum decad. iii. lib. 4—7. Albert Crantz, Vandal, 245—277. Solignac, iv. 1—21. Zielinski, i. 321—330. Dlugoss says that the catastrophe of the king was owing to the desertion of Huniades and the Hungarians: this shows how little a contemporary (the author was born in 1415) may know of what does not pass immediately under his own eye. Sarnicki justly describes the sensation produced over Europe by this event: " Mirum est quanta fama et celebritas sit istius pugnæ, ut fere nullus sit historicus, nullus poeta, nullus jurisconsultus, nullus denique theologus, qui hujus nobilissimi regis vicem querulis vocibus non deploret et lugeat." (In fin. reg. Uladis.)

CASIMIR IV.

1445—1492.

WHEN thé Poles were constrained to believe that Ula-dislas was no more, they met to elect another king. Their suffrages fell on his brother Casimir, grand duke of Lithuania, not because that prince had very great qualities to recommend him, but solely because, during the absence of the deceased monarch, he had contrived to separate Lithuania from Poland,— countries which they were naturally anxious to re-unite. For some time he refused to accept the vacant dignity; he thought it better to exercise a despotic sway in his grand duchy * than to fill a throne subject to the all-powerful control of the nobles. They were preparing to elect another candidate, when he signif·d his intention to reign.

This prince, however, long refused to accept the con-ditions imposed on his predecessors: instead of swearing to the *pacta conventa*, and to the indissolubility of the union between the kingdom and the grand duchy, he precipitately fled into Lithuania to escape the persecu-tions of his new subjects; and when compelled to be present at the Polish diets, he adhered to his purpose with an obstinacy which occasioned them equal indigna-tion and surprise. In vain did they reproach him, in vain stigmatise him as a tyrant and a traitor; he bore their vociferations, their howls of execration, with provoking coolness. A confederation of the chief nobility at length met, and resolved in his very presence to depose him, if

* " Tel était sur eux " (the Lithuanians) " l'empire de leur grand duc, qu'un historien presque contemporain raconte, que condamnés par lui à mourir, ils dressoient eux-memes la potence, et, de peur de déplaire par des retards, consommaient leur supplice en tout hâte: sujets si dociles qu'ils craignaient la disgrace jusque sur l'échafaud." *Salvandy, Histoire du Pologne,* &c. i. 95. This, like most other things in this conceited writer, is a gross exaggeration ; but even exaggeration proves the despotism. Most of the Lithuanians at this day have no great desire for liberal institutions. The tranquillity they enjoy under the Russian sceptre, they consider (and justly) as superior to the stormy liberty they once possessed.

he persisted in his obstinacy. This menace had the
desired effect. From this moment Poland was in truth
a republic, — a name which she already began to assume; and her kings were but the lieutenants of the
diet.

The sway of the Teutonic knights had always been
tyrannical; it had long been intolerable. The Prussians
resolved to cast it off. In a simultaneous rising they
seized on all the fortresses of the order, except Marienburg, the residence of the grand master. Deputies
arrived in Poland to propose the incorporation of Prussia
with the republic, and to stipulate in return for a community of privileges. Their proposal was eagerly
accepted, their homage received, and ambassadors sent to
exact the usual oaths from the nobles of the country.
Casimir himself soon followed. He was received as a
deliverer: he conferred privileges on the chief towns with
great facility, and thereby secured their attachment. In
the mean time the knights were not idle. With the
money raised on their few remaining possessions, they
raised troops in Bohemia and Silesia, and advanced
against Casimir. The Poles were signally defeated:
they levied new forces. But money did more than their
arms: for a sum amounting nearly to half a million of
florins, they obtained possession of Marienburg from the
mercenaries of the order, which was unable to pay its
soldiers. The knights had no longer a foot of ground
in all Prussia; being conducted to the frontiers, they
were told to depart in peace. They speedily spread
throughout Germany, the courts of which looked with
no favourable eye on this sudden aggrandisement of
Poland. Means were furnished them for asserting their
claims to the country whence they had been expelled.
A desolating war followed, in which the successes of the
two contending parties were nearly balanced: smoking
ruins, and fields laid waste, alone remained. At length
both parties, from their mutual losses, sighed for peace.
It was made on conditions sufficiently advantageous to
the republic. Western Prussia, comprising Pomerania,

Culm, Malborg, with the important cities of Dantzic, Marienburg, Elbing, Thorn, &c. which had been dismembered, were restored to Poland; Eastern Prussia, or Prussia Proper, the cradle of that fierce race, was left to the knights who were to hold it as a fief of the crown, and every future grand master to do homage for it to the king and senate. These advantages, however, had been dearly purchased: in this war 300,000 men had fallen, 17,000 villages and hamlets were burnt [*], and immense sums expended.

From his accession, Casimir had exhibited gross partiality for the Lithuanians, to the prejudice of his Polish subjects. Yet as a Pole had the boldness to reproach him in full senate, they had deserved little favour at his hands; they had betrayed his predecessors and himself; they had recently formed the design not only of dismembering Podolia from the republic, but of choosing another ruler: it was by money, by entreaties, by promises lavished on the chiefs of the revolt, that he had succeeded for a time in tranquillising them; but though their purpose slumbered, it was sure to be renewed whenever Poland was engaged in a war more than usually serious. At their instigation the Tatars invaded Polish Russia; but the misunderstanding between the two people was suspended by the appearance of an enemy whose arms threatened the subjugation of both.

Under Ivan Vasilevitch the Muscovites freed themselves from the yoke of the Tatars. Without any other assistance than his own courage and genius, this extraordinary man not only secured the independence of his country, but amplified it by important conquests: his subjects he was the first to discipline, and prepare for that career of ambition which his successors have ever since pursued. He took Novogorod the Great, which Witold had joined to Lithuania, and which paid an annual revenue of 100,000 roubles; Siewiertz, and a portion of White Russia, were next subjugated. Casimir

---

[*] So say the historians; but few readers will believe a statement so extravagantly exaggerated.

hastened to stop his progress by suing for a peace, as the
condition of which he was allowed to retain his conquests.
Lithuania soon learned, by dear-bought experience, that
she was unable alone to resist her formidable neighbours,
and that a union with the republic was the only means
left by which her subjugation could be averted. She
found that the Tatars, whom she had so criminally drawn
into the country, were not easily to be dismissed. These
barbarians laid waste several flourishing provinces, and
committed the most horrible depredations. The Poles
under John Albert, son of Casimir, advanced to the relief of the Lithuanians: two decisive victories won by
that prince, freed the grand duchy from the fierce invaders.

On the death of Ladislas, king of Bohemia and Hungary (the posthumous son of Albert), both kingdoms
were thrown into confusion; both had to choose a ruler
in critical times. Casimir, as the husband of one of the
daughters left by Albert, was the legitimate heir of both
crowns. In the interim the government of Bohemia was
seized by Podiebraski, who, though he professed to hold
the reins only until a king should be crowned, evidently
aspired to render it hereditary in his family; and who,
as a Hussite, was sure of the support of a numerous party.
The catholic party, the Silesians, the pope, pressed Casimir to ascend the throne; but he was then engaged in
the war with the knights, and he was too conscious of
his inability to struggle with a second enemy, to bring
on his hands Podiebraski and the Hussites. The Bohemian catholics, however, on the excommunication of
that aspiring ruler, elected him (Casimir), or, if he declined the dignity, one of his sons, as their king. Still
he refused to engage in another war. Matthias, son of
the famous Huniades, whom the Hungarians had raised
to their throne, now contended for that of Bohemia.
Resolved to disarm one at least of his enemies, Podiebraski, on whom the papal thunders fell harmless, declared Uladislas, the eldest son of Casimir, his successor
to the crown. Thus both Hussite and catholic acknow-

ledged the rights of the Polish royal family,—the former, it must be observed with regret, and with the intention of one day disputing them. He was, in fact, preparing to exclude Uladislas from the accession in favour of Matthias, whom this measure had disarmed, when death put a period to his stormy and unprincipled career. Uladislas was crowned at Prague, notwithstanding the opposition of the Hungarian king.

Irritated at the heavy contributions they had been compelled to raise, and at the progress of the Turkish arms on their frontiers, the Hungarian nobles combined to dethrone Matthias, and to put in his place Casimir, second son of the Polish king. Twenty thousand Poles proceeded to Hungary with the young prince; they were expelled by Matthias, to whom a strong party still adhered. On the death of that king the Hungarians elected—not Casimir *, but John Albert, the third son of the Polish monarch, whose victories over the Tatars had given lustre to his name. Uladislas aspired to the same throne, and was proclaimed, through the intrigues of the widow of Matthias. A war followed between the two brothers, in which John Albert was taken prisoner, and was not set at liberty until he had renounced all claims to the Hungarian crown. The aged Casimir strongly reprobated the ambition of Uladislas, whom one kingdom could not satisfy, and whom he disinherited at his death.

Under this monarch aristocracy made rapid progress in Poland. When, on the conclusion of the war with the knights, he assembled a diet to devise means for paying the troops their arrears, it was resolved to resist the demand in a way which should compel him to relinquish it. Hitherto the diets had consisted of isolated nobles, whom the king's summons, or their own will, had assembled: as their votes were irresponsible, and given generally from motives of personal interest or prejudice, the advantage to the order at large had been purely accidental. *Now*, that order resolved to exercise

---

* This prince was more ambitious of a celestial than of an earthly crown. He died in 1482, and was canonised by pope Paul V.

a new and irresistible influence over the executive. As
every noble could not attend the diet, yet as every one
wished to have a voice in its deliberations, *deputies* were
elected to bear the representations of those who could not
attend. Each of these deputies was strictly bound down
by the instructions he received from his constituents; he
had no longer the power to preserve his own interests
separate from those of his order ; he had, in fact, no will
of his own, except in so far as it coincided with the will
of those who sent him : he was their servant, though
their equal. Each palatinate sent two deputies ; so also
did each district.*

The success of this first representative diet astonished
all Poland ; it was the first in which the members did
not openly quarrel. It was resolved that all future ones
should be representative also. Thus, what accident alone
occasioned, was perpetuated from its convenience, and
its admirable adaptation to the purpose for which it was
intended — the diminution of the royal prerogative. It
soon became too powerful for the crown, which it tram-
pled under foot; and for the senate of prelates and barons,
whose measures it controlled. What in England was
the foundation of rational freedom, was in Poland subversive of all order, all good government : in the former
country, representation was devised as a check to feudal
aristocracy, which shackled both king and nation; in the
latter, it was devised by the aristocracy themselves, both
to destroy the already too limited prerogatives of the
crown, and to rivet the chain of slavery on a whole nation. This very diet annulled the humane decree of
Casimir the Great, which permitted a peasant to leave
his master for ill usage, and enacted that in all cases such
peasant might be demanded by his lord; nay, that whoever harboured the fugitive, should be visited with a heavy
fine. This, and the assumption of judicial authority
over his serfs, for peasants they can no longer be called,

* See the last chapter of the present work, in which the number of palatinates, of senators, and deputies will be found.

was a restoration of the worst evils of feudality. But the most ruinous effects of the new system were the factions which soon began to reign in these assemblies, the depression of the executive authority, and the indecision which accompanied the public acts. The deputies, as a celebrated historian well observes[*], considered themselves, in their representative character, the highest order in the republic. Merely to show their independence, they frustrated the designs of the king, or opposed the advice of the senate with perfect impunity; in fact, they annihilated all power other than their own. Instead of adjusting the balance of the state; instead of repressing on the one hand the encroachments of royalty, and on the other those of popular license, they looked only to the interests, or prejudices, or passions of their order. Reason and moderation, nay, the very appearance of deliberation, were banished from their assemblies; clamour alone, or noisy presumption, could obtain a hearing. Thus it has been, and thus it ever will be, whereever the popular voice has an undue preponderance, — wherever that voice is not awed by superior authority. [†]

The feeble though obstinate Casimir IV. was regretted by nobody. Whatever good appeared under his reign, says a national writer, must be referred to the favour of Heaven; whatever bad, to the weakness of his administration. Idle, indifferent to the welfare of his Polish subjects, and blindly partial to the Lithuanians; without knowledge of men or business; without economy or method either in public or private life, he seems to have been the passive creature of impulse, and to have resigned himself to the stream of circumstances, whereever no prejudice interfered. He was too weak to have a character.[‡]

* Rulhière, Anarchie de Pologne.
† The system of deputies, in its commencement, was not adopted by *all* the palatinates; some openly resisted it, and adhered to their ancient privileges of appearing at the diet *en masse.*
‡ Dlugoss, lib. xiii. 1—592. Cromer, xxii. 502—657. Sarnicki, vii. cap. 7. Neugebaver, 319—428. Kojalowitz, Historia Lituaniæ, 194—256. so-

The throne of Casimir was successively filled by three of his sons.

JOHN I. (ALBERT.)
1492—1500.

On the death of Casimir, efforts were made to raise to the throne Sigismund, the youngest son of that prince ; but the deputies, who remembered the exploits of John Albert, being sustained by a body of cavalry furnished by the queen, secured the triumph of their favourite. This choice was in conformity with the last wishes of Casimir ; and so was the election of another son, Alexander, to the grand ducal throne of Lithuania. Neither people, however, had yet learned to lay aside their national jealousies, and unite their suffrages in favour of a common ruler.

The first expedition of this monarch proved that his merit by no means corresponded with his reputation. At the head of a considerable force of Poles, of Lithuanians, and of Teutonic auxiliaries, he penetrated into

---

lignac, iv. 122—238. Zielinski, i. 330—358. Bonfinius, Rerum Hungar. decad. iii. lib. 7, 8.

The history of Dlugoss ends in 1480; a work in which this excellent old man was occupied near twenty-five years. It contains many superstitions, many legends, many things utterly improbable; but these must be placed to the age, much more than to the man : in him the true is easily distinguished from the fabulous. As a record of Polish history from the earliest times down to 1480, it is beyond all comparison the best work of the kind : preceding writers are too meagre to afford much information ; subsequent ones, such as Cromer, Sarnicki, Neugebaver, &c. have done no more than abridge him. At the close of his labours, he is exuberant in his gratitude that his life had been spared to complete them. "Immensas autem gratias ago, infinitasque et immortales, sanctæ et immortali Trinitati, Patri et Filio et Spiritui Sancto, et Dei genetrici, excellentissimæ Virgini Mariæ, sanctæ theotocos, et omnibus angelis, patriarchis, prophetis, apostolis, martyribus, confessoribus, virginibus, omnibusque coelestium virtutum ordinibus, præsertim tam beatis Michaeli archangelo, utrique Joanni patriarchæ et apostolo, beato Stanislao, Venceslao, Adalberto, Floriano, Hedvigi, patronis regni Poloniæ gloriosis, et beato Vincentio martyri famoso, et beatis virginibus et electis Annæ, Mariæ Magdalenæ, Dorothæ, Margarethæ, Barbaræ, et beatis confessoribus Hieronymo, Augustino, Ambrosio, Gregorio, Basilio, Benedicto, et omnibus sanctis quorum suffragiis et auxiliis et intercessione credo me librum præsentem scripsisse et dictasse." He exhorts the clergy, doctors, masters, scribes, &c. to continue his work after him. — Dlugoss was canon of Cracow, and preceptor to the sons of Casimir : he constantly refused church dignities. He died the very year in which he finished his labours.

Wallachia, without intimating whether his hostilities were to be directed against the voivode of that province, or the Turks, or both. He had soon reason to repent of his temerity: the Wallachians, unable to oppose him openly, hid themselves in their forests, but emerged from time to time to harass his detachments: provisions, too, failed; the invaders were discouraged; and an armistice was obtained, by favour of which they turned their way homewards. But the sequel of this inglorious expedition is still more disastrous. As they were returning through a thick forest, and a country full of defiles, where they could not draw out their forces in line, they were suddenly assailed by the perfidious voivode: trees, which had been previously sawn asunder, yet so contrived as to remain in an upright position, were made to fall on them, and crush their crowded and encumbered masses: the scene was horrid; all were eager to escape destruction; the king was with difficulty extricated by some of his devoted followers; great numbers were made prisoners, and relentlessly massacred. Probably all would have been cut off, but for the eagerness of the enemy to pillage, and their inability, from lassitude, to join in a vigorous pursuit. The fugitive remnant of a once mighty host was cordially welcomed on its return. The king seemed to become more dear to the nation from his very disasters.

But John Albert could be loved only so long as his character was unknown. Entirely governed by a favourite, who was also odious as a foreigner, he had not the wish any more than the ability to repair the evils he had occasioned. Others, of a nature still more to be dreaded, menaced the murmuring kingdom. Aided by the Turks and Tatars, the voivode of Wallachia penetrated into Podolia and Polish Russia, the flourishing towns of which he laid in ashes, and returned with immense booty, and 100,000 captives. A second irruption of these barbarians would have been as fatal and as little resisted, had not a season unusually rigorous (it was December) saved Poland and Lithuania. Forty thousand of the invaders perished, alike from the intensity of the cold and the want of provisions. Many were found dead in the bellies of their horses, which they had ripped open in the expectation of finding warmth within. The voivode and sultan, in consternation at so terrific a misfortune, were glad to sue for peace.

But the kingdom was no sooner rid of one enemy than it was assailed by another. The formidable Ivan, under the pretext that his son-in-law Alexander had not, according to contract, erected a chapel, and procured a Greek priest for his daughter Helen, fell on Lithuania. At the same time a khan of the Tatars, in concert with the Muscovites, ravaged Beltz and Lublin. Both triumphed; for no serious opposition was made to either, except in Lithuania, where a handful of the natives were exterminated by the Muscovites. — During these incursions, John Albert tranquilly remained in his capital, which he fortified.

Hitherto the king had exhibited weakness only; he now showed that he could be perfidious. He had prevailed on a Bulgarian khan beyond the Volga to advance with a host of Tatars, and assist him in making head against the Muscovites and the other khan. The treaty between them, which was offensive and defensive, had been cemented by the most solemn oaths on the part of the Poles, who engaged to meet Shah Achmet on the confines of the Ukraine. In pursuance of his treaty the shah advanced, but received no aid from the Polish king, who, though he had made peace with Ivan, was compelled by honour, justice, and truth, not to abandon his ally. Through the Machiavellian counsel of his Italian favourite, John Albert left that ally to his fate; considering that the weakening of the Tatars by the hands of each other could not but be advantageous to the republic. Achmet was soon assailed by the rival chief: in one battle he was victorious; in a second he was completely routed, and obliged to flee for safety into the states of his allies. The melancholy result of this detestable policy will appear in the next reign.

This feeble, despicable prince died just as his kinsman Frederic, grand master of the knights, refused to do him homage. Nobody regretted him: he was one of the most deplorable of human beings. Under his reign not only was the national independence in great peril, but internal freedom, the freedom of the agricultural class, was annihilated. At the diet of Petrikau (held in 1496), the selfish aristocracy decreed that henceforth no citizen or peasant should aspire to the ecclesiastical dignities, which they reserved for themselves alone. The peasantry, too, were prohibited from other tribunals than those of their tyrannical masters: they were reduced to the most deplorable slavery. The deputies at the same diet took care to preserve the confirmation of their own exemption from all direct contributions. But they not only put the finishing hand to the degradation of the people: they still further diminished the royal prerogative, by decreeing that in future no king should be allowed to declare war without their permission.*

ALEXANDER.

1501—1506.

This prince was elected, like his father Casimir IV., not because his talents were judged worthy of the honour, but in the fear of losing Lithuania, which he would probably have dismembered, had his claims as a candidate been rejected. Before his coronation by his brother, the cardinal Frederic, archbishop of Gnesna, it was agreed that the two nations should henceforth be more closely united; that Lithuania should no longer be governed by separate dukes; that its deputies should attend the diets of election in Poland; and that both the crown and the

* Cromer, 658—674. Sarnicki, vii. cap. 8. Neugebaver, 429—441. Kojalowitz, 259—289. Solignac, iv. 239—276. Zielinski, i. 358—370. Karamsin, Histoire de Russie, tom. vii.

duchy should enjoy the same laws, privileges, interests, and metallic currency. This was the only wise measure adopted during three consecutive reigns.

Alexander was scarcely seated on his throne when the unfortunate Achmet, after wandering through vast deserts, came to demand hospitality and protection from his selfish allies. He soon found that his friends had vanished with his empire. The palatin of Kiow seized his person, and conducted him to Wilna, to await the pleasure of the king. During three years he was confined a prisoner. Alexander was then too much occupied with his favourite Glinski, and in his negotiations with Russia, to cast a look on misfortune. On the conclusion of a treaty with that power, a diet was held at Radomski, before which the sultan was required to appear. He was met by the king, who received him with much appearance of pomp, as if purposely to insult him in his adversity. Before the senate the Tatar stood as firm and majestic as if he still commanded 100,000 men. His noble deportment, his dignified complaints, proved him to be truly royal, and must have covered his base allies with confusion, had virtue enough been left for such a sentiment as shame. " I have no wish," said the sultan, " to rail at the insults you have offered me ; by so doing I should deserve them. My reverses, my captivity, your own remorse, must convince you of your injustice. Was it only to destroy me that you enticed me so far into these inhospitable regions? I trusted to your promises, your oaths, your urgent necessities ; for you I have lost my subjects, troops, glory, and nation: where is my recompense? Where is the people who would treat an enemy as you treat an ally and a friend! But he who is false to his God can never be true to man!" He concluded by beseeching the senate to permit his return home ; he offered to forgive the past. " If you repent of your injustice, it is enough ; I am not disposed to revenge ; benefits only impress my heart." It was feared, however, that if he were permitted to return, he *must* seek revenge : he was detained at Troki, and obliged to promise that he would not attempt to escape. Hopes were held out to him that his detention would be only temporary. But his personal enemy, the khan of the Crimea, urged his perpetual imprisonment; as the price of which that prince offered peace, and threatened war in the event of his enlargement. Seeing that no hope of his freedom remained, Achmet had the weakness to break his parole, by precipitately flying from Troki. To this rash step he was urged by some of his countrymen who arrived to demand his deliverance, and who appear to have convinced him that he owed little fidelity to a perjured nation. He was overtaken, brought back, and guarded with greater caution than ever in the fortress of Kowno, in Samogitia. He submitted to this new trial with the same unbending constancy, and predicted that iniquity would be its own punishment,—that the Tatar khan, for whose gratification this violence was committed, would soon turn against them.

The result approved the foresight of Achmet. Podolia, Polish Russia, and a portion of the Grand Duchy, were ravaged by a flying army of Tatars, immediately after the ratification of the treaty. Glinski, the favourite, who had some talents for war, advanced with 7000 horse to meet the invaders. (Alexander had for some time lain sick at Wilna, while on his passage to meet the enemy.) They were defeated, their booty and prisoners retaken; and hope again revisited the long desponding hearts of the Poles. The victory was indeed a signal one, considering the small numbers on both sides: that of the enemy might amount to 20,000.

The king was in the agonies of death when this intelligence reached him. He had no longer the use of his speech; but his eyes, his upraised hands, his quivering lips, bespoke his satisfaction, and his gratitude to heaven for this unexpected success.

Thus ended a reign more deplorable, if possible, than that of John Albert. It is, however, remarkable for some things that ought not to pass unnoticed. In a diet held at Radom a few burgher deputies were admitted with the nobles. In the same diet it was decreed that nothing important should be undertaken without the common consent (*communi consensu*) of the deputies ; a concession made by the senate, or prelates and barons of the realm. But one obvious thing was overlooked : the decision of the deputies was not defined to depend on the *majority*, but was received as implying *unanimity* of suffrages. This fatal omission gave rise to the *veto*, which involved in its exercise the ruin of the nation.

Alexander is known as something of a legislator. He commanded a number of scattered ordinances to be collected into one body, and rendered their observance binding on all orders of the state.[*]

SIGISMUND I.

1506—1548.

THIS prince, who had been hitherto known as duke of Glogau, and had been sent for by his dying brother, arrived at Wilna a few hours after Alexander's death. He was immediately acknowledged by the Lithuanians, who thus already disregarded the contract made with the Poles, — that no ruler should be chosen without the consent of both nations. The latter, however, ratified the choice the more readily, as Sigismund was now the only prince of the house of Jagello eligible to the throne. Uladislas had crowns enough already ; and Frederic, as an ecclesiastic, could not well be proposed.

Having resumed certain domains of the crown which the blind profusion of his predecessors had alienated, and ordered his judges to proceed to the trial of Glinski, the favourite of Alexander, he proposed to chastise the presumption of the Muscovites. Glinski, however, does not appear at this time to have deserved such rigour. Pros-

---

[*] Cromer, 674—688. Sarnicki, vii. cap. 2. Neugebaver, 441—451. Kojalowitz, 289—315. Solignac, iv. 276—310. Zielinski, i. 371—380. Karamsin, Histoire de Russie, tom. vii.

parity might have made him overbearing to his equals,
but we are not told that he had done any thing worthy
of condemnation: on the contrary, his victory over the
Tatars should have procured him the gratitude, though
it only increased the envy, of the Poles. Perceiving
that the nobles were thirsting for his destruction, he now
became really criminal: he opened a correspondence
with Vasil Ivanovitch, whose designs on Lithuania he
well knew, and offered to aid that Muscovite prince with
his counsel and arms. His traitorous proposals were
eagerly accepted. An army of Muscovites invaded the
palatinate of Micislaf: he joined them, and was immediately invested with the chief command. The
Lithuanians advanced to meet him; the Muscovites
retreated, and sued for peace, but with the deliberate
purpose of renewing hostilities as soon as they had collected a greater force. Accordingly, Vasil soon returned
with a formidable host; he subjugated Livonia, which,
as the Polish armies were engaged in Transylvania, they
could not relieve. Two years afterwards, at the instance
of the emperor Maximilian, he penetrated into Lithuania.
Glinski, however, who conducted his army, and whom
remorse had long afflicted, exhibited little disposition to
forward his views. Smolensko was not so much taken by
force as persuaded to submit; but Glinski intended to
restore it to Sigismund, whose pardon he had obtained,
and whose arms he had resolved to rejoin.

This double treachery proved fatal to its framer: it
had long been suspected; it was now discovered; and
Glinski was undone. As the Polish king was now able
to send a considerable force into these regions, success
abandoned the Muscovites. One of his generals routed
80,000 of them on the banks of the Borysthenes *; but,
as usual, the victory was stained by horrible cruelty.
No mercy was shown to the survivors; the whole plain,
for the space of four miles, was strewn with dead. This
disaster was long felt by the Muscovites, yet the ad-

* The Russian historians, probably with great justice, much reduce the
formidable numbers of their countrymen in their contests with the republic.

vantages of the war were theirs: the acquisition of Smolensko, and a great portion of Livonia, was more agreeable to Vasil than the honour of victory to Sigismund. The Poles have seldom derived much advantage from success in the field: if they have won many battles, they have taken few cities; and their conquests have often been lost almost as soon as gained.

The Wallachians were no less humbled. Incensed at being refused the hand of a Polish princess, Bogdan, their chief, entered Podolia, and laid siege, first to Halitz, and next to Leopol. Both places vigorously resisted. At the approach of Sigismund, Bogdan retreated, and wreaked his vengeance on the towns through which he passed. He was pursued by the castellan of Cracow, who vanquished him in a decisive action on the banks of the Dniester or Borysthenes. Again were the Polish arms sullied by vindictive fury. During more than twenty years the Wallachians respected the valour of the republic. Their renewal of hostilities was not less unfavourable to their hopes. At Oberstein, in the province of Pokucia, they were again signally defeated by the palatine Tarnowski. Sigismund, it is said, meditated the entire subjugation of Wallachia, which he proposed to incorporate with his kingdom, and assembled a mighty force at Leopol to effect his purpose; but the dissensions of his nobles and the intrigues of his queen occupied him too closely to permit him to think of conquests.

A third and more implacable enemy was the military order, which had already occasioned such disasters to Poland. Unmindful of the conditions which his predecessor had subscribed with Casimir, the grand master, Frederic of Saxony, had refused homage to the republic, and even insisted on the restoration of Pomerania, and the other conquests formerly made by the knights. Pretensions so astounding show that he had resolved on war: his audacity had been increased by the emperor Maximilian, who promised to aid him in his efforts at independence. Neither his death, nor the secession of Maximilian from the interests of the order, could damp the ambition of his successor, Albert of Brandenburgh.[*] For some years the Poles were too much occupied in their wars with the Muscovites and Wallachians to punish his rebellion. In the design of amplifying his possessions, Albert carried his arms into Samogitia, which he would have subdued but for the prompt resistance of the palatine Radzivil. This check did not discourage him. He had recourse to some princes of the empire, who were ever ready to sell the blood of their subjects to the highest bidder. With the troops thus acquired, he laid siege to some Pomeranian fortresses. He was at length opposed by Firley, palatine of Sandomir, one of the ablest generals of Sigismund. Not only did he lose the few conquests he had made, but he had the mortification to see the last possessions of his order in peril. In dismay he now sued for peace: he waited on Sigismund, then at Thorn, whom he had little difficulty in disarming: his near connection with the royal family of Poland, and the peaceable disposition of his uncle, will account for his success. But his perfidy was at least equal to his ambition. While arranging with the king the conditions of a peace which he professed his earnest wish to be perpetual, he heard that a considerable reinforcement of Danes and Germans had arrived at Königsberg. He hastily broke off his negotiations, and requested permission to return. At first the Poles, who well knew his design of renewing the war, hesitated whether they ought not to detain him as a prisoner; but he had received a safe-conduct, and Sigismund scorned to take advantage of his situation at the expense of honour. The gates of Thorn were opened, and hostilities recommenced. But though the German auxiliaries were headed by the celebrated Schonenberg, and occasional success shone on the banners of the knights, the result of the war was unfavourable to them, and Albert was again compelled to invoke the magnanimity of his uncle. A

* Albert was the son of Sophia, sister of Sigismund. He was only in his twenty-fifth year when elected grand master of the order.

truce of four years was willingly granted, until the basis of a lasting peace could be formed.

On the expiration of this period, Europe was surprised at the singular treaty made between Albert and Sigismund. The Teutonic order was abolished; the grand master and most of the knights having embraced the doctrines of Luther, and separated from the Romish communion. In resigning his dignity, Albert was created prince of Eastern Prussia,—of the territories ceded to the order by Casimir II.,—and the principality was made hereditary in his family: it was to be held for ever as a fief of the crown; homage and military service were to be performed for it; every new prince was to receive the investiture from the hands of the Polish monarch, and to have a high place in the senate: it could not be sold, alienated, encumbered, or dismembered, without the consent of the diet: an appeal lay from the decision of the prince to the tribunal of the kingdom; and, finally, in case the male posterity of Albert, or that of his brothers, became extinct, the fief should revert to the crown. By this important treaty, Albert, who had already taken a wife, congratulated himself as the founder of a new dynasty, and of a sovereignty which he foresaw his measures would not fail to amplify; and Sigismund, that he had dealt the death-blow to an order which had long been the scourge of the country, and which no valour could extirpate. Perhaps, too, he exulted in the aggrandisement of his family; he might even hope that it would ultimately prove advantageous to Poland, since, in case his own posterity should fail, Prussia might furnish a successful candidate for the crown, and be incorporated, as Masovia and other duchies had been, with that country. If, as will be hereafter seen, the consequences of such a concession have been fatal to the republic, assuredly the blame is not his: he may be forgiven for not foreseeing what no human prudence could have predicted.

The other wars of Sigismund were few and unimportant. One of his generals aided the Hungarians against the Turks; but the Christian army was signally defeated. By pope Julius II. he was urged to march against those formidable barbarians, and was offered the chief command of the European forces. But the offer, however brilliant, made little impression on one whose uncle had perished through a misplaced confidence in Christian co-operation, and who saw the two greatest potentates in Europe (Charles V. and Francis I.) more eager to destroy each other than to oppose the infidel,—nay, in strict league with that great enemy of their faith. To war he appears to have entertained a great aversion, though he never shunned it when it was required by the interests of his people. This moderation met with its reward. He had the consolation to see among his subjects an abundance to which they had hitherto been strangers : private feuds, too, became less frequent and vindictive. Many laws were made at his suggestion ; but a more solid benefit to both Poles and Lithuanians was his assimilating the codes of the two people, and thereby promoting the great end of their union. He had, however, many obstacles to encounter : neither the patriotism of his views, nor the influence of his character, could always restrain the restless tumults of his nobles, who, proud of their privileges, and secure of impunity, thwarted his wisest measures whenever caprice impelled them. The intrigues of his queen (daughter of Sforza, duke of Milan, whom he had received at the hands of the emperor Maximilian, one of the most mercenary, ambitious, and unprincipled of women, even in a country where such epithets may be universally applied to her sex,) embarrassed him still more, and frequently brought his administration into disrepute. Then the opposition of the high and petty nobility ; the eagerness of the former to distinguish themselves from the rest of their order, by titles as well as riches ; the hostility of both towards the citizens and burghers, whom they wished to enslave as effectually as they had done the peasantry ; and, lastly, the fierceness of contention between the adherents of the reformed and of the old religion, filled his court with factions, and his cities with discontent.

The doctrines of Luther must have made considerable progress in the Polish dominions, before a powerful order of monks would consent to strip themselves of their numerous advantages, and descend from sovereignty to a private station. From the number of proselytes made by the disciples of Huss,—proselytes, however, whom fear of persecution caused outwardly to conform with the established faith,—these doctrines gained a speedy triumph, especially in Pomerania and Prussia. To extirpate them, Sigismund had recourse to the very worst of arguments,—fire and sword. It must not, therefore, be concluded that such measures were congenial to his disposition; he was naturally much more inclined to mildness; but the spirit of the age was one of persecution, and he ought not to be blamed with undue severity for not rising superior to it. His fulminating decrees were lost on the Dantzickers, who, not satisfied with deriding his bigotry, openly resisted his authority, and refused to allow the very toleration which they claimed for themselves. They deposed their magistrates, created new ones, profaned the churches, expelled the priests, pillaged the monastic establishments, and committed many other excesses. For a time they were too formidable to be opposed, especially as they were under the protection of the grand master Albert; but, on the conclusion of his treaty with that aspiring prince, Sigismund resolved to punish them,—rather for their revolt than for their opinions. He might yet be pardoned for confounding the two, as he evidently did, and for concluding that obedience and heresy were inconsistent, if not irreconcilable. Fourteen of the principal ringleaders were beheaded, the rest banished, and the ancient worship was restored. Afterwards he had the good sense to relax from his severity: though he refused to admit the protestants into public offices, he connived at their toleration.

Sigismund lived to the age of eighty-two, the effect of temperance, of exercise, and of bodily vigour. His strength was prodigious; he could break in his hands the hardest metals. Modest, humble, humane, enlightened, indefatigable, the father of his people, he had strong claims on their affection and gratitude. But his character will be best known from the success of his administration. When he ascended the throne, he found the eastern provinces of his kingdom little better than deserts; the Teutonic knights in open revolt; strife and poverty within. His victories taught his enemies to respect his territories, which soon smiled with abundance: industry brought comfort and content to his people, who loved him in life, and revered his memory after death. At no previous period of her history could Poland boast of so much wealth, nor, consequently, of so much general happiness; never before did she number so many able generals, or such valiant nobles. The esteem of four successive pontiffs, of the greatest potentates in Europe, not even excepting the grand signior, who respected his character still more than his power, rendered him a striking contrast to the despicable princes his immediate predecessors.[*]

SIGISMUND II. (AUGUSTUS.)

1548—1572.

As a mark of respect to his father, and because he was the last male heir of the house of Jagello, Sigismund Augustus had been declared successor to the throne many years before its vacancy. There was consequently no interregnum, no election.

From the early dissipation into which the prince had plunged, and his effeminate education under his Italian

[*] Cromer, 688—709. (The work of this author properly finishes with Alexander, but his funeral oration of Sigismund may be regarded as a continuation until 1548). Sarnicki, vii. cap. 10. Neugebaver, 452—570. Vita Petri Kmithæ (ad calcem Hist. Dlugossi, tom. ii. col. 1607—1632). Kojalowitz, 316—408. Solignac, iv. 311—430. Zielinski, ii. 1. 31.

mother*, the nobles flattered themselves with the prospect
of a feeble reign. A clandestine marriage, into which
he had entered while at Wilna, with a young widow, a
Radzivil, was the first subject of contention between
him and them. At the diet of Petrikau, they deliberated
about annulling it, on the ground that it was a contract
made without their knowledge, or that of the late king,
and therefore illegal. They justly argued, that a monarch
should be compelled to sacrifice private affections to the
good of the state; that the indulgence of a weak passion
was a poor compensation to the republic for the loss of a
powerful foreign alliance. They insisted that the union
should be dissolved, and another contracted more in
harmony with the interests and honour of the nation.
The result showed that in calculating on his presumed
easiness of temper they had wofully erred. He steadily
refused to hear their proposal: he observed, that a faithless husband must necessarily make a faithless king;
'that his vows to his queen were indissoluble; and that
no power on earth should induce him to violate them.
In vain did they entreat, expostulate, menace; he was
inflexible. In a transport of rage they threatened his
deposition, and would probably have proceeded to that
extremity, had he not suddenly exhibited a stroke of
policy that silenced the leading members of the senate
and diet. By proposing to restore the ancient laws
against pluralities either in the church or state; by
inveighing against the prelates and barons who usurped
a multitude of dignities and starosts, to the prejudice of
obscure merit, he gained over to his side most of his
hearers, — all, in fact, except the few who were interested in the present unequal mode of distribution.
Praises of the king, and bitter curses against the plural-
ists resounded in the assembly. His object was completely secured: not only was all opposition hushed, but
the queen was crowned with acclamation. And well she

* " Mater enim hunc puerum habuit indulgenter, nec facile patiebatur
illum a suo latere, etiam cum esset grandior, discedere." *Stanisl. Orichov.
Annal.* 1—5. Mothers are every where much the same.

deserved the honour. Her piety, her charity, her intercession for oppressed innocence, her unostentatious
virtues, soon rendered her the delight of the Poles; and
her premature death was regarded as a national cala-
mity.

From this domestic affliction the king was roused,
not so much by the progress of the reformation, as by
the dissensions between its adherents and those of the
ancient faith. The disciples of the new doctrines had
amazingly increased. Not only the burghers and citizens,
but nobles, senators, nay, even priests and bishops *, were
among the number. Many of the latter had thrown off
the unnatural obligation of celibacy, had married, not
secretly, but in the face of the world, and were now
prepared to defend the justice of the change. The
prelates, also, who still continued within the pale of the
established church, were at a loss what measures to
devise in this emergency. For a time they had recourse
to severity. The bishop of Cujavia had condemned to
the flames a priest of his diocese for administering the
Lord's supper under both kinds. A lady of some distinction had suffered the same fate, by command of the
bishop of Cracow, (the Polish prelates, like the barons,
had judicial powers even in cases of life and death,) for
denying the real presence. Great numbers were visited
with the milder doom of banishment and loss of property.
Measures so opposed to humanity, and even to sound
policy, could not be long employed with impunity. In
another diet held at Petrikau, they were forcibly assailed
by several members, who spared not the prelates themselves. A powerful baron, Raphael Lesczynski, who
had resigned a palatinate to follow the bent of his
conscience (no dignity could yet be held by a Lutheran),
distinguished himself above the rest in his hostility to
the Roman catholic hierarchy.† This voluntary renun-

* Cosmin and Prasnicki, both preachers of the king; Lismanini, confessor
to the queen-mother; Direwiski, canon of Cracow; the bishops of Culm,
Warmia, Cujavia (not the persecutor), Kaminiec, and Kiovia, were all
either open or secret protestants.
† He refused to kneel, or even to uncover, at the customary mass before
the opening of the diet: he regarded the ceremony with smiles of contempt,

ciation of senatorial dignity and immense wealth, instead
of lessening, increased his influence. The speech which
he made in answer to the chancellor, who called on the
diet to invest the bishops with new powers to check the
growing heresy, displayed almost as much eloquence as
intrepidity. He inveighed against the rulers of the
church as men who had obtained their stations by birth,
faction, bribery, or favour — by any thing rather than
their own merit: he represented them as luxurious in
their living, as scandalous in their morals, as overbearing
in their pretensions. " Through their idleness, their
bad example, religion has suffered, its exercise has been
degraded, its purity has been sullied by childish superstitions. Hence their aversion to such believers as
ascend to the first ages of the church to acquire a knowledge of its doctrines and practice : hence these pro-
scriptions, these murders, this right of life and death,
which they assume over free citizens, whose only offence
is a refusal of their guidance lest the flock be lost with
the shepherd." Language like this was admirably adapted
to its object : it roused not only the protestant members
of the diet, but the catholics, to whom the pomp of the
hierarchy had long been displeasing ; it was applauded
both by deputies and senators. Tarnowski, castellan of
Cracow, and a catholic, followed on the same side. He
defied the bishops to produce any law which authorised
them to assume the power of life and death over the
people. He did not, however, distinguish (because to
do so did not suit his purpose) between their ecclesiastical and temporal privileges : as *bishops*, they had no
such power ; as *barons*, they were as much enabled to
hold courts as any palatine or castellan in the realm.
Such authority was, doubtless, objectionable, since the
sword of justice should never be wielded by ministers of
peace. Hence he argued with greater truth and force

and preserved throughout a standing posture. Orichov. lib. v. p. 1538 (in
calc. Dlugoss, tom. ii.). The fervour of zeal is seldom united with discretion. Would this man have submitted to the same irritable disrespect if
shown in a *conventicle ?* Not often has dissent been distinguished for a tolerant spirit.

in saying, that, if such power existed, it ought no longer
to be recognised, since it was at variance with that
equity which forbade the same party to be both accuser
and judge, and subversive of a freedom which king and
republic were bound equally to respect. In conclusion,
he disclaimed all intention of favouring heresy :—" Let
our prelates oppose it, but let them use no other arms
than such as become their characters—good example,
reason, persuasion." An incident lent additional force
to what was now become the popular cause.

Orzechowski, canon of Przemysl, and probably inclined to the reformed religion, had publicly married.[*]
Sentence of degradation and of banishment had been
pronounced against him by his diocesan, a zealous stickler
for ecclesiastical discipline and the privileges of his order.
In the process, however, some customary formalities had
not been observed; the priest appealed to the senate
against the illegality, no less than the unreasonableness,
of the conviction ; he even appeared in person to expose
both. An animated and a noisy debate arose : the bishop
in question defended his jurisdiction : it was opposed, as
contrary to the laws of the state. Several prelates admitted that the punishment awarded exceeded the guilt
of the crime, and appeared to doubt their own competency to decide in any case except where heresy was
concerned :- even breaches of discipline serious enough
to require condign punishment, they seemed to think
within the exclusive province of the lay tribunals. But
in the present temper of the nation those tribunals would
have acquitted Orzechowski : the deputies were evidently
resolved to vote for it, and many of the senators were
similarly disposed. Rather than see their privileges
usurped by the lay members, the bishops at length released him from all canonical penance, and restored him
to his clerical functions. In return for such extraordinary indulgence, they only required from him a confession of the orthodox faith, and a promise that he would
visit Rome to procure the confirmation of their absolu-

* Author of the six books of Annals referred to in the notes.

tion, or, in case it could not be had, to renounce the
engagement he had formed.* This was a cowardly, we
may add, a highly criminal subterfuge. Whether celibacy
was right or wrong, they had sworn to enforce it.

The conduct of Sigismund at this remarkable diet was
any thing but decisive. On one side, he feared the power
of the prelates; on another, he reprobated their vices,
and inclined towards toleration. Probably, in his heart
he was not much averse to the new doctrines. He openly
protected them in Lithuania; he permitted Calvin to
dedicate to him a commentary on St. Paul's epistle to
the Hebrews, and Luther an edition of the translation
of the bible. He had even sent the Franciscan Lismanini into Switzerland to obtain more certain information
as to the tenets of the reformers †; tenets, which both
Melancthon and Calvin believed he was about to embrace.
But the majority of his people were still catholics, and
as such were liable to the influence of their priesthood:
then the arrival of a papal legate with powers to end the
distractions of the bishops, and with the design of watching the king's measures, added to the difficulties of his
situation. After long deliberation, bigotry, or rather
rashness, prevailed: the sectarians of the kingdom were
subjected to the episcopal tribunals. This event was
wholly unexpected: it was too bold not to surprise even
the prelates themselves, and it filled the converts with
more indignation than alarm. Its impolicy was soon
evident: though the fires of persecution began to burn
with great fury, they were speedily quenched,—not by
the humanity of the ecclesiastical judges, but by the
amazing increase of proselytes, whose numbers inspired
the hierarchy with dread. To punish hundreds of thousands was impossible. In despair, the prelates abandoned
the exercise of their odious jurisdiction, and silently permitted what they had not power to prevent.

The report of Sigismund's barbarous policy soon

* We are told that he ultimately obtained a papal dispensation for keeping his wife. The story is incredible.
† This worthy never returned to give an account of his mission. He
married and settled in Geneva. *He returned ... in Poland from 1556 to 1563*

reached the inhabitants of Dantzic, who had been among
the first converts to the reformed faith.   To escape its
effects, or to be revenged on him who had framed it,
they were preparing to transfer their allegiance to another master, when Sigismund suddenly arrived amongst
them : his presence only, as he well knew, could recall
their fidelity.   He was received with outward respect
indeed, but with great distrust.   Lest his escort, which
was as numerous as it was well armed, should fall on
the people, burgher guards were placed in the streets at
every twenty paces, and sentinels were posted in the bel-
fries, to summon the whole population to arms at the
first signal.   The situation of the king was critical, but
he knew how to extricate himself from it.   His easy
manners, his candour, his apparent regard for the inhabitants, soon disarmed their hostility.   He asked them
what advantage they could possibly hope to gain from
submission to the emperor ; whether in such a case they
could rationally expect privileges so ample as they
already possessed.   He reminded them that they were
almost sovereigns in their own city, and assured them
that by himself and the Poles they were regarded with
brotherly affection.   As to their change of religion, he
neither authorised nor approved it ; but he would not
imitate his father ; he would not attempt by force what
reason was unable to accomplish.   His wise and dignified and affectionate remonstrance had its effect.   The
inhabitants were now eager to testify their attachment to
his person and fidelity to his government.   No doubt
he really felt the moderation he professed ; for thenceforth he ceased to interfere with the faith of his people,
whom he permitted to worship God in the way most
agreeable to themselves.   Dissidents were allowed to
hold their synods openly : in one held at Kozmin, the
Hussites and Calvinists, who had previously weakened
themselves by their animosities, effected a union.   Their
number and credit was so great that many were returned
as deputies to the national diet, and had the hardihood
to propose the abolition of clerical celibacy, the celebra-

tion of the Lord's supper under both kinds, that of the mass in the vulgar tongue, and that first-fruits should no longer be sent to Rome. Assuredly there was nothing unreasonable in any one of these demands; but we cannot avoid expressing our surprise that in so short a time as had elapsed since the first preaching of the reformation, it should have gained so firm a footing in one of the most bigoted countries in Europe.

From religious dissensions Sigismund was at length summoned to others of a more formidable character. William de Furstenburg, grand master of the knights sword-bearers in Livonia *, made war on the archbishop of Riga, whom he took and imprisoned. As this prelate was brother to duke Albert of Prussia, and cousin to the Polish king, the latter sent an ambassador to demand his enlargement. The messenger was assassinated, probably, as was believed, by the contrivance of the grand master. The Poles cried for vengeance; an army was raised, with which the king marched into Livonia. The knights of the sword were immediately dispersed; Furstenburg was obliged to make a humiliating submission, to liberate his captive, and to acknowledge his victor as lord paramount of his dominions. Without the consent

---

* In 1158 the faith of Christ was carried into Livonia by some merchants of Lubec. The first bishop, Meinhard, was consecrated, in 1170, by the archbishop of Bremen. He was succeeded, in 1193, by Berthold, abbot of Lucca, in Saxony, who founded Riga. Many Germans who had taken the cross for the Holy Land followed him into this pagan region, on being promised by Celestine III. the same indulgences as if they warred with the Mussulmans. Berthold was slain in an engagement with his infidel flock. His successor, Albert, raised an army, whose zeal was so great that it led them to form an association on the plan of the Templars. They took nearly the same vows, and engaged to subdue and convert the pagans. Their habit was white, on which two swords were crossed in red; hence their appellation of *Ensiferi*, or sword-bearers. The order was approved in 1204 by Innocent III. The first grand master was Vinno, who founded several towns. In 1238 the knights united with the Teutonics. Thenceforth the Livonian knights were governed by a provincial master deputed by the chapter in Eastern Prussia. They soon acquired sovereign power in Livonia, obliging even the archbishop of Riga to acknowledge it. That prelate and his suffragans at length assumed the habit of the order. When Albert, grand master of the Teutonics, commenced his war with the Poles, he borrowed money of Walter de Plettenberg, provincial of Livonia, whom he rendered free and independent, and whom Charles V. afterwards made a prince of the empire. Under Plettenberg, Riga, Revel, Dorpat, and other towns embraced the reformed religion. He was succeeded by Henry de Galen, and the latter by Furstenberg. Dlugoss, iv. 318. Alberti Krantzii Saxon., vii. cap. 13. Sarnicki, vi. cap. 18.

of Poland he could make neither peace nor war; least of all with Muscovy.

The union of so considerable a province with the republic roused the envy of Ivan Vasilevitch, commonly called Ivan the Terrible.* He poured 120,000 men into Esthonia, which they ravaged: several towns of Livonia were taken, the knights massacred or dispersed, except a few who were led captives to Moscow. The cruelties committed by these ferocious barbarians in this expedition, not on their prisoners only, but on all that fell in their way—on women and children and helpless age—are frightful. Streets were deluged with blood; women every where violated before they were murdered; their children's brains dashed out before their eyes; every thing combustible committed to the flames, and thousands led away to hopeless slavery.† The unhappy Livonians had no help from the Poles, who, with their usual want of foresight, had disbanded immediately after receiving the homage of the grand master. In vain did Kettler, who had been just raised to that dignity, wait on their king at Cracow: Sigismund had the will but not the power to aid them; the Poles were not to be roused,—perhaps they were not very eager to encounter the vast forces of the tsar. The Lithuanians were more easily persuaded. At a diet convoked at Wilna, Kettler and the king appeared. In consideration of several privileges bestowed on them by Sigismund, the nobles decreed that Livonia should be relieved. A treaty was made, in which the superiority of the king was again recognised, or rather Livonia was declared a portion of the republic; Courland and Semigallia being ceded to the grand master, who engaged for himself and successors to do homage for these possessions. It also guaranteed the privileges of the people, their toleration in matters of religion (they were mostly protestants), and

---

* For an account of the strange actions of this ruler—the most extraordinary man, perhaps, to be found in all history—see Karamsin, Histoire de Russie, tom. viii.

† So say the Polish historians, doubtless with great truth; but why do they not confess their own atrocities?

their defence against all enemies. It was ultimately approved in the castle of Riga, where Kettler solemnly renounced his rights as grand master, surrendered the insignia of his order, and was immediately declared hereditary duke of Courland and Semigallia; as such he received the oaths of the nobles of those countries. Thus ended the order of the sword, which during three centuries and a half had ruled over these remote regions. Like Albert and the Teutonics, Kettler and most of his knights had embraced the doctrines of Luther.

The result of this treaty was far from corresponding with its solemnity. The Swedes, who had some pretensions over Livonia, and who already possessed Revel and one or two other fortresses, invaded the duchy. The Muscovites followed the example, at the head of an amazing force. A bloody war ensued, in which the Poles acquired the honour but not the advantages of victory. Though they defeated the Russians in three successive actions, yet the latter subjugated and retained the palatinate of Polotsk; and Esthonia fell to Sweden.

Under this monarch, the union between Lithuania and Poland was cemented more strongly than before. From this time the two people were conjoined in every treaty with foreign powers, in every war, and were considered as forming one indivisible republic, under a chief elected by both in the general diet at Warsaw. The Lithuanians had their two separate chambers, — senators and deputies, — like the Poles, for their own internal administration. Before the time of this king, their privileges were not so great as those enjoyed by their neighbours. They had often and vainly complained, and had as often been promised redress; but Sigismund Augustus was the first of their princes who fulfilled their just expectations. By him the nobles of the grand duchy were placed on an equal footing with those of the crown.

Sigismund Augustus died without issue: with him was extinguished the male line of the Jagellos, who had ruled the two nations with glory during one hundred and eighty-six years.* The refusal of the pope to annul his marriage with his last wife, an archduchess of Austria, from whom he separated, prevented his intended union with a younger princess, and cut off all hope of posterity. His reformed subjects, indeed, were willing enough to annul it, and by so doing to burst asunder the ties which bound the realm to the see of Rome ; but he was too timid or too prudent to adopt their advice. He contented himself with showing greater favour than ever to the protestants, to whom, in revenge for the pope's obstinacy, he opened the way to the dignities of the state, The same circumstance, doubtless, contributed to his laxity with respect to women, — the only vice (yet that is great enough) with which history can charge him. As a king, he ranks very high. He was possessed of no great military talents; but by his prudence, his penetration, his activity, his enlightened views, his patriotism, his love of justice, and his generosity, he procured advantages for his people which well compensated for their absence. The happiness of his reign appears with greater lustre when contrasted with those which followed. With him ended the greatness of Poland. Though succeeding monarchs often covered their brows with laurels, the extinction of an hereditary line of princes, the anarchy inseparable from an elective crown, and from the gradual diminution of its prerogatives, and, above all, the increasing power of the tsars, sapped the foundations not merely of its prosperity, but of its security, and with fearful rapidity accelerated its ruin. In about two centuries from this period, and Poland will be no more. †

* " Les princes de Lithuanie avaient regné sur la république cent soixante-dix ans. *Salvandy,* i. 28. This writer is correct in nothing.
† Neugebaver, 570—640. Kojalowitz, 410—495. Orichov. Annal. lib. vi. Vita Petri Kmitæ (ad calc. Dlugoss, tom. ii.) Lubieniec, Historia Reformationis Polon., lib. i. et ii. Sarnicki, vii. cap. ii. Solignac, v. i. 165. Zielinski, ii. 31—56. Karamsin, Histoire de Russie, tom. ix.

BOOK II.

THE CROWN ELECTIVE.

CHAP. I.

FROM THE EXTINCTION OF THE JAGELLOS TO THE DEATH OF JOHN SOBIESKI.

INTERREGNUM.—HENRY DE VALOIS.

1572—1574.

THE death of Sigismund Augustus gave the Polish nobles, what they had long wanted, the privilege of electing their monarchs, and of augmenting their already
enormous powers by every new *pacta conventa*. Those
of Great Poland, Little Poland, Polish Russia, and Lithuania, first assembled in their *dietines*, in which they
formed a *confederation**, for the twofold purpose of pre-
serving internal tranquillity and of defending the republic
against the incursions of any neighbouring state. In the
preliminary diet, held always at Warsaw,—called also
the *diet of convocation*, — a dispute arose whether the
primate or the crown-marshal was to exercise some of
the most important functions of the *interrex*. That
they had always rested with the archbishop of Gnesna,
was too notorious to be denied ; but the marshal, John
Firley, was a protestant, and his partisans were naturally
anxious to invest their champion with authority. It was
constitutionally decided that the power of convoking diets
and dietines, and of *nominating* the successful candidate,
rested with the prelate ; but the privilege of *proclaiming*
the new king should be left with the marshal. A day
was appointed for the *diet of election ;* the *place* was not
so easily settled. The Poles proposed Warsaw, the Lithuanians a village on the frontiers of Poland and the

* See the last chapter in this work.

grand duchy, as still more central. It was at length decided that the nobles should meet on the plains of Praga, opposite to Warsaw, and on the eastern bank of the Vistula. At first it was expected that the election would be made by deputies only; but on the motion of a leading palatine, that as all nobles were equal in the eye of the law, so all ought to concur in the choice of a ruler, it was carried by acclamation that the assembly should consist of the whole body of the equestrian order, —of all, at least, who were disposed to attend. This was another fatal innovation: a diet of two or three hundred members (exclusive of the senators) might possibly be managed; but what authority could control one hundred thousand?

In this preliminary diet the protestants were not inattentive to their own concerns, which they were, indeed, bound by duty to promote. What they wished was ample toleration; but as they were the weaker party in point of numbers, and as some of the Polish prelates, no less than the papal legate Commendoni, were averse to their just claims, they were compelled to act with great caution. Under the general name of *dissidents* *, — a name which comprised themselves, Socinians, members of the Greek church, and even such Roman catholics as were opposed to persecution, — they concluded an alliance with the heads of the latter, by the terms of which the amplest toleration was secured to all who differed from the established faith. The odious zeal, however, of the legate and the primate procured the dissolution of so salutary a covenant, and left open a field for the display of religious rancour, no less than of the other bad passions, which could not fail to agitate the congregated mass. The Greeks, schismatics as they are insolently termed by a predominant church, from their numbers and weight, (they comprised a great

* In its original import this term included the Polish Christians of *every* denomination: " Nos dissidentes in religione," or " We differing in religion," was the language of their confederations. It was subsequently renounced by the Roman catholics, and its signification restricted within the limits of the text.

majority of the Lithuanians, and nearly all the inhabitants of Polish Russia,) were secure against persecution,
but the Lutherans had no aid but in their own policy
and were constrained to watch with scrutinising attention the measures of their adversaries.

At the time appointed for the holding of the elective
diet, such numbers of nobles arrived that the circum-
ference of the plain (twelve miles in extent) where they
were stationed by palatinates for the greater facility of
collecting their suffrages, was scarcely able to contain
them * ; and as they were all armed, they looked like
men assembled to conquer a kingdom, rather than to
exercise a peaceful deliberative privilege.   In the centre
of the circle or *kolo* was the tent of the late king, where
the senators and ministers of the crown were met in
consultation. †

The candidates for the vacant crown were Ernest
archduke of Austria, Henry de Valois duke of Anjou, a
Swedish prince, and the tsar of Russia.   The arrogance
of the last, and the inability of the third to offer any
considerable advantage to the republic in support of his
pretensions ‡, occasioned the rejection of both, and left
the contest between the two rival powers of France and
Austria.   There was, indeed, some intention of proposing a *Piast*, a term thenceforth applied, not to a prince
of the ancient family of that name, for none remained,
but to a *native*, in contradistinction to a *foreign* candidate;
but the jealousy of the great barons, who dreaded nothing
so much as the elevation of *an equal*, immediately scouted
the suggestion.

The protestant party were in favour of the archduke;

* Yet they comprised only the nobles of the crown and the grand duchy
with the incorporated palatinates of Polish Russia. The dukes of Courland,
Prussia, and Pomerania claimed to be present by their deputies, but the
claim was not admitted by a selfish diet. With respect to the duke of
Prussia, this refusal was clearly an infraction of the treaty made with
Albert of Brandenburg.

† The royal tent was contained in an immense building of wood, capable
of holding five or six thousand persons. It was subsequently called the
Szopa.

‡ Either John III., however, or his son Sigismund (who was in fact afterwards elected), had acquired a claim to the Polish crown in virtue of their
connection with the family of Jagello. John had married a sister of the
late king of Poland, and Sigismund was the issue of that union.

as belonging to a house of acknowledged tolerance, to one which, whilst the fires of persecution were burning almost every where else, honourably distinguished itself by moderation, and that, too, in spite of papal entreaties or remonstrances. In every other respect, indeed, the pretensions of Ernest were immeasurably superior to those of his rival; but two causes occasioned his failure — the tolerance of his house, which displeased the bigots, and the aversion entertained towards the empire by the Poles from the earliest period of their history. The factitious reputation which Henry had acquired in the civil wars òf France, his known hostility to the reformation, and the wily manœuvres of his ambassador Montluc bishop of Valence, secured his triumph; yet that triumph was not obtained without great labour, and the obstacles which intervened would have been insurmountable to an agent less unprincipled than the prelate. News of the horrid massacre of St. Bartholomew long thwarted his designs. At first, with an effrontery peculiarly his own, he denied that such an event had happened at all.[*] When doubt as to that most perfidious and most infamous of transactions could no longer exist, he extricated himself from the dilemma in which his falsehood had placed him, by pretending that he had received no account of it from his government. If his honour was lost, his impudence was exhaustless, and it served him well on the present occasion. He reluctantly admitted that there had been *an execution,* but he reduced the number of victims to *forty,* and contended that they had met their fate — not because they were hugonots, but because they were implicated in a

---

[*] Yet he himself, prior to leaving France, was near falling a sacrifice to the bloodthirsty fury of his court. As his inclination towards the doctrines of the reformers was well known, orders were sent down into Lorraine to arrest and put him to death before he could pass the frontier. He was accordingly intercepted, and would immediately have been executed, had not his impudence averted the catastrophe. By exhibiting his letters of credence, by contending that the order for his arrest was a forgery, and by loudly threatening them with the vengeance of Catherine de Medicis and the duke, he actually intimidated the soldiers, and made them doubtful of the instructions they had received. He was detained at Verdun until the court, with characteristic duplicity, disavowed the violence, and sent him permission to proceed. See Daniel, Histoire de France, tom. v ; also Anquetil, Histoire des Guerres de la Ligue.

L 4

conspiracy to dethrone Charles IX., to make way for the prince of Condé. The sincerity of the Poles made them his dupes; they could not imagine that the ambassador of a Christian country could utter a deliberate falsehood. Even the protestants were taught to believe that their co-religionists were treated in France with peculiar mildness. After exacting some stipulations for themselves — stipulations which they procured by means of an armed confederation, and which they compelled even Montluc to sanction *, Firley, their chief, no longer hesitated to proclaim the duke of Anjou. Throughout this hollow negotiation, the conduct of the agent was suitable to the infamous government he represented.

　The chief articles of the *pacta conventa*, as proposed to each of the candidates previous to the election, and intended as the basis of all future covenants between the Poles and their new sovereigns, were: — 1. That the king should not in the remotest degree attempt to influence the senate in the choice of a successor; but should leave inviolable to the Polish nobles the right of electing one at his decease. 2. That he should not assume the title of *master* and *heir* of the monarchy, as borne by all preceding kings. 3. That he should observe the treaty of peace made with the dissidents. 4. That he should not declare war, or dispatch the nobles on any expedition, without the previous sanction of the diet. 5. That he should not impose taxes or contributions of any description. 6. That he should not have any authority to appoint ambassadors to foreign courts. 7. That in case of different opinions prevailing among the senators, he should espouse such only as were in accordance with the laws, and clearly advantageous to the nation. 8. That he should be furnished with a permanent council, the members of which (sixteen in number; viz. four bishops,

---

* " Il promit, il signa, il jura même, tout ce qu'on voulut; et persuadé qu'il n'accordait rien à force de ne rien refuser, il ne douta point que son prince, ainsi que tous ceux qui l'avoient précédé, ne se dégageât aisément, dès qu'il seroit sur le trône, des obligations qu'il avoit fallu contracter pour lui en ouvrir le chemin." *Solignac*, v. 339. It is not easy to express our sense of such infamy, nor of the indignation we feel at the historian who can relate such infernal policy, without at the same time reprobating it as it deserves.

four palatines, and eight castellans) should be changed every half year, and should be selected by the ordinary diets. 9. That a *general* diet should be convoked every two years, or oftener, if required. 10. That the duration of each diet should not exceed six weeks. 11. That no dignities or benefices should be conferred on other than natives. 12. That the king should neither marry nor divorce a wife without the permission of the diet. The violation of any one of these articles, even in spirit, was to be considered by the Poles as absolving them from their oaths of allegiance, and as empowering them to elect another ruler.   Besides these important concessions to the nobles—concessions which virtually annihilated the power of the crown, and which are known as the *articles of Henry*, Montluc engaged that France should send a fleet into the Baltic, to ensure for the Poles the dominion of that sea; that in the event of a war with Muscovy, she should furnish the republic with 4000 of her best troops, and pay them herself; that in case of war with any other power, she should aid her ally with money instead of troops; that Henry should annually apply, for the sole advantage of the republic, a considerable portion of his hereditary revenues in France; that he should pay the debts of the crown; and that either at Paris or Cracow he should be at the expense of educating and supporting 100 young Polish nobles.

When these conditions were laid before Henry by the Polish ambassadors, who were despatched to Paris for that purpose*, he was staggered at their number and extent.   He had evidently no wish to accept the honour awarded him — to become, as he expressed it, a mere judge, a mere minister of state to the sovereign diet: and his aversion to it was increased by the lingering, hopeless condition of his royal brother, and by an incident sufficiently characteristic of the fierce people he was about to manage.   To the article respecting the dissidents,

---

* The appearance of these ambassadors with their bows and quivers, their *shaven crowns* (see p. 12. Introduction), their flowing garments, and rich equipages, made a singular impression on a people so fond of novelty as the Parisians. *De Thou, Hist. Univ.* vi. 699.

moderate as were its terms, he hesitated to swear.
Montluc durst not acknowledge that he had sanctioned
it.   The Polish ambassadors, who were one day present
with their new king, were highly indignant at the prelate's cowardice.   One of them, Zborowski, who severely
upbraided him for it, no less than for his lack of sincerity, being asked by Henry the reason of his vivacity,
fearlessly replied, " I am telling your majesty's ambassador, that, if he had not undertaken to procure your sanction to the article in question, your majesty would never
have been elected king of Poland ; and I say more, that
unless you *do* sanction it, our king you never shall be ! "
The king at length did swear to it; but he had no intention of being bound by its obligations : he was resolved
to invent, if possible, some decent pretext for remaining
in France.   The delays which he eagerly sought in com-
mencing his journey irritated the Poles, who began openly
to talk of a new election — the very end to which his
efforts were directed ; but his brother, jealous of his
popularity, and, perhaps, fearing his ambitious designs
nearer home, actually forced him to leave the kingdom.*

The new king was crowned at Cracow, February 21.
1574.   The ceremony did not pass without opposition
from Firley and his fellow protestants, who openly insulted him, and insisted on new concessions to their
body.   Perhaps the very cathedral in which it was
solemnised would have been stained with blood, had not
one of the palatines had presence of mind sufficient to
avert the dreaded catastrophe : the ceremony was allowed
to proceed unmolested.   But their hostility to their
monarch was too bitter to be long restrained.   They

* The mortifications Henry was doomed to support in his passage through
Heidelberg from the elector of Saxony have been described by the French
historians.   A large picture in the palace of Frederic represented the
horrible details of the recent massacre : the curtain which covered it was
suddenly withdrawn ; and he was asked, in no pleasing tone, if he recol-
lected Coligni and other personages there exhibited.   At table he was purposely served by French refugees ; and the conversation between the elector
and his friends spared neither " the Lorraine butchers," nor " the Italian
traitors."   De Thou. Daniel. Anquetil, Histoire des Guerres de la Ligue,
tom. i.   Varillas, Histoire de Charles IX. tom. i. et ii.   The reproof was
merited, but the way in which it was given was below the dignity of the
elector.

showed it on every occasion, and were joined by not a few of the leading catholics ; by all who had been refused a share in the distribution of crown favours.

The fickleness of Henry, his superficial qualities, his duplicity with respect to the protestants whom he sought occasions to humble, if not openly to persecute, his inapplication to the duties of royalty, and his childish ostentation, soon convinced the Poles that they had chosen an unworthy ruler ; one little fitted to grasp the sceptre of the Piasts and the Jagellos. An incident added to his unpopularity. Samuel Zborowski, a young noble of great riches and still greater arrogance, one day struck his lance into the ground opposite the apartment of Henry, and in a loud voice challenged any one who might be zealous for their new master, to remove the weapon from its place. The challenge was accepted by an obscure gentleman, who bore away the lance in triumph. The latter was a domestic of count Tenczyn, a circumstance which mortified still more the pride of Zborowski, who asserted that the count had sent the man on purpose to insult him, and also loudly insisted that the hand which had dared to remove the weapon should instantly replace it. Tenczyn refused to interfere ; high words and hostile messages ensued. At the head of some armed horsemen Zborowski fell on the partisans of Tenczyn ; the king hastened to the spot ; the combatants removed, to end the affray in some other place ; and in the struggle which followed, the castellan Wapowski, while endeavouring to establish peace between the disputants, was mortally and wantonly wounded by the sabre of Zborowski. The bleeding body was immediately borne into the presence of Henry, and vengeance loudly demanded on the homicide. The king promised that justice should be done ; but, whether through fear or partiality, he merely banished the assassin, without depriving him of either honours or riches. A sentence so little in conformity with the laws, and so inadequate to the offence, raised universal indignation ; nor was this indignation lessened, when, on the death of Firley, the palatinate of Cracow was conferred on a brother of Zborowski.

This feeble prince soon sighed for the banks of the Seine: amidst the ferocious people whose authority he was constrained to recognise, and who despised him for his imbecility, he had no hope of enjoyment. To escape their factions, their mutinies, their studied insults, he shut himself up within his palace, and with the few countrymen whom he had been permitted to retain near his person, he abandoned himself to idleness and dissipation. He had resolved to escape from his bondage, and he cared not whether the vessel of the state, which he thus left to itself, sailed or sunk. He drowned the complaints of the people in shouts of revelry. Their menaces would probably have roused him, had not an event which he had long foreseen afforded him an opportunity of flight.

By the death of his brother, who died on the 30th of May, 1574, he was become heir to the crown of the Valois. His first object was to conceal the letters which announced that event, and to flee before the Poles could have any suspicion of his intention. The intelligence, however, transpired through another channel. His senators advised him to convoke a diet, and, in conformity with the laws, to solicit permission of a short absence while he settled the affairs of his new heritage. Such permission would willingly have been granted him, more willingly still had he proposed an eternal separation; but he feared the ambition of his brother the duke of Alençon, who secretly aspired to the throne; and he resolved to depart without it. He concealed his extraordinary purpose with great art; it was not so much as suspected by the Poles, who, indeed, would not readily have believed that the man they had deigned to honour by their choice, could be so base and so ungrateful as to imitate a criminal escaping from justice. The truth is, no criminal ever longed to flee from his fetters so heartily as Henry from his imperious subjects. On the evening of the 18th of June, he gave a grand entertainment to the sister of the late king Sigismund, and graced it with his best smiles. At the usual hour he retired to his apartment, and the lights were extinguished; but at the same moment one of his confidential domestics entered, conducted him by a private passage out of the palace, and hastened with him to the appointed rendezvous, which was a chapel in the suburbs.* Here he was joined by several horsemen, and all set out with full speed towards the frontiers of Silesia, which they reached early on the following day. His flight was soon made known; the whole city of Cracow was thrown into commotion; the streets were instantly filled with inhabitants who had left their beds, and whose murmurs, if not curses, were rendered more awful amidst the faint glimmer of torches. The friends of the fugitive were insulted, and narrowly escaped being victims to the popular indignation. A pursuit was ordered; but Henry was already on the lands of the empire before he was overtaken by the grand chamberlain Tenczyn, accompanied by five Polish horsemen. Being asked by one of the prince's attendants whether he came as a friend or foe? and having replied, as a *friend*, he was admitted to speak with the king, but not until he had put off his armour. The chamberlain addressed him with respectful firmness, represented the injury which by a precipitate and inglorious flight he was doing, not only to the republic, but to his own character, and pressed him to return, that he might take possession of his new kingdom with the consent of the diet, and in a manner worthy the ruler of two great states. He was, however, inexorable. Having presented the chamberlain with a ring, which he drew from his finger, he continued his journey, with a promise that he should not fail to return as soon as he had restored France to tranquillity,—a promise which, it is almost needless to observe, he never intended to fulfil. Some letters found on a table in his apartment attempted

---

* Solikovius says the rendezvous was at the royal stables:—" Extinctis luminibus, per posteriorem arcis januam ad stabulum pervenit; ubi equo parato conscenso, cum octo comitibus, tota nocte effuso equi cursu, Oswiecismo prima luce transito, ad Poznam oppidum Silesiæ pervenit." *Rerum Polon. Com.* p. 31. The variation is almost too slight to be noticed.

to account for his precipitate departure by the urgency of the troubles in his hereditary kingdom; yet he did not reach Lyons till the following year.

In a diet assembled at Warsaw, it was resolved that if the king did not return by the 12th May, 1575, the throne should be declared vacant. Deputies were sent to acquaint him with the decree. His return, indeed, was neither wished nor expected; but in a matter of so much importance, and so unparalleled, the Poles were unwilling to act with precipitation, or to afford the world any reason for concluding that justice had less sway over them than their national resentment. After the expiration of the term, the interregnum was proclaimed in the diet of Stenzyca, and a day appointed for a new election.*

STEPHEN.

1575—1586.

AFTER the deposition of Henry, no less than five foreign and two native princes were proposed as candidates for the crown. The latter, however, refused to divide the suffrages of the republic, wisely preferring the privilege of electing kings to the honour of being elected themselves. The primate, many of the bishops, and several palatines, declared in favour of an Austrian prince; but the greater portion of the diet (assembled on the plains opposite to Warsaw) were for the princess Anne, sister of Sigismund

* Joannis Dem. Solikovii Archiep. Leop. Commentarius Brevis Rerum Polonicarum à morte Sigismundi Augusti, p. 1—47. Histoire des Diètes de Pologne, p. 1—43. Neugebaver, 642—660. Sarnicki, lib. viii. col. 1223, 1224. Solignac, v. 166—493. Zielinski, ii. 56—78. See also the histories of France by Daniel and Anquetil, the Universal History of De Thou, and the History of Charles IX. by Varillas. The best authority for the subsequent life of Henry de Valois is to be found in the Mémoires et Correspondance de Duplessis Mornay, the celebrated *fac-totum* of Henry de Bourbon, king of Navarre.

The unfinished work of Solignac ends with the inglorious flight of Henry. To the industry with which he has consulted the original authorities, and to the agreeableness of his powers of narration, we have already done justice; but he abounds with details too trifling to be recorded, — a circumstance which frequently renders his work tedious; a still stronger objection to it is, that he was almost unacquainted with the constitution, laws, and policy of the Poles. In this, however, he is partly excusable, as, at the time he wrote, the national writers had not learned to apply the torch of criticism to the darkness of their historic literature.

Augustus, whose hand they resolved to confer on Stephen
Batory, duke of Transylvania. Accordingly, Stephen was
proclaimed king by Zumoyski starost of Beltz, whose
name was soon to prove famous in the annals of Poland.
On the other hand, Uchanski the primate nominated the
emperor Maximilian, who was proclaimed by the marshal
of the crown : this party, however, being too feeble to
contend with the great body of the equestrian order, despatched messengers to hasten the arrival of the emperor;
but Zamoyski acted with still greater celerity. While
his rival was busied about certain conditions, which the
party of the primate forced on Maximilian, Batory arrived in Poland, married the princess, subscribed to every
thing required from him *, and was solemnly crowned.
A civil war appeared inevitable, but the death of Maximilian happily averted the disaster. The primate and
his party at length submitted, but not until they were
menaced by the activity of the new king, who made vigorous preparations to subdue them.

But though Poland and Lithuania thus acknowledged
the new king, Prussia, which had espoused the interests
of the Austrian, was less tractable. The country, however, was speedily reduced to submission, with the exception of Dantzic, which not only refused to own him,
but insisted on its recognition by the diet as a free and
independent republic. The inhabitants confided in the
strength of their fortifications, in their own courage, and
in the known inability of the Poles to press a siege with
vigour. They did not sufficiently attend to, perhaps
in their yearnings after sovereignty they disregarded,
the military reputation of Batory, whom merit alone had
raised from an humble station † to the government of

* He had confirmed by his ambassadors the *articles of Henry;* had
engaged to recover the conquests made by the Muscovites; to pay the debts
of the state; to pour 200,000 florins into the Polish treasury; to redeem the
captives made by the Tatars; not to employ Polish troops in foreign wars;
to maintain, in case of need, at his own expense, 1500 infantry; and to
marry the princess Anne. The last condition had been evaded by Henry:
it was made obligatory on Batory, who had naturally no great liking to a
lady of fifty-two.
† The family, however, of Batory was ancient, as appears from Bonfinius,
Historia Pannonica, *passim.*

Transylvania, and for whom it had secured the respect
and alliance of the Porte. Enthusiasm seldom reasons;
that enthusiasm least of all which is the offspring of religious fervour and of aspiring freedom. Here, as in
religion, faith is believed capable of moving mountains:
its very intensity not unfrequently leads to its realisation,
in cases where human wisdom would predict a very different result. Had the Dantzickers sought no other
glory than that of defending their city, had they resolutely kept within their entrenchments, they might have
beheld the power of their king shattered against the bulwarks below them; but the principles which moved them
pushed them on to temerity. Not satisfied with behold-
ing from their ramparts the ineffectual assaults of the
Poles, they issued from their gates to contend in the open
plain, where that people have seldom appeared without
victory. Their rashness cost them dear; the loss of
8000 men compelled them again to seek the shelter of
their walls, and annihilated their hope of ultimate success. Fortunately they had to deal with a monarch of
extraordinary moderation, who wished to correct, not to
destroy them, and who deemed clemency superior to the
honour even of a just triumph. Their submission disarmed his resentment, and left him at liberty to march
against other enemies.

During this struggle of Stephen with his rebellious
subjects, the Muscovites had laid waste Livonia. To
punish their audacity, and wrest from their grasp the
conquests they had made during the reign of his immediate predecessors, was now his object. War, however,
was more easily declared than made; the treasury was
empty, and the nobles refused to replenish it. Of them
it might truly be said, that while they eagerly concurred
in any burdens laid on the other orders of the state, —
on the clergy and the burghers, — those burdens they
would not so much as touch with one of their fingers.
It was not without exceeding difficulty that the deputies
to the diet at Warsaw were induced to sanction a contribution of a florin an acre, — a contribution considerable

certainly, but inadequate to the purpose for which it was raised, and far inferior to that which the clergy had voluntarily imposed on themselves. Three of the most considerable palatinates persisted in their opposition. With the supplies, however, thus afforded, he opened a brilliant campaign at the head of his combined Poles, Lithuanians, and Hungarians. Success every where accompanied him. Polotsk, Sakol, Turowla, and many other places, submitted to his arms. The investiture of the duchy (Polotsk, which the Muscovites had reduced in the time of Sigismund I.) he conferred on Gottard duke of Courland. On the approach of winter he returned, to obtain more liberal supplies for the ensuing campaign. Nothing can more strongly exhibit the different characters of the Poles and Lithuanians than the reception he met from each. At Wilna his splendid successes procured him the most enthusiastic welcome; at Warsaw they caused him to be received with sullen discontent. The Polish nobles were less alive to the glory of their country than to the preservation of their monstrous privileges, which, they apprehended, might be endangered under so vigilant and able a ruler. With the aid, however, of Zamoyski and some other leading barons, he again wrung a few supplies from that most jealous of bodies, a diet: Zamoyski was rewarded with the chancellor's seal, and the marshal's baton. Stephen now directed his course towards the province of Novogorod: neither the innumerable marshes, nor the vast forests of these steppes, which had been untrodden by soldier's foot since the days of Witold, could stop his progress; he triumphed over every obstacle, and, with amazing rapidity, reduced the chief fortified towns between Livonia and that ancient mistress of the North.* But his troops were thinned by fatigue, and even victory; reinforcements were peremptorily necessary; and though in an enfeebled state of health, he again returned to collect them. On this occasion he reproached the diet, with something like indignation, that his measures were so

* " Who can resist God and Novogorod the great? "

M

coolly supported; and that, through their absurd jealousy, his valiant followers were constrained to pause in the career of conquest. The succeeding campaign promised to be equally glorious, when the tsar, by adroitly insinuating his inclination to unite the Greek with the Latin church, prevailed on the pope to interpose for peace. To the wishes of the papal see the king was ever ready to pay the utmost deference. The conditions were advantageous to the republic. If she surrendered her recent conquests, — which she could not possibly have retained, — she obtained an acknowledgment of her rights of sovereignty over Livonia; and Polotsk, with several surrounding fortresses, was annexed to Lithuania. Stephen divided Livonia into three palatinates, over which he placed three palatines, three castellans, and other functionaries, as in the palatinates of the crown: he appointed the times and places of the dietines, and granted entire liberty of conscience to the protestant inhabitants.*

But from his wise policy with respect to the Cossacks Batory derived more glory than from all his victories. This singular people were originally deserters from the armies maintained by the republic, near the banks of the Borysthenes, to arrest the incursions of the Tatars. The almost inaccessible isles of that river, and the vast steppes of the Ukraine, served for secure places of retreat. As their numbers increased by propagation and desertion, — and they opened their arms to the people of every nation who arrived among them, — they made frequent predatory incursions into the Ottoman territories; they sometimes ventured as far as the suburbs of Constantinople, and in rude boats, consisting merely of trees hollowed out, they did not hesitate to trust themselves on the Black Sea, every shore of which they visited and ravaged. Their soil, — the richest in corn of any in Europe, — required little cultivation, and they were con-

* In his organisation of Livonia, Stephen was indirectly aided by the historian Sohkowski, whom he promoted to the archbishopric of Leopol. For his valour in the preceding campaign, Zamoyski, crown marshal, was presented with the hand of Batory's niece.

sequently at liberty to pass most of their time in plunder, piracy, or open war.

As they were Christians in their origin, they preserved a sort of Christianity among themselves, but so mingled, in time, with idolatrous and Mahommedan notions, that its fair characters were almost lost. The Polish gentleman, whom infamy had branded or justice threatened; the Polish serf, who fled from the iron despotism of a haughty rapacious master; the Greek schismatic, the persecuted Lutheran, either imperfectly remembered or but negligently practised the rites of their respective churches: hence a sort of mongrel worship prevailed, of which the leading features more resembled the eastern than the western church. But they did not much trouble themselves with either the doctrines or the duties of Christianity. Robbers by profession, and cruel by habit, they were the terror of surrounding countries. Strong, hardy, of indomitable courage, fond of war even more for the dangers which attended it than for the plunder it procured them, their alliance was eagerly sought by Lithuanians, Poles, Muscovites, Tatars, and Turks. To the former people, as the stock whence the majority were derived, they long bore sentiments of affection: indeed, they acknowledged themselves vassals of the republic, though their chief obedience was owing to their own grand hetman. Ostafi Daskiewitz, a peasant on the estates of a Lithuanian noble, (many nobles both of the crown and the grand duchy had extensive estates in the Ukraine,) was the first who divided them into regiments, and taught them discipline. As a reward for his exertions, he was presented by Sigismund I., who appeared sensible of the advantages which these formidable warriors might procure for the kingdom, with the starosty of Tserkassy, and the jurisdiction of some fortresses near the Borysthenes. Had the advice of this simple but strong-minded man been taken, Poland would have been effectually screened against the incursions of the Tatars. He counselled Sigismund to maintain 10,000 armed men on the banks of the river, who in their rude rafts could easily prevent the enemy from crossing: a few troops of horse might forage for this stationary little army. A still more important suggestion was to build forts and little towers on the islets of that magnificent stream. What Sigismund had not the spirit, perhaps not the means to accomplish, Batory might and should have effected. The latter monarch, however, did much towards so desirable an end. He diligently cultivated the affection of the Cossacks; and they are among the most grateful of men. He gave them the city of Trychtymirow, which became their chief magazine, and the residence of their grand hetman: he introduced among them the useful arts of life, and greatly improved their discipline: he formed them into six regiments, each consisting of 1000 men (ten companies of 100), and commanded by a hetman (*hattaman*). Each grand hetman, whom the whole force obeyed, received his investiture at the hands of the king: the symbols were an ensign, a horse tail (*bonzuk*), a baton resembling a club, and a looking-glass. The Cossacks being thus attached by new ties,—those of gratitude and allegiance,—to the republic, were well disposed to fulfil the purpose assigned them: their fidelity was striking; until from friends they were transformed into enemies by the most intolerable wrongs.*

In his internal administration Stephen was not less wise or vigilant. The establishment of a supreme tribunal at Cracow remedied the inconvenience of a multiplicity of appeals from the inferior courts to the assemblies of the palatines, and from the latter to the king. From his infirm state of health, Sigismund Augustus had found it impossible to decide on many of these appeals: hence the nobles arrogated to themselves the privilege of appointing judges from their own body to exercise a final jurisdiction, but it was one which that monarch refused to sanction. It was, however, extorted from Henry. Batory, like Sigismund, opposed it, and still more the

* Chevalier, Histoire de la Guerre des Cossacs contre la Pologne, &c. p. 302, &c.   Malte-Brun, Tableau de la Pologne ancienne et moderne, tom. i. p. 464, &c.

dangerous practice of self-election by the inferior judges in each palatinate. He decreed that in future each great palatinate should elect two nobles, each small palatinate one, who at Petrikau should decide on the affairs of Great Poland, and at Lublin on those of Little Poland ; and that from the decisions of those courts an appeal should lie open to the supreme tribunal before mentioned, in the proceedings of which he could constitutionally share. Similar tribunals he also established in Lithuania.

But however signal the services which this great prince rendered to the republic, he could not escape the common lot of his predecessors,—the jealousy, the opposition, and the hatred of a licentious nobility ; nor could he easily quell the tumults which arose among them. From the family of Zborowski he was doomed to experience the most trouble. Samuel, who, as observed in the preceding reign, had been banished for the murder of Wapowski, had not only ventured to return on the accession of Stephen, but had formed or joined a faction for the destruction of Zamoyski, starost of Cracow. He was informed by his intended victim, that if he continued to disturb the peace of the state, or to appear openly while subject to the punishment decreed against him, justice should lay hands on him. Instead of profiting by this judicious warning, he hastened his preparations for revenge: he posted armed satellites to waylay the starost; but his measures were watched, and he himself was arrested. Zamoyski submitted the affair to the king, who ordered the culprit to be judged according to the laws. In his examination he implicated his two brothers, Andrew and Christopher, in a conspiracy, the object of which was to dethrone or assassinate the best of monarchs. Samuel was beheaded at Cracow, and the senate assembled at Lublin to examine into the truth of the charges against the other two. They appeared at the trial, but, like Orgetorix of old, with such a number of armed followers and friends, that they hoped to overawe the proceedings. Stephen, however, was not to be intimidated in the discharge of a solemn duty. His firmness, and still more their own consciousness of guilt, daunted these haughty nobles, who vainly appealed to his clemency.

After an impartial trial, in which they were clearly convicted of high treason, Christopher, as the more criminal of the two, was condemned to death, and the decision concerning Andrew was postponed to the following diet. In vain did the nobles, who could not but respect the justice of the sentence, and who were yet alarmed at the courage with which the king ventured to punish one of the most powerful members of their order, solicit the pardon of the criminals: he was inexorable. But Christopher escaped into Germany, and the well deserved chastisement of the other was averted by an unexpected event.

Batory had resolved to chastise the perfidious aggressions of the tsar, and was busied in his preparations for a vigorous campaign, when death suddenly seized him at Grodno. His last words, " *In manus tuas, Domine, commendo spiritum meum,*" were evidence of his religious sincerity,—a sincerity which some of his enemies had endeavoured to dispute.* His character ranked him among the greatest and best monarchs of Poland. In early life he had been instructed in that most salutary of schools — adversity: for vigilance, for perseverance, for vigour, for enlightened views and patriotic intentions, he yields to no prince in Polish history. To science and letters he was a constant benefactor. He founded the university of Wilna, and stimulated young students to increased diligence, by holding out to them the prospect of honourable employments. He was himself no mean proficient in literary pursuits ; he was acquainted with several languages, and was familiar with (to a prince) that most important of subjects,—history and the policy of nations: his Latinity was unequalled by any writer of his kingdom. What does him much more

* " In templo plus quam sacerdos," was the character of Batory's piety, as drawn by a contemporary.

honour is his tolerant spirit. When urged to severe measures with the dissidents, he replied, " I reign over persons ; but it is God who rules the conscience. Know," he would add, " that God has reserved three things to himself ;—the creation of something out of nothing, the knowledge of futurity, and the government of the conscience."

Some months before his death he advised the diet to make the crown hereditary, and thereby to avert the doom which the abuses of an elective one would infallibly bring on the country. He foresaw that doom ; and so might any one, without much claim to the gift of prophecy. Though his great qualities, for a time, averted the evil, it was rapidly approaching.*

SIGISMUND III.
1586—1632.

As usual, the interregnum afforded ample opportunity for the gratification of individual revenge, and of the worst passions of our nature. The feud between the Zborowskis and Zamoyskis was more deadly than ever. Both factions appeared on the field of election with numerous bodies of armed adherents : the former amounted to 10,000 ; the latter were less strong in number, but more select. The two armies occupied positions within sight of each other, and would soon have come to blows, had not the primate and the senate decreed that no armed individual should be suffered on the field. To this hostile demonstration must be added the murmurs of the Lithuanians, who insisted on the incorporation of Livonia, Podolia, and Volhynia with their grand duchy; and who complained that the two last elections had been

---

* Solikovius, 49—171. Heidestein, Rerum Polonicarum Hist. lib. ix. Sarnicki, viii. col. 1224—1230. (in calce Dlugossi, tom. ii.) Zielinski, ii. 78—106. Karamsin, ix. 279. *et passim.* " Fuit vir," says Sarnicki, " tam in pace quam in bello, excelso et forti animo ; judicii magni, præsertim ubi ab affectibus liber erat : in victu et amictu parcus, ab omni jactantiâ et ostentatione alienus, eruditione insigniter tinctus ; sermonis Latini valdè studiosus, et prorsus Terentianus." In person, this author compares him to Attila ; but the description does not exactly tally with that given by Procopius.

made without their participation. Then the Prussians submitted a long list of grievances, of which most were imaginary, but which were admirably calculated to increase the confusion already existing. In short, discordance ran so high, that unless the great body of the nobles, who had no interest in the dissensions of a few ambitious leaders, had threatened to sweep away all before them, no election would probably have been made for many months.

Such was the inauspicious temper of the diet when the candidates were proposed. There were one or two Austrian princes, as usual; Feodor Vasilevitch the tsar, and Sigismund prince royal of Sweden. Of course Zamoyski and the Zborowskis espoused opposite interests: the former, with the great bulk of the palatines and nobles, declared for Sigismund; the latter supported the archduke Maximilian; the Lithuanians favoured the pretensions of the tsar. The current of feeling was so strong in behalf of a scion of the Jagellonic dynasty, that the Swedish prince was nominated by the primate, and proclaimed by Zamoyski, in the absence of the marshals. With the same formalities did the opposite party proclaim Maximilian. The former reached Cracow, December 1.; the latter, on the 16th of the same month, arrived at Mogila. A contest was now inevitable. Zamoyski defeated the adherents of the archduke, and Sigismund was crowned on the 27th. The *pacta conventa*, to which he swore, guaranteed the articles of Henry, an alliance offensive and defensive between Poland and Sweden; the free navigation of the Baltic to the Poles; the erection of five fortresses on as many weak points of the frontiers; the discharge of the national debts; and the preservation of the national privileges.*

But though the new king was thus seated on the throne, it could be secured to him only by another victory. If the party of his competitor had been checked, it had not

* The Poles also required the cession of Esthonia; but as the Swedish king was naturally averse to the dismemberment of his states, the subject was postponed until the death of that monarch. Subsequent events rendered its consideration at that time useless.

been humbled : with considerable reinforcements Maximilian seized Lublo, but was compelled to retreat by the active Zamoyski, who pursued him into Silesia, defeated and took him prisoner. He was conducted to a Polish fortress, to await the pleasure of Sigismund. Zamoyski on this occasion behaved with real magnanimity. He gave liberty to his inveterate enemies, the Zborowskis, and the other partisans of the archduke, and treated his prisoners with the utmost deference. The only revenge which he took on the Austrian prince for refusing to sit at his table, and for adhering, with a pride less dignified than puerile, to the formalities of etiquette, was to seat his captive at a separate one, surrounded with a golden chain. Nor did Sigismund himself act with less greatness of mind. He refused to exact a ransom from his rival; he declared that he would never add insult to misfortune: the only conditions which he required were, that Maximilian should restore some domains on which he had unjustly seized, and for ever relinquish all claim to the Polish crown. If the latter remained a prisoner longer than was expected, his own obstinacy was the cause.

Sigismund, however, though he had some good qualities, had likewise some defects; he was very unfit to fill the throne of Batory. He did not strive to cultivate the good-will of the nation; he adhered, with a weak pertinacity, to the usages of the Swedes; he passed much of his time with a chemical enthusiast, in pursuit of the philosopher's stone; he testified something like indifference to his new duties, and dissatisfied some of his best friends by mistaken pride. Even Zamoyski, the hero of the republic, to whom he was indebted for his crown, he treated with marked disrespect. He soon violated the *pacta conventa*, first, by espousing, contrary to the wishes of his subjects, an Austrian princess; and, secondly, by persecuting the dissidents. He found, however, that he could do neither with impunity: secret rumours gave way to open hostility; an extraordinary diet was convoked, by the marshal of the crown and

some senators, to enquire into the nature of his correspondence with the court of Vienna. He was present.
The sight of a king on his throne, subject to the reproaches of his assembled nobles, and constrained to
acknowledge their justice, was new to Europe, and even
to Poland. The venerable primate Karnkowski, who
glowed for the honour of his country, used little ceremony with this royal delinquent. After upbraiding him
with the odious connection he had formed, the prelate
intimated to him that the Poles knew how to deal with
one who forfeited his word. " Your majesty must remember that you reign over a free people; over nobles
who have no equals under heaven. Your dignity, sire,
is far above your father's, who reigns only over peasants.
Think of what was said by Stephen Batory, of glorious
memory, — ' I will one day teach these little Swedish
kings to know themselves.' " This mortifying disparage-
ment of his country, and this purposed display of the
honour which Poland, by deigning to choose him, had
conferred on " the little king," incensed him highly.
Zamoyski next adduced the heads of accusation, supporting each by documentary or verbal evidence. However, proceedings ceased for this time, on Sigismund's
promising to be in future more mindful of the obligations
he had contracted, and of doing nothing without the
concurrence of the diet. But some years afterwards the
flame of discontent burst forth with increased fury. Two
ambitious nobles openly headed a confederation, which
insisted that Sigismund should not only promise amendment in presence of a diet, but should publicly ask pardon
of the members for his infringement of the *pacta conventa*. He had the firmness to scorn so humiliating a
proposal, and to vindicate his authority by arms. The
rebels were not slow to meet him. At Guzaw, in an
engagement of some importance, from the numbers arrayed on both sides, he subdued the rebels, chiefly
through the means of his general, Chodkiewicz, whose
name was afterwards to become so famous in the wars
of Livonia, Muscovy, and Turkey. The rebellion was

extinguished by the submission of its framers; but the dissatisfaction with him and his government ended only with his reign.

To these civil commotions succeeded a war with the Tatars, whom the incursions of the Cossacks, the acknowledged vassals of the republic, armed for revenge. Zamoyski, after defeating the duke of Transylvania, who had seized on Wallachia, and appointing a palatine who should rule that principality (Wallachia), as the tributary of Poland, hastened to oppose their khan. The khan was at the head of 70,000 combatants; and, what was still more threatening, an army of Turks was only waiting for the success of its Tatar ally to fall on Kaminiec (in Podolia), one of the great bulwarks of the republic. The Polish hero triumphed: the khan was constrained to sue for peace, as the price of which he agreed to evacuate Moldavia, and to acknowledge the new hospodar. The Turks were held in respect by this signal humiliation of their allies, and were eager enough to prolong the peace with the republic. For his conduct in this astonishing campaign,—in which he had routed 60,000 Transylvanians and Servians, humbled the aspiring ambition of the Transylvanian duke Michael Batory, changed the governors of Wallachia and Moldavia, annihilated rather than routed a great army of Tatars, and held in check the whole power of the sultan,—Zamoyski was enthusiastically cheered by the diet at Warsaw.

If the weakness and bigotry of Sigismund rendered him unpopular in Poland, they did him still more injury in Sweden: they lost him the crown of the Goths. His injudicious zeal for the re-establishment in that country of the Roman catholic religion; his imprudent deportment towards the Lutherans during two successive visits to his native kingdom, his negligence in repressing the ambitious designs of his uncle Charles, whom he appointed regent, and the ultimate usurpation of that politic prince, are subjects belonging to Swedish history.

Sigismund had little difficulty in interesting the Poles in his quarrel with his relative. War was decreed on the Swedish possessions in Livonia, whither Charles hastened in person. The veteran Zamoyski defeated him in several actions; and when, through disgust with his prince and the growing infirmities of age, he relinquished the command to his lieutenant Chodkiewicz, the honour of the Polish arms was nobly supported by that general. With less than 4000 men, the latter inflicted a terrible defeat on 17,000 Swedes, with Charles at their head. In consequence of this signal event, Livonia remained in the power of the victors. The theatre of war was now changed to Muscovy.

Boris, marshal of the court of Moscow, had married his sister to the feeble tsar Feodor, and had in consequence of this alliance been permitted to exercise unbounded power. As the monarch was without offspring, and as another prince, brother of the tsar, alone remained of the race of the mighty Ruric, the minister soon formed the design of securing the succession for himself. He caused the heir apparent, Demetrius (Dmitri), to be assassinated, and after the death of Feodor seated himself on the imperial throne.* He speedily entered into relations with Poland: he made an alliance of twenty years with Sigismund; yet, with the barbarian duplicity of his character, he secretly favoured the kindred usurper of Sweden. Sigismund had soon an opportunity of revenge: an adventurer appeared in Poland, pretending to be the real Demetrius, who told a plausible story of the way in which he had escaped the bloody purpose of Boris. As, in person, manner, and age, he resembled the murdered prince, he gained credence with many. The pope and Sigismund regarded, or professed to regard, him as the unquestionable heir of the tsars. Two of the greatest houses in the republic, with one of which he solicited the honour of an alliance, openly armed in his behalf, and

* Boris, in many points of his character, and still more in his actions, resembles our Richard III.; the same unprincipled ambition, the same cold-blooded cruelty, the same successful attempt to gain plebeian favour, the same pretended unwillingness to accept the throne, the same tyranny when the object of that ambition was secured, distinguished both; and though the end of both was not the same, it was in neither peace. History is but a picture of God's moral justice. See Karamsin, tom. x. xi.

enabled him to set out for Moscow at the head of some forces. In vain did Boris adduce evidence to prove the death of prince Demetrius, and that the impostor who had assumed the name and character was one Otrepieff, a deserter from the monastery of Cudnow: in vain did he menace Poland with the whole force of the empire, if any assistance were afforded to the adventurer. Whether the pretensions of the latter were real or false, they were too favourable to the views of the Polish king, and, to the palatine of Sandomir, whose daughter Marina was to be raised to an imperial throne, not to be espoused with ardour: both were convinced that a host of discontented Muscovites would join his standard. Their confidence was well founded. This Warbeck of the North was soon strong enough to contend on the field with the armies of the tsar. He was defeated, indeed, but only to re-appear with greater hopes of success. Such were his courage and conduct, and such the favourable combination of circumstances, that he triumphed in an undertaking which sober reason would have pronounced as worse than Quixotic. Sudden death removed Boris, and a brilliant victory precipitated from the throne the youthful son of that monarch. He ascended it, and fulfilled his engagements with the palatine by placing the diadem on the brow of Marina. Still more extraordinary than this success is the fact, that one who had been so base as to invent and practise so great a deception, should yet exhibit qualities well worthy of his exaltation — generosity, clemency, magnanimity, enlightened views, and patriotic sentiments. But his span of empire and of life was brief: a party, which raged at the sight of successful imposition, and still more at the favours with which a grateful ruler rewarded the instruments of his elevation, his Polish adherents, silently raised its head. Demetrius was assassinated amidst the entertainments of his marriage. The head of the conspiracy, Vasil Shouiski, remotely related to the imperial race of Ruric, was proclaimed tsar; and Marina with her Polish attendants was transferred from a palace to a dungeon.

The strangest passage, however, in this strange history remains to be read. Though the body of the murdered emperor had been exposed to the populace of Moscow, his name and person were assumed by another impostor, who boldly asserted that he had been almost miraculously preserved from death, and that he now re-appeared to claim the support of his faithful subjects: he was immediately recognised by thousands as the twice-murdered Demetrius, and by Marina herself as her royal husband. The Poles and Cossacks flocked to his standard; and Shouiski, to fix a tottering throne, called in the assistance of Sigismund's most implacable enemy, the king of Sweden.

As yet the Polish king had not openly taken a share in the troubles of Russia; he had only connived at the armaments of his nobles. Now war was decreed by the diet, and he himself set out to conduct it. At no time had Poland braver troops or abler generals. The Muscovites were defeated in several engagements; and, after a siege of eighteen months, though strongly defended, Smolensko became the prize of the victors. Afterwards the marshal of the crown, Zolkiewski, a worthy successor of the illustrious Zamoyski, with no more than 8000 Poles, utterly routed Shouiski at the head of 30,000 Muscovites and 8000 Swedes. This splendid success enabled the marshal to effect a junction with Demetrius, and to march on Moscow, which he closely invested. In consternation at their menaced destruction, the Muscovites placed all their hopes of escape from it in a misunderstanding between Demetrius and his allies. Cunning served them better than force: they opened the gates to the Poles, delivered up to Zolkiewski (Sigismund still remained at Smolensko) their tsar Shouiski with his two brothers, and professed their readiness to place on the imperial throne Uladislas, son of Sigismund. Being thus left without foreign support, Demetrius retired from Moscow. The young prince was proclaimed, and actually invited to take possession of the dignity. But one condition displeased the father: before Uladislas could ascend the throne, he was required to embrace the Greek religion. Sooner than see his son a schismatic, the conscientious monarch would willingly have sacrificed even a more brilliant diadem. His imprudent return to Warsaw, and his still more imprudent indecision, lost a crown. Incensed at both, and still more that he could obtain no money for the payment of his troops, Zolkiewski also returned. His triumphant entry into the capital with his imperial captive was but a poor compensation for the valour which had been displayed, and the sacrifices which had been sustained. The Muscovites rose against the Polish garrisons: in the contest which followed, a great part of Moscow was laid in ashes. This wanton outrage raised the indignation of the natives to the highest pitch; the Poles were expelled from the country ; Michael Federovitsh, descended on the maternal side from the ancient dukes of Russia, and ancestor of the present autocrat, was raised to the throne ; Marina was drowned, and her infant son strangled. In vain did Sigismund and his son endeavour to re-establish their affairs: the nation showed little disposition to gratify their personal ambition by engaging in a new and hopeless war. With the few troops they were able to collect, they could do no more than obtain an. honourable peace, as the price of which they acknowledged the new tsar.

The wars of Sigismund with the Turks were more splendid than advantageous. The first campaign, indeed, was disastrous: the Poles, unable to support their ally, the voivode of Moldavia, who at their instigation had refused to pay tribute to the Porte, were compelled to desist from their pretensions over that principality, to see it governed by a nominee of the sultan, and their strongest barrier against the ambition of the Ottomans thus demolished before their eyes. Gratiani, indeed, the new voivode, attempted to throw off the Moslem yoke, and to place the country in its ancient dependence on Poland ; but a formidable army of Turks soon expelled him from his capital, and forced him to implore the aid of the republic. The favour which Sigismund now showed to Batory, voivode of Transylvania, to whom the Porte was inimical, increased the breach between Poland and Turkey. Zolkiewski, who had been censured, perhaps not without justice, for the disasters of the preceding campaign, for treating with the enemy instead of defeating him, was again ordered to take the field. No more than 8000 Poles, however, and some Cossacks, accompanied him in his expedition; and Gratiani could not furnish him with more than 600 followers, instead of the thousands which had been promised. Though his entire force fell short of 20,000, this great captain did not hesitate to measure arms with his 70,000 opponents*, among whom were the flower of the Ottoman army. For a whole day he opposed a wall of adamant to the overwhelming masses of the infidels, on whom he inflicted a terrific slaughter. Even victory, however, had so diminished his numbers, that he was forced to retreat; a measure rendered still more necessary by the murmurs of his officers, who refused to be led like sheep to the slaughter. That retreat he conducted in a masterly manner; and as often as he turned about to face his pursuers, he taught them to respect him. The intrepid chief, however, with his little army, were cut off at Cecora, near the banks of the Dniester: his head was sent to Constantinople, and all Podolia was ravaged by the enemy.

To avenge this disaster, the Poles now armed in greater numbers; and under the brave Chodkiewicz, conqueror of the Swedes, opened a new campaign. The present struggle promised to be more terrific than any which had preceded it: at the head of the whole force of Turkey, and of the Tatars, amounting, it is said, to 300,000 men, the sultan Osman advanced with the resolution of crushing Poland at one blow. Christendom

---

* Some modern Polish historians reduce their own force to 8000, and increase that of the enemy to 100,000. On most occasions where the Turks are concerned, they calculate with the same unfairness. Had the Ottomans historians of their own, the numbers, no doubt, would be materially altered. Nevertheless, the Poles must be admitted to be the bravest among brave nations — as having exhibited more splendid feats of valour than any people in Europe

trembled for the republic; but, under such a leader, and with an army (including Cossacks) above 60,000 strong, the Poles feared not for themselves. On the plains of Kotzim the infidels sustained a fearful slaughter: the veteran Chodkiewicz was present in the thickest of the affray; he spread consternation even to the sultan's camp. But his fatigues were too much for his age and strength. Feeling his last hour approach, he caused himself to be carried to his tent; and from his bed of death he resigned the command to Lubomirski, whom he exhorted to conquer or to die. His death only inflamed his countrymen to greater deeds. On the morning of September 28. (1622), 30,000 infidels fell in an attack headed by their sultan. Disease and famine aided the sword, and forced the Turkish monarch to sue for peace. As from his numbers he was still formidable, it was readily granted by the Christians. The conditions were advantageous to the republic: the treaty made with Zolkiewski was confirmed; the Tatars and Cossacks were to desist from their inroads into the territories of their respective enemies; and the hospodar of Moldavia, though subject to the Porte, was to be a Christian, and an ally of Poland. Osman returned to his capital, to be assassinated by the Janizaries for losing 60,000 of his best troops.

The reign of Sigismund is a strange mixture of splendour and weakness — of splendour on the part of his great generals, of weakness in his neglecting to profit by the advantages procured for him. While Chodkiewicz was acquiring immortality on the banks of the Dniester; another Polish captain was nobly supporting the military honour of the republic in Livonia against the youthful Gustavus Adolphus, successor to Charles. To detail the events of this nine years' war would require a volume; it must suffice to observe, that whatever success was gained by arms, was lost by the imbecility or obstinacy of Sigismund, and that peace could not be obtained without sacrificing a portion of Livonia to the Swedes. Still less can we dwell on the famous thirty years' war between the catholic and protestant interests of Europe; a war in which the few Polish troops who were engaged, and who fought, not as principals, but as allies of the emperor, performed prodigies of valour.

The same year witnessed the deaths of the two Vasas, of the northern lion on the plains of Zutphen, and of Sigismund in his palace at Warsaw. It would be difficult to say which of the two was the greater enemy to Poland; whether Gustavus by his victories, or the Polish monarch by his bigotry, his weakness, his obstinacy, his inactivity, and above all by his indifference to a people indifferent to him in return. He had, however, some good qualities: pious, just, merciful, the same in prosperity and adversity, he could not but win the respect, though he could never obtain the esteem, of his subjects. His reign, as might be expected from his character, was disastrous. The loss of Moldavia and Wallachia, of a portion of Livonia, and perhaps still more of the Swedish crown for himself, and of the Muscovite for his son, embittered his declining years. Even the victories which shed so bright a lustre over his kingdom were but too dearly purchased by the blood and treasure expended. The internal state of Poland, during this period, is still worse. It exhibits little more than his contentions with his nobles, or with his protestant subjects, and the oppression of the peasants by their avaricious, tyrannical, and insulting masters; an oppression which he had the humanity to pity, but not the vigour to alleviate.*

By his two wives, both archduchesses of Austria and sisters, Sigismund had several sons, of whom two were destined to sway the sceptre of Poland.

* Sulikovius, 171—224. Puffendorf, Introduction à l'Histoire, &c. tom. iv. v. vi.   Karamsin, tom. x. xi.   Zielinski, ii. 136—191. Schiller, Histoire de la Guerre de Trente Ans, tom. i. ii.

ULADISLAS VII.* (VASA.)
1632—1648.

AT the present election the number of candidates was fewer, and the proceedings less violent, than for some time past. Both Uladislas and John Casimir, sons of Sigismund, were closely connected with the house of Austria; and either would have been supported both by that power and the empire. The only disturbance arose from the claims of the dissidents, and the obstinacy of the catholics in resisting them. The former insisted on a perfect community of privileges, without calling to mind that, as they were so much inferior in respect to numbers and influence, their demands, however just, could only lead to intestine dissension; and the latter, with all the haughtiness of a dominant church, scarcely condescended to allow simple toleration. Both appeared armed on the field of election; but both concurred in choosing the elder prince. Uladislas, the successful candidate, long become the idol of the nation, had the address to reconcile them. The chief articles of the *pacta conventa* were, that the king should supply the public depôts with arms; recover the conquered provinces; settle the disputes with Muscovy and Sweden; fortify some places, and construct others, and maintain a fleet in the Baltic; that he should not presume to marry without the sanction of his people, nor confer posts on strangers, &c.† Some of the conditions were impracticable, most were subsequently disregarded; their very unreasonableness occasioned their nullity.

Having pacified the dissidents, established a mathematical and military college at Leopol, and by a union of moderation with firmness given promise of a brilliant

---

* The modern Polish historians term Uladislas *the fourth* monarch of the name. Though three princes of that name were but *dukes*, they were, nominally at least, sovereigns of Poland.

† These conditions were added to the " articles of Henry," which always formed the basis of the covenants between the Polish monarchs and their subjects.

reign, the new monarch, in compliance with the declared wish of his diet, prepared for war with the Muscovites, who had made several destructive incursions into the eastern provinces of the republic, and were now investing Smolensko. In the absence of money and troops, such preparations were not made without much difficulty. Having at length collected a small army in Lithuania, he proceeded to Smolensko, the siege of which he soon raised, and pursued the fugitive enemy. Within an entrenched camp, and in the depths of their forests, the Muscovites during five months resisted his attacks. The extreme severity of the weather (it was now winter), the scarcity of provisions, and the want of suitable accommodations, thinned the ranks of the assailants, but could not damp the ardour of their chief, who took up his abode in a wretched hut, and submitted to the same privations as the meanest of his followers. Sehin, the general of the tsar, was at length compelled to own, with bended knees, the ascendant of Uladislas, to whom he abandoned his camp, and at the same time engaged to take no further part in the present war. The reduction of some places, among which Viazma was the most considerable, added to the glory of the king. Moscow itself began to take the alarm; the tsar Michael Federovitsh sued for peace, as the price of which he proposed to renounce all pretensions over Livonia, Esthonia, Courland, Smolensko, Severia, and Tsernichof; but in return he required a renunciation on the part of Uladislas of the imperial throne. Several reasons urged the king to accept the conditions. If he had ever seriously resolved to obtain possession of a dignity to which he believed he had a claim, he found his troops,—originally but 20,000, and now greatly reduced in number,—unequal to his purpose, and, still more, unwilling to effect it. From the severity of the season, and much more from inability to obtain their arrears of pay, they were become mutinous. On the conclusion of peace they returned home, but not without ravaging the estates of the nobles and the richer clergy, and inflicting as great injury on their country as could have been done by the Muscovites themselves.

On his return, Uladislas found reason for rejoicing that he had so happily concluded the recent war. At the instigation of the Turks, and with the concurrence of the tsar, the Tatars had penetrated into Podolia, the southern portion of which they laid waste with their usual barbarity. They were met and routed on the plains of Moldavia, by the grand general of the crown, who next discomfited an army of Turks which advanced to support them. The sultan, Amurath IV., in consternation at this unexpected check, and still more at the result of the Muscovite expedition, hastened to disavow the hostility of his pachas, one of whom, Ali, he punished with death, as if that general had not acted by his own orders. Where his own reputation or interest is concerned, an act of injustice, however cruel, costs little to a tyrant. Both Muscovy and Turkey were now convinced that the councils of Poland were directed by a vigorous hand, and both were taught to respect the faith of treaties.

The success of Uladislas in his policy with Sweden was highly advantageous to the republic. During the wars of his predecessors with the two princes who had successively borne the crown of the Goths, many places in Polish Prussia had been reduced by the enemy. To regain them was now the firm resolution of the king. The opportunity was favourable to his purpose: an infant princess filled the throne of the great Gustavus, and the regency, in its struggles with the empire, was unwilling to draw on Sweden another enemy; one, too, so formidable as the republic. The storm was averted by negotiation. While Uladislas was marching his troops into Prussia, proposals were made him of relinquishing, as the condition of peace, every place held in that country by the Swedish forces. He thus acquired all that he could have obtained by a fortunate war, without resigning his title to the crown of his ancestors.

But all the glories of this reign, all the advantages it

procured to the republic, were fatally counterbalanced by
the haughty and inhuman policy of the nobles towards
the Cossacks.   Of late, the grant of lands in the Ukraine
to these rapacious landlords had been more frequent.
In the central provinces of the republic their unbounded
power was considerably restrained in its exercise by their
habitual residence among their serfs; but these distant
possessions never saw the face of the proprietors, and
were abandoned to Jews, the most unpopular and hateful
of stewards.   These Israelites had, in most cases, advanced money on the forthcoming produce of the soil;
and were naturally anxious to make the most of it;
nor were they likely to show much indulgence in its
collection.   The Cossacks were still less likely to
submit with patience to the extortions they were made
to endure.   They insisted, not only on the entire abolition of these grievances, but that their chiefs should
have a seat in the diet.   Their remonstrances, their
cries, their demands of justice, were received with
insulting indifference or with open refusal: the abuses
so loudly complained of were aggravated by new imposts, or by insults still more intolerable to a people resolved to be free.   Obtaining no redress from the diet,
the members of which, however jealous of their own
liberties, would allow none to the people, they had laid
their complaints before the throne of Sigismund III.
With every disposition, that monarch was utterly powerless to relieve them; Uladislas was equally well-inten-
tioned, and equally unable to satisfy them.   On one
occasion the latter prince is said to have replied to the
deputies from these sons of the wilderness, " Have you
no sabres?" Whether such a reply was given them or
not, both sabres and lances were speedily in requisition.
Their first efforts were unsuccessful; though they destroyed the fortress of Kudak, which had been erected to
overawe them, they were surprised and defeated by
Potocki, grand hetman of the crown.   This failure
rather enraged than discouraged them, and their exas-
peration was increased by the annihilation of their religious hierarchy, of their civil privileges, of their territo-

rial revenues, and by their degradation to the rank of serfs, — all which iniquities were done at the diet of 1638. Nay, a resolution was taken at the same time to extirpate both their faith and themselves, if they showed any disposition to escape the bondage doomed them. Again they armed, and by their combination so imposed on the troops sent to subdue them, that a promise was made them of restoring the privileges which had been so wickedly and so impolitically wrested from them. Such a promise, however, was not intended to be fulfilled: the Cossacks, in revenge, made frequent irruptions into the palatinates of the grand duchy, and no longer prevented the Tatars from similar ravages. Some idea may be formed of the extent of these depredations when it is known that from the princely domains of one noble alone 30,000 peasants were carried away and sold as slaves to the Turks and Tatars. Things were in this state when a new instance of outrageous cruelty spread the flames of insurrection from one end of the Ukraine to the other, and lent fearful force to their intensity.

There was a veteran Cossack, Bogdan Chmielnicki by name, whose valour under the ensigns of the republic was known far beyond the bounds of his nation. His success twenty years before, in defending Zolkiew against the assaults of the Tatars, had given lustre to his character. This man had a windmill, with some lands adjacent, situated near the banks of the Borysthenes, on which the steward of a great Polish family had cast a longing eye: this steward thought that the surest way of obtaining the mill and estate would be through the ruin of the owner. On some frivolous charge or other, Bogdan was summoned before the tribunal of the steward's master, Alexander Koniecpolski, grand ensign of the crown, was thrown into prison, and would probably have been sacrificed but for the interference of the castellan of Cracow.* On the death of that dignitary, the poor

* James Sobieski, father to the heroic John III., whose lady Bogdan had saved from slavery by the defence of Zolkiew. Bogdan, however, was no saint. To escape the punishment of homicide, he had fled from the neighbourhood of Zolkiew, his patrimonial residence, to seek an asylum among

Cossack was left without a protector, and his mill was unceremoniously seized by his enemy : his indignant remonstrances were met by blows, or by attempted assassination.   In vain did he appeal to the diet sitting at Warsaw ; neither justice, nor a consideration of his former services, could touch the members.   Resolved to humble himself no longer before these insulting tyrants, he fled to the Tatars, with the intention, no doubt, of interesting them in his behalf.   It does not appear that he had ever seriously resolved to make war on the republic ; his design was merely to procure the redress of his personal wrongs, until Czapalinski, the infamous steward before named, not satisfied with violently usurping his property, first violated, next murdered, his wife, and set fire to his habitation, amidst the flames of which his infant son perished.   Another son, Timothy, who had grown up to man's estate, was publicly scourged for venting a natural indignation.*   The bolt of vengeance, so long suspended, at length fell.   At the head of 40,000 Tatars, and of many times that number of Cossacks, who had wrongs to be redressed as well as he, and whom the tale of *his* had summoned around him with electric rapidity, he began his fearful march.   Two successive armies of the republic, which endeavoured to stem the tide of inundation, were utterly swept away by the torrent ; their generals and superior officers led away captives, and 70,000 peasants consigned to hopeless bondage.

At this critical moment expired Uladislas, a misfortune scarcely inferior to the insurrection of the Cossacks ; for never did any state more urgently require the authority of such a monarch.   He is chiefly known for his love of justice, his abilities as a captain, his great valour, and his amiable manners.   Under him the republic was pros-

---

the Cossacks, the usual resort of men answerable to the laws. The property he possessed in the Ukraine was the reward of his military services, conferred on him by the grand-general of the crown.

* There must have been some provocation for this monstrous behaviour of Czapalinski. If, as some accounts state, he had once been ignominiously whipped by the servants of Bogdan, we shall feel less surprise at his dreadful revenge. The Cossack had incurred the hostility of Koniecpolski by his bravadoes, and probably by threats of revolt.

perous, notwithstanding her wars with the Muscovites and Turks; and had his advice been taken, the Cossacks would have remained faithful to her, and opposed an effectual barrier to the incursions of the Tatars. But eternal justice had doomed the chastisement of a haughty, tyrannical, and unprincipled aristocracy, on whom reasoning, entreaty, or remonstrance, could have no effect, and whose understandings were blinded by hardness of heart. In their conduct during these reigns there appears something like fatality, which may be explained by a maxim confirmed by all human experience: — *Quem Deus vult perdere, prius dementat.*[*]

Uladislas died without issue by either of his wives; the former an Austrian archduchess, the latter Maria Louisa, daughter of the duke of Mantua.

INTERREGNUM.   JOHN CASIMIR.
1648.

NEVER was interregnum more fatal than that which followed the death of Uladislas. The terrible Bogdan, breathing vengeance against the republic, seized on the whole of the Ukraine, and advanced towards Red Russia. In his destructive march through Podolia and Volhynia, his chief vengeance was made to fall on the Jesuits and the Jews; the former as the persecutors of the Greek church, no less than of the Arians and anabaptists, who every where flocked to his standard, the latter as the iniquitous oppressors of every class of Christians. He was joined by vast hordes of Tatars from Bessarabia and the Crimea, who longed to assist in the contemplated annihilation of the republic. This confederacy of Mussulmans, Socinians, and Greeks, all actuated by feelings

---

[*] Hartknock, Repub. Polon. lib. i.   Puffendorf, lib. iv.   Pastorius de Hirtenberg, Florus Polonicus, &c. lib. v. Salvandy, i. 171—215. Kwiatowski, (as condensed by Zielinski, tom. ii. 195—220.), in his reign of Uladislas IV., p. 1. 427. Little assistance can be obtained from the general historians of Europe during these times: numerous as they are, they are little conversant with Polish affairs. For some reigns past we have had to lament the gradual falling off of Polish guides: now we feel their loss more than ever. Salvandy is so full of inaccuracies, that nothing he says can be received unsupported by other authority.

of the most vindictive character, committed excesses at which the soul revolts : the churches and monasteries were levelled with the ground, the nuns were violated; some priests were forced, under the raised poniard, not merely to contract, but to consummate a marriage with the trembling inmates of the cloisters, and in general both were subsequently sacrificed; the rest of the clergy were despatched without mercy.* But the chief weight of vengeance fell on the nobles, who were doomed to a lingering death; whose wives and daughters were stripped naked before their eyes, and, after violation, were whipped to death in sight of the ruthless invaders. As Bogdan advanced into Red Russia, he was joined by the serfs, whose fetters he broke, and whose champion he loudly proclaimed himself. The chivalry of Poland were with difficulty brought into the field; whether struck by fear or conscience, they fled without striking a blow before the resistless hetman. Leopol opened its gates to him; the whole palatinate acknowledged his power except Zamosk, within the bulwarks of which the braver portion of the Polish chivalry had shut themselves up, resolved to defend it or to die: this last act of despairing courage would have been useless, had not his Tatar allies abandoned Bogdan to deposit their treasures and captives in their own country, and caused him to prosecute the siege with less vigour.

At this critical period the diet of election assembled (that of convocation had been previously held) to appoint a successor to a throne which appeared about to fall for ever. The candidates were the tsar Alexis, father of Peter the Great, Ragotski, voivode of Transylvania, and two sons of Sigismund III., both ecclesiastics. The elder, John Casimir, had, with the pope's sanction, resigned his dignity of cardinal, assumed the title of hereditary king of Sweden, and become a suitor to the widow of his brother, the late monarch. The younger, the bishop of

* These atrocities were not unprovoked. The soul of the catholic party, prince Jeremiah Wisnowiecki, had, in Lithuania, inflicted terrific torments on the Arian and anabaptist dissidents. This man was a monster of cruelty.

Breslaw, was no less eager to obtain a wife and a crown: for the first time Europe beheld two brothers, invested with the higher honours of the priesthood, rivals for two objects so foreign to their original vocation ; both procuring absolution from a twofold vow, and seeking a dispensation for marrying a sister-in-law. The cardinal was the favourite both with the queen and nobles ; his mildness, his amiable manners, his tolerant disposition, contrasted greatly with the stern bigotry of the bishop. John Casimir was so sure of his election (neither of the foreign candidates had any chance of success) that he opened a correspondence with Bogdan, condemned the injustice done to the hetman, and professed his desire to see the pacification of the republic, in terms sufficiently advantageous to Pole and Cossack. (This correspondence accounts for the inaction of Bogdan during the period of election.) His confidence was justified by the event ; on the 20th of November he was elected, and early in the following year he led to the hymeneal altar the wife of his brother.*

One of the new king's first acts was to renew his negotiations with Bogdan, who still lay in the vicinity of Zamosk. The hetman showed his respect to the head of the republic by pressing the royal letter to his lips, and countermanding the assault which he had prepared on the walls of that fortress. Every thing presaged peace, when the savage Jeremy Wisnowiecki, general of the grand duchy, unmindful alike of the national honour and that of his king, surprised the camp of the unsuspecting besiegers, and committed a horrible slaughter. Bogdan retreated, his heart big with ven-

---

* It was disgust with the world, not a celestial vocation, which drew John Casimir to the cloister. As he was proceeding to Spain (this was during the reign of Uladislas) he was seized at Marseilles by order of the French government, and closely confined in the fortress of Sisteron, built on the summit of a steep rock. From thence, after two years of rigorous captivity, he was transferred to the château of Vincennes, to meet with even worse treatment. It was not without great difficulty that the pope and the republic succeeded in procuring his liberation. Whether the detestable Richelieu, in this vindictive proceeding, wished to punish the Polish monarch for joining with Austria, or John Casimir himself, for having borne arms against France in the thirty years' war, is unknown. From his depressed spirits and enfeebled frame, both occasioned by his imprisonment, the prince renounced the world, and became an ecclesiastic.

geance, to prepare for a new campaign ; and naturally
refusing all further communication with a people whose
perfidy was at least equal to their other qualities.   In
vain did the king upbraid his nobles for their past and
present misdeeds ; in vain did he strive to avert the
evils which impended ; war was inevitable, and he was
reluctantly compelled to share in it.   He encountered
Bogdan, with a powerful ally, the Tatar khan Islaf,
whose combined forces amounted, it is said, to 160,000
men *, on the plains of Zborow.   By this formidable
host was the faithless Jeremy invested within an entrenched camp.   The besieged had long baffled the
assaults of the barbarians, and had been encouraged to
hold out by a letter, which an arrow had brought to
them, and which announced the approach of the king
with the flower of Polish chivalry.   But though the
army of John Casimir was 20,000 strong, he could not
effect a junction with the 9000 shut up in the camp.
He trembled for the republic, which he well saw no
human valour could save.   But policy saved her : the
khan of the Tatars was persuaded by his offers, one of
which was the restoration of the annual tribute formerly
paid by the Poles, to withdraw them from the confederacy.   By the desertion of so powerful an ally, Bogdan
himself was induced to accept the terms proposed by the
king.   But the peace was of short continuance : instead
of gratitude to Heaven for an escape from utter destruction, the Polish nobles felt only the shame of receiving
the boon from a people whom a long habit of oppressing
made them despise.   The hetman had scarcely reached
the Ukraine when his ears were assailed with the notes
of preparation for a new war.   The nobles in full diet
at Warsaw, and in opposition to the prayers of their
monarch, refused to ratify the conditions of Zbarras,
and decreed the renewal of hostilities by the whole
equestrian body.   Bogdan was somewhat startled at the

* Doubtless an exaggeration. Another account has 110,000 ; a third,
with that random calculation, and that disregard to accuracy. so frequent in the Polish computations of the enemy, impudently raises them
to 340,000.

magnitude of the danger: he applied for aid to the sultan, but in vain, as the Turkish forces were then occupied in the war of Candia: the Tatars, however, were directed to support one whom the Porte recognised as prince of the Ukraine. His best supports were his Greek co-religionists, with the Lutherans, Arians, and anabaptists, who now flocked to his standard, from Red Russia, and the heart of Lithuania, to the Borysthenes; and the peasants, who, whether catholics or dissidents, were now determined to be free. Again did the two hostile armies meet in Red Russia, near Berestecko; the Poles amounted to 100,000; the enemy, it is said, to three times that number. Here was at length decided the conflict between schism and orthodoxy, between slavery and tyranny. After an obstinate battle, in which the king exhibited equal bravery and skill, the forces of Bogdan were totally routed with great slaughter. The hetman retreated towards the Borysthenes, but still opposed a formidable front to the Polish generals. A multitude of petty contests followed, in which the success was nearly balanced, until a body of 40,000 Poles, who were waiting to intercept the son of Bogdan as he was hastening to his Moldavian bride, were almost exterminated in a sudden charge by father and son.* This disaster was a terrific one to Poland; every man expected to see clouds of Cossacks and Tatars hovering on the banks of the Vistula; thousands retired to Dantzic, or into Germany, to escape the portentous storm believed to be impending.

There was, unhappily, reason enough for despair: the internal state of the kingdom was no better than its external. The gallantries of the king, especially with the wife of his vice-chancellor, raised him up a host of

---

* Scarcely any two writers agree either as to the occasion of this battle of Batowitz, or the extent of the loss sustained by the Poles. Some accounts assign the disaster to the Tatars, not to the Cossacks; others, to the latter alone; one says it was Bogdan, another his son, who inflicted this severe blow on the republic: in short, it is a subject on which we find nothing but contradiction or confusion. The modern historians of Poland reduce the numbers of their countrymen before the action to 9000. This is highly disingenuous: the loss of so small a number could not have occasioned the consternation which followed throughout the republic.

enemies. While the injured husband fled to the Swedish court, to embroil that power with his native country, a deputy, by his single *veto*, dissolved a diet which had been summoned for the express purpose of providing for the defence of the menaced kingdom. This novelty (for though the dangerous power existed in every individual member, no one hitherto had been hardy enough to exercise it,) filled the assembly with equal surprise and consternation; by this fatal measure, all the preceding deliberations of that diet were nullified. From this period the dangerous privilege was exercised as often as any individual could be found bold enough to run the risk of his life—for assassination was generally his doom if he could not escape in time, or, as was often the case, if he had not protectors powerful enough to screen him from the consequences of his temerity,—by thus setting aside the unanimous resolutions of the other members. Strange state of things, in which one equal was admitted to tyrannise over the many! in which one dissentient voice could arrest the proceedings of a whole deliberative body, and thereby plunge a great nation into woes irremediable! in which, while all power was denied to the king, the most despotic degree of it was allowed to rest in the humble menial — for such were many of the nobles — of any baron, prelate, or gentleman, in the realm!

With forces wholly inadequate to the undertaking, without money or supplies, the dejected king hastened to the relief of Kaminiec, invested by Bogdan. In one of the obscure contentions which followed — for no general action could be dreamed of by the Poles — the son of the hetman was killed. This event, however, was more likely to exasperate than to pacify the father; but the defection of his Tatar allies again weakened him too much to permit him to think of immediate vengeance. Though induced to accept the terms of a truce, he prepared for new hostilities. He applied for aid to the tsar Alexis, whose vassal he offered to become, on condition that 200,000 Muscovites were poured into Lithuania. For some time Alexis hesitated to enter into

war with a power which had all but,dethroned his father
Michael.   To know whether such a war were agreeable
to Heaven, and consequently likely to issue fortunately,
he opposed to each other two wild bulls, the one christened Poland, the other Muscovy ; and had the mortification to behold the Polish brute triumphant.   The
patriarch, however, removed his superstitious fears, and
war was declared.   The acquisition of a vast territory
from the lake Ilmen to the Black Sea, — for the submission of Bogdan rendered him lord of those extensive
regions, probably influenced him more than the interests
of his religion, which his patriarch taught him he was
bound to support.   In the present distracted state of
Poland his arms could not fail to be invincible.   Smolensko, with its 300 towers, fell before him ; Witepsk,
Polotsk, Mohilof, all Severia and Semigallia, acknowledged
his sway ; whilst on the Moldavian frontier his Cossack
allies reduced Haman, Bratslaw, and other fortresses. In
vain did the Poles endeavour to oppose so many and
such formidable enemies.   Their best generals were
worsted ; their finest armies routed ; and the pit of destruction seemed already opened before them, when the
appearance of a third enemy rendered all resistance hopeless.

On the abdication of queen Christina, and the accession of Charles Gustavus, the Polish monarch beheld
with indignation and regret his own exclusion from the
throne of his ancestors.   As the last scion of the house
of Vasa, he directed his ambassador at Stockholm to
protest against the election of the duke.   This incon-
siderate act, at a time when, in the eyes of all Europe,
Poland was undone, filled Charles with equal indignation and surprise.   His ambition for military fame, and
the representations of John Casimir's personal enemy, the
vice-chancellor Radzichowski, who longed for the destruction of one that had deprived him of wife and
country, and who showed that Poland was a prize at
once brilliant and unable to resist, did the rest.   Sixty
thousand Swedes landed in Pomerania, and, without loss

of time penetrated into Great Poland. As the Greek religionists had joined the arms of the tsar and of the Cossack, so from that same motive,—revenge for past sufferings,—the Lutherans joined those of Charles Gustavus, who loudly proclaimed himself the champion of protestantism, the redresser of all grievances originating in religion. He was immediately strengthened by the adhesion of several palatinates: his march was one triumphant career, to the walls first of Warsaw, and next of Cracow, which submitted without resistance. The example was speedily followed by the rest of the country as far as Leopol in Red Russia. The nobles of the grand duchy felt the universal panic, and acknowledged the Swede; but from community of religion the Lithuanian clergy declared for the tsar. The terrified John Casimir fled into Silesia; all Poland obeyed Charles, from the Carpathian mountains to the duchy of Courland. Successes so astoundingly rapid scarcely leave the mind time to breathe, but are yet sufficiently explicable. Religious animosities influenced the dissidents more powerfully than love of country; the peasants, whether catholic or Lutheran, were no less moved by the hope of emancipation; many nobles thought the Swede might prove as good a ruler as the present monarch; but panic fear, the utter hopelessness of resistance when so many armies of the republic had been annihilated by Cossack and Muscovite, and when but a handful of troops remained, flying from fortress to fortress to escape destruction, did more than all the rest, and blotted Poland for a time from the list of nations.

But, in human affairs, evil has its tide, as well as good. The very spirits which the sudden and apparently miraculous successes of Charles Gustavus had humbled to the dust, now began to rise. The haughty behaviour of the victor, who despised the very Poles to whom he was in a great measure indebted for his success; the exhortations of the catholic clergy, whom bigotry much more than patriotism rendered averse to the sway of a foreigner and a heretic; the pillage and depredations committed by the Swedish troops, especially in the catholic

churches, the peculiar objects of their fury, fermented
in the minds of the people the leaven of discontent.
Thousands began to flock into Silesia, to rally round the
standard of their fugitive monarch.   The opportunity
was propitious in other respects.   Alarmed at the
triumph of Charles, the tsar, satisfied with his present
conquests, had arrested his troops in the full career of
victory ; and even Bogdan had been persuaded by a
suppliant messenger from John Casimir to suspend his
blows.   All Europe, too, began to feel commiseration
for a gallant people, or rather to dread the aspiring views
of the conqueror.   Charles was not a little astonished to
find that his work was to recommence ; on every side
small armies rose to harass his motions, and confederations were formed for the defence of the rightful king,
who hastened to reclaim his crown.   The Swede was
defeated in several engagements ; but he still contrived
to retain possession of the chief palatinates, and even to
invest John Casimir in Dantzic, the inhabitants of which,
though protestants, nobly fulfilled their duty.   But what
can control a whole nation resolved to be free ?   While
the heroic Dantzickers were astonishing all Europe by
their defence, Ragotski duke of Transylvania, whom
Charles had allured by promising to partition the republic, was utterly routed by Potocki, grand general of the
crown.   John Casimir was soon conducted from his critical position at Dantzic, to the midst of his subjects,
now taught loyalty by misfortune.   The Swedes were
again defeated, and so were their allies the adherents of
Brandenburg, whom the same views as those of the
Transylvanians had joined with the invaders.   The sun
of Charles's fortune now declined with as great rapidity
an it had risen.   The alliance of Holland, of Denmark,
of the empire, Hungary, nay, even of the Brandenburger,
—who, as the reward of his adhesion to the cause of the
republic, was exempted from all homage in his original
Pomeranian possessions *, and was presented with the

* This is denied by some writers on the first partition (1772), but it is now
generally admitted by the Poles.

fiefs of Lawemburg and Butow,—enabled the republic again to rear her head among nations. The invasion of Sweden itself by the Danish king, recalled Charles to the defence of his hereditary states, and Poland was freed from the foot of the foreigner. The war, however, lingered in Pomerania, and along the shores of the Baltic, until the death of Charles, and the peace of Oliva, when the Polish king renounced his vain claim to the crown of the Goths, and ceded almost all Livonia to Sweden,— a country occupied by the troops of that power, but menaced every hour by the arms of the tsar.

Two years before the death of Charles Gustavus, a fit of apoplexy removed from the busy scenes in which he had delighted the celebrated Bogdan, after ten years of empire. By the Polish writers he has been stigmatised as rebel and traitor, as distinguished alike by malignity and perfidy. The annihilation of their finest armies, and the defeat of their ablest generals, by this extraordinary man, have forced them reluctantly to confess his surpassing military talents, and the well-judged policy which enabled him, in spite of the republic, to retain his power to the close of life. The charge of rebellion will scarcely attach to him : the Cossacks were the allies, more than the subjects, of Poland; and in seeking to escape from the intolerable yoke of that country, they did no more than patriotism and justice to themselves sanctioned. The truth is, that though he owed nothing to Poland except the accident of his birth; though his wrongs were such as would have armed the most loyal of subjects; though, to use his own expressions, in turning against his wanton persecutors he had done no more than the trodden worm would have done, he was singularly indulgent to his native land. At all times he professed his readiness to submit, on condition that his reasonable proposals were sanctioned by the diet : he testified great respect for the king, whose subject he long considered himself; and he more than once arrested the march of his victorious troops when resistance by the Poles was utterly hopeless. Had he been less moderate, we may say less magnanimous, the banks of the Vistula, not those of the Borysthenes, would have been the seat of his empire. So much for his rebellion and malignity. As to his perfidy, the charge comes with exceedingly bad grace from men who, in their transactions with the Cossacks, exhibited little else.

But the empire which Bogdan had raised was dissolved after his death. His son, George Chinielniski, was recognised beyond the Borysthenes; another chief, Wyhowski, reigned on this side: the former, to secure his dominion, acknowledged himself the vassal of the tsar; the latter, of the republic. A long war desolated these fine regions; a war in which both protecting powers took a part. Wyhowski being treacherously shot by order of the Polish monarch, the remaining Cossacks submitted to the Muscovite. Thus it is that retribution follows crime, as notoriously as effect follows cause. In general, the Poles were successful in the Ukraine; but that success procured them no solid advantage, while the Muscovites ruled at pleasure in the grand duchy: even Wilna was long in the power of the tsar. At length two splendid but dearly bought victories freed Lithuania and Volhynia from the invaders; the one obtained at Polouka, by Czarniecki, the ablest perhaps of the many able generals of John Casimir; the other by Lubomirski and Potocki, at Cudnowa. Still many provinces, from Courland to Muscovy, and on the left bank of the Borysthenes, with the important fortresses on the frontiers, for ever remained in the giant grasp of the autocrat. These vast possessions were ceded to the Muscovite by the peace of 1667. But if one enemy was pacified, others remained. An army of Cossacks and Tatars, raised up by the Porte, entered into Podolia, and vigorously invested Kaminiec. They were signally defeated by John Sobieski, who, on the death of the generals before mentioned, was intrusted, as grand hetman of the crown, with the supreme command of the Polish armies. Though with but a handful of troops,—no more than 10,000,—this wonderful man routed 80,000 of the

enemy, and freed his country from the scourge of invasion. In the preceding battles, while serving in a
subordinate capacity, he had been the right hand of the
generals in chief, and had powerfully contributed to their
triumphs. The conqueror of Podhaie was now known
beyond the bounds of the republic; his name was repeated with admiration by all Europe.

Scarcely an evil can be mentioned which did not
afflict the kingdom during the eventful reign of this
monarch. To the horrors of invasion by so many enemies, must now be added those of civil strife. The
queen, in opposition to the *pacta conventa*, had long and
not very secretly endeavoured to bring over the great
barons to acknowledge a son of the famous Condé as
the successor of Casimir. Such was her influence over
her husband, that he hesitated not, in full diet, to propose the young prince to the suffrages of the nobles.
Their silence, so contrary to their usual howls when any
thing peculiarly disagreeable was introduced, afforded the
royal pair a momentary prospect of success; but the
vehement opposition of Lubomirski undeceived them.
The vindictive queen vowed the destruction of the marshal. Summoned before the diet, on no less a charge
than that of an understanding with the Cossacks and
Tatars to overturn the state,—a charge for which there
was not even the shadow of a foundation,—he refused
to appear, and was condemned by a few court creatures
to lose his honours, his substance, and his life. But
the victor in so many battles, the saviour, in conjunction
with the deceased Czarniecki, of his country, was not to
be sacrificed with impunity to a woman's hatred. From
his asylum in Silesia he perceived the indignation which
his sentence had produced. Great Poland loudly declared for persecuted innocence. He returned, and a
civil war followed, in which the king was twice defeated by him, and obliged to renounce the interests of
the French prince. The victor again departed for Breslaw, where he ended his days. Though innocent of the
crimes imputed to him, it may be doubted whether his

past services to his country were not more than counterbalanced by the disasters of which he was the cause:
no wrongs assuredly could justify his armed opposition
to his sovereign; still less the carnage which his desire
of vengeance inflicted on the nation.[*]

In this beautiful picture of disasters abroad and
anarchy at home,—of carnage and misery on every side,
—the disbanded military took a prominent part. On
their return from their expeditions against the Muscovites and the Cossacks, they loudly demanded their arrears of pay; and when unable to procure any money,—
such was the exhausted state of the treasury,—they indemnified themselves by indiscriminately plundering the
houses of all who fell in their way,—of noble, priest, or
burgher; and murder was not unfrequently added to
robbery. These disorders were very common in Lithuania.

No wonder that such a sceptre should have become
too heavy for the enfeebled hand of John Casimir, or
that he should have little delight in a dignity which
twenty years of incessant troubles had attended. The
loss of so many provinces, the rebellion of his nobles,
the disobedience of the army, the inconceivable indifference of his people to calamities which it required no
prophetic powers to foresee[†]; and, finally, the death of
his queen made him resolve on bidding adieu to his
sceptre and the world. His abdication was not without
dignity. In the diet convened for that purpose, he stood
for the last time on the steps of the throne; and, in the
midst of an assembly profoundly affected at his resolution,—a resolution from which he could not be made to
swerve,—he explained the reasons of so extraordinary
a step:—" Poles! the time is come when I consider it

* The decree of attainder issued against him was reversed after the
abdication of the king.
† His speech at the diet of 1661, in which he denounced the partition of
Poland as the inevitable consequence of the existing anarchy, has been
considered prophetic. Rulhière (Histoire de l'Anarchie de Pologne, tom. i.)
has proved, that in using so fatal a word as *partition*, the king alluded to a
fact. The dismemberment of the republic during the invasion of Charles
Gustavus had, as before related, been seriously entertained by the surrounding powers.

my duty to discharge the debt of gratitude contracted by
my ancestors, during more than three centuries, towards
the republic.   Enfeebled by age, exhausted by many
campaigns, filled with sorrow at the contradictions I
have long endured in your debates, I, your king and
father, resign into your hands what the world most
values—a crown.   Instead of a sceptre and a throne,
give me a simple habitation; a few feet of earth, the
last possession of us all: and let me leave among you
the remembrance, that I was always the first to combat,
the last to retreat; that from love to you and my coun_
try, I resigned the crown into the same hands which had
honoured me with it." He concluded by begging pardon
of any one he might have offended, as from his heart he
forgave all who had ever offended him; and expressed
in strong terms his affection towards Poland, and his
assurance that his last prayers should be for her welfare.
He then bade an affectionate adieu to his people, and
shortly afterwards retired to France, where he died in
about five years.

Under John Casimir, the Arians were expelled from
the republic, and the Lutherans were persecuted.   Persecution, however, is sure to meet its reward.   The
adhesion of the Greeks to the tsar, and of the other dissidents to Charles Gustavus, was its inevitable conse_
quence.   The king was the unresisting instrument of
the Jesuits, whose bigotry would not suffer the country
to remain in peace.   Ineffectual attempts were made to
unite the Greek and Latin Christians: their only effect
was to aggravate the hostility already subsisting between
them.   In short, the reign of this monarch, while it
exhibits a continued succession of the worst evils which
have afflicted nations, is unredeemed by a single advantage to the republic: its only distinction is the fearfully
accelerated impulse which it gave to the decline of Poland.   The fact speaks little either for monarch or diet:
but he must not be blamed with undue severity; his
heart was better than his head; and both were superior
to those of the turbulent, fierce, and ungovernable

men who composed a body at once legislative and executive. *

MICHAEL.
1668—1673.

THE first act of the diet of convocation was to declare that no Polish king should hereafter abdicate : the fetters he might assume were thus rendered everlasting.

The candidates were three : — the prince of Condé, supported by the primate and the great barons; the prince of Neuberg, an ally, or rather a creature, of Louis XIV.; and Charles of Lorraine, a prince in the interests of Austria. The first of these candidates, however illustrious his exploits, could not be acceptable to a nation which detested alike the tyranny and arrogance of the French monarch, and which remembered but too well the disasters inflicted on the republic by one of that nation, — Henry de Valois. Though the grand marshal of the crown, Sobieski, left the fields on which he had hitherto reaped his laurels, to swell the partisans of Condé, the cause was hopeless : vast bodies of armed nobles flocked round the *kolo,* and insisted that the Frenchman should be excluded. The contest, which now lay between the French and Austrian interests, promised to be ruinous, and to end in blood : the adherents of each were nearly equal in number, and perfectly so in obstinacy. One morning, however, before the great dignitaries had arrived, and while the electors were ranged round the plain, under the banners of their respective palatinates, the cry of a *Piast* proceeded from that of Russia, and an obscure prince, Michael Koributh,

* Puffendorf, Historia Caroli Gustavi. Idem, Rerum Brandenb. Hist. lib. viii. This author, however, is ill informed in Polish affairs. Pastorius de Hirtemberg, part ii. This work is as meagre as the epitome of the writer in whose manner it was composed,—Florus. Hartknock de Republica Polonica, lib. i. : a meagre work also, and one, therefore, which we forbore to quote, so long as authorities were numerous : it is, however, a judicious abbreviation. The letters of our countryman Dr. Connor on the ancient and modern state of Poland are worth consulting. Salvandy, i. 229—424. Zielinski, xi. 221—258. We omit the immense herd of contemporary German historians, whose works, however diffuse on the affairs of France and the empire, exhibit a deplorable ignorance on those of Poland.

was proclaimed by those immediately at hand. The cry spread with electric rapidity: it was echoed by the electors of the other palatinates, who by this unexpected nomination saw an escape from the greatest of all evils, —civil war. As the senators approached, they were surprised at the universal clashing of sabres, and the howls of approbation which accompanied the name of *Michael!* They were compelled to join in the vast chorus, and "Michael! Michael!" resounded with deafening acclamations. In less than two hours he was proclaimed king of Poland.

Prince Michael Koributh Wisnowiecki was the son of the ruthless Jeremy, so infamous for his persecution of the dissidents. Infirm in body and weak in mind, without influence, because without courage and riches, he saw that if he was now made the scape-goat for the hostile factions, both would afterwards unite in his pursuit. With tears in his eyes he begged to decline the proffered dignity; and when his entreaties were received with howls of "Most serene king, you *shall* reign!" he mounted his horse, and precipitately fled from the plain. He was pursued, brought back, forced to accept the *pacta conventa* which had been prepared for the successful candidate, and to promise before the assembled multitude, whose outrageous demonstrations of homage he well knew were intended to insult his incapacity, that he would never seek to evade his new duties. To relieve his extreme poverty, some of the wealthier barons immediately filled his empty apartments with household furniture, and his still emptier kitchen with cheer, to which he had never before been accustomed. In these studied attentions there was more of contempt than of good nature. The mockery was complete, when in the diploma of his elevation it was expressed that he was the sun of the republic, the proudest boast of a mighty line of princes, one who left the greatest of the Piasts, the Jagellos, or the Vasas far behind him.

With the commencement of his reign Michael began to experience mortification within and danger from without. Though the public treasury was empty, though Poland had no army, even when the Cossacks and Tatars were preparing to invade her, two consecutive diets were dissolved, and their proceedings consequently nullified, by the veto. Then the quarrels of the deputies— quarrels which were not unfrequently decided by the sword—introduced a perfect contempt for the laws, as well as for all authority other than that of brute force. The poor monarch strove in vain to reconcile the hostile factions; his entreaties—he was too timid or too prudent to use threats—were disregarded, even by such as the distribution of crown benefices had at first allied with his interests. Without decision, without vigour, without money or troops, and consequently without the means of commanding respect from any one of his subjects, he was the scorn or jest of all. A resolution was soon taken to dethrone this phantom of royalty. The turbulent primate Prasmowski was the soul of the conspiracy, which was rendered still more formidable by the accession of the queen Eleanor, an Austrian princess. In the view of obtaining a divorce, and of procuring the elevation to the throne of one who had long been her lover—the prince of Lorraine,—she scrupled not to plot against her husband and king. It was, in fact, but exchanging one lord for another, a beloved for a despised one; and whether the plot failed or succeeded, she was sure of a husband and a throne. Fortunately for Michael, there was another conspiracy, the object of which was to transfer the queen and the sceptre to a French prince. Thus one faction neutralised the other; but in the end one of them would doubtless have triumphed, notwithstanding the adhesion of the small nobles to the reigning king—an adhesion, however, not the result of attachment to the royal person, but solely of hostility to the great barons—had not the loud notes of warlike preparation drowned for a moment the noisy contentions of the rebels.

During these melancholy transactions, the heroic Sobieski was gathering new laurels on the plains of

Podolia and Volhynia. By several successes, though obtained with but a handful of troops, chiefly raised at his own expense, he preserved the frontier provinces from the ravages of the Cossacks, the allies now of Muscovy, now of the Porte, as best suited their ideas of interest or of revenge. He was now opposed, however, to a new and apparently resistless enemy — the Turks, whom the perfidious policy or revenge of Louis XIV. raised up against the republic. The advanced guard of that enemy, consisting of Cossacks and Tatars, whom the Porte had ordered to pass the Borysthenes, he utterly routed, retook the important frontier fortresses, and by every where opposing a movable rampart to the barbarians, he kept them in check, fixed the wavering fidelity of the Volhynians, who were ready to join the Muscovites, and re-established his communications with Moldavia. Europe termed these preliminary operations *the miraculous campaign*. But Mahomet IV. now approached, accompanied by the veteran army which had reduced Candia, and which under its general, Cuprugli, had triumphed over the Venetians, the Hungarians, and the empire. About 300,000 Osmanlis crossed the Dniester, and advanced into Podolia. In the deplorable anarchy which reigned at the diet, no measures whatever had been taken to oppose the enemy. Sobieski had but 6000 men ; and notwithstanding his energetic remonstrances, he could obtain no reinforcements. He had the mortification to see the fall of Kaminiec, the reduction of all Podolia, and the advance of the Turks into Red Russia, the capital of which, Leopol, was soon invested by Mahomet in person. What man *could* do — what no man but himself could have *dared*—he accomplished. He cut off an army of Tatars, leaving 15,000 dead on the field, and releasing 20,000 Polish captives, whom the robbers were carrying away. But however splendid this success, it could not arrest the arms of the Turks. As the panic-struck nobles removed as far as possible from the seat of war, Michael hastened to make peace with the Porte ; as the price of which he ceded

Kaminiec and the Ukraine to the victors, acknowledged the superiority of the Porte over the Cossacks, and agreed to pay an annual tribute of 20,000 ducats.

Such was the humiliating state to which the republic was reduced by its own dissensions. In vain did Sobieski exclaim against the inglorious peace of Budchaz; in no Polish breast could he awaken the fire of patriotism. It is impossible not to suspect that the money of France or of the Porte had corrupted the leaders of the various factions: a nation renowned beyond all others for its valour, would surely not have thus coolly beheld its glory sullied, its very existence threatened, unless treachery had disarmed its natural defenders. At this time no less than five armed confederations were opposed to each other,—of the great against the king; of the loyal in his defence; of the army in defence of their chief, whom Michael and his party had resolved to try, as implicated in the French party; of the Lithuanians against the Poles; and, finally, of the servants against their masters, of the peasants against their lords.

Though Sobieski despised Michael, he scorned to take revenge on so poor a creature; his country still remained though humbled and degraded, and he swore to exalt her or to die. Through his efforts, and the mutual exhaustion of the contending parties, something like tranquillity was restored; and, in a diet held at Warsaw, the renewal of the war was decreed. As no tribute was sent, the grand vizier did not wait for the hostile declaration: followed by his imperial master, he crossed the Danube. At the head of near 40,000 men, Poles, Lithuanians, and German auxiliaries, Sobieski opened a campaign destined to be for ever memorable in the annals of the world. His plan was to meet and annihilate Caplan Pacha, who was advancing through Moldavia; to return and fall on Hussein, another Turkish general, who, with 80,000 men, held the strong position of Kotzim, on the Moldavian side of the Dniester, opposite to Kaminiec: the destruction of these two leaders, he hoped, would lead to the fall of the latter fortress, and enable him to contend with the sultan in person, should the monarch persist in advancing. The mutiny of his troops, however, especially of the Lithuanians, who exclaimed that he was leading them to utter destruction, and who refused to advance into an unknown country, compelled him to begin with Hussein. With difficulty he prevailed on them to pass the Dniester, and to march on Kotzim: he found the Turkish general so strongly fortified, that Paz, the Lithuanian hetman, refused at first to join in the meditated assault; but he had done such wonders in preceding campaigns with a handful of troops, that with 40,000 he thought nothing impossible. Paz, his personal enemy, he persuaded to co-operate, and the bombardment commenced, while the grand assault was preparing. Fortunately for the Christian arms, the night of the 10th of November, 1673, was one of unexampled severity: the snow fell profusely, and the piercing blasts were still more fatal to the besieged, most of them from warm Asiatic climes. On the morning of the 11th, Sobieski led the attack: ere long his lance gleamed on the heights, and the struggle was renewed in the heart of the Turkish entrenchments. In vain did the Janizaries endeavour to prolong it; they fell in heaps, while the less courageous or more enfeebled portion of the enemy sought safety in flight. The bridge, however, which connected the two banks of the river, was in the possession of the Christians, and thousands perished while endeavouring to swim over. The carnage was now terrific; 40,000 of the Moslems now lay on the plain, or floated in the stream, and an immense booty fell to the victors. Poland was saved; the fortress of Kotzim capitulated. Caplan Pacha retreated beyond the Danube;. Moldavia and Wallachia declared for the republic, and would perhaps have been incorporated with it, had not the grand hetman been recalled from his career of conquest by an important, though not an unexpected, event.

This was no other than the death of Michael, who expired at Lemberg (Leopol) the night before the great battle of Kotzim, while on his way to join the army.

His demise was very agreeable to the Poles, who longed for a prince capable of restoring their ancient glôry. Let him not, however, be judged with undue severity : his feebleness was no more than his misfortune, while his intentions were good. Though without vigour of understanding, he was accomplished, and even learned ; he was acquainted with several languages, and addicted to literary pursuits. Knowing his own incapacity to rule so fierce a nation, compulsion alone made him ascend the throne; and if his reign was disastrous, the reason has been sufficiently explained. On the whole, he should be pitied rather than condemned.*

JOHN III. (SOBIESKI.)
1674—1696.

THOUGH, on the death of Michael, the number of candidates was greater than it had been on any preceding occasion, from the state of parties in the republic, no one could doubt that the chief struggle would be between those of France and the empire. The dukes of Lorraine and Neuberg were again proposed : the former was zealously supported by a queen lover; the latter by the money and promises of Louis. (The electors had long been sufficiently alive to the *value* of their votes.) That a stormy election was apprehended, was evident from the care with which the *szopa*, or wooden pavilion of the senators, was fortified. The appearance on the plains was exceedingly picturesque : every where were seen small bands of horsemen exercising their daring feats ; some tilting; some running at the ring ; others riding with battle-axes brandished to the entrance of the szopa, and with loud hurras inciting the senate to expedition ; others were deciding private quarrels, which always ended in blood; some were listening with fierce impatience to the harangues of their leaders, and testifying by their howls or hurras their condemnation or approval of the subject. At a distance appeared the white tents

* Puffendorf, tom. iv. lib. iv. Hartknock, lib. i. cap. ii. Connor, vol. i. book iii. Salvandy, ii. 1—156. Zielinski, xi. 258—272.

of the nobles, which resembled an amphitheatre of snowy mountains, with the sparkling waters of the Vistula, and the lofty towers of Warsaw.

The appearance of the Lithuanians was hostile: perhaps they had some reason to suspect the nomination of Sobieski, with whom their hetman, Paz, had long been at variance; certainly they seemed resolved to support the Austrian to the last extremity. Sobieski, who in the mean time had arrived from Kotzim, proposed the prince of Condé, another candidate; whether in the hope that such a proposition would succeed, or with the view of distracting the different parties, and making way for his own elevation, is not very clear. He soon found, however, that the prince was no favourite on the *kolo*; and his personal friend, Jablonowski, palatine of Russia, commenced a harangue in support of his pretensions. The speaker, with great animation, and not without eloquence, showed that the republic could expect little benefit from any of the candidates proposed, and insisted that its choice ought to fall on a Piast; on one, above all, capable of repressing domestic anarchy, and of upholding the honour of its arms, which had been so lamentably sullied during the two preceding reigns. The cry of "A Piast! a Piast! and God bless Poland!" speedily rose from the Russian palatinate, and was immediately echoed by thousands of voices. Seeing their minds thus favourably inclined, he proposed the conqueror of Slobodisza, of Podhaic, of Kalusz and Kotzim; and the cry was met with "Sobieski for ever!" All the palatinates of the crown joined in the acclamation; but the Lithuanians entered their protest against a Piast. Fortunately for the peace of the republic, the grand duchy was not, or did not long continue, unanimous; prince Radzivil embraced the cause of the crown; Paz was at length persuaded to withdraw his unavailing opposition; and John III. was proclaimed king of Poland.*

* The *pacta conventa* signed by this king differed little from those of his predecessors. In the article that offices should be conferred on native nobles only, it was added, and on such only as have worn their honours three gener-

Before the new king would consent to be crowned, he undertook an expedition to rescue Kaminiec, Podolia, and the Ukraine, from the domination of the Moslems. To preserve these, and if possible to add to them, Mahomet IV. had taken the field with a formidable army. Kotzim was retaken, the Muscovites who contended with the Porte for the possession of the provinces on the Borysthenes were expelled from the Ukraine, and several Cossack fortresses carried; but here the sultan, thinking he had done enough for glory, returned to Constantinople. John now entered on the scene, and with great rapidity retook all the conquests that had been made, except Kotzim, and reduced to obedience most of the Cossacks on the left bank of the Borysthenes. But this scene was doomed to be sufficiently diversified: the wicked desertion of Paz, who, with his Lithuanians, was averse to a winter campaign, prevented the king from completing the subjugation of the Ukraine, and even forced him to retreat before a new army of Turks and Tatars: 20,000 of the Tatars, however, were signally defeated at Zlotsow; and the little fortress of Trembowla made a defence worthy the best ages of Roman bravery. The Lithuanian soldiers being compelled by their countrymen to rejoin the king, that monarch again entered on the career of victory. The Turks were defeated at Soczawa, and were pursued with great loss to the ramparts of Kaminiec. With the exception of that fortress and of Podhaic, which they had stormed, Poland was free from the invaders.

Sobieski having thus nobly earned the crown of a kingdom which he had so often saved, returned to Cracow, where his coronation was performed with the accustomed pomp, but with far more than the accustomed joy. At the diet assembled on this occasion, a standing army of 30,000, and an extraordinary one of three times that number, were decreed; but nothing more was done;

---

ations. Every third year he was to pass into Lithuania: it had before been decreed that every third diet should be held at Grodno. A pension was to be paid to queen Eleanor.

and the republic remained defenceless as before. Other salutary proposals submitted by the king, whose talents were as conspicuous in government as in the field, had no better success. The fate of the republic, however it might be delayed by monarchs so enlightened and conquerors so great as he, was not to be averted.

From these harassing cares John was summoned by a new invasion of the Turks and Tatars, amounting in number to 210,000*, and commanded by Ibraham Pacha of Damascus, whose surname of *Shaitan*, or the devil, was significant enough of his talents and character. The Polish king, with his handful of 10,000, was compelled to entrench himself at Zuranow, where he was well defended by sixty-three pieces of cannon. His fate was considered — perhaps even by himself — as decided; all Poland, instead of flocking to his aid, hastened to the churches, to pray for his deliverance. For twenty days the cannonading continued its destructive havoc, occasionally diversified by still more destructive sorties from the camp. The advantage rested with the Poles, but they were so thinned by their very successes, that their situation became desperate. The Tatar khan, however, who knew that the Muscovites were laying waste that part of the Ukraine subject to Doroszensko, the feudatory of the Porte, and were menacing his own territories, clamoured for peace. It was proposed by the pacha, but on the same humiliating terms as those of Budchaz. The enraged Sobieski threatened to hang the messenger who should in future bring him so insulting a proposal. Hostilities recommenced ; though the Poles were without provisions or ammunition, he scorned to capitulate. He rode among his dismayed ranks, reminded them that he had extricated them from situations even worse than the present one, and gaily asked whether his head was likely to have suffered by the weight of a crown. When the Lithuanians threatened to desert, he only replied:—" Desert who will — alive or dead I remain !" But to remain in his camp was no

* Probably exaggerated.

longer safe: one morning he issued from it, and drew up
his handful of men, now scarcely 7000, in battle array
as tranquilly as if he had legions to marshal. Utterly
confounded at this display of rashness or of confidence,
the Turks cried out — " There is magic in it!" a cry
in which Shaitan, devil as he was, joined. Filled with
admiration at a bravery which exceeded his imagination,
the pacha sued for peace on less dishonourable conditions.
By the treaty two thirds of the Ukraine were restored to Poland, the remaining third being in the power of the Porte;
the question as to Podolia was to be discussed at Constantinople; all prisoners, hostages, &c. were also restored.
The conditions, indeed, were below the dignity of the
republic; but that such favourable ones could be procured at such a crisis, is the best comment on the valour
of the king. This was the sentiment of all Europe,
which resounded more than ever with his praises.

This peace was followed by the prolongation of the
truce with Muscovy. Neither were the conditions of
the latter so advantageous as could have been desired.
Three insignificant fortresses were restored; but Severia,
Smolensko, Kiow, and other possessions, remained in the
iron grasp of the autocrat. In vain would the king have
endeavoured to wrest them from it: without money or
troops, with anarchy also before his eyes, it was no slight
blessing that he was able to preserve, from day to day,
the independence, nay the existence, of the republic.

During the four following years the king was unable
to undertake any expedition for the reconquest of the lost
possessions. Though he convoked diet after diet, in the
hope of obtaining the necessary supplies for that purpose
diet after diet was dissolved by the fatal veto; for the
same reason he could not procure the adoption of the
many salutary courses he recommended, to banish
anarchy, to put the kingdom on a permanent footing of
defence, and to amend the laws. His failure, indeed,
must be partly attributed to himself; since, great as he
was, he appeared as much alive to the aggrandisement of
his own family as to the good of the republic. There

P

can be little doubt — and he ought to be praised for it —
that he had long meditated the means of rendering the
crown hereditary in his offspring; but the little caution
with which he proceeded in this great design, and the
criminal intrigues of his queen, a Frenchwoman of
little principle, whose influence over him was unbounded,
roused the jealousy of the nobles, especially of the Lithuanians, and compelled him to suspend it. Had he
shown more prudence, as well as more firmness, in his
administration, and within his palace, his object might
have been attained, and Poland preserved from ruin,
under the sway of his family.

John Sobieski had always belonged to the faction or
party in the interests of France, and, consequently,
averse to that of Austria ; but there was one thing in
which he would not gratify the perfidious Louis XIV.
As a Christian knight, and a noble Pole, he had vowed
inextinguishable hostility against the Moslems ;— a feeling, in his case, deepened by the memory of his maternal
grandfather, his father, and his brother, who had all
perished under the sword of the misbelievers, — and he
could not consequently band with the Porte against the
empire.   While the Turks were arming for the invasion
of Germany, his alliance was eagerly sought by Louis
and Leopold : he entered into a treaty offensive and defensive with the latter.   To this turn in his policy he
was said, perhaps injuriously, to have been not a little
disposed by the promise of an archduchess for his eldest
son, and by the resentment of some insults shown by
the *grand monarque* to his queen.

But the money of Louis, and the venality of the
Polish barons, opposed great obstacles to the ratifications
of this treaty by the diet.   A conspiracy was soon set on
foot, the object of which was, either to turn the king
from the Austrian cause, or to dethrone him.   Fortunately the correspondence of the French ambassador with
the unprincipled court of Paris fell into his hands, and
he was enabled to frustrate the criminal design.   To
escape detection, the very conspirators voted for a war

with the infidels, and preparations were made for a great campaign. It was time. Vienna was invested by 300,000 Turks and Tatars, under Kara Mustapha, the vizier; the dastardly Leopold had retreated to Lintz, and despatched messenger after messenger to hasten the departure of Sobieski. Germany looked to him as its saviour, and Europe as the bulwark of Christendom. Having beheld at his feet the ambassadors of the empire and the nuncio of the pope, he left Cracow, August 15th, with a small body of Polish troops, and without waiting for the Lithuanians: the chief part of his army, amounting in all to about 30,000 men, he had previously ordered to rendezvous under the walls of Vienna.

The king found the affairs of the imperialists in a worse situation than he had conceived. The Turkish artillery had made a practicable breach, and the terrified inhabitants of the capital were in momentary expectation of an assault. One evening, however, their despair was changed to joy, as they perceived from their telescopes the appearance of the Polish hussars on the heights of Kalemberg. Sobieski was enthusiastically invested with the chief command of the Christian army, consisting of Poles, Saxons, Bavarians, and Austrians, amounting to 70,000 men. One who had been his rival as a candidate, the duke of Lorraine, gave a noble example of magnanimity by this submission, and by zealously co-operating in all his plans. On the morning of Sept. 12. commenced the mighty struggle between the crescent and the cross. Throughout the day the advantage rested with the Christians; but the vast masses of the Turks remained unbroken. Towards nightfall the Polish king had fought his way to the entrenched camp of the vizier, whom he perceived seated in a magnificent apartment tranquilly drinking coffee with his two sons. Provoked at the sight he rushed forward, followed by an intrepid band. With the loud war cry of " *God for Poland!*" and his pious repetition of the well-known verse of Israel's prophet king, — " *Non nobis, non nobis, Domine exercituum, sed nomini tuo da gloriam!*" was united

that of "*Sobieski!*" Shouts of "*Sobieski! Sobieski!*"
caught the ears of the Moslems, who, for the first time,
now certainly knew that this dreaded hero was with the
Christians. "Allah!" exclaimed the Tatar khan, "the
king is with them sure enough!" The consternation
among the infidels was extreme: but, true to the bravery
of their character, they made a vigorous stand. In vain;
their ranks strewed the ground; six pachas fell with
them; the vizier fled, and with him the remnant of his
once formidable host. The Turkish camp, with its immense riches, became the prey of the victors; not only
Germany but Europe was saved. The hero of Christendom hastened to the cathedral of St. Stephen to join in
a solemn *Te Deum* for the success of this memorable day.

It is painful to dwell on the subsequent conduct of
Leopold. Instead of clasping the knees of his saviour
with joy, and of blushing at his own cowardice, he met
the king with coolness, nay, even with insult. His empire was saved, and as he had no more need of further
aid, he took care to exhibit no further gratitude. His
behaviour astonished no less than incensed the Poles,
many of whom, without their king's permission, returned
to their homes; but Sobieski, with the rest, proceeded
into Hungary in pursuit of the fugitive Moslems. By
two subsequent victories won at Parkan and Strigonia,
he freed most of that kingdom from the foot of the invaders, and would have extended his successes far beyond
the Danube, had not the Lithuanians delayed to join
him, and his Polish troops insisted on returning to their
country.

On his arrival, he had the additional gratification of
finding that one of his generals had obtained some signal
successes in the Ukraine, over a combined army of Turks
and Tatars; had dethroned one hospodar of Wallachia, and elevated another better disposed to the views
of the republic.

But while pursuing the splendid successes of this
Christian hero, posterity must blush at the weakness of
his policy, at the blindness with which he pursued the

aggrandisement of his family; implicitly followed the counsels of his despicable queen ; and trusted to the protestations of Leopold, who, when his aid was required, never hesitated at promises, and when that aid was furnished, never · thought of performing them.   Though the archduchess promised to his son was resigned to the elector of Bavaria *, the imperial lure of assisting him to subdue Wallachia, which was to become a permanent sovereignty in his family, again armed him against the Turks.   To be freed from all apprehensions on the side of Muscovy, he for ever confirmed to that power the possession of Smolensko, Siewierz, Tsernichof, and the greater portion of Kiovia, with Kiow the capital.   These possessions, indeed, he could not hope to recover ; but voluntarily to have resigned them, and for ever, justly excited the indignation of many, especially when they found that the tsarina Sophia refused to perform conditions to which she had agreed, — to join the general crusade against the Porte, and to pay the republic 200,000 rubles in return for these concessions.

Having raised about 40,000 men, the king entered into Wallachia, to conquer it for one of his sons.   But the expedition had no effect, owing partly to the exceeding dryness of the season, and to the consequent sufferings of his army ; and partly to the non-appearance of the contingents promised by Leopold and the hospodar. He returned, but not without loss, both from the reason already assigned, and from the activity of the Turks in his rear ; who, however, dared not attack him. A second expedition was but partly successful; in fact, the infirmities of age had overtaken him, and had impaired his mental no less than his bodily vigour.   His failure, however, in both expeditions was owing to circumstances over which he had no control; in neither did it dim the lustre of his martial fame.

No two men could be more unlike than Sobieski in the field, and Sobieski at his palace of government : in

* The young prince, by means of Leopold, was afterwards married to the princess of Neuberg ; a union which connected him with the royal families of Spain, Portugal, and Austria.

the former he was the greatest, in the latter the meanest, of men. He was justly despised for his tame submission to his worthless queen. To her he abandoned all but the load of administration; her creatures filled most offices in the state; all, too, were become venal,—all conferred on the highest bidder. The bishop Zaluski, on this subject, relates an anecdote, sufficiently characteristic of the court where such a shameless transaction could take place. The rich see of Cracow being vacant, the queen one day said to the bishop of Culm, " I wager with your sincerity that you alone will have the bishopric of Cracow." Of course the prelate accepted the challenge, and, on being invested with the see, paid the amount. Zaluski himself opened a way to the royal favour by means equally reprehensible. He presented the queen with a medicine-chest, together with a book of directions for employing them, valued at a few hundred ducats: she received it with contempt. The offer of a silver altar, estimated at 10,000 crowns, of a valuable ring, and two diamond crosses, gratified her avarice, and made the fortune of the giver. Her temper was about equal to her disinterestedness. On one occasion the king had promised the great seal to Zaluski; the queen to Denhoff: of course the latter triumphed.— " You are not ignorant," said the king to the disappointed claimant, his intimate friend, " of the rights claimed by wives; with what importunity the queen demands every thing that she likes: you only have the power to make me live tranquilly or wretchedly with my wife. She has given her word to another, and if I refuse her the disposal of the chancellorship, she will not remain with me. I know you wish me too well to expose me to public laughter, and I am convinced that you will let me do what she wishes, but what I do with extreme regret." Can this be the victor of Slobodyssa, Podhaic, Kotzim, and Vienna?

It cannot be matter of much surprise that such a prince should have little influence in the diets, or that his measures should form the subject of severe scrutiny by many of his nobles. French money raised him up enemies on every side; so also did that of his queen, whenever he ventured on such as were unpalatable either to her or to her creatures. The man who could not preserve peace in his own family, who could not prevent his wife and eldest son, nor mother-in-law and daughter-in-law, from bringing disgrace on his palace by their unnatural quarrels, could not be expected to have much influence any where. In full senate he was often treated with marked disrespect: the words *tyrant! traitor!* were lavished on him ; and he was once or twice invited to descend from a dignity which he dishonoured. That he seriously entertained the design of abdication, notwithstanding the decree against it during the interregnum of Michael Koributh, is certain ; but if he had many enemies, he had more friends, and he was persuaded to relinquish it.

The last days of John Sobieski were passed in literary or in philosophical contemplation. Sometimes, too, he migrated from scene to scene, pitching his tent, like the Sarmatians of old, wherever a fine natural prospect attracted his attention. His last hours were wrapped in mystery. He spoke to Zaluski of a dose of mercury which he had taken, and which had occasioned him intense suffering in mind and body. " Is there no one," he abruptly exclaimed, while heavy sobs agitated his whole frame, " to avenge my death ! " This might be the raving of a sickly, nervous, distempered mind ; but a dreadful suspicion fixed on the queen. Her subsequent conduct confirmed it. Scarcely was the breath out of his body, when she seized on his treasures, and renewed her quarrels with her eldest son, prince James, with a bitterness that showed she felt no regret for his loss.*

The character of John Sobieski has been unjustly treated by some Polish historians. No one can vindicate his deplorable weakness, his unaccountable submis-

---

* Yet this was the woman to whom he was devoted through life with more than a lover's fidelity, and to whom his letters, which breathed the utmost affection, uniformly commenced, " Seule joie de mon âme, charmante et bien aimée Mariette ! "

sion to the caprice of a shameless woman, his eagerness
to advance the interests of his family, his want of firmness, as well as of caution, in his administration. But
when the contraction of the boundaries of the republic
is imputed to him as a crime, he is most harshly judged.
That he acted with imprudence, at the most, in ceding to
Muscovy the possessions before mentioned, cannot be
denied : they had long been held by the tsar, and were
for ever lost to Poland. As to Podolia and the Ukraine,
let those be blamed who, with criminal negligence, forbore to support him in his campaigns, who threw on him
the responsibility of the war, while they rendered it utterly impossible for him to procure for that war a successful issue. Our only surprise must be, that the limits
were not much farther narrowed, that the republic had
a province left. Under any other monarch Poland would
have been erased from the list of nations. His vigorous
arm for a time arrested her in her rapid fall.* He was
the last independent king of Poland. His enemies could
not but allow that he was one of the greatest characters.
in royal biography, the greatest beyond comparison in
the regal annals of his country.

CHAP. II.

FROM THE DEATH OF SOBIESKI TO THE ANNIHILATION OF THE REPUBLIC.

FREDERIC AUGUSTUS I.†
1696—1733.

THE eldest son of the deceased monarch was so sure of
the crown, that he began to use his baptismal name

* Connor, vol. i. b. iii. iv. Puffendorf, Hist. Germ. iv. lib. iv. Zaluski,
tom. i. ii. Daleyrac, Anecdotes de Pologne, tom. i. ii. Lettres du Roi de
Pologne Jean Sobieski à la Reine Marie Casimire pendant la cumpagne de
Vienne, &c. in one volume. Salvandy, tom. ii. iii. Zielinski, ii. 272—312.
Malte-Brun, Tableau de Pologne, as enlarged by Chodzko, tom. i. p. 457, &c.
See also an article on *Poland under Sobieski*, in No. XIV. of the Foreign
Quarterly Review.
† By the Polish historians usually termed Augustus II., the first being
Sigismund Augustus. The first baptismal name ought to be taken wherever
there are two. but both, perhaps, are preferable.

only; to promise benefices and dignities to his creatures, and to act the sovereign as confidently as if the
power were already his. But though he had at first
many adherents, whom respect for his father's memory
rallied round him, he had soon more opponents, among
whom the most bitter was his own.mother. In hope
of procuring the election of her second son, Alexander, a prince of easy disposition, and of reigning
under his name, she employed the immense treasures
she had amassed, to destroy the sanguine expectations
of prince James. Nor was the behaviour of the latter
prince less unnatural. Scarcely was the breath out of
his father's body, when a series of vindictive quarrels
disgraced a family which had never been distinguished
for harmony. In the apprehension of her dangerous
intrigues, James refused her access to the palace. He
flew to Zolkiew, to secure his father's treasures; and,
when followed by his mother and brothers, he turned
the cannon of that fortress against them. Such scenes
so scandalised the capital and the country, that a re-
action took place in the minds of those who had shown
a disposition to continue the crown in the royal family.
Several dietines formally voted for its exclusion; and
the old queen herself, seeing that there was no hope
of her favourite son's elevation, strongly exhorted
the nobles to set aside her offspring, and choose some
worthier ruler. " If you elect any of my sons, your
republic is at an end. Above all, beware of prince
James!" Her object was now to fix the crown on the
head of a bachelor, and secure the continuance of her
authority by a husband. She was, however, so universally detested, that the diet insisted on her removing to
Dantzic until the election was ended.

The chief candidates were two; a nephew of Louis
XIV., and the elector of Saxony; the one a French,
the other an Austrian partisan. As usual, the crown
and the grand duchy, the great and the small nobles
espoused opposite sides: the former inclined to the
prince of Conti, the latter to the elector, who had just

abjured Lutheranism, as a necessary step to the dignity
he coveted. The party of James having joined that of
the royal convert, the elector's became more powerful;
still the other was more imposing. Unanimity being
found impossible, both proclaimed their respective candidates: the primate sung *Te Deum* for the prince in the
cathedral of Cracow; the bishop of Cujavia in the same
place, and in the archbishop's presence, for the elector.
The following day, however, the party of Frederic Augustus received considerable accessions, and still greater
when it was·generally known that he had communicated
at the altar of Rome. But his chief advantage over
his competitor, was his proximity to this scene of political contention. While the prince of Conti awaited the
result in France, *he* was in Silesia, ready to assist his
partisans with money, or to confirm such articles of the
pacta conventa * as had been signed by his ambassador.
And no sooner was he acquainted with the double election than he hastened to Cracow, where he was solemnly crowned, notwithstanding the opposition of the
French party. When the prince of Conti subsequently
arrived at Dantzic, he found Augustus too firmly seated
to be shaken, without the aid of a considerable army;
and Poland showed no inclination to aid him with one.
Eventually the primate and the chiefs of his party
submitted: they could not well do otherwise, as the pope
had recognised the elector; but some of the Lithuanian nobles were never well affected to his cause: a few
refused to do homage, until the invasion of Charles XII.
enabled them to rebel with impunity. His election was
irregular, and therefore null according to the laws; but
laws are regarded only so long as there is force to invest them with the necessary vigour.†

* These were about thirty in number, the most important of which regarded the recovery of Kaminiec and the Ukraine, &c.; to support, at his
own expense, 6000 troops. These conditions are not worth the trouble of
enumerating, as few of them were ever fulfilled.
† Si on s'en rapportait aux relations différentes qui furent publiées dans le
tems, il ne seroit pas facile de dire laquelle des deux élections étoit légitime,
ni même de quel côté se trouvait le grand nombre, tant les divers écrivains
ont pris de plaisir à déguiser de part et d'autre pour raconter les choses à
l'avantage de celui de deux princes pour lequel ils s'intéressoient.—Parthenay, *Histoire de Pologne sous Auguste II.*, tom. i. *Neither* election was
legitimate.

Frederic Augustus lost no time in fulfilling one of the conditions imposed on him at his accession, in re-taking Kaminiec. He invested that fortress with an allied army of Poles, Lithuanians, and Saxons; but the presence of the foreigners was so disagreeable to the natives, that his efforts were long abortive. In the end, however, the place capitulated; and by the peace of Carlowitz, the Porte renounced all pretensions over Podolia and the Ukraine. This was an important service to the republic; for though a portion of the Ukraine was in the power of Muscovy, the Podolian frontier was now ensured against the incursions of the Turks. But this success was counterbalanced by the loss of the district of Elbing. The elector of Brandenburg besieged and took the city of Elbing, which he proposed, however, to surrender, as soon as he should receive the sum of 400,000 crowns lent to the republic by his father. In this he certainly was justified by existing treaties. The republic instantly commenced negotiations, and promised, after the separation of the diet, then sitting, to pay him 300,000, on the condition of its immediate evacuation. The jewels of the crown were placed in his hands, as security for the due performance of the convention. He *did* evacuate it by torchlight, and it was at the same moment entered by the Polish army. But the money was not paid; and Frederic Augustus, to indemnify himself, took possession of the district: he ever afterwards retained both it and the jewels. In little more than a year this able and ambitious man assumed the title of king, and as such was immediately recognised by Frederic Augustus* without the concurrence of the republic.

The Polish monarch was not very anxious to perform the conditions of the *pacta conventa*, or to comply with the wishes of his nobles. In his secret treaty with the tsar, the famous Peter I., he acted as if no diet were ever to be called; and in detaining his Saxon subjects in the kingdom, he exasperated the Poles to such a pitch

* Of course, as elector of Saxony, not as king of Poland.

that numbers of these foreigners were daily massacred
whenever they ventured beyond the precincts of the capital. That treaty, however, the object of which was to
wrest from Sweden Livonia and Ingria, brought its own
punishment. Though the arms of Augustus were at first
successful in the former country, his prosperity was soon
checked by the youth whom he had ventured to despise.
After the affair of Copenhagen, Charles XII. entered on
a career of conquest perhaps unrivalled in modern history. The signal victory of Narva, and the subsequent
reduction of Courland, opened the way for the invasion
of Lithuania.

At this time the grand duchy was a prey to two
rival factions, the Oginskis and the Sapiehas, whose
quarrels deluged it with blood. These vindictive princes
made war on each other with as much acrimony, and
with forces almost as numerous, as crowned heads ; nor
did they condescend to receive the expostulations of their
king, who vainly endeavoured to reconcile them. The
republic now exhibited a strange spectacle ; the king at
war with the Swedes, not only without the consent, but
in direct opposition to the loudly expressed wishes, of
the diet ; the grand duchy one scene of bloody commotion ; and Poland uncertain what steps to take in a
conjunction so unusual. A confederation was at length
assembled to repress this anarchy ; but its efforts only
added to the disorder. Seeing themselves proclaimed
enemies of their country, and their domains subject to a
sentence of confiscation, the Sapiehas joined the Swedish
invader, whom they instigated to more vindictive proceedings. They were but too well aided by the ambitious primate, who had never been friendly to the elevation
of Frederic Augustus, and who now urged Charles to
dethrone him. The result is in the memory of every
reader. After a decisive victory over his enemy, the conqueror penetrated into Poland, obtained possession of
Cracow and the capital, and by his policy as much as
by his victories procured the deposition of Frederic Augustus. The interregnum was proclaimed May 2. 1705,

by the cardinal primate. His object was to place the crown on the head of a son of Sobieski; but the captivity of two of the princes in Saxony, the magnanimous refusal of a third, Alexander, to profit by the misfortune of an elder brother, and, above all, the absolute will of the Swedish king, raised Stanislas, palatine of Posnania, to the vacant dignity.

But though Stanislas had virtues enough to shed a lustre on any crown, he could not be expected to reign undisturbed in a country which the humiliation of being compelled to receive him rendered averse to his sway. Many of the great barons joined the Muscovites, who laid waste the grand duchy, and who advanced or retreated according to the inverse movements of the Polish and Swedish armies. At length, while Charles was in Saxony, an assembly at Leopol, over which the archbishop of Gnesna presided, declared null the abdication of Frederic Augustus. The whole country was infested by armed partisans, not only of the two kings, but of such as wished neither; and by a still greater number, who aimed only at procuring some advantage from the anarchy which prevailed. To this desolating scourge must be added the plague, which in two months carried off, in Warsaw alone, about 15,000 souls, and in Dantzic above 24,000. Poland, in fact, was cursed with every possible evil, except a bad king; nor could the humane, enlightened Stanislas atone for the tithe of the mischiefs of which he had been the unwilling cause. The disaster of Pultowa relieved him from a load which he had long sighed to lay down; and while gratitude called him to share the fate of his benefactor and friend, a captive in Turkey, Frederic Augustus was restored by the diet of Warsaw.

But the restoration of Frederic Augustus did not restore peace to Poland. His armed auxiliaries, the Saxons and the Muscovites, were quartered in different parts of the country, both to overawe the adherents of Stanislas and to receive Charles, should the Porte be ever reduced to release a captive whose chains he endeavoured to perpetuate. These foreigners were charged with heavy excesses; their presence was the greatest offence: the Poles confederated against them, and for two years Polish and Saxon blood deluged the country. The efforts of the king to reconcile his hostile subjects were vain: nothing but the absence or the destruction of the Saxons would satisfy the republic. Through the interference of the tsar—and from this reign Muscovite influence acquired irresistible strength—the foreign troops were at length dismissed, and the king reconciled with the Poles.

Nor was the republic more prosperous in her foreign relations. After the death of Catherine, the widow of Peter, Courland became so intimately connected with Muscovy as to be for ever lost to Poland. Anne, a niece of Peter, had been married to Kettler, sovereign of that duchy. After his death, the reigning duke, Ferdinand, being without male issue, the fief would naturally in time revert to the crown. The Poles meditated the incorporation of the duchy with the republic, and the consequent abolition of the feudal dignity; the king hoped to preserve it in his own family; and the Courlanders themselves were tenacious enough of their ancient privileges. In opposition to the remonstrances of Ferdinand, the nobles elected as their future ruler prince Maurice of Saxe, a natural son of Frederic Augustus. The king, however, was forced by a diet held at Grodno to withhold the instrument of investiture, and even to reprimand the Courlanders for attempting to secure the perpetuity of their government. Maurice for some time refused to abandon the people who had elected him; but there was a third party, which had not yet been consulted, and which was resolved that neither of the two should succeed in their views. Muscovy laid pretensions to the sovereignty, in virtue of the claims (chiefly of a pecuniary nature) possessed by the grand duchess Anne; her troops entered the country, and expelled Maurice. Anne was soon afterwards called to the imperial throne; and one of her first acts was to invest her favourite, Biron, with the fief.

The reign of Frederic Augustus was still further disgraced by the persecution of the dissidents. The laws in favour of the Lutherans had gradually weakened, probably owing to their numerical decrease; so that in a diet held at Grodno, in 1718, access was refused to a Calvinistic deputy. The sectarians were even prohibited from filling offices in the administration of justice. An incident set fire to the combustible spirit of indignation which existed in Polish Prussia and Pomerania, more than any where else, because there the protestants had a numerical preponderance. In a procession of the host to the church belonging to the nuns of St. Benedict, at Thorn, some Lutheran children, while gazing on the spectacle with the curiosity natural to their years, were ordered by a Jesuit student to kneel; and such as refused were visited with a box on the ear. The parents of the children hastened to chastise the student; the brethren of the latter, to support orthodoxy. Stones and other missiles flew about, until the soldiers of the guard arrived, and safely lodged the original offender in prison. The following day, a body of students proceeded to demand the enlargement of their comrade, and insulted the citizens as they passed along. The ringleader of this second mutiny was also seized and confined. At the solicitation of the principal of the order, the first delinquent was discharged, but the latter was detained. The students assembled a third time, pursued a Lutheran citizen sword in hand, and on his escape they seized a German scholar, whom they dragged to their college by way of reprisal, and confined; they next assaulted the spectators whom this disgraceful scene had assembled. The chief magistrate sent an officer to pacify the two parties, and at the same time to demand the release of the innocent German. The rector of the institution refused to surrender him, unless the young Jesuit were also discharged. This contempt of the laws so enraged the populace, that a tumultuous battle ensued, in which the students were armed with muskets, their assailants with whatever was at hand. It ended in the forcing of

the college by the burghers, and the utter destruction of
the furniture, books, &c., in a huge fire kindled for the
purpose.

Such is the account given of these transactions by the
senate of Thorn; but, as may be easily conceived, it
differs materially from that drawn up by the Jesuits
themselves, who throw the whole blame on the populace.
To arrive at the exact truth is impossible: it is sufficient to observe, that both parties deserved punishment,
since both had wantonly violated the laws; the populace
in a greater degree than even the Jesuits.

On hearing the report of the fathers, all Poland was
in commotion. Commissioners were sent to examine
into the truth of the charges. In the discharge of their
functions, they exhibited, we are told, gross partiality.
From the depositions of the witnesses, sixty-six offenders,
all Lutheran burghers, were committed to prison, and an
extraordinary tribunal formed at Warsaw, to try and
pass sentence on them. Its severity astonished all Europe. The president and vice-president of the munici-
pality were ordered to be beheaded, for not having shown
sufficient vigour in repressing the tumult; the property
of the former, also, was confiscated in favour of the
Jesuits; two magistrates were to be imprisoned for a
short period; seven ringleaders of the populace were
also to lose their heads; and four others, convicted of
dishonouring the images of the saints, were to lose their
right hands before decapitation; finally, about forty
others were sentenced to various periods of imprisonment. These sanguinary proceedings were solemnly
sanctioned by a national diet; and thus all Poland shared
in the guilt. The executions were hurried, to prevent
the effects of the energetic remonstrances, which the
neighbouring powers, catholic as well as protestant, the
pope and the emperor, as well as the king of Prussia
and the tsar, began to make. Those remonstrances were
treated with contempt; and Europe saw with horror the
speedy catastrophe of this infernal tragedy. With one
or two trifling exceptions, all the sentences were exe

cuted, and with such circumstances of wanton barbarity
as must stamp both the republic and its agents with
everlasting infamy. But history is full of retribution:
the time was at hand when the insulted, persecuted
Lutherans were to obtain the great object of their
hopes — to be transferred from the odious sway of these
despicable tyrants, to that of Prussia: nay, the las·
hour of the nation was about to sound; and whom woulc
its dying notes either surprise or grieve?*

Frederic Augustus died early in 1733. He had a few
virtues, but more vices. His reign was one continued
scene of disasters; many of which may be imputed to
himself, but more, perhaps, to the influence of circumstances.†

FREDERIC AUGUSTUS·II.‡
1733—1763.

AFTER passing a severe law against the Lutherans, who
were not only deprived of their civil rights, but insultingly forbidden to leave their odious country, the
diet of convocation resolved that a Piast only should be

---

* One cannot help feeling indignant at the way in which the atrocities of
Thorn are noticed by the modern historians of Poland.

† Voltaire, Histoire de Charles XII. Parthenay, Histoire de Pologne
sous Auguste II., tom. i. et ii. Proyart, Histoire de Stanislas I. Roi de
Pologne, tom. i. Rulhière, Histoire de l'Anarchie de Pologne, i. 65—140.
Malte-Brun, Tableau de Pologne (as enlarged by Chodako), tom. i. *passim*.
Zielinski, ii. 312—342.

It may be doubted how far reference to Voltaire's work is justifiable. It
is a perfect romance. "Mons. de Voltaire," says the second of the authorities just quoted, " avait fait un poëme en vers sur les guerres civiles de
France arrivées du temps d'Henri IV. Il a été charmé d'en faire un en prose
sur les guerres du roi de Suède."—" Il ne s'est point embarrassé d'éplucher
beaucoup son sujet. Il l'a pris en gros, l'a effleuré, et assaisonnant le tout
de cette rapidité de style et d'images qui attache le lecteur, il ne s'est guères
embarrassé si les descriptions des villes, des sièges, et de batailles, soient
vraies."—" Tout l'ouvrage de monsieur de Voltaire est plein de négligences
qui déshonoreroient une histoire, mais que l'on excuse dans *un poëme.*" The
celebrated Swedish senator who spoke of the book with most sovereign contempt was wrong, because " il ne considéroit son livre que comme une histoire, au lieu qu'à le regarder comme un poëme, il n'auroit pu lui refuser des
éloges." All this is true. When Voltaire presented his work to Stanislas,
ex-king of Poland, who had retired to France, " il se promettoit des com-
plimens flatteurs; il ne reçut que des reproches humilians. Le roi lui de-
manda de quel front il osoit présenter à un témoin, et à un acteur, un livre
qui outrageoit la vérité en mille manières."—*Lettre du Père Louis de Poix
à l'Abbé Proyart.* It is time that this arch-impostor—the greatest that
ever disgraced the literature of any country—should be unmasked.

‡ Usually termed *Augustus III.*

elected. This exclusion of foreign candidates was intended to open the way for the second elevation of
Stanislas, now father-in-law of Louis XV., who, in
his peaceful court of Lorraine, was too philosophic to
be tempted by ambition. Overcome, however, by the
French court, and by the pressing entreaties of his former subjects, he reluctantly proceeded to Warsaw, to
support by his presence the efforts of his friends. He
was received with acclamation, and in the diet of election sixty thousand voices declared him king of Poland.

But the republic had ceased to control her own destinies; her independence had vanished, and she was no
longer allowed either to choose her own rulers or to
take any other important step without the concurrence
of her neighbours. Both Austria and Muscovy had
resolved to resist the pretensions of Stanislas, and to
enforce the election of a rival candidate, Frederic
Augustus, elector of Saxony, son of the late king. The
grounds of this arbitrary interference on the part of
either power would be vainly sought in the recognised
principles of international law. The treaties formerly
in force between the crowns of Poland and Hungary
afforded a pretext to the Austrian emperor, as king of
the latter country, to watch over the internal peace of the
republic; but the absurdity of such a plea will appear
gross enough, when we consider that neither of the
powers had ever dreamed of mutual interference in
circumstances purely internal, but of mutual aid only
against foreign aggressions; and that even if such an
extraordinary agreement had ever existed, it must long
since have fallen into oblivion, with the treaties which
involved it. The pretensions of Muscovy were still
more preposterous; since the treaty between Frederic
Augustus and the tsar, in 1717 — the basis on which
these pretensions were founded — regarded only the evacuation of the Polish territory by the Saxon troops under
the auspices of Peter, who, as the friend alike of the
republic and her king, was permitted on this occasion to
interpose his good offices between them. It must not,

indeed, be concealed, that the interference of Muscovy
had been demanded by the bishop of Cracow and the
palatine of Sandomir, as the heads of a party which refused to acknowledge Stanislas, and which had even
taken up arms against the adherents of that prince;
yet, to render such interference legitimate, it should
have been demanded by the majority of the nation in
diet assembled, not by a faction after the election had
been legally made. But power does not often condescend to reason with weakness. An army of Muscovites
arrived in the neighbourhood of Warsaw; and at the
village of Kamien, in a wretched inn in the depths of
a forest, the party of nobles opposed to the French interest, proclaimed Frederic Augustus king of Poland.
On the 9th of November the elector left Saxony. At
Tarnowitz, on the Silesian frontier, he swore to the
pacta conventa, and entered triumphant into Cracow,
where he and his queen were solemnly crowned. The
Muscovite troops pursued the fugitive Stanislas to Dantzic, where that prince hoped to make a stand until the
arrival of the promised succours from France. Though
aid arrived from that country, it was too slender to avail
him. The bravery of the inhabitants, however, enabled
him to withstand a vigorous siege of five months : when
the city was compelled to capitulate, he stole from the
place, and, in disguise, reached the Prussian territories
after many narrow escapes.*

After receiving the oaths of the Dantzickers, and assisting at the diet of pacification — the only diet which,
during his reign, was not dissolved by the veto — Frederic Augustus appeared to think he had done enough
for his new subjects, and abandoned himself entirely to
his favourite occupations of smoking or hunting. To
business of every description he had a mortal aversion :
the government of his two states he abandoned to his
minister count Bruhl. The minister, indeed, strove to
resemble him in idle pomp and dissipation, and by that
means obtained unbounded ascendancy over him; an

* See note A.

ascendancy, however, which was rather felt than seen, and which he who exercised it had art enough to conceal. The king had not the capacity, or would not be at the pains, to learn the Polish language; another source of discontent to the people. But the forests of Saxony were more favourable to the royal sports than those of Poland; Saxony, therefore, had more of the royal presence. Wherever was the king, there also was Bruhl. Both, we are told, would spend whole mornings together without uttering a word: indeed, the respect paid by the minister was too servile to permit him the liberty of speech unasked; all his ambition was to answer, in the fewest possible words, the solitary laconic demands of his master. As the latter paced his apartments or his gardens with his never-failing attendant, a pipe, he would sometimes let his half-open eyes carelessly fall on his minister, and would ask — "Bruhl, have I any money?" — "Yes, sire," was the constant reply. But to satisfy the expensive whims of the king, he was obliged to employ some unpopular if not dangerous expedients. The bank of Saxony had more notes than bullion; and in Poland all offices, all benefices, were sold to the highest bidder. The magnificence of the servant was equal to that of the master. If we may believe a contemporary writer *, Lucullus himself, the object of astonishment to the Romans, who on one occasion lent five thousand of his dresses for a public spectacle, would have appeared miserably poor to this Saxon minister. "Were it not for my profusion," said Bruhl, "the king would leave me destitute of even necessaries." The pride of the monarch might indeed be gratified by the service of so pompous a menial; but he himself was but the menial of the tsar, who ruled at Warsaw, not indeed so despotically, but certainly with as much effect, as at St. Petersburg.

Nothing can more clearly prove this absolute depend-

* Rulhière, Histoire de l'Anarchie de Pologne, l. 178. This is an excellent work, but not wholly free from the defects of the French school. Its continual aim at effect, and its consequent exaggerations, sometimes render it an unsafe guide.

ence of the republic on the northern empire, than the
fact, that though Frederic Augustus, in virtue of his
rights over Courland, permitted his third son, Charles,
whom the states of that duchy had ventured to elect for
their sovereign, to accept the precarious dignity, his
timidity was absolutely ludicrous; nor would he grant
the permission, until assured that the choice would be
agreeable to the empress Elizabeth. But Peter III.,
the successor of that princess, refused to acknowledge
duke Charles, who, in fear of the consequences, precipitately fled from Courland to await the course of
events. In his contempt for the republic, the new tsar
would not even condescend to acquaint Frederic Augustus with his accession. So completely did he consider Poland within his grasp, and in reality a province
of his empire, however his policy might induce him to
permit a little longer the show of national independence,
that, in a treaty with the Prussian monarch, he insisted
on three great objects: 1. The election of a Piast, and
consequently a creature of his own, after the death of
Augustus; 2. The protection of the dissidents against
the declared will of the diet; and, 3. The possession of
Courland as a fief of the imperial crown. St. Petersburg, in short, was the great focus where the rays of
Polish intrigue were concentrated, and where the more
ambitious natives resorted to obtain, by flattering the
imperial confidants, the dignities of the republic. Every
intimation, however slight, from the northern metropo-
lis, was an imperious obligation on the feeble king and
his servile minister; and not on them alone, but on
the great body of the nobles, who had lost all sense of
the national dishonour, and who transferred their homage from Warsaw to St. Petersburg without shame or
remorse. Among these unprincipled Poles none was
more conspicuous than count Stanislas Poniatowski, who,
in the reign of Elizabeth, formed a criminal intrigue
with the grand duchess Catherine; and who, by favour
of the connection, was taught to regard the Polish crown
as his own. The father of this adventurer had been

the confidant of Charles XII. in Turkey, and had been
singularly favoured by that monarch. "Charles," wrote
the archduchess to the old count, "knew how to distinguish your merit: I also can distinguish that of your
son, whom I may one day raise, perhaps, above even
Charles himself." The confidants of the two lovers had
little doubt that, when the grand duchess was seated on
the imperial throne, she would contrive to set aside her
husband, and bestow both her hand and sceptre on one
whom she had resolved to place over the republic. Finally, the Muscovite armies traversed the kingdom,
whether to oppose the Germans or the Turks, or to
support the plots of their avowed adherents, with perfect impunity, and in contempt of the humble supplications of court and diet.

It must not, indeed, be concealed, that the republic
had a few true sons, who endeavoured to rouse the nation to a sense of its humiliation, and to arm it against
the interference of its neighbours. At the head of these
was Branicki, grand general of the crown, who belonged
to no faction, and who aimed only at the redemption
of his country. But his efforts could avail little against
those of two rival factions, whose dissensions were espoused by the great body of Polish nobles. The court,
aided by the Radzivils and the Potockis, laboured to
preserve the ancient privileges of the republic, — in other
words, the abuses which had brought that republic to
its present deplorable state; and the Czartorinskis to
establish an hereditary monarchy, the trunk of which
should be, not Frederic Augustus, but their kinsman the
young count Poniatowski. The cause of the latter was
naturally more acceptable at the court of St. Petersburg,
especially after the elevation of Catherine; and the
Muscovite generals were ordered to protect it, in opposition to the king, and, if need were, to the whole
nation.

Catherine II. was no less decisive with respect to
Courland. She ordered 15,000 of her troops to take

possession of the duchy in favour of Biron, who had been exiled by Peter and recalled by her. At a meeting of the senate, indeed, over which the feeble king presided, some members had the boldness to dispute the rights of Biron, and to insist on the restoration of Charles; and, what is still stranger, they prevailed on a majority to adopt the same sentiments. They even resolved to cite the Muscovite governor before the tribunal of their king. But this was no more than the empty menace of cowards, who hoped to obtain by blustering what they dared not attempt by open force. A thundering declaration of the tsarina, and the movement of a few Muscovite troops towards the frontiers, so appalled them that they sought refuge in the obscurity of their sylvan abodes; and the king, with his minister Bruhl, precipitately abandoned Poland, never to return. With no less speed did duke Charles, who had stood a six months' siege by the Muscovite troops, follow that exemplary pair to Dresden. It is true, indeed, that the empress arrested the march of her troops in Lithuania; that she found cause to fear the determined opposition of the lesser nobles; and that she resolved to wait for the king's death before she proceeded to declare the throne vacant, and secure the elevation of her former lover: but her purpose was immutable; and if her moderation or policy induced her to delay its execution, she knew her power too well to distrust its eventual accomplishment. However, " to make assurance doubly sure," she sought the alliance of the Prussian king, with whom she publicly arranged a portion of the policy that was afterwards adopted in regard to this doomed nation.

Nothing could be more mortifying to the Czartorinskis than this stroke of policy on the part of the tsarina. They had long planned the deposition of Frederic Augustus, and the forcible elevation of their kinsman; and their vexation knew no bounds at the delay thus opposed to their ambitious impatience. The young count, in particular, who had traitorously boasted that the last hour of the king was come; that Poland was about to enter on new destinies, behaved like a madman on the occasion, but he became more tractable on learning the indisposition of Frederic Augustus. The death of that prince restored him to perfect equanimity.

Though, under Frederic Augustus, Poland entered on no foreign war, his reign was the most disastrous in her annals. While the Muscovite and Prussian armies traversed her plains at pleasure, and extorted whatever they pleased; while one faction openly opposed another, not merely in the diet but on the field; while every national assembly was immediately dissolved by the veto; the laws could not be expected to exercise much authority. They were, in fact, utterly disregarded; the tribunals were derided, or forcibly overturned; and brute force prevailed on every side. The miserable peasants vainly besought the protection of their lords, who were either powerless, or indifferent to their complaints: while thousands expired of hunger, a far greater number sought to relieve their necessities by open depredations. Bands of robbers, less formidable only than the kindred masses congregated under the name of soldiers, infested the country in every direction. Famine aided the devastations of both: the population, no less than the wealth of the kingdom, decreased with frightful rapidity.*

INTERREGNUM. — STANISLAS AUGUSTUS.

1763—1795.

Though Catherine had long determined on the election of her former lover, she was at first prudent enough

---

* Rulhière, liv. 4. et 5. tom. i. et ii. Proyart, i. *passim.* Malte-Brun, by Chodzko, tom. ii. 89—92. Zielinski, ii. 342—364. Such is the meagreness of this last writer, that his work appears to be a hasty compilation of notes on which it was intended afterwards to dilate. Yet of this work the celebrated M. de Jouy writes thus to the author :—" Vous avez, monsieur, élevé un monument durable à la gloire de votre patrie, et à la vôtre, dans un ouvrage où vous avez rempli toutes les conditions imposées à l'historien digne de ce nom." This novelist should mind the proverb, "Ne sutor," &c.

to employ address in preference to open force. She had no wish, by her example, to procure the armed interference of Austria; a power which could not regard without alarm the growing preponderance of her empire; and the great Frederic might possibly be no less disposed to preserve Poland independent, as a barrier against her progressive encroachments westward. Her ambassador at Warsaw had orders to repeat her resolution to defend the integrity of the republic; but he was at the same time instructed to say, that a Piast only would be agreeable to his sovereign. Who that Piast was, there was no difficulty in surmising; but the count, from his unprincipled manœuvres during the late reign, and still more, perhaps, from the comparative baseness of his extraction, was odious to the whole nation.*   Here was another obstacle, which required alike great art and unflinching firmness to remove. Entreaties were first to be tried, then remonstrances, next menaces, but actual force only when other means should fail.

In the dietines assembled in each palatinate, to choose the members for the diet of convocation, and to draw up such laws, regulations, and improvements, as it was intended to propose in the general diet, the necessity of a radical change in the constitution was very generally expressed. But if the members agreed in this self-evident proposition, they differed widely in every other matter. While one party inclined to the establishment of an hereditary monarchy, and the abolition of the veto, another contended for the formation of a government purely aristocratical; a third, with equal zeal, insisted that the constitution should only be slightly modified, to meet the wants of a new and improved society. All dispute, however, was soon cut short by

---

* When one of her emissaries told Catherine that the Poles were indignant at the bare proposal of having a king whose grandfather had been a steward on a small estate of the Sapiehas, she blushed for a moment to think that one so base had been her lover; but the news only confirmed her purpose. " Were he a steward himself," she replied, " I wish him to become a king; and a king he shall be!"

the united declaration of the Prussian and Muscovite ambassadors, to the effect that their sovereigns would not allow any change at all in the existing system. The Poles now *felt* that they were slaves.

To a Piast—in other words, a mean dependant on the tsarina — Austria opposed the young elector of Saxony, son of the late king. A great number of nobles, on the promise that the freedom of election should be guaranteed by the forces of the empire, and the Muscovites taught to respect the republic, espoused the interests of this candidate ; and probably his death was the only event which averted from the country the scourge of war. It was an event so favourable to the views of Muscovy, that her triumph was secure. So convinced of this was the sagacious Frederic, that he hastened to confirm Catherine in her design, which he offered to support with all his power ; and he thereby acquired all the advantages he expected,—a confirmation of the favourable treaty he had before made with Peter III. Poniatowski received the riband of the black eagle, which he regarded as an earnest of his approaching elevation.

As the period appointed for opening the diet of convocation drew near, the two allied powers took measures to secure their common object. 40,000 Prussians were stationed on the Silesian frontier ; and 10,000 Muscovites, regardless alike of decency and justice, and actuated by no other principle than a consciousness of their own strength, quickly occupied the positions round Warsaw. Their creatures, the Czartorinskis, were no less active in distributing money with amazing prodigality, and in promising places, pensions, and benefices, to all who promoted the success of their kinsman. But on some neither fear nor seduction had any influence : twenty-two senators and forty-five deputies, at the head of whom were the grand hetman and Mokronowski, a Pole zealous for his country's cause, signed a declaration to the effect that the diet of convocation could not be held so long as foreign troops were present. On the 7th of

May, however, it was opened, but under circumstances
deeply humiliating to the nation. The Muscovite
troops were posted in the squares, and at the ends of
the streets leading to the place of deliberation ; while the
armed adherents of the Czartorinskis, some thousands in
number, had the audacity to occupy not only the ave-
nues to the house, but the halls of the senators and the
deputies. Of the fifty senators then in Warsaw, only
eight proceeded to the diet, which was to be opened by
the aged count Malachowski, marshal on the occasion.
Instead of raising his staff—the signal for the commencement of proceedings — this intrepid man resolutely
held it downwards, while his no less courageous companion, Mokronowski, conjured him, in the name of the
members who had signed the declaration, not to elevate
it at all so long as the Muscovites controlled the free
exercise of deliberation. As the speaker concluded by his
veto, a multitude of soldiers, with drawn sabres, rushed
towards him. For a moment the tumult was hushed,
when the marshal of the diet declared his intention
of departing with the symbol of his office. Immediately
a hundred armed creatures of the Czartorinskis exclaimed, in a menacing tone, " Raise your staff! "—
" No," cried Mokronowski, in one still louder; " do
no such thing !" Again the soldiers endeavoured to
pierce through the crowd of deputies, to lay their victim
low, while several voices exclaimed, " Mokronowski,
retract your veto ; we are no longer masters ; you are
rushing on certain death !"—" Be it so !" replied he,
as he folded his arms in expectation of the catastrophe ;
" I will die free !" The elevation of his purpose was
read in the energy of his look, and could not but strike
a deep awe into the assailants, who began to hesitate in
their design ; especially when they reflected that their
bloody deed must bring inevitable disgrace on their
cause, and, perhaps, rouse all Europe against them.
As the marshal refused to erect his staff, he was called
on to resign it into other hands. " Never ! " replied
this noble octogenarian : " you may cut off my hand, or

you may take my life; but as I am a marshal elected
by a free people, so by a free people only can I be deposed. I wish to leave the place!" He was surrounded on every side by ferocious soldiers and deputies
resolved to prevent his egress. Seeing him thus violently detained, Mokronowski exclaimed, "Gentlemen,
if a victim is wanted, behold me; but respect age and
virtue!" At the same moment, the younger of
these heroic patriots forcibly opened a way for the
marshal, whom he succeeded in conducting to the
gate. The undaunted deportment of both seemed to
have made its due impression on the members, who
opposed no further obstacle to their departure. As they
passed through the streets, however, they were exposed
to new dangers; and there is little doubt that Mokronowski would have been sacrificed, had not a man, whose
name history conceals, closely followed his heels, ex-
claiming at every step, " Make way for general Ga-
domski!"

But this admirable display of firmness led to no corresponding result. Though 200 members of the diet
had resolved to have no share in this lawless force, and
left Warsaw for their respective habitations, those who
remained—the creatures of Muscovy and the Czartorinskis, scarcely eighty in number—were but the more
encouraged to betray the liberties of their country.
Another marshal was speedily elected, and measures
passed in this illegal assembly, alike injurious to freedom and tranquillity. The dissidents were deprived of
the few remaining rights left them by former persecutors; the Prussians were also forbidden to assemble at
the diets, otherwise than by deputies — and these to be
few in number. (On its union with the crown, Prussia
had been guaranteed in its privileges of sending as
many nobles to the national assemblies as might be willing to attend.) No folly, surely, ever equalled that of
men, who, in such a desperate situation, laboured to
alienate an important portion of the people from the
government, at a time when the most perfect harmony

and the closest union were required to avert the threatened destruction of the republic. In some other things they exhibited a little common sense. They abolished the veto, making the success of the measures proposed depend on the majority, not on the unanimity, of suffrages; and they recognised in the elector or Brandenburg the long-disputed title of the king of Prussia.* Finally, the diet of election opened August 27.; and on the 7th of the following month, Stanislas Augustus Poniatowski was declared king of Poland.

The first acts of Stanislas were almost sufficient to efface the shame of his elevation. Not only was the abolition of the veto confirmed, and the arbitrary powers of the grand marshals and hetmans greatly restrained; but enlightened regulations were introduced into the commerce of the country and the finances of the state; the arts and sciences were encouraged, especially such as related to war. The dissidents, however, could not obtain the rights which they claimed, notwithstanding the representations of the Muscovite ambassador, whose sovereign was ever on the alert to protect the discontented and to urge their confederations. But the tsarina was in no disposition to see her imperial will thwarted; her attachment to the king had long been weakened by new favourites; and she could not behold, without anxiety, the changes introduced into the constitution of the Poles, — changes which, she was sagacious enough to foresee, must, if permitted to take effect, entirely frustrate her views on the republic. Her ambassador declared to the diet, that these innovations must be abandoned, and the ancient usages restored. The assembly was compelled to give way, especially as numerous confederations were formed by the small nobles, no doubt in the pay of Catherine, for the same object. The conviction felt by the humblest member of the equestrian order, that *he* by his single protest could

---

* They also recognised the sovereign of Muscovy as " empress of all the Russias," thereby supporting the claim of the tsarina to the dominion over Red Russia, and the other Russian provinces possessed by Poland.

arrest the whole machine of government, was a privilege too gratifying to self-love to be abandoned without reluctance. Hence Muscovy had little difficulty in nullifying measures, which, however advantageous, and even necessary to the republic, were less prized by the majority of the nobles than their own monstrous immunities.

It must not, however, be supposed that this dictatorial interference of Muscovy was admitted without opposition. In the diet of 1767-8, it was courageously denounced by several senators, especially by two bishops and two temporal barons : but the fate of these men was intended to deter all others from following the example : they were arrested by night, and conveyed into the heart of Muscovy. Liberty of discussion had long been forbidden by the haughty foreigners ; but as mere menaces had produced little effect, to the astonishment of all Europe, unblushing violence, and that too of the most odious description, was hereafter to be employed. It was now evident that nothing less than the entire subjugation of Poland, than its reduction to a province of the empire, was resolved. The forcible removal of these heroic champions of independence was to secure the triumph of the ancient anarchy.

But however appalling the fate of these men, it had not the effect designed by its framers : it roused the patriotic and the bold to a more determined and effectual opposition. A confederation of a few influential nobles was formed at Bar, a little town in Podolia, of which the avowed object was to free the country from foreign influence, and to dethrone the poor creature who so dishonoured the nation. At the same time the Turks declared war on the tsarina. A memorable struggle ensued, which during four years desolated the fairest provinces of the republic. But unassisted patriotism, however determined, could do little with the veteran armies of Russia : the small bands of the natives were annihilated one by one. An attempt of the confederates to carry off the king by violence did no

good to their cause. Finally, the Turks were unsuccessful, the Muscovites every where triumphant; circumstances which led to a result hitherto unprecedented in
history, — the partition of the republic by the three
neighbouring powers.

It is not difficult to fix the period when this abomi-
nable project was first entertained, or with what power
it originated. Notwithstanding the cautious language
of the king of Prussia in his Memoirs, there is reason
enough for inferring that *he* was its author, and that the
subject was first introduced to Catherine, in 1770, by his
brother prince Henry. More than twelve months, however, elapsed before the two potentates finally arranged
the limits of their respective pretensions; and although
they agreed, without difficulty, on guaranteeing each
other's claims, would Austria calmly witness the usurpation? If the Poles themselves were not easy to reduce,
what hope of their subjugation would remain, should
they be supported by the troops of the empire? — that
power must be permitted to share the spoil. Unscrupulous, however, as Catherine often was, she refused
to be the first to mention such a project to the court
of Vienna. Frederic had less shame. After some he-
sitation, the Austrian court acceded to the alliance.
The treaty of partition was signed at St. Petersburg,
August 5. 1772.

By this treaty Prussia acquired the palatinates of Malborg, Pomerania, and Warmia, Culm, except Dantzic
and Thorn, and a part of Great Poland. Austria had
Red Russia, or Galicia, with a part of Podolia, Sendomir,
and Cracow. Muscovy had Polotsk, Witepsk, Micislaf,
and Polish Livonia.

It must not be supposed that these monstrous usurpations were made without some show of justice. Both
Austria and Prussia published elaborate expositions of
their claims on the countries invaded; claims which, as
they would require a volume to state and confute, can have
no place in the present compendium.* All that can be

* For the exposure of these pretended claims, the curious reader may consult " Les Droits des trois Puissances Alliées sur les Provinces de la Répub-

here observed on the subject is, that Austria claimed in virtue of rights said to have been once possessed by the Hungarian crown, and Prussia in virtue of the con‑ nection between the electors of Brandenburg and the dukes of Pomerania. In neither case have these claims either justice or reason to support them; but if they had both — if their force were as convincing as their weakness — they had been annulled by subsequent treaties. If, in contempt of the whole course of diplomatic in‑ tercourse between nations, claims drawn from the depths of antiquity are to be advanced, what throne would be safe? England might assert her right to Normandy with far greater appearance of reason than either of the powers in question to the countries they usurped. As to Muscovy, she had no treaties to mystify; and she claimed the vast provinces on which she seized in con‑ sideration of sacrifices pretended to have been made, and expense to which she alleged herself to have been put, in so long endeavouring to serve her ally, in pre‑ serving the republic from foreign invasion, and from utter destruction by the native confederations. A claim at once so ludicrous and so impudent could be advanced only by a power conscious of its own overbearing might.

The powers thus allied in iniquity were not satisfied with the success of their violence; they resolved to add insult, by forcing a diet to sanction the dismemberment of the country. The great body of the deputies, how‑ ever, refused to attend this diet of 1773; the few who did were chiefly creatures of Russia, the mercenary be‑ trayers of the national independence. But among these few, nine or ten showed considerable intrepidity in de‑ fence of their privileges; none so much as Thaddeus Reyten, deputy of Nowogrodek, who, from incorruptible,

lique de Pologne, avec l'Exposition de l'Insuffisance et de la Nullité de leurs Droits," 2 vols. 8vo.; and Malte‑Brun, "Tableau de Pologne," by Chodzko, tom. i. *passim.* The mere English reader will find the said claims suffici‑ ently exposed in "Letters concerning the Present State of Poland,"(London, 8vo. 1773,) which proves from historic evidence, and from the treaties pre‑ served in Dumont (Corps Diplomatique), that the manifestos published by the usurping powers are a tissue of sophistry, of perverted facts, of state‑ ments at variance with the whole course of history, and that they are fur‑ ther disgraced by artful omissions.

daring integrity has been surnamed *the Polish Cato*. As *unanimity* could not be expected, wherever one true patriot was to be found, the foreigners laboured to change the *diet* into a *confederation*, where the great question might be decided by a majority of votes. To prevent this was the great end of the patriots : each party endeavoured to produce the election of a marshal from among themselves; since the powers with which that officer was invested, made his support or opposition no slight object. Corrupted as were a great number of the members, they could not tamely see one Poninski, a creature of Russia, forced on them ; and they exclaimed that Reyten should be their marshal. Poninski immediately adjourned the diet to the following day, and retired into the king's apartments. Reyten also, after exhorting his countrymen to firmness, declared the sitting adjourned. Thus passed the first day. Throughout the night, the gold of the three ambassadors was lavishly distributed, and more traitors made. The following day both marshals resorted to the hall of assembly ; but as neither would give way, nothing was done, and the sitting was again adjourned. Seeing no prospect of unanimity, Poninski drew up the act of confederation at his own hotel, and sent it to Stanislas to be signed. The king replied that he could not legally sign it without the consent of his ministers and senators. The menaces of the ambassadors, however, soon compelled the weak creature to accede to the confederation ; but that illegal body was debarred from the hall of deliberations by the intrepid Reyten, who, with four companions, persisted in keeping possession of this sanctuary until he saw the confederation held in the open air. As longer opposition, where the very shadow of law was disregarded, would be useless, he returned to his own residence, with the melancholy consolation of reflecting that he was almost the only one who had withstood the torrent of intimidation or corruption.* After his de-

* This great patriot became soon afterwards insane, the effects of his country's dishonour. His death was singular. In a paroxysm of his disorder he broke a wine glass with his teeth, and swallowed the pieces.

parture the partition treaty was ratified, and a permanent council was established, which, under the influence
of the Russian ambassador, governed king and republic.

During the few following years, Poland presented the
spectacle of a country exhausted alike by its own dissensions and the arms of its enemies.   The calm was
unusual, and would have been a blessing could any
salutary laws have been adopted by the diets.   Many
such, indeed, were proposed, the most signal of which
was the emancipation of the serfs ; but the very proposition was received with such indignation by the selfish
nobles, that Russian gold was not wanted to defeat the
other measures with which it was accompanied, — the
suppression of the veto, and the establishment of an
hereditary monarchy.   The enlightened Zamoyski, who
had drawn up a code of laws which involved this obnoxious provision, was near falling a sacrifice to his
patriotic zeal.

But what no consideration of justice or policy could
effect, was at length brought about by the example of
the French.   In the memorable diet which opened in
1788, and which, like the French constitutional assembly, declared itself permanent, a new constitution was
promulgated, was solemnly sanctioned by king and nobles, and was enthusiastically received by the whole
nation.   It reformed the vices of the old constitution —
offered a new existence to the burghers and peasants —
destroyed all confederations, with the fatal veto, and
declared the throne hereditary in the house of Saxony.
It had, however, two great faults ; it limited the royal
authority, so as to make the king a mere cipher * ; and
it came too late to save the nation.   The elector of
Saxony refused to accept the crown, unless the royal

* We need not be surprised that such enemies to thrones as Tom Paine
and Volney, or that such hot-headed zealots for popular immunities as
Fox, should have praised the Polish constitution of May 3. (1791); but
the rhetorical praises of Burke *must* surprise us.   Surely that celebrated
man could not have read the articles.   If the reader will be at the pains to
consult them, (they are to be found in Oginski, "Mémoires sur la Pologne
et les Polonnais, depuis 1788 jusqu'à la fin de 1815," tom. L p 130.) he will
perceive that they are inconsistent with the due powers of the crown, so
essential not merely to the welfare, but to the existence, of a nation.

prerogatives were amplified; and Catherine resolved to destroy both it and the republic. The king of Prussia, indeed, announced his entire satisfaction with the wholesome changes which had been introduced; and pretended that he had nothing so much at heart as the welfare of the nation, and the preservation of a good understanding with it: but with his usual contempt of oaths, with his wonted duplicity and perfidy, he renewed his alliance with the tsarina, the basis of which was a second partition of the republic!

The first object of Catherine was to form the leading discontented Poles into a confederation to destroy the new constitution, and to call in her assistance to reestablish the ancient laws. The confederation of Targowitz struck the nation with terror, but inspired the bold with more ardour. Resistance was unanimously decreed, and the king was invested with dictatorial powers for the national defence. He even promised to take the field in person, and triumph or fall with his people. Yet, in August 1792, a very few weeks after this ebullition of patriotism, he acceded to the infamous confederation; ordered his armies to retreat, and to leave the country open to the domination of the Russian troops. His example constrained all who had property to lose; since all preferred the enjoyment of their substance under arbitrary government, to independence with poverty or exile. The Russian troops entered the kingdom, and restored the ancient chains; the perfidious Prussian followed the example, and began his second career of spoliation by the reduction of Dantzic. A diet was assembled at Grodno; but none were admitted as members except such as had opposed the constitution of 1791; none, in fact, but the slaves of the tsarina. The feeble Stanislas was compelled to attend it. It was converted into a diet of confederation, the better to attain the ends for which it was convoked: yet some of the members were intrepid enough to protest against the meditated encroachments on the territories of the republic; nor did they desist until several were arrested, and the remainder threatened with Siberia. The Russian troops which had hitherto occupied the approaches to the hall of assembly, and had exercised a strict surveillance over every suspected person, were now introduced into this sanctuary of the laws. Another treaty of partition was violently signed, by which Prussia acquired the remainder of Great and a part of Little Poland; and the Russian boundary was advanced to the centre of Lithuania and Volhynia. The territory of the republic was now reduced to little more than four thousand square miles; and its army, by the menaces of the tsarina, to 15,000 men. The previous manifestos of the two powers (Austria had nothing to do with this second iniquity) on the forcible occupation by their troops of the provinces to be dismembered, are not worth attention. Their attempts to justify the violence were too absurd to be received; they exhibit nothing but insulting unmitigated violence.

No one acquainted with the warlike character of the Poles, and their fierce spirit of independence, could suppose that such unprincipled aggressions would be tamely borne by the great bulk of the nation. An insurrection was organised; and Thaddeus Kosciusko was placed at the head of the native army. The general was every way worthy of the choice; combining great firmness of purpose with moderation of manner, a cool judgment with the most ardent bravery, he devoted himself heart and hand to the redemption of his beloved country. Cracow and Warsaw caught the flame of patriotism, and opened their gates to him. Wilna, with all the grand duchy, rose in the same cause. Detached bands of the Russians were exterminated; and even an advantage gained over them in two considerable engagements. Finally, Great Poland adhered to the national cause; and an army of Prussians, under the king in person, was obliged to raise the siege of Warsaw, which he had hastened to invest. But here was the term of Kosciusko's success. The inhabitants of Warsaw, by imitating the bloody scenes of Paris, by slaughtering, without the appearance of trial, such as they merely suspected unfavourable to *Jacobinism*, and the similar atrocities committed in Wilna and other places, convinced the sounder portion of the Poles, that the hellish doctrines of the French revolution had made fearful progress among their countrymen. They, and the whole body of the clergy, stood aloof from the insurgents; especially when they found that the latter had sent deputies to the national convention of Paris, and had made proposals of *fraternising* with the French people. Besides, the insurgent armies had no organisation, no discipline, no supplies; and the state had no head except a tribunal of terror. (As for Stanislas, though he remained in Warsaw, no one thought of him. Had success attended the popular cause, his head would probably have fallen, notwithstanding the moderation of the general in chief, who, though a republican, exerted himself ably to prevent the excesses of the mob.*) Such a case, aided by such narrow means, could not be expected to succeed. Wilna was retaken; Lithuania again subjected; Suwaroff arrived from the Ukraine, where he had obtained a high reputation in the Turkish war, and commenced his resistless career. Two decisive victories, in the latter of which the Polish Generalissimo, the only hope of his country, was taken prisoner, enabled him to march on the capital (Cracow had fallen some weeks before). The last remains of the national army were concentrated at Praga, on the right bank of the Vistula, immediately opposite to Warsaw; but in a few minutes they were broken by the furious charges of the Russian general, who sullied his reputation by a frightful carnage. The fate of Poland was now decided; Warsaw capitulated, and the remaining portion of the territory was divided among the three invading powers. Austria had Cracow, with the country between

---

* The lamentations of this chief to Oginski on the bloody scenes which had been committed in the capital before his eyes, proves how impossible it is for the best-intentioned men to prevent popular excesses. Man, alas! is to be governed only by fear.

the Pilitsa, the Vistula, and the Bug.   Prussia had the
capital, with the territory as far as the Niemen.   The
lion's share, as usual, fell to Russia.   As to the feeble
despicable Stanislas, his lot was such as had long been
foreseen ; but such as, with an infatuated confidence in
the *magnanimity* of the empress, he would never con-
template as possible, until it was actually consummated.
Being ordered to resign a dignity which he had so un-
worthily filled, he retired to Grodno ; and on the death
of Catherine, in 1796, to St. Petersburg, where he ended
his days in 1798.

The republic was thus erased from the list of nations
after an existence of near ten centuries.   Perhaps no
people on earth have shown so much personal bravery
as the Poles : their history is full of wonderful victories.   But how little the most chivalrous valour, or the
most splended military successes, could avail with such
a vicious frame of society, has been but too well seen.
That a country without government (for Poland had
none, properly so called, after the extinction of the
Jagellos), without finances, without army, and depending
for its existence year after year on tumultuous levies,
ill disciplined, ill armed, and worse paid, should so long
have preserved its independence,—in defiance, too, of the
powerful nations around, and with a great portion of
its own inhabitants, whom ages of tyranny had exasperated, hostile to its success,—is the most astonishing fact
in all history.   What valour must that have been, which
could enable one hundred thousand men to trample on a
whole nation naturally prone to revolt, and bid defiance
to Europe and Asia, to Christian and Mussulman, both
ever ready to invade the republic !   But valour, though
almost super-human, could not enforce obedience to the
laws ; it could not preserve domestic tranquillity ; it
could not restrain the violence of petty feuds and intestine commotions ; it could not preserve the proud
nobles from unbounded dissipation, nor, consequently,
from temptation to corruption, from receiving bribes
to repair their shattered fortunes ; it could not prevent

the powers which lavished this means of corruptions from interference in the affairs of the kingdom; it could not dissolve the union of these powers with the discontented parties at home; it could not inspire the slow-moving machine of government with vigour, when the humblest partisan, corrupted by foreign money, could arrest it with a word; it could not avert the entrance of foreign armies to support the factious and rebellious; it could not, while divided in itself, uphold the national independence against the combined effects of foreign and domestic treason; finally, it could not effect impossibilities, nor, therefore, for ever turn aside the destroying sword which had so long impended over it.[*]

CHAP. III.

POLAND PARTIALLY RESTORED.

1796—1831.

GRAND DUCHY OF WARSAW.—KINGDOM OF POLAND. — REPUBLIC OF CRACOW.

THE extinction of the Polish republic afforded ample scope for the exercise of political declamation: the tribunes of France, the parliament of England, and the press of both countries, abounded with eloquent invectives against the perfidious violence of the partitioning powers; and a widely spread, if not deep, sympathy was called forth in favour of a people who, whatever might have been their errors, or even crimes, were entitled to admiration from their great deeds, and to pity from their fate. The troubled state of affairs, however, throughout

[*] Rulhiere, i. 2, 3, 4. Malte Brun, by Chodzko, xi. 93—134. Ferrand, "Histoire des Trois Démembremens de la Pologne, pour faire suite à l'Histoire de Rulhiere,"*passim.* Oginski, "Mémoires sur la Pologne et les Polonnais, depuis 1788 jusqu'à la fin de 1815," i. ii. Zielinski, ii. 364—391.

Europe did not permit any power to interfere in behalf of the oppressed. Every prince was too intent on securing his own preservation to dream of breaking a lance for another. Hence the impunity with which the three potentates proceeded to perfect their common wickedness; to repress the indignant efforts of the sufferers; and to fill their prisons with, not only those who had distinguished themselves during the recent struggle, but with such as either ventured to complain, or were even suspected of dissatisfaction at the new state of things. The inhabitants of the great towns, especially of the three most influential (Warsaw, Cracow, and Wilna), were rigorously disarmed, and formidable garrisons of foreign troops were every where ready to crush all attempts at insurrection.

But if the cry of vengeance was smothered where the conquerors were present, other countries were soon made to resound with it. If Turkey and Sweden, two powers equally alarmed at the aggrandisement of Russia, Austria, and Prussia, felt their own feebleness too sensibly to oppose it by arms, France and the countries which French influence pervaded, were ready to combine in any measure that might distract, the enemies of the revolution. To France and Italy, therefore, the eyes of the Poles were now turned for aid, both to recover their independence and to gratify their resistless feeling of revenge. A secret confederation was formed at Cracow, the members of which offered to the French directory to sacrifice their fortunes and lives at the first call of the republic. This was not a vain offer: hundreds of the warlike nobles continued, notwithstanding the strict surveillance observed by their new masters, to escape from their bondage, and proceed to Venice or to Paris. In pursuance of the compact made between their leader, Dombrowski, and the directory, Polish legions were formed in aid of the new Italian republics, and ready to act wherever the French government might require. Their pay and subsistence were to be furnished by the Italian states: that of Lombardy was the first to hire their services. They preserved their native uniform and arms, but assumed the revolutionary cockade; and their motto, of " *Gli uomini liberi sono fratelli*," showed how completely they harmonised with the fearful spirit which shook Europe to its centre. That both the directors and Bonaparte held out to them the prospect of their country's restoration, is well known; but their credulity must have been equal at least to their hopes, or they would never have placed the shadow of reliance on the promises of a people by whom they had been so often betrayed. Their martial prowess—confined chiefly to Italy—contributed greatly to the success of the republican cause. Their number amounted to some thousands, and their valour was unabated. But they were soon taught to distrust the fair professions of the republican hero. When anxious to preserve, by his influence, an entrance to the congress of Rastadt for a Polish representative, they were coolly answered, " that the hearts of all friends of liberty were for the brave Poles; but time and destiny alone could restore them as a nation." Hope seldom reasons well; if the time of regeneration was deferred, might it not arrive—perhaps at no distant period,—when a more favourable conjuncture of circumstances would render it impossible that the French government should refuse to urge their claims? So thought the Poles, who still continued under the banners of the republic.

The same unvaried picture of services performed, and of hopes deceived, is exhibited throughout the connexion of the Polish legions with France. Their adherence to a foreign cause,—for in no sense could it be called their own,—so stedfastly and devotedly maintained, can be explained only by the resistless passion of the Poles for military fame: to them the battle-field is as much a home as the deep to the Englishman. Though, during the absence of Bonaparte in Egypt, they were literally exterminated by the Austrians and Russians, they repaired their losses with astonishing promptitude: in 1801 they amounted to 15,000. Their blood flowed in vain: in every treaty which their valour had been so instrumental in winning, themselves and country were forgotten. However dishonourable this fact may render their ally and protector, their fate in this case is scarcely to be pitied: they were at all times the willing, unscrupulous instruments of the most unprincipled of governments. They hesitated at no breach of faith; they revolted at no atrocity: with them obedience to orders the most unjustifiable was a point of honour; and their movements were everywhere perceptible by the sanguinary traces left behind them. But, seeing the disappointment of their hopes, many of them, after the peace of Luneville (1801), bade adieu to the French service, and returned to their own country, where an amnesty had been recently proclaimed. A considerable number, indeed, remained: some entered into the service of the king of Etruria; others departed on the ill-starred expedition to St. Domingo; and the few who survived returned to their country after the formation of the grand duchy.*

While the Polish soldiers were thus exhibiting a useless valour in foreign climes, their countrymen at home must not be overlooked.

The condition of the inhabitants varied according to the characters of the sovereigns under whom they were placed. The aim of Prussia and Austria was to Germanise their respective portions, and gradually to obliterate every trace of nationality. Each, accordingly, introduced German laws and usages; the language of the public schools and of the public acts was German; Germans alone were intrusted with public employments. Russia pursued a more politic or a more generous policy: with the view, perhaps, of one day extending her Polish possessions, she strove to attach the inhabitants to

* Will the reader believe that the French bulletins, during the wars of Italy, Russia, &c. passed over in silence the valiant deeds of their Polish allies, and attributed the whole glory of success to their countrymen alone? Such, however, is the truth. The same mean, despicable policy was adopted with respect to the Italians: it has been sufficiently exposed by the authors of "Gli Italiani in Russia, Memorie d'un Ufiziale Italiano, per servire alla Storia della Russia, della Polonia, e della Italia nel 1812;" and of "La Storia delle Campagne e delle Assedj degli Italiani in Ispagna." A history —poorly written, but containing some interesting facts—of the Polish legions in Italy under the command of Dombrowski has been recently published by Chodzko, Paris, 2 tom. en 8vo.

her government. The preservation of the Lithuanian statutes,—the influence in the general administration possessed by the native marshals elected in the dietines of the nobles,—the publication of the acts of government in the native tongue,—and the admission of the people to the highest dignities,—rendered the condition of Russian Poland much less galling than that of the portion subjected to either of the two other powers. Since the accession of Alexander, especially, great encouragement had been given both to the great branches of national industry, and to the diffusion of education. An imperial ukase of April 4. 1803, had conferred extraordinary privileges on the university of Wilna; and in no case had the tsar neglected any opportunity of improving the temporal or moral condition of his new subjects. The conduct of Austria in this respect was less liberal. Under the plea,—a true one no doubt, but not sufficient to justify so arbitrary a measure,—that the spirit of the students of Cracow was too revolutionary to consist with a monarchical government, she destroyed that venerable seat of learning, which during more than four centuries had supported the religion and the civilisation of Poland; and though in lieu of it she founded a college at Leopol, the jealous regulations and vigorous surveillance introduced into that seminary were not likely to fill its halls with native students. Nor were the circumstances of the people in other respects more enviable. Galicia, which had served as a granary to Austria in her endless wars with the French, and where her losses of men had been repaired, was now exhausted; so that the nobles of this province — the richest, perhaps, in Poland — have not even yet been able to recover from the misery into which they were plunged by the exactions of the government. Those of Polish Prussia were scarcely treated with more indulgence: but though the state was rapacious, their enterprising spirit, and the superior facilities they enjoyed for commerce, neutralised the severity of their imposts, and rendered their condition one of comparative comfort. In all the three, the minds of the inhabitants were freed from all apprehension on political accounts; government prosecutions had long ceased; the general amnesty had covered all anterior events with the veil of oblivion.

Such was the condition of the Poles when the French emperor endeavoured to attach them to his interests by loudly proclaiming himself their restorer,—the breaker of the yoke under which they groaned. That sickness of heart occasioned by hope deferred, caused many to turn a deaf ear to his summons; but the majority, electrified at the promise of approaching freedom, flew eagerly to arms, and devoted themselves, with heart and hand, to the will of Napoleon. The brilliant campaign of 1806,—the victory of Jena, and the advance of the French into Poland to oppose the formidable masses of Russians, who appeared as the allies of Prussia,—seemed an earnest of future success; a sure pledge of approaching restoration. Polish regiments were organised with amazing rapidity. To increase the general enthusiasm, Napoleon was unscrupulous enough to proclaim the near approach of Kosciuszko; though, but a few months before, that general, who knew his character, had refused to espouse his views,—in other words, to deceive the still confiding Poles. On the 27th of November he entered Posen in triumph; the following month Warsaw received him with no less enthusiasm. The inhabitants of the latter were still more overjoyed when he proceeded to organise a supreme commission of government,—a measure which they hailed as the dissevering of the last link that bound them to Prussia. His purpose was announced; his armies were recruited by thousands of the bravest troops in Europe; Friedland bore witness to the talents and valour of Dombrowski and the heroes he commanded; and the opening of negotiations at Tilsit was hailed by the Poles as the dawning of a bright futurity.—Will posterity readily believe that this very man, in his celebrated interview on the Niemen with the emperor Alexander, seriously proposed to unite Warsaw, and the conquests which the Poles had assisted him to wrest from Prussia, *with the Russian empire;* and that the tsar refused to accept them—not so much through consideration for the Poles, as from an unwillingness to profit by the misfortunes of an ally? Yes; this very man proposed thus infamously to betray his warm, confiding, staunch adherents,—to betray them too beyond the possibility of redemption; and it was only when he found the tsar too moderate or too conscientious to receive the infernal overture that he began to make a parade of generosity, and to form a small portion of his conquests into the grand duchy of Warsaw, which he united with Saxony! *

The duchy of Warsaw consisted of six departments, —Posen, Kalisch, Plock, Warsaw, Lomza, and Bydgoszez: its population somewhat exceeded two millions. The Poles were highly dissatisfied with "this mockery of a country," as they called it. They had been taught to regard the ancient kingdom, if not Lithuania itself, as about to become inevitably their own; and their mortification may be conceived on finding not only that Prussia was allowed to retain several palatinates; that Austria was guaranteed in her Polish possessions; that the provinces east of the Bug were to remain in the power of Russia; but that a considerable portion of the ancient republic on this side that river was ceded, as the department of Bialystok, in perpetual sovereignty to the tsar. The peace of Tilsit they regarded as the grave of their hopes.

According to the new constitution granted by Napoleon, the virtual master of the duchy, the Catholic religion was properly declared the religion of the state; but ample toleration, and even a community of civil rights, were wisely allowed to the dissidents. Serfage was abolished. The power of the Saxon king, as grand duke of Warsaw,

* With their usual unfairness, the French writers have affected to doubt the fact above recorded. Hear Oginski, who had opportunities enough of learning the truth: " Quoique tous les partisans de Napoléon aient révoqué et mis en doute cette proposition, il n'est pas moins vrai qu'elle a été faite, et j'en ai eu depuis les témoignages les plus authentiques sous les yeux." Tom. ii. p. 344.

Dantzig was also wrested from Prussia, and made an independent republic.

was more extensive than had been enjoyed by his royal predecessors since the time of the Jagellos. With him rested the initiative of all projects of law; the nomination, not only of the senators, but the presidents of the dietines, and of the communal assemblies; and the appointment of all officers, civil and military. The code Napoleon was subsequently admitted as the basis of judicial proceedings.

The duchy soon felt the might of its new existence. The exertions of the government of Napoleon, who retained *military* possession of the country, and whose infamous lieutenant, Davoust, occupied Warsaw as headquarters, added to the inevitable expenses of the civil list, impoverished the small proprietors. Many, wisely preferring easy circumstances under an absolute but paternal government, to ruin with nominal freedom, removed into the Polish provinces subjected to Russia or Austria; for, even in the latter, rapacity was yielding to moderation and mildness. Those who remained consoled themselves with the belief, that eventually Poland would be recalled into existence, and her independence reestablished on sure foundations. That they should have been made dupes to the emissaries of a man who had never promised but to betray them, can be only explained by the well-known truth, how easily do we believe what we hope! For this reason many native regiments continued in the alliance of France. In the Austrian war of 1809, they covered themselves with renown, and rendered the greatest benefits to the cause of their imperial ally. They conquered Galicia without the smallest aid from France, while the emperor was proceeding elsewhere in his splendid career of victory. They reduced Cracow and the adjacent territory; and though for forty days—days during which the Polish leaders were arrayed in mourning—they were compelled to abandon Warsaw to the archduke Ferdinand, they regained triumphant possession of that capital, and humbled their enemies on every side. They considered that what their own arms had won, they had a right to retain; and they regarded as inevitable the incorporation of these conquests with their infant state. They were soon undeceived: they were not allowed to retain a foot of Galicia; and half of their other conquests, between Warsaw and the Austrian frontier, was wrested from them. Four departments,—Cracow, Radom, Lublin, and Siedlec,—were indeed incorporated with the grand duchy; but this advantage was a poor compensation for the immense sacrifices which had been made,—for the loans which had been forcibly raised, for the lives which had been wasted, and for the misery which afflicted every class of the inhabitants. Military conscription had depopulated their towns; the stern agents of despotism—the despotism, not of the Saxon king, but of Napoleon—had carried away the produce of the soil, and hostile armies had laid waste their plains. So utterly exhausted was the country, that the state could not reckon on the usual contributions; and a royal decree exempted from them the agricultural and mechanical classes.

Such were the benefits which the grand duchy derived from her connection with Bonaparte! His policy with regard to the Poles was not even judicious, much less generous.

Previous to opening the Russian campaign, Napoleon, in the view of interesting the Poles in his behalf, had resource to his usual arts, and, strange to say, with his usual success. The reflecting portion, indeed,—but, alas! how few are *they* in *any* nation!—scorned to be deluded again. "We are flattered," said a rough old soldier, "when our services are required:—is Poland always to be fed on hope alone?" But the mob,—such as do not *think*, be they high or low,—were persuaded, from the representations of the imperial agents, that their ancient republic was speedily to be restored in all its glory; that Lithuania was to be wrested from the tsar, and Galicia exchanged by Austria for Illyria. Who could refuse to arm for a potentate so regardless of his own interests, and so eager to avenge the wrongs of the oppressed? Yet, while

the deluded people were meeting at Warsaw to prepare
for their approaching high destinies; while the French
emperor was enthusiastically hailed as their regenerator;
while the abbé de Pradt, by *his* authority, added fuel
to the patriotic flame, a *secret* treaty with the emperor
Francis had again guaranteed the integrity of the
Austrian possessions in Poland.   But it *was secret*, and
his purpose was realised: at his voice more than
80,000 Poles took the field, while a general confederation of the nobles declared the republic restored, the
act of declaration being signed by the Saxon king, in
whose house the hereditary monarchy was to be vested.
At the same time, all Poles in the Russian service were
recalled to participate in the joyful event, and, if need
were, to seal their new liberties with their blood.   This
intoxication, however, was of short duration; the reply
of Napoleon to the Polish deputation, which had followed him to Wilna, left them no room to hope for
his aid: he exhorted them to fight for their own independence; assured them that if *all* the palatinates combined, they might reasonably expect to attain their
object; and insultingly added, — "I must, however, inform you that I have guaranteed to the Austrian emperor the integrity of his states, and that I cannot
sanction any project or movement tending to disturb
him in the possession of the Polish provinces which
remain to him."   So much for Galicia : as to Lithuania,
which he was expected to treat as an ally, and to unite
with the ancient republic, he not only considered it, but
proclaimed it, an hostile country, and ravaged it with
perfect impunity.   Thus the Lithuanians received an
avowedly open enemy, instead of an ally and a friend.
Both people had abundant reason to curse their blind
credulity.   This insulting perfidy was unknown to the
Polish troops, who were advancing on the ancient
frontiers of Muscovy, or they would surely have for-
saken the cause of one whom no services could affect,
no promises bind.
    It is useless to dwell on the valour displayed by the

deluded Poles in this disastrous expedition, of which the details are in the memory of every reader. The work of Bonaparte — the formation of the grand duchy —was destroyed; the king of Saxony, who had adhered to his cause with extraordinary fidelity, was stripped at once both of it and a portion of his hereditary dominions; the three powers again took possession of the towns which they had held previous to the invasions of Bonaparte, until a congress of all the sovereigns who had taken a prominent part in the war against the common enemy of Europe should assemble, to decide, among other matters, on the fate of the country.

After the fall of Bonaparte, the attention of the allied sovereigns was powerfully demanded by the state of Poland. The re-establishment of the kingdom in all its ancient integrity was not merely an act of justice to a people whose fall is one of the darkest pages in the history of the world, but it was, of all objects, the one most desirable towards the security of central Europe against the ambition of the tsars. But for Poland, a great portion of Christendom might have been subject to the misbelievers; but for her, the northern emperors would probably long ago have poured their wild hordes into the very heart of Germany: the nation which had been, and might again become, the bulwark alike of civil and religious freedom, could not fail to be invested with interest of the very highest order. Public opinion, the interest of rulers, and the sympathy of the governed, called for the restoration of injured Sarmatia. The side of humanity, of justice, and of policy, was powerfully advocated by France and England: their able plenipotentiaries, Talleyrand and Castlereagh, did all that could be done, short of having recourse to actual hostilities, to attain this European object. But neither power, nor both combined, could contend with success against those which were interested in the partition. France was exhausted by her long wars, and weakened by a restriction

within her ancient limits : England could have furnished
no more than a handful of troops ; nor could all her
wealth have hired mercenaries sufficiently numerous or
brave to justify her in throwing down the gauntlet of
defiance to two such military nations as Prussia and
Muscovy.   To the honour of the Austrian emperor, he
not only disapproved the projected union of the late
duchy with Russia, but he expressed his desire for Polish independence, and even his willingness to surrender
a portion of his own territories to make the new kingdom more respectable.   At this juncture, however,
Napoleon escaped from Elba ; and Alexander, finding
that his aid was indispensable in the approaching contest,
was able, not indeed to make his own terms, but to
insist on a measure he had long meditated,—the union of
the grand duchy, *as a separate kingdom,* with his empire.   Not less effectual was his policy with the Poles
themselves.   By persuading them that his great object was
to confer on them a national existence and liberal institutions, he interested them so far in his views, that they
would willingly have armed to support those views as they
had so often done those of Napoleon.*   In this state of
things, all that France and England could do was to
claim a national existence for the whole body of Poles,
and to stipulate for their political freedom.   Their representations were powerfully supported by the emperor
Francis, who again expressed regret that Poland could
not be re-established as an independent state with a
national representation of its own.†   Owing to these
energetic appeals *to his liberality,* and to the influence
of public opinion so widely diffused by the political

* In a proclamation addressed by the archduke Constantine to the Polish
army, December 11. (O. S.) 1814, he invites them to arm in *defence of their
national existence,*—to aid, if need were, the efforts of their powerful protector, who was zealously labouring for *their* good alone.   The proceedings
of the congress — three members of which were decidedly favourable to the
restoration of Poland — were thus artfully rendered suspicious to the Poles
themselves.
† Throughout this affair the conduct of the emperor Francis was as honourable as it was politic.   Austria was the last to join the coalition against
Poland ; she was the first to propose the reversal of that iniquity.

press, the autocrat showed no reluctance to make the concessions required. Prussia was no less willing. The result was a solemn engagement formed by the three partitioning powers in concert to confer on their respective Polish subjects a national representation, and national institutions regulated after the form of political existence which each of the respective governments might think proper to grant them.*

By the celebrated treaty of Vienna the following bases were solemnly sanctioned : —

1. Galicia and the salt mines of Wieliczka were restored to Austria.

2. The grand duchy of Posen, forming the western palatinates bordering on Silesia, and containing a population of about 800,000 souls, was surrendered to Prussia. This power was also confirmed in its conquests made at the period of the first partition.

3. The city and district of Cracow was to belong to none of the three powers, but to be formed into a free and independent republic, under the guarantee of the three. Its extent is 19½ geographical miles, inhabited at that time by a population of 61,000 souls.†

4. The remainder of ancient Poland, comprising the chief part of the recent grand duchy of Warsaw (embracing a country bounded by a line drawn from Thorn to near Cracow in the west, to the Bug and the Niemen in the east ‡), reverted to Russia, and was to form a kingdom for ever subject to the tsars. Population about 4,000,000.

The new kingdom of Poland was proclaimed June 20. 1815; and on December 24. in the same year, a constitutional charter was granted to the Poles.

The articles of this charter (in number 165) were of

---

* Les Polonais, sujets respectifs des hautes parties contractantes, obtiendront une représentation et des institutions nationales, reglées d'après le mode d'existence politique que chacun des gouvernemens auxquels ils appartiennent jugera utile et convenable de leur accorder.

† The population has since greatly increased.

‡ The district of Bialystock is not included.

so liberal a description as to astonish all Europe. They
abundantly prove, that at the time of their promulgation Alexander was no enemy of liberal institutions. He
seems, indeed, from the lessons of his tutor Laharpe,
from his acquaintance with the political literature of
Europe, and from his frequent intercourse with liberal
society, to have imbibed notions free enough for the at-
mosphere of Paris or London. He was certainly a most
extraordinary autocrat. Though the charter in question
has probably for ever passed away, the nature of the
dispute between the Poles and their monarch cannot
be understood without adverting to some of its provisions.

Though the Catholic religion was declared the religion of the state, all dissidents were placed on a footing
of perfect equality, as to civil rights, with the professors
of the established faith (Art. 11.). The liberty of the
press was recognised in its fullest extent (16.). No
subject could be arrested prior to judicial conviction
(18.). The inviolability of person and property, in the
strictest sense, was guaranteed (23. to 26.). All public
business to be transacted in the Polish language (28.) ;
and all offices, civil or military, to be held by natives
alone (29.).* The national representation to be vested
in two chambers, — senators and deputies (31.). The
power of the crown (35. to 47.) was not more than sufficient to give due weight to the executive : all kings to
be crowned at Warsaw, after swearing to the observance
of the charter : during his absence, the chief authority
to be vested in a lieutenant and council of state (63. to
75.). The great public departments to be presided by
responsible ministers (76. to 82.). The legislative
power to rest with the king and the two chambers: an
ordinary diet to be held every two years, and sit thirty
days ; an *extraordinary* diet whenever judged necessary

* Strangers, however, might be naturalised and admissible to public employments after five years' residence, if in the interim they should acquire
the Polish language (33.) ; and the king reserved to himself the privilege of
appointing distinguished foreigners to certain employments (34.).

by the king (86. to 88.). No member could be arrested during a session, except for great offences; and not even then, without the consent of the assembly (89.). The deliberations of the diet extended to all projects submitted to it by the ministry, affecting the laws and the whole routine of internal administration (90. to 94.). All deliberations to be public, except when committees were sitting (95.). All projects of law to originate with the council of state, and to be laid before the chambers by command of the king; such projects, however, being previously examined by committees of both houses (96. to 98.). All measures to be passed by a majority of votes (102.). The senators to be nominated by the king, and to exercise their functions for life (110.). The deputies (128 in number, or about double that of the senators) were 77 for districts (one for each), and 51 for so many communes (118. and 119.). To become a member of this chamber the qualifications were, citizenship; the age of thirty; possession of some portion, however small, of landed property; and the payment, in annual contributions, of 100 Polish florins * (121.). No public functionary eligible to sit without the consent of the head of his department (122.). The nobles of each district to meet in dietines, for the purpose of electing one of their body to the general diet, and of returning two members to the palatine assemblies † (125.), all dietines being convoked by the king (126.). The class of electors was numerous; comprising — 1. All landowners, however small, who paid any contribution whatever towards the support of the state; 2. Every manufacturer or shopkeeper possessing a capital of 10,000 florins; 3. All rectors and vicars; 4. All professors and teachers; 5. All artists or mechanics distinguished for talent (131.). Every elector to be enrolled,

---

* The Polish florin is about *sixpence*. The qualifications for a senator were, 35 years, and a contribution of 2000 florins.

† These assemblies were held in every palatinate, and were somewhat similar to our county courts, only the nobles had the choice of advocates and certain judges for the despatch of local business.

and to have reached twenty-one years (132.). The tribunals to be filled with judges, part nominated by the king, and part elected by the palatinates (140.); the former being appointed for life, and unremovable (141.).

Such were the chief provisions of this remarkable charter, which left only two things to be desired,—the trial by jury, and the competency of either chamber to propose laws: the initiative was confined to the executive, consisting of the king and the council of state.

The enthusiasm of the Poles towards their sovereign, for some time after the promulgation of this charter, was almost boundless. His lieutenant, Zayonczek, imitated his example, and strove with success to attach the Poles to his sway. Prosperity, the result of a settled and an enlightened government, followed in the train of peace. Innumerable improvements introduced into the public education; the establishment of a university at Warsaw, and of an agricultural society at Mount Maria; the rapid increase of trade; the diffusion of wealth, and the consequent advance towards happiness by the nation at large; might well render his government popular. That prosperity, indeed, is his noblest monument. On taking possession of the country, he found nothing but desolation and misery. So enormous had been the force which the grand duchy had been compelled to maintain, so heavy the exactions of the treasury, that no country could have borne them, much less one whose two chief outlets for her produce, Dantzig and Odessa, were long closed by the continental system of Napoleon, and by the Turkish war. The finances of the duchy, indeed, were unable to pay more than an insignificant portion of the troops; either the remainder was raised by forced loans, or the men went unpaid. Twelve millions of francs, in addition, were borrowed at Paris, on the security of the mines of Wieliczka. Still all would not do: the revenue did not reach one half of the expenditure: in time, no functionary, civil or ecclesiastical, and scarcely any soldier, was paid. The contractors fled;

troops traversed the country at pleasure, plundering indiscriminately all who fell in their way. In short, there was little money or food any where, and a total stop was put to all branches of industry.—To repair these evils was the emperor's first object. By opening the country to foreign merchants ; by providing the husbandmen with oxen and horses; by suspending the payment of some taxes and suppressing others, and by providing for the support of his army from his hereditary dominions; he recalled industry and the means of subsistence, and laid the foundation of that prosperity which went on increasing until the breaking out of the present insurrection. *

So satisfied was the Polish nation with its new situation in the year 1818—near three years after its union with Russia—that the opposition to ministers in the chamber of deputies was utterly insignificant. The benefits of the government had disarmed the prejudices and antipathies of the people. The emperor himself appears, at this time, to have been no less satisfied : he congratulated himself on the liberal policy he had adopted towards his new subjects ; and declared in full senate at Warsaw, that he was only waiting to try the effect of the free institutions he had given them, to extend those institutions over all the regions which Providence had confided to his care.

Having now reached the term of the good understanding between the Poles and their monarch ; it is necessary to advert to the causes which led first to mistrust, then to hatred, and lastly to open hostility between the two parties.

On the first view of the case, it could not rationally be expected that any considerable degree of harmony could subsist between people who, during eight centuries, had been at war with each other, and between

* For an account of the deplorable state of the grand duchy under the Saxon reign—or rather under Napoleon—see the abbé de Pradt, *Histoire de l'Ambassade en Pologne*, p. 86. &c. : the Discourse of count Mostowski on opening the diet of 1818 ; and the Mémoires de Oginski, tom. iv.

whom, consequently, a strong national antipathy had
been long fostered.   And even had they always lived in
peace, they were too dissimilar in manners, habits, sentiments, and religion, ever cordially to coalesce.   For
ages the Pole had idolised a liberty unexampled in any
country under heaven : the Muscovite had no will of
his own, but depended entirely on God and the tsar :
the one was the maker and master of kings ; the other
obeyed, as implicitly as the voice of fate, the most
arbitrary orders of his monarch, whom he considered
Heaven's favourite vicegerent.   The one was enlightened by education, and by intercourse with the polished
nations of Europe ; the other, who long thought it a
crime to leave home, was brutified by superstition and
ignorance : each cursed the other as schismatic, — as
out of the pale of God's visible church, and doomed to
perdition.   The antipathy which ages had nourished,
had been intensely aggravated by late events.   The
unprovoked violence of Catharine ; the haughtiness of
her troops ; the excesses accompanying the elevation
and fall of Stanislas ; the keen sense of humiliation —
so keen as to become intolerable to a proud people,—
were causes more than sufficient to neutralise the
greatest benefits conferred by the tsars.

Another and, if possible, weightier consideration
arises : — How could the most arbitrary monarch in
Europe — one whose will had never been trammelled
by either the spirit or the forms of freedom ; whose
nod was all but omnipotent, — be expected to guide the
delicately complicated machine of a popular government ?
Would he be very likely to pay much regard to the
apparently insignificant, however necessary, springs which
kept it in motion ?   Would the lord of fifty legions, whose
empire extended over half the old world, be likely to hear
with patience the bold voice of freedom in a distant and
(as to territory) insignificant corner of his vast heritage ?

Under no state of things, however, would the Poles,
as long as they were subject to foreign ascendency, have

remained satisfied. The recollections of their ancient glory would give a more bitter pang to the consciousness of present degradation. Alexander, indeed, had held out to them the hope of uniting Lithuania under the same form of government: but even in this case, would either Poles or Lithuanians be less subject to the autocrat? Besides, what guarantee had they that even their present advantages would be continued to them? None, surely, but the personal character of the autocrat, who, with the best intentions, was somewhat fickle, and who might any day abandon the reins of empire to a more rigorous, or less scrupulous hand. " What have we to *hope*," exclaimed the celebrated Dombrowski at the period at which this compendium is arrived; " what have we not to *fear?* This very day might we not tremble for the fate which may await us to-morrow? " The general expressed his conviction that if the Poles, instead of being disunited, would cordially combine, they would recover their lost greatness. " Let them," added he, " retrieve their ancient nationality ; let them combine their opinions, their desires, their wishes ! " In other words, he meant that the whole nation should enter into an understanding to permit the existence of the present order of things no longer than they could help. " If the same fortune," he concluded, " which has given us a sovereign, should one day turn round on him, Poland may recover her liberty and independence, and acknowledge no king but the one of her own choice."

Words like these, and from such a quarter, could not fail to produce their effect. They flew from mouth to mouth ; the press began to echo them. The opposition in the chamber of deputies assumed a more formidable appearance. The success, however transient, of the liberal party in Spain and Italy, was hailed with transport. Were the Poles, the bravest of the brave, to despond at such a crisis? The anti-Russian party, comprising the army, the students in the public schools, the populace of the capital, began to act with greater boldness and decision: no very obscure hints were thrown out that the glorious example of other countries would not be lost nearer home. The newspapers, which followed the current of public opinion, however changing, as inevitably as the shadow does the substance, adopted the same resolute if not menacing tone. It was evident that a revolution was meditated, and that the minds of the people, not merely of the kingdom, but of the countries under the sway of Austria and Prussia, as well as those of the grand duchy, were to be prepared for it by sure though apparently insensible degrees. Privileges were now claimed, and principles promulgated, of a tendency too democratic to consort with the existing frame of society. That Russia should take alarm at the fearless activity of the press, — an engine which, however powerless over the few who venture to think for themselves, will always have tremendous influence over the multitude, — was naturally to be expected. Accordingly, by an ordinance of July 31. 1819, the censorship was established, in violation of art. 16.

If men have no opportunity of expressing their opinions publicly, they will do so privately. When the journals, the legitimate outlets of popular feeling, were thus arbitrarily and impoliticly closed, secret societies began to multiply. A sort of political freemasonry connected the leaders of the meditated movement, and its ramifications extended as far as Wilna. Their avowed object was not merely to free their country and the grand duchy from the Russian yoke, but to unite their brethren of Gallicia and Posen in one common cause, and then openly to strike a blow for their dearest rights. But however secret their meetings and purposes, neither could long escape the vigilance of the police, which, since the arrival of Constantine as commander in chief of the Polish army, had acquired alarming activity. Why this personage should have interfered in a branch of administration beyond his province—why he should have stepped out of his own peculiar sphere to hire spies, to collect information, and to influence the proceedings of the tribunals against the suspected or the accused—has been matter of much conjecture. Perhaps he proposed to render himself necessary to his imperial brother; perhaps he could not live without some bustle to excite him; perhaps his mind was congenially occupied in the discovery and punishment of treason. However this be, he acted with amazing impolicy. His wisest course—and the Poles themselves once hoped that he would adopt it— was to cultivate the attachment of the people among whom he resided, and thereby prepare their minds for one day seconding his views on the crown. Instead of this, he conducted himself towards all whom he suspected of liberal opinions—and few there were who did not entertain them—with violence, often with brutality. At his instigation, the secret police pursued its fatal career: arbitrary arrests, hidden condemnations, the banishment of many, the imprisonment of more, signalised his baneful activity. That amidst so many sentences, some should be passed on individuals wholly innocent, need not surprise us. Where spies are hired to mix with society for the purpose of detecting the disaffected, if they do not find treason, they will make it: private malignity, and a desire of being thought useful, if not indispensable, to their employers, and of enjoying the rewards due to success in procuring informations, would make them vigilant enough. As this is a profession which none but the basest and most unprincipled of men would follow, we cannot expect that they would always exercise it with much regard to justice. In such men, revenge or avarice would be all-powerful.

The university of Wilna was visited with some severity by the agents of this dreaded institution. Twenty of its students were seized and sentenced to different punishments—none, however, very rigorous. Those of Warsaw were not used more indulgently. A state prison was erected in the capital, and its dungeons were soon crowded with inmates—many, no doubt, not undeserving their fate, but not a few the victims of an execrable system. The proceedings, however, which are dark, must always be suspected: of the hundreds who were dragged from the bosom of their families, and consigned to various fortresses, all would be thought innocent, since none had been legally convicted.

By art. 10. of the constitutional charter, the Russian troops, when required to pass through Poland, were to be at the entire charge of the tsar's treasury: for years, however, they were stationed at Warsaw — evidently to overawe the population — at the expense of the inhabitants. Then the violations of individual liberty (in opposition to art. 18. to 21.); the difficulty of procuring passports; the misapplication of the revenue to objects other than those to which it was raised, — to the reimbursement of the secret police, for instance; the nomination of men as senators without the necessary qualifications, and who had no other merit than that of being creatures of the government; were infractions of the charter, as wanton as they were intended to be humiliating.

The army was as much dissatisfied as the nation. The ungovernable temper, and the consequent excesses, of Constantine; the useless but vexatious manœuvres which he introduced; his rigorous mode of exercise, fitted for no other than frames of adamant; and, above all, his overbearing manner towards the best and highest officers in the service; raised him enemies on every side. His good qualities—and he has many—were wholly overlooked amidst his ebullitions of fury, and the unjustifiable, often cruel, acts he committed while under their influence. On ordinary occasions, when his temper is not ruffled, no man can make himself more agreeable: no man can exhibit more—not of courtesy, for he is too rough for it—but of warmheartedness; and his generosity in pecuniary matters is almost boundless.

But the worst remains yet to be told. Russian money and influence were unblushingly employed in the dietines, to procure the return to the general diet of such members only as were known to care less for their country than for their own fortunes. Then, instead of a diet being held every two years (in accordance with art. 87.), none was convoked from 1820 to 1825, and only one after the accession of Nicholas. Finally, an ordinance (issued in 1825) abolished the publicity of the debates in the two chambers; and the most distinguished members of opposition were forcibly removed from Warsaw the night preceding the opening of the diet.*

In examining these and a few minor complaints urged with much force by the Polish organs, no one will hesitate to admit that, however the colouring in this painful picture may be overcharged,—and overcharged it unquestionably is,—the nation had but too much cause for discontent. No wonder that the government and the people should regard each other first with distrust, then with hatred; that the former could not behold with much favour institutions which, however liberal, were not considered sufficiently so by those on whom they had been conferred; or that the latter should have much confidence in a power which had violated the most solemn engagements, and might violate them again. The conflict—long a moral one—between the two, was too stormy to be hushed. It was vain to whisper peace: to remind the one party, that if wrongs had been endured, they had not been wholly unprovoked; or the other, that necessary caution had degenerated into an intolerable, inquisitorial surveillance, and justice into revenge.

Yet with all this irritation, it may be doubted whether the majority of the nation were at any time inclined to proceed to extremities. The condition of the country had continued to improve beyond all precedent: at no former period of her history was the public wealth so great, or so generally diffused. Bridges and public roads constructed at an enormous expense, frequently at the expense of the tsar's treasury; the multitude of new habitations, remarkable for a neatness and a regard to domestic comfort never before observed; the em-

* To the preceding recapitulation of national grievances, individual ones need not be added. Some of the latter have been laboriously exaggerated in this country. But the cause of the Poles stands in no need of exaggeration: it is strong in its own righteous justice.

bellishments introduced into the buildings, not merely
of the rich, but of tradesmen and mechanics ; the encouragement afforded, and eagerly afforded, by the government to every useful branch of industry ; the
progress made by agriculture in particular, the foundation of Polish prosperity ; the accumulation on all sides
of national and individual wealth ; and, above all, the
happy countenances of the inferior classes of society;
exhibited a wonderful contrast to what had lately been.
The most immense of markets, Russia — a market all but
closed to the rest of Europe—afforded constant activity
to the manufacturer.   To prove this astonishing progress from deplorable, hopeless poverty, to successful
enterprise, let one fact suffice.   In 1815 there were
scarcely one hundred looms for coarse woollen cloths :
at the commencement of the present insurrection there
were six thousand.*

   In contemplating the recent history of Poland, it
cannot but be matter of regret to the philanthropic mind
that the nation should, so soon after its union with
Russia, have brought on itself the ill-will of that power.
Though some slight infractions were made on the spirit
rather than the letter of the charter, during the four first
years of the connection, these might have been remedied
by an appeal to the emperor.   On the part neither of
Alexander nor of his lieutenant did there exist the
slightest wish to violate its provisions, until experience
had taught both that individual freedom was not so
much the object in pursuit, as a total separation from
the empire.   Then it was that liberal institutions became
odious in the cabinet of St. Petersburgh ; that the tsar
resolved to prevent their extension, on the plea — a mistaken but not unnatural plea—that they were inconsistent with a settled monarchy, and consequently with
long continued social security : then it was that the imperial ministers and their underlings commenced their
unwise system, — a system but partially known to the
tsar, and one that would never have been approved by

* See Appendix C.

him,—of exasperating the Poles, first by petty annoy-
ances, next by depriving them of privileges to which
they had a sacred right,—of adding fuel to a fire already
too intense to continue long harmless.

The seeds of hatred, thus unfortunately sown, germi-
nated with silent but fatal rapidity. A vast number of
soldiers (especially of unemployed officers); of ardent
patriots and students; of all whom Russian haughtiness
had provoked, or Russian liberality had failed to visit; and
more than all, of that fickle and numerically speaking imposing class so prone to change; were gradually initiated
into the great plot destined to concentrate the scattered ele-
ments of resistance to imperial violence, and to sweep its
framers and abettors from the face of the kingdom. The
society, numerous as were its ramifications, was well organised, and its proceedings were wrapt in more than ma-
sonic mystery. That not a few of its members were
implicated in the conspiracy which exploded on the accession of Nicholas — utterly unknown at present as were the
subjects and nature of that conspiracy—appears both
from the numerous arrests on that occasion (no fewer
than two hundred took place in Poland and Lithuania),
and from the very admission of their organs. Though
the commission of enquiry, consisting chiefly of Poles,
failed to discover the clue to that dark transaction, evidence enough was adduced to prove the existence of a
formidable national association. Two years afterwards
(in 1828), that association gained over the great body
of Polish officers, and silently waited the progress of
events to watch for an opportunity of striking the blow.

It has often been matter of surprise to most thinking
foreigners, that the Poles did not take advantage of the
Turkish war to erect the standard of independence.
Evidently, however, their plan was not at that period
sufficiently matured. That it was so even in 1830 may
be reasonably doubted. But the French insurrection—
which appears not to have been wholly unexpected in
the Polish capital—its daring character, its splendid
success, had an electric effect on the whole nation, and

disposed the initiated to anticipate the time of their
rising. It is well known—it has, indeed, been admitted by both Poles and Frenchmen, including the
political organs of the latter—that emissaries from
Warsaw held confidential meetings with the leaders of
the revolution of July, and were instigated to rouse
their countrymen by the promise of immediate aid from
the government of the citizen king. That such aid was
relied on with the fullest confidence, by the Polish
patriots themselves, must be known to all who have recently mixed with Polish society, or who hold any correspondence with the country. The best authority for
such a fact is to be found in the universal impression of
the people. At this moment no feeling is more prevalent at Warsaw, no complaint more bitter, than that the
Poles, on this occasion, have been betrayed.

Two other circumstances powerfully contributed to
hasten the long-meditated catastrophe. The army began
to entertain the notion—whether justly founded or not
cannot yet be determined—that it was to be removed to
the south of Europe to assist in extirpating the alarming
doctrines of the French politicians, and that its place
was to be supplied by an army of Russians. The youths
of the military school, too, found or fancied excuse for
apprehension. That their design of rising was not unknown to the authorities, appears from the eagerness
with which one of the hired agents of police endeavoured
to win their confidence, professing his devotion to their
cause, and imploring permission to share in the execution of their project. Though this fellow overshot his
mark ; though his eagerness caused him to be suspected
and shunned ; he learned enough to be convinced, not
only that an insurrection was resolved on, but that it
was actually at hand.

The apprehensions of the army and the students, —
of whom the latter had every thing to fear from the
grand duke, should he, as he was believed to have
threatened, arrest and try them by martial law—the
conviction that the whole populace of the capital were

friendly to the project; the secret encouragement of France; the eagerness of the enterprising to court danger for its very sake; the assumed approbation of the free towards the cause at least, if not towards the time and circumstances, of the insurrection, — hastened the opening of the great tragedy. The first object of its actors was to seize on the person of the grand duke, their most obnoxious enemy, — to use him, perhaps, as a hostage for their safety, should fortune prove unpropitious. The students — as the young and the rash will always be in such cases — were the authorised leaders of "the movement." On the evening of November the 29th, one of them, in accordance with a preconcerted plan, entered the school, and called his comrades to arms. The call was instantly obeyed. On their way to the residence of Constantine, which stands about two miles from the city, their number was increased by the students of the university and public schools. Two or three companies — not a regiment, as has been usually stated — of Russian cavalry, they furiously assailed and overpowered. This first success they did not use with much moderation: towards a few of the officers, who appear to have been personally obnoxious, they exhibited great animosity; three or four were cruelly massacred after the conflict was over. They forced the palace, flew to the grand duke's apartments, but had the mortification of finding their victim fled: the intrepid fidelity of a servant had first concealed, then assisted him to escape. As their first object had thus unexpectedly failed, the conspirators now resolved to gain the city. Their retreat was opposed by the Russian guards; but such was the spirit which animated them, — such were the skill and courage they displayed, that, after a struggle continued over a space of two miles, they accomplished their purpose.

During this desperate affray, the efforts of another party within the city were more successful. A considerable body of cadets and students paraded the streets, calling on the inhabitants to arm for their country's freedom. They were joined, as had been previously arranged, not by hundreds, but by thousands, of native troops ; and their force was augmented by several pieces of cannon. The Russian posts, which were now attacked, were carried ; the prison doors were opened, and criminals as well as debtors invited to swell the assailants ; the theatre was speedily emptied of its spectators ; and the great body of citizens were provided with arms from the public arsenal. In the excitement consequent on this extraordinary commotion, every part of which was conducted with a regularity that could only be the result of a maturely formed design, no reader will be surprised, how much soever he may lament, to find that several excesses were committed. Many Russians were massacred ; many Poles, known to have been on terms of intimacy with the grand duke, shared the same fate. But some dark deeds were done for which no excitement can apologise, — some which will for ever disgrace this memorable night. While a number of Russian and a few Polish superior officers were laudably exerting themselves to calm the ferocity of the people ; while they fearlessly rode among them, and urged them to desist from their violent proceedings, to lay their grievances before the emperor, who would readily redress them, and, above all, to remember that the Russians and themselves were fellow-subjects, and refrain from bloodshed, — these very peace-makers, whose heroism should have commanded the respect, and whose kind-hearted intentions should have won the affections, of the populace, were barbarously massacred. Some other officers of rank — all Russians, except one — were made prisoners.

By the morning of the 30th, all the Polish troops, with the exception of one regiment and a few companies who held for Constantine, and remained with him, had joined the insurgents. Near 30,000 armed citizens swelled their dense ranks. To oppose so formidable a mass would have been madness. In twelve hours the revolution was begun and completed. In vain did the grand duke, who lay without the walls, meditate the recovery of the intrenchments and fortifications. His isolated though desperate efforts to re-enter the city were repulsed with serious loss; and when he became acquainted with the number of his antagonists, he wisely desisted from his purpose. He removed to a greater distance from the walls, as if uncertain what steps to take in so extraordinary an emergency.

In a few hours an administrative council was formed, to preside over the destinies of the infant state. It was composed of men distinguished for their talents, character, or services. At first they evidently entertained no intention of throwing off their allegiance to the tsar; all their proclamations were in his name, and all their claims bounded to a due execution of the charter. As their ambition or their patriotism rose with their success, they insisted on an incorporation of Lithuania, and the other Polish provinces subject to Russia, with the kingdom. Some months after, they declared the throne vacant,—a declaration highly rash and impolitic.

The behaviour of Constantine in his retreat was not without generosity. At the request of the provisional government, he agreed to send back the Polish troops who still remained faithful to him; and proposed that, if the people would submit, he would endeavour not only to procure an amnesty for all, but the redress of their alleged grievances. It was too late, however, to think of such submission, or such security; the die was irrevocably cast. If the Poles were guilty of rashness in what they had just effected, they were not likely to commit the folly of undoing it. On the 3d of December his imperial highness evacuated the vicinity of the capital; about the middle of the month he crossed the Bug. He was perfectly unmolested in his retreat.

As nothing less than unconditional submission will satisfy the tsar, and as the Poles would rather perish than make it, they are now fully and irrevocably embarked in the most fearful of contests. That they have a right to vindicate their national independence,—that

to do so is their highest duty,—will not be denied on
this side the Berezina; but whether they have chosen
the proper time for rising, is a very different consideration.   Their plans were evidently not matured.   Neither from Lithuania, nor from any other of the provinces
incorporated with Russia, have they received the aid on
which they relied.   So far, indeed, the honour of the
campaign has been theirs; their efforts have been stu-
pendous; their bravery worthy the age of their Boleslas
and Sobieskis: but even success has fearfully diminished
their numbers, and impaired their resources.   It must
be clear to every unimpassioned observer, that Poland
has not the means to contend with her great antagonist.
Where the valour and discipline of two nations are about
equal, the weaker must in the end give way to the
stronger, unless there are countervailing circumstances
in favour of the former.   Now, in Poland, where are
such circumstances to be found?   She has no moun-
tain fastnesses, like the Asturias, Scotland, or Wales, in
which her sons can take shelter when overpowered by
numbers, and emerge on the enemy's retreat: she has
no fortresses, like the Netherlands, capable of arresting
and breaking the force of her assailants.   That she will
nobly perform her duty, as she has hitherto done, is un-
doubted; that she will prefer annihilation to submission,
is not improbable.   Nothing appears able to save her
but European interference.   Is such interference probable?   Will Austria and Prussia, the only powers
which could have much weight on the occasion, interfere?   With what face could they propose to Russia
the independence of her revolted subjects, unless they
were prepared to confer the same boon on their own,—
on the inhabitants of Posen and Gallicia?   Whatever
may be said of Austria,—the least criminal of the
powers concerned in the odious partition,—Prussia
must greatly have changed, if she abandon one inch of
her territories without compulsion.   As to the representations of England or France, they would probably be
disregarded.

It is, however, useless to anticipate: time is on the wing. Though the author of this compendium *knows* that the result is regarded with apprehension by the Poles themselves, he is not so little read in history as to be ignorant that a " Providence rules in the affairs of men," and that a righteous cause is often made to prosper against all human calculation, when even its warmest friends despair of its success. May that of the Poles be one of these!

But if the Christian may faintly hope, the philanthropist must grieve at the contrast exhibited by Poland during the last and present year. Her plains are covered with ruins, or washed with blood; her resources are exhausted, her industry destroyed; her abundance has given way to wretchedness; the countenances of her children, once so happy, are now wan, squalid, and despairing; her peasants, her landowners, and not a few of her chief nobles, now curse the thoughtless precipitation which hurried the nation into so awful a contest before her means of defence were fully organised. The majority of the Poles are heartily sick of the war, however anxious the army, " the youths of the military schools," and " the students of the university," may be to continue it.

Of the republic of Cracow, whose existence and independence are guaranteed by the congress of Vienna, little need be said. From 1795 to 1809, the city had belonged to Austria: by the peace of Schoenbrunn it had been united with the grand duchy of Warsaw. A charter of twenty-two articles, almost as liberal as those of the Poles, was granted by the three powers most interested. The government of the republic is vested in a senate of twelve, and a president: nine (including the president) are elected by the deputies, the remaining four by the episcopal chapter and the academy. Persons of landed property paying a contribution of fifty Polish florins, priests, members of the academy, distinguished artists, and merchants, may elect, or in

certain cases become, senators. The deputies are chiefly
elected by the citizens : three prelates, six magistrates,
sit there in virtue of their offices ; three doctors in the
faculties of law, medicine, and divinity, and three
senators, are deputed by their respective bodies. The
law declares all citizens to be equal ; confers on the
deputies the power of controlling the finances, and of
inspecting public functionaries. All proceedings in the
courts are public : the judges are elected partly by the
people, partly by the senate and representatives ; all are
independent, because unremovable.*

CHAP. IV.

SOCIETY, CONSTITUTION, MANNERS, ETC. OF THE ANCIENT POLES.

IN their infancy the Poles, like the other branches of
the great Slavonic family, were split into independent
tribes, each governed by its own kniaz, or judge, whom
age or reputed wisdom had raised to that dignity. His
attributes, however, were entirely of a civil nature, as
the command of the troops was confided to another
dignitary, the voivod, whose authority terminated with
the war.

Even after the establishment of a kingly government,
these judges and generals long continued the chief, if
not the only, officers in the monarchy. In the general
assemblies of the tribes, convoked to deliberate on peace
or war, their voices were the expressed organs of their
countrymen. Such assemblies, before the establishment
of a senate, and while the kings were limited in power,
were of frequent occurrence, and as they were attended
by all who bore arms (the cultivation of the soil was

* Mémoires d'Oginski, tom. iii. et iv. *passim.* Malte-Brun, Tableau de
Pologne. Précis Historique, cinquième époque, by Chodzko, ii. 135—230.
" Annual Retrospect of Public Affairs," (in Dr. Lardner's Cabinet Library,)
ii. 289. I forbear to quote the French pamphlets, or the newspapers, which
are no authority at all. Much of the information in the last twenty pages
is derived from private sources.

abandoned wholly to slaves and captives), they were necessarily numerous.

As the royal authority acquired strength, especially after the division of the country into palatinates by Miecislas II., these national meetings were discontinued. The palatines, on their appearance at court, or wherever they fell in with the king, and in all warlike expeditions, were his privileged advisers. So, also, were the bishops, who, after the introduction of Christianity, were joined with the temporal barons in the exercise of this privilege. And when, from the natural progress of society towards civilisation, he found it impossible to decide on the cases submitted to his wandering tribunal, when even the palatine courts were found insufficient for the same purpose, he granted first to his leading barons, and gradually to the great bulk of that military body, the exercise of the *jus ducale*, or of the judicial power, as hitherto held by the prince himself. Every baronial residence thus became a tribunal of justice, and, what is worse, was authorised to be held *jure hereditario*. From these tribunals, the decisions of which, in the absence of written law *, were founded on natural equity and traditionary prescription, there was long no appeal. Each of the palatines had an assistant invested with the same judicial powers; and so probably had the other barons. The bishops had a similar jurisdiction; but as it was considered unbecoming in a minister of peace to pass sentence of death on any human creature, the painful duty devolved on a vicar, who uniformly presided in the episcopal court.

Though each of these palatines, bishops, and barons, could thus advise his sovereign, the formation of a regular senate was slow, and completed only when experience had proved its utility. At first, the only subjects on which the monarch deliberated with his barons related to war: what he originally granted through

* Legum scriptarum nullus fuit usus apud Polonos vetustioribus temporibus: nec ullæ extant antiquiores iis, quas Casimirus magnus rex condidit.—*Polonia, sive de Situ, Populis, Moribus, Magistratibus, et Republicâ Regni Polonici libri duo*, by the historian Cromer, lib. ii. p. 105.

courtesy, or through diffidence in himself, or with a
view to lessen his responsibility in case of failure, *they*
eventually claimed as a right.

But among a free, ferocious people, the decisions of
the king and senate were not permitted long to have the
force of absolute law.   The barons and prelates, nay,
the whole body of the nobles or warriors, tenacious of
the privilege they had exercised in the infancy of their
society, often collected together to deliberate on affairs
more than usually momentous, and alike by their numbers and attitude imposed on the government.   Absolute as was the king's authority, he could not but quail
before this formidable body ; he could not but be unwilling to undertake any thing likely to displease it; and
to know the sentiments of his people, he often convoked
them to lay before them his meditated designs, and, if
possible, to gain their sanction.   This mark of confidence,
or of policy, at first flattered their pride ; but soon, as
in the case of the senators, it was regarded as a mere
act of justice towards themselves.   Their will, thus
irresistibly pronounced, became the first and most absolute law of the state.

While the three estates of the realm were thus gradually acquiring organisation and strength, the mul-
tiplication of towns, and still more their increase in
population and riches, gave rise to another change in
the internal administration.   These, finding the national
or feudal law no longer applicable to their circumstances,
procured, by petition or purchase, their exemption from
it, and adopted the Teutonic or burgher law, so much
more favourable to industrious communities.   As the
new jurisprudence was less arbitrary in its character, as
well as less severe in its operation, the free peasants
and artisans resorted to these municipal abodes.   They
gained much by an escape from the rude barbarous institutions of the Slavi, — from torture, and the various
modes in which recourse was had to the judgment of
heaven, — and by their incorporation into communities
where justice, however encumbered with interminable

formalities, and obscured by an endless nomenclature of technical terms, was more favourable to individual liberty. Town after town procured, from the avarice or the favour of the monarch, charters which empowered them to change the feudal for the burgher law,—which transformed them from vassals to citizens; and many of the great landowners were no less eager to encourage a change that, while it hastened the acquisition of individual wealth, increased their own revenues. (At all times a vast proportion of the Polish towns have belonged to the great barons.) Some communties, and even districts, assimilated, as much as they could, the native with the foreign jurisprudence. The result was a strange mixture of the two,—in many cases, a mass of contradictions. In fact, uniformity of laws was unknown until Casimir the Great introduced it. *

In the code of Wisliza, the place where Casimir held this memorable legislative diet, we find mention made of palatines, castellans, starosts, judges, &c., and a careful limitation of the jurisdiction possessed by their respective tribunals, as well as of the cases in which appeals could be carried, either to the king and senate, or to the supreme Teutonic tribunal established by that prince. Criminal affairs lay within the cognizance of the starosts and castellans; the question of disputed boundaries, &c. belonged to the *succamerarii*, or provincial chamberlains; more important disputes about property, affecting inheritance, partition, and redemption, and crimes of high treason, were carried either before the palatinal or the royal courts. The statute of Wisliza, which guaranteed alike the jurisdiction of the feudal and Teutonic tribunals, continued the basis of Polish legislation until the close of the last century; though some of its provisions were modified, abrogated, or amended, and others added, by succeeding diets. It must not, however, be forgotten, that brute force, not law, held its empire over the republic; that the peasants, or serfs, were judicially, though unconstitutionally, subjected to their masters; and that,

* See the reign of Casimir, p. 91.

while the nobles set all laws affecting themselves at
defiance, and enjoyed an unbounded licentiousness, the
rest of the nation was miserably enslaved, excepting
some of the more powerful municipalities, over which
these haughty tyrants could obtain no control. In no
European country has the peasant had to complain of
wrongs so revolting, yet so patiently borne. Down to
the destruction of the republic, his condition was infinitely more wretched than that of the Russian boor.

Of the three orders into which the state was divided,
the king, though his authority had been anciently despotic, was the least important. His dignity was un-
accompanied with power; he was merely the president
of the senate, and the chief judge of the republic. His
station, however, was not without its influence, since he
alone could nominate to all dignities and benefices. As
he was thus the fountain of honour, and, to a considerable
extent, of wealth, his favour was eagerly sought by the
ambitious and the needy. But as, when offices were
once conferred, the holders were unremovable during life
(unless in cases of convicted delinquency), that influence usually continued no longer than while he had
them to bestow.

The *senators*, or counsellors of the king, were the most
respectable of the three orders of government; but, like
his, their power was bounded. They were indeed en-
trusted with the different branches of the executive,
(they were all judges within their respective districts),
with the control over the numerous offices of administration; and they served as a superior court of appeal
from the tribunals of the republic; in concert with
the king, they could also ratify laws, and correspond with
foreign powers; but their proceedings were subject to
the rigid supervision of the diet, which kept a keen
and steady eye upon them. Their number was 139 *,
consisting of two archbishops, thirteen bishops, thirty-
five palatines (including three or four castellans who

* At one period the number amounted to one hundred and forty-four;
at another, it scarcely exceeded a hundred. The changes in the limits of
the republic will account for the difference.

ranked as palatines), seventy-nine castellans, and ten great officers of state. All these senators were nominated by the king, and could not be displaced during life. They were sworn to advise him with all sincerity and boldness; and they were seldom backward in so doing. No one could be a senator except in virtue of some office, nor except such as were of noble birth, and were land-owners to a considerable extent, either in the provinces of the crown or of the grand duchy.

Of the two archbishops, Gnesna and Leopol, the former was primate of the kingdom, and ex officio apostolic legate. During the interregna he was also the head of the republic, and invested with more powers than were ever permitted to the monarch. In the senate, the bishops took precedence of all the temporal barons.

The *palatines* were the generals of the forces raised in their respective palatinates during warlike expeditions; and in peace, they were the presidents of the judicial tribunals and political assemblies of their provinces. They also determined the price of provisions and merchandise; regulated weights and measures; judged and protected the Jews. A vice-palatine was associated with each of these great dignitaries.

The *castellans* were considered as the lieutenants or deputies of the palatines, and were invested with the same powers, though in an inferior degree. Like the palatines, they held their tribunals, presided over the assembled nobility of their district, and headed them in war. (The castellan of Cracow had no jurisdiction; but in rank he took precedence of all the palatines, and of all the temporal dignitaries in the republic.) Though all castellans were considered as members of the senate, the least influential portion, amounting to full one half, were seldom summoned to attend. The ten great officers of state were, the grand marshal, the chancellor, the vice-chancellor, the treasurer, and the marshal of the court; one of each for the kingdom and for the grand duchy.

The *starosts* had no seat in the senate, yet many of them had a civil jurisdiction; they held a common court every fortnight, and a great one every six weeks : they were, besides, the collectors of the king's revenue, one fourth of which they reserved to pay the expenses of their bailiffs, secretaries, &c. The word *starost* signifies aged ; and the crown lands attached to each starosty were originally intended as benefices to which old and deserving servants of the republic might retire to end their days in comfort, with few duties to be discharged. Soon, however, they were conferred on the young as well as the old,— on such chiefly as had been fortunate enough to obtain favour at court.

The *diet* consisted of the senators already mentioned, and of the deputies returned by each of the palatinates and districts of the republic ; the number of both amounted to about four hundred. These deputies were chosen in the *dietines*, or provincial assemblies of the nobles, (one held in each palatinate,) to represent in the general diet the interests and wishes of their constituents. Their name of *nuntii*, or messengers, sufficiently denoted the absence of all discretionary power in the discharge of their function. They were so strictly bound down by the instructions they received, that no individual deputy could be said to have either will or power of his own, except in so far as either concurred with the general interests of his order. On the dissolution of the diet, he was required to appear before his constituents, and give a strict account of the manner in which those instructions had been followed. Woe to the poor wretch, whom fear or favour had induced to deviate from them ! he was almost sure to be massacred. As the choice of deputies was so important to the nobles, who thus surrendered their dearest privileges for a time into the hands of their representatives, so it was often a subject of fierce dispute. At these elections sabres were sure to clash, and blood to flow, before that choice was ratified.

The diets were of two descriptions—the ordinary,

which were held biennially, and the extraordinary, which
were summoned on any urgent occasion : the duration
of the former was about six weeks, of the latter, three.
The diets by deputies were termed the *comitia togata*,
because the members were to meet without arms or
horses ; but the *comitia paludata*, which assembled
during an interregnum, consisted of the whole body of
the nobles, who attended in the open plain, armed and
equipped as if for battle.   It was seldom, indeed, that
such meetings were confined to mere deliberation : they
almost invariably ended in tumult and blood.   All diets
(except those held during the interregna) were convoked
by the king, in writs addressed to the palatines, which
the latter communicated to the castellans, starosts, and
other officers, commanding them on a given day to assemble the nobles in dietines, for the election of deputies to the general diet.   In these dietines, every *gentleman* possessing an estate of three acres could vote ;
and every deputy was chosen by the majority of suffrages.

The necessity of unanimity in the general diets, and
the power possessed by any deputy, however humble, of
arresting their proceedings, was the great curse of these
representative assemblies.   As the nuntii were impera-
tively enjoined to insist on certain given points, as they
were liable to so rigorous an examination of the way in
which they discharged their trust, they usually brought
obstinacy enough to these ill-regulated scenes.   Hence
unanimity was found impossible ; and the baneful veto
not only paralysed the operations of government, but
often left the army without pay, and the state without
defence, at a time when vigour and promptitude were
alike necessary to save the national independence,—
when hostile armies were ravaging the frontier provinces.
Another manœuvre, scarcely less diabolical than the
veto itself, was the habit of wasting the time of the diet
in frivolous disputes, until the day of its dissolution arrived.   This was called *drawing out the diet*.   If a few
members wished to oppose the passing of any particular

resolution, and were yet afraid to do so openly, they had only to propose something which they were sure would be rejected, but which would have the effect of dividing the members, and of causing them to lose their time in acrimonious disputes. This was called *blowing into the nest to vex the flies.* Apprehensive of such a result, or of the veto, or of both, the army, which could receive no pay without an express vote of the diet, would frequently approach the capital to keep the factions in awe. At other times a great body of the nobles, distrustful of their delegates, would openly encamp in the plain outside the walls of the city, and by this means secure the fidelity of their representatives. But all would not do ; diet after diet was dissolved, and the republic, as we have seen in the course of this history, reduced to the very brink of destruction. It must inevitably have perished long before the last partition, but for an experiment as singular as any other thing in this most singular of constitutions. This was the *confederations.*

The *confederations* were meetings in which measures were carried by the *majority* of suffrages, and in which, consequently, the veto could have no place. When successive diets were dissolved by this fatal privilege,— when the machine of the state was thereby completely arrested, perhaps at some critical moment,—a few leading nobles formed themselves into a body, and by their manifestoes, addressed to the whole of their order, invited all who valued the king, the constitution, or the country, to unite with them in devising such means as appeared necessary for the occasion. The nobles who attended at the appointed time and place,—and all who failed so to do were menaced with the confiscation of their property, — were bound by oath to defend each other's honour, possessions, and life, against all opponents. If a majority of the Poles attended it, it was approved by the king, who presided at its sittings ; and its proceedings were thus legalised. So jealous were the people, however, of destroying their favourite law of unanimity, that the authority of the confederations could not extend beyond the time of their actual existence : the moment these bodies separated, their powers ceased; and their measures, how transient soever the purposes for which they were devised, were always to be laid before the next· diet, for the approbation of that truly constitutional assembly.

Of confederations there were various kinds. Those which were formed with the consent of the senate, and of the equestrian order, were called *general.* These were always useful, often necessary. Another class sprung from rebellion to lawful authority, or an extreme zeal for measures which the regular diets could not be persuaded to adopt. Sometimes several such confederations were sitting at the same time—with views, of course, directly opposite, and treating each other as rebels and traitors. A third species of confederation was that of the army, which often rose against its officers, or even against the king and diet : the most frequent cause was want of pay. The *Rokosz* was the last and most dreaded of these self-elected assemblies. At its voice the nobles were obliged to have recourse to arms, to obtain the object proposed by open force. This was usually the last resource of a desperate minority ; and though the present evils occasioned by it might be great, its influence was short-lived. None of these confederations, it is evident, were legal,— none in strict accordance with the spirit of the constitution, except those which were denominated *general.* As their measures were clearly for the good of the state,— usually, indeed, for its salvation,— there was no difficulty in procuring their ratification by the following diet. Generally, however, such sanction was unnecessary. The confederation did not separate until its objects were attained : what *had been* done could not be recalled ; and it was not safe to blame proceedings which had been adopted by an overwhelming majority of the nobles,— and such a majority was necessary to constitute a legal general confederation.

The confederation had its marshal, in imitation of the diet; but the authority of the former was usually more extended than that of the latter; it was almost equal to that possessed by the ancient dictators.

The *dietines*, or little diets, were, as before observed, assemblies of the nobles in each palatinate, where *nuntii* were elected to the general diet. Most of the local business of the palatinate was also transacted at these meetings. As unanimity was not here necessary, as the partisans of different candidates were often nearly balanced in number, and as all who attended were armed, they seldom separated without bloodshed. To the ancient Poles, as to the modern Irish, nothing could be more agreeable than a bloody affray.

Such were the more remarkable institutions of the ancient Poles. It now remains to say something of their *manners*.[*]

Before the seventh century of the Christian era, the Slavi led a nomadic life. The fathers of the Sarmatians, living, if we may thus express it, in the primitive state of nature, possessed their territory in common. But this state could not continue for ever. As early as the sixth century, the Slavi began to live in society. "They do not," says Procopius, "obey one master; they live in democracy; they continue isolated, and lead a nomadic life. The god of thunder is their chief divinity; they sacrifice to him oxen and other beasts; they also honour the rivers and the nymphs. When they proceed to battle, their only arms are a lance and shield." — "They all speak the same barbarous language, and resemble each other in conformation of body; all are tall and strong; their complexion is brown, their hair light; their character is not wicked or perfidious: in many respects they remind us of the simple manners of the Huns." To the democratic habits of this people the same testimony is borne by the imperial historian Constantine Porphyrogenitus.

[*] Much of what follows is abridged or altered from Malte-Brun's *Tableau de Pologne*, by Chodzko, i. 76.

" Anciently," says Dlugoss, " the Poles had no intercouse with other nations either by land or sea. Their clothing was rude, and fabricated by their own hands. Their food was flesh, fish, and milk: they had no riches, and were not therefore envied by their neighbours. After their incorporation into a people, the contributions they paid to their ruler were the skins of such animals as they found in their forests; sometimes fish, cattle, and corn were added. The orders of the chief had all the force of law. Their huts were thatched with straw. Free and tranquil, they lived at peace both with their neighbours and with one another. This was the golden age — the age of simplicity and happiness — to our fathers."

The good Dlugoss, in this short but graphic sketch of ancient simplicity and happiness, — drawn wholly from imagination, — has only fallen into the universal error. What nation is there which does not boast of its golden age? yet in what nation did it ever exist?

After the first union of Chrobatia with Poland by Ziemowit, the manners of the Poles began to change, — to follow the impulse given them by the opening of an intercourse with the west, and by the introduction of Christianity. At that time the pagan deities of these people, such as *Jessa* (Jupiter), *Liada* (Mars), *Dziezlia* (Venus), *Nia* (Pluto), who had a temple at Gnesna, *Dzievana* (Diana), *Zyvia Marzana* (Ceres), and others, were put to flight by the holy sign of man's redemption. The temples of Cracow, and the altars of Lelum Polelum (Castor and Pollux), gave way to the Christian altars erected by Miecislas I., which were farther multiplied by his son, the great Boleslas.* This last prince was the true founder and legislator of the Poles. By him justice and civilisation were diffused over the country. He introduced the Benedictines, who rendered immense services to Poland; many cities were then built; the equestrian order was then instituted, whose valour was destined to exalt to such a

* See the reign of Boleslas I.

U

pitch the greatness of the country, before the abuse of
their privileges brought anarchy and disorder.

The manners of this period are thus described by
Dlugoss: — " The Polish nobles thirst for military
fame; dangers, and even death, they despise; they are
lavish of their revenues, faithful to their sovereign, taking
pleasure in agricultural pursuits and the breeding of
cattle.   They are open towards strangers, and afford to
other nations the finest example of hospitality and beneficence; but they oppress their peasants.   The country
people are much addicted to drunkenness; hence quarrels, wounds, sometimes murder.   They are, however,
patient, and accustomed to the most rigorous labours;
they support, without complaining, hunger, cold, and
every óther privation; they believe in magic, are fond
of novelty, and never scruple at robbery or plunder.
They care little about comfort in their dwellings."

· After the fortunate issue of the war with the Teutonic
knights (1466), the re-union of Pomerania with Poland
made commerce flourish: from this time, as the national
writers justly observe, may be dated the introduction of
luxury, and the first inroads on the severe manners of
the ancient Sarmatians.   Seventy years after the time
of Dlugoss, Decius, secretary of Sigismund I., bears
witness to the change which was in progress in the
habits of the people.   " Luxury and indulgence," says
he, " succeeded to the severity of the warlike virtues."
This author, however, rather praises the change, since
it was transforming savage ferocity into something like
humanity.   Under Albert, things remained in the same
state; under Alexander, the luxury of the table was
carried to an enormous height; every body was impoverished by foolish expenses, especially in dress.   But
amidst all this, something good may be discovered;
the sanctity in which promises were held, and the inclination of all classes for reading, were characteristic of
the times.   Under Sigismund I., instruction flourished
beyond example: few gentlemen were to be found who
could not speak three or four languages; all, without

exception, spoke Latin, which was as much the language of the court and of diplomacy as French is at the present day. When the Polish deputation arrived at Paris, to offer the crown to Henry, what most astonished the French, says De Thou, " was the facility with which they expressed themselves in Latin, French, German, and Italian. These four languages were as familiar to them as their native tongue." Their superior information was humiliating to the Gallic nobility, of whom no more than two could converse in Latin, and these had to be brought from their estates in the country for the purpose of upholding the honour of the French nobility. " They spoke our language with so much purity, that they might have been taken for men educated on the banks of the Seine or the Loire, rather than in countries watered by the Vistula and the Dnieper. Our courtiers, who know nothing, and who are declared enemies of every thing called learning, were sadly humbled; when spoken to, they could only blush, or answer by signs." Muretus bears the same honourable testimony to the acquirements of the Poles of his day, whom he contrasts with the Italians.

In the time of Cromer (the 16th century), the Poles are represented, — but some allowance must be made for the favourable colouring of a native, — as free and open ; as preferring to be the dupes of deception rather than deceivers ; as inclined to peace even more than to war (the reverse, however, is notoriously the fact) ; as directed by mildness and magnanimity ; as devoted to their king and leaders (untrue) ; as hospitable and warm-hearted (most true) ; as strongly inclined to imitate the modes of other people ; as fond of literature, but averse to the mechanical arts ; as still more fond of pomp.

There is a singular conversation, in MS., preserved by Minucci, in the account of the journey he undertook, in 1659, to negotiate for his master, the duke of Tuscany, the succession to the Polish crown ; — a conversation characteristic enough of the Polish rustics. " What think you of this country ?" enquired the

Polish queen of the envoy. " What surprises me most, madam," was the reply, " is to see that, notwithstanding the war which has brought such desolation on the country, I find fertility on every side : every where do I see the peasants actively employed in repairing them." " Know," said the queen, " that these are people who complain of the present without remembering the past, or caring for the future. Whenever the enemy sacks a town and departs, the inhabitants of that town return the following day to rebuild it. This you have seen in the case of Wratislaw, which has been rebuilt in so short a time, and within sight too of the enemy stationed on the opposite side of the Vistula." Her majesty spoke the real truth : no people on earth so soon forget their misfortunes as the Polish peasantry ; they were, and are now, as light-hearted as the French.

Under succeeding princes, the Poles, the most imitative of human beings, conformed to the fashion of the court, whether that fashion was German or French ; but the former they merely tolerated, while in the latter their souls were wrapt. As foreign kings, and still more as foreign queens, thenceforth presided over the festivities of the capital, the national manners were confounded with the novelties introduced. In the country, however, amidst nature's everlasting forests, ancient usages remained in all their vigour, until the Russian and French troops, who overran or were quar- in every part, by their intercourse with the people greatly weakened the nationality which had hitherto prevailed. That nationality is every where decaying more and more. The partition of the people under three different governments has done more to produce this effect than any other cause, or all other causes combined. The citizens of Warsaw are already French or Russian, while the inhabitants of Posen and Galicia find no difficulty in assimilating in manners with their Prussian and Austrian fellow-subjects.

In contemplating the state of society in Poland during the progress of ages, to omit all mention of the Jews, a people more numerous here than in any other country of the same extent under heaven, and bearing so great a proportion to the whole population, would be unpardonable. The influence of these people is to be found in every thing, — in the laws, the history, and the condition of the Poles.

In the tenth century, a great number of Jews, attracted by the fertility of the soil, the abundance of minerals, and the facilities for commerce, afforded by Poland, removed into that country from various parts of Germany. Their example was followed by their brethren of Bohemia (which at that time could scarcely be called a part of Germany); there they found protection and repose. Probably a few of that nation had long been settled in various parts of the country, as we know they had been in Russia; but we have no historic account of the circumstance, unless the Jewish traditions are admitted as history, prior to the period under consideration.

The first charter granted to the Polish Jews was by Boleslas II. in 1264. It was renewed and greatly amplified by Casimir the Great, whose celebrated mistress, the Jewess Esther, knew how to interest him in behalf of her nation. Witold, of Lithuania, also encouraged them : by Lewis king of Poland and Hungary, however, they were persecuted. Under some princes they were not allowed to have any intimate connection with Christians. As they certainly gave unwonted activity to commerce, they appear to have been suffered as a necessary evil. They were treated with rigour under Sigismund : they were accused — probably not unjustly — of being concerned in a plot for the occupation of the eastern provinces by the Turks ; but their money, it is believed, turned aside the gathering storm. Their riches must indeed have been considerable, if any estimate is to be drawn from the fact, that nearly all the trade of the country was in their hands. In 1540 they boasted that, while the Christians could number only 600 dealers, *they* had 3200 ; and that they gave employment to near 10,000 mechanics, artisans, and manufacturers.

Though the wealth of the Jews often exposed them to the avarice of the great, there can be no doubt that the hatred with which they were always regarded in Poland, as every where else, was to a certain extent deserved. By practising usury, and dealing in contraband commodities, — both forbidden by the ancient church of Poland, — by lending money on the most iniquitous terms to the heirs of the rich, they rendered themselves obnoxious to the people. But habituated to insults; accustomed to proceed straitforward to their end — the accumulation of wealth, no matter the road which led them to it; industrious beyond all precedent; always sober, and pressed by few wants, they seldom failed to grow rich. Nothing can more fully expose their exceptionable mode of dealing, than the fact, that by the Polish laws they have at all times been forbidden to keep wine shops, to sell brandy, or to traffic with the peasantry, lest they should not only impoverish, but corrupt that thoughtless class. Subsequently they were prohibited from dealing in horses.

The numerical increase of this people has long surprised the Poles; the ratio of that increase, compared with that of the Christians, being usually as two, or even three, to one. Sigismund Augustus was astonished at the fact: perhaps, too, he began to be alarmed lest in time they should outnumber the Christian population. He subjected them to a capitation tax, from which, at a florin per head, he calculated on receiving about 200,000 florins. His surprise, and that of his court, was extreme on finding that the roll did not contain 17,000 names, though both sexes, old and young, were included. Of course, not one tenth of their actual number had been given in by the Israelites, who have always entertained a particular aversion to such a census. Sigismund complained of this to his intimate friend, the bishop of Cracow, a prelate famous for a tolerant spirit, and — in that age a more remarkable proof of understanding — for an utter disbelief in magic. "Bishop," said the king,—"you who do not believe that the devil has any thing to do with human affairs, and who have no faith in witchcraft,—tell me, I beseech you, how the Jews, who *yesterday* were 200,000, have been able to conceal themselves under ground, so as to reckon scarcely 17,000 *to-day*, when the capitation tax is wanted." — " Your majesty must be aware," replied the prelate, " that the Jews do not want the devil's help to become wizards."

Under Sigismund III. this people had increased so much in number and riches, that they instituted a little state in the country. They printed works, in which they had the boldness to ridicule some ceremonies of the church, and to propose that the whole nation should follow the Mosaic law : they promised to make Poland a second Idumea, if the proposal were accepted. A decree by the diet that whoever spake with disrespect of the Christian rites should be banished, silenced them for this time. Ere long, however, they engaged in a controversial war with the other party, and published an incredible number of pamphlets in support of their civil and religious rights ; nor did the contest end until both parties were tired of conducting it.

Mention has already been made, in the course of this history *, of the rapacious tyranny of the Jewish agents over the Cossacks of the Ukraine. Though, however, they were among the prime causes of Bogdan's rebellion, they appear to have been too formidable for punishment, at least by the state; but the Cossack chief massacred them wherever he found them. They were generally attached to the government which left them unmolested to the acquisition of wealth; but their feeling, when persecuted, was vindictive enough. Under Michael they entered into a treasonable correspondence with their old friends, the Turks : under Sobieski they were remarkable for loyalty. They were, indeed, special favourites of the latter prince, whose elevation to the throne they are said to have predicted—(they might have done so without much knowledge of the occult sciences). In

* See the reigns of Uladislas V. and John Casimir.

1682, the senate remonstrated with him for his indulgence towards them. Their condition under the three succeeding sovereigns was not materially altered.

The Polish Jews have sometimes had to contend with greater enemies than the Christians,—with one another. Messiahs have not been wanting to sow division among them. One of these, Sabatayzavi, drew after him nine tenths of his nation, and at one time seemed disposed to dispute the possession of the country with the Poles themselves. An armed force, however, at length expelled him from the republic, and obliged him to seek refuge among the Turks, by whom—for reasons not explained—he was arrested. But, even in his disgrace, he was not without consideration; for thousands of the sons of Israel resorted to Constantinople to honour him. To expose his impositions, a Polish Jew, of great learning and courage, undertook the same journey: whether, as he purposed, he convinced the divan that the fellow was more of a knave than of an enthusiast, does not appear.

In 1750, one Frank, a neophyte of Wallachia, formed a new sect. He maintained the essentials of the Jewish doctrines, but preserved the Roman ritual. Arriving in Poland, his preaching soon brought him into contact with the tribunals of the country, and consigned him to a fortress. Being released by the Muscovite troops, he went to Vienna, and from thence into Moravia, actively disseminating his new opinions as he passed along. Joseph II. expelled him from Austria. He then proceeded to Offenbach, where he soon collected a considerable number of followers. He at length encountered a rival in a Jewish rabbi, Israel Hirszowicz, who founded a new sect after the doctrines of Maimonides. To secure his influence, he now formed his disciples into a sort of politic association, of which he constituted himself the hereditary chief. When this man died, he was interred with royal honours. His daughter is now the sovereign of the faithful.

The chief maxim of this sect is, that a Jew must of necessity always be a Jew, and observe the law of Moses;

but that he may publicly follow the profession of the dominant religion: he has only to observe the Mosaic rites *in secret.* In the fear that this strange tenet should be made known, and lead, as it inevitably must have done, to the destruction of those convicted of entertaining it, all marriages with orthodox Jews as well as with Gentiles are prohibited. The members of this sect are believed to be exceedingly numerous, and to fill important posts in the administration of the countries they inhabit. Their chief place is Appenheim; but they assume so much mystery, that they have hitherto eluded the investigation of the police.

Since the occupation of Poland by the three powers, the Jews have been placed on the same footing of equality as the Christian inhabitants. They do not trouble themselves with the tribunals of the country, so long as disputes happen among themselves; their elders are their judges. But between Jews and Christians law-suits are common enough: out of every ten cases brought before the courts, a Jew is said to be concerned in nine. In many cases, however, they are merely the agents of others. At this day, as in the seventeenth century, they are the stewards, or managers, or agents of the great landed proprietors, to whom they have made themselves indispensable. Almost all the coin of the kingdom is in their hands; and they are ever ready to advance it to spendthrifts — and such are most of the Polish nobles — who have any thing in the shape of security to offer.

There is no trade too vile, or even too dangerous, for a Polish Jew, if he can profit by it. In 1806 and 1812, they were the hired spies of the French and Polish armies; but they are charged, probably on good grounds, with betraying their employers whenever they found it their interest to do so. They are said on these occasions to have rendered far more signal services to the Russians, whom they were hired to watch, than to either French or Poles; and their perversity in this respect is viewed as having occasioned no light disasters in the last fearful

expedition.   They are now, however, much less attached
to Russia, since Nicholas, by an ukase of April, 1827,
has rendered them liable to the military conscription.
Those which live under his yoke now curse both him
and his cause, and heartily wish success to the Poles.
Two regiments of Jews now swell the forces of the
brave republic.   To their conduct on this occasion,
as in 1794, when they raised and supported a regiment
of their own nation, it is impossible for their worst enemies to deny the meed of praise. *Then* they exhibited
as much bravery as the most patriotic of the Polish
chivalry ; *now*, they will do no less honour to themselves
and cause.

The amazing fecundity of the Jews has been charged
to their early marriages : most of them are parents at a
very early age, and grandfathers before many English
gentlemen even think of marrying.   It may, however,
be reasonably doubted, whether such marriages are
favourable to population.   But one thing is certain, that
the proportion they bear to the Christians is alarming.*
As they are not producers, but live on the produce raised
by others, their existence in no state—at least in any
considerable numbers —can be other than a national injury.   That they have been a curse to Poland, is loudly
proclaimed by all the native writers.   Besides their
usurious dealings and general unfairness, they are reproached with always contriving to fail when their children are full grown, and of previously consigning their
property to them, to the prejudice of their creditors.

The Polish Jews acknowledge one universal head,
whom they call *the Prince of Bondage*, and who constantly leads a wandering life in Western Asia.   He is
evidently waiting the redemption of his people.

* See Appendix C, where the number of Polish Jews is computed. The
real number much exceeds it.

APPENDIX A. Page 10.

DESTRUCTION OF POPIEL.

THE substance of the following extract having appeared in the text, there is no necessity for translating it. It is here exhibited as a specimen of the style of an author not very common in this country.

" De cadaveribus siquidem patruorum et procerum quæ tyrannus abjici jusserat inhumata, insolitæ quantitatis murium multitudo ebulliens, sedentem in convivio et voluptate dantem operam *Pompilium* non sine aliorum stupore, in unum duntaxat tyrannum *Pompilium,* et suam consortem, duosque filios *Pompilium,* et Leszkonem cœpit continuatis et rabidis morsibus infestare desævireque. Quos etsi militum servorumque sedula cura abigeret, recentesque succederent fatigatis: Vincebat tamen perseverans murium, et noctu et interdiu, nullo spatio ad quietum concesso, multitudo omnium suffragiis aut defatigatis, aut se ab ejus tutela sub ducentibus. Cùm et in defensores rabies sæpius murium verteretur, nova remedia præparantur, extruuntur frequentes et ardentes foci, et in medio eorum *Pompilius* cum uxore et filiis consistit, si forte incendiis mures arcerentur, sed et ignes quantumcunque flammantes, muribus pervii nullum præstabant Pompilio auxilium. Sic ad aliud elementum reversus, in late patentia stagna deportatur per naves Pompilius cum consorte et liberis, et turri locatur lignea, undis undique ambita, sed nihilo plus undæ tulerunt remedii, quàm ignes. Singulos enim gurgites, in quos se *Popiel* contulerat, mures natando variis itineribus illum persequebantur, consecutique navem assiduis corrosionibus infestabant: Milites autem et nautæ, ne simul navi a muribus perforata aquarum suffocatione interirent, ipso etiam *Pompilio* mandante, in litus navem reducunt. Cui è navi egredienti, nova murium caterva occurrit,

et cum his qui illum in stagna consecuti fuerant, simul con-
juncta tyrannum vehementius infestant.   His itaque et aliis
pluribus remediis, ne quicquam proficientibus, virtutem divi-
nam universi agnoscentes, ab eo diffugiunt.   Qui videns se
ab omnibus desertum, in turrim castri *Crusviciensis* excellen-
tiorem cum conjuge et duobus filiis conscendit, ubi à super-
abundante murium multitudine, a quibus sine intervallo
oppugnabantur, duo primùm filii, eo et infelice matre inspec-
tante, nullamque ferre valentibus opem, deinde crudelissima
conjux, et ipse ad extremum tyrannus Popiel adeò lacerati et
corrosi, et cum singulis partibus artubusque devorati sunt, ut
neque, alicujus ossis vel nervi vestigium reliquerent.   In
hunc modum scelestus et impius *Popiel* cum suggestrice iniqua,
altera *Jesabel* et filiis, ultione divina deletus et insolito novoque
genere mortis consumptus, manibus necatorum patruorum
et procerum justas pœnas dedit." — *Dlugoss*, lib. i. col. 76
et 77.

APPENDIX B. Page 221.

ESCAPE OF STANISLAS LECSZINSKI.

The escape of this prince from Dantzic is one of the most romantic incidents in either history or biography ; if possible, it exceeds in interest that of the equally unfortunate Prince Charles after the battle of Culloden. The following account is abridged from one drawn up by the king himself : I preserve as much as possible the very words of the royal relater.

THE king, having procured a peasant's dress, left his hotel in Dantzic, in which he had been so long and so closely invested by the Muscovite troops, about ten o'clock in the evening of June 27. 1734, just as the city resolved to capitulate. After passing the ditch surrounding the rampart, he and his companions, all peasants, except one of his generals, proceeded in a boat, (the whole country was then inundated by the waters of the Vistula,) to seek the bed of that river, in the hope that by dawn of day they would have gained the bank opposite to the posts held by the Russians. But daylight surprised them before they had sailed an English mile, and they were compelled to pass the day in a mean cabin within sight of the city, and in momentary risk of being surprised by the enemy. At nightfall they resumed their precarious voyage ; and at midnight the general and two companions left the others to sail over the marsh, while they endeavoured to find a more practicable route by land. He saw the general no more. He was now left with two guides only, on whose discretion he could not place much reliance, and whose fidelity appears to have been more than once, though, as the result proves, unjustly, suspected by him.

At daybreak, the little party were again anxious to procure some hiding-place until night ; but as the houses were likely to be filled with Cossacks, there was great peril in the attempt. They found a hut belonging to an acquaintance of the two countrymen. Here the king was ushered into a small chamber the only one in the house; and left to his reflections, on a bundle of straw, while his conductors went out to reconnoitre; and, if possible, to discover some trace of the general and their companions. These reflections were not of the most pleasing description: every moment he feared to be taken, by the arrival of the Russians, or through the treachery of his guides. He could not sleep. — " I rose up, and on looking out at a loop-hole, perceived a Russian officer gravely pacing the meadow, and two soldiers watching their horses graze. The sight stopped my breath. The thoughtful air of the man, who seemed intent on something, — the horses, which he continually approached, as if impatient to make use of them, — the armed soldiers, and their appearance in a place so far distant from their camp, — all made me apprehensive that I had fallen into the net I had been so careful to avoid. There is something more valuable than courage, — something which I was near losing, — I mean *hope*, by which that courage is often inspired and supported. My alarm was still further increased on perceiving, about a hundred paces behind, several Cossacks galloping along the fields : they were approaching the wretched shelter in which I had expected to find more security than any where else. The unexpected sight made me draw back from my window to my straw pallet. I thought of nothing but how to escape the pursuit of the men who surrounded me. I expected to see the house invested in a moment : more than this was done ; it was not blockaded, but instantly occupied ; and steps were heard on the stair ascending to my loft."

This, however, was a false alarm : the Cossacks, indeed, were in the house, but only to take refreshment ; and the steps on the stairs were those of the hostess, whom his conductors, just arrived, had sent to desire him to lie quiet. In about two hours the Cossacks departed ; but he had great difficulty in satisfying the inquisitiveness of his hostess, who, though simple enough, could easily perceive he was no peasant.

" Towards night, being heartily tired of my situation in the loft, I descended to converse with my conductors. They knew, they said, that the general was only a quarter of a league off, and that he purposed to join us at night on the border of the Vistula, where a boat was ready to take us over ; but they

doubted whether the passage could be made in the high wind
then blowing, and in a boat so small, and so unfit for the object, as the one they had procured.　'Let us try, at any rate,'
said I: 'I see no danger so great as remaining longer where
we are.'　I could no longer distrust men who, having eat and
drunk with my enemies, had preferred my safety to their own
interests; who, amidst the smoke of tobacco, and with a kind
of beer well fitted to muddle their senses, had courage and
honesty enough to preserve the fidelity they had promised me.
My resolution was opposed by them.　At nightfall we re-
entered the boat, which, however, we left a short distance from
the hut, on the verge of the inundation.　We now travelled some
miles on foot: the ground was so soft and muddy that we
were often knee-deep in it, and were constantly obliged to aid
each other in getting out of it: sometimes our efforts to do so
only plunged us the more deeply into the mire.

　"At length we gained the brink of the Vistula.　Here
one of my conductors desired me to wait a moment, while he
went to see if the boat was ready at the place appointed.　He
kept us in suspense a full hour; and when he returned, we
learned that no boat was in sight, and that the Russians had
probably taken it away.　All that we could now do, was to
re-enter the marsh we had just left.　We followed another
route, and after walking a league, — as painful a walk as the
one we had just supported, — we arrived at a house in which
I was instantly recognised.　"What do I see!" exclaimed
my host, the moment he saw me.　"One of our comrades to
be sure!" replied one of the conductors: "dost thou see any
thing extraordinary in him?"　"I am not deceived," rejoined
the man: "it is king Stanislas!"　"Yes, friend!" said I, in
a firm tone, "I am he; but if I may judge from your coun-
tenance, you are too civil to refuse me the aid I want in my
present situation."　This simple confession had the best possible effect: I understood my man at once.　His free and
decided manner announced to me either an enemy, — perhaps
a dangerous one, if I refused him my confidence; or a man
prompt to undertake any thing or every thing, if I testified as
much openness as himself.　He promised to provide me with
a boat for passing the Vistula; and he fulfilled the promise.

Full of zeal, he left his house to seek one, and to ascertain in what part the passage could be made with the least danger."

In the meantime the fugitive king was unexpectedly joined by the peasant — the leader, indeed, of the rest — from whom he had separated the night following his escape from the city, and to whom his safety had been intrusted by the French ambassador in that place. He learned that the Cossacks were every where beating the bushes in search of him; and that the general, with another companion, had with difficulty escaped from them the preceding night, while waiting for him on the borders of the Vistula. These active emissaries of the enemy stopped and strictly examined every person they met. The trusty host now returned, with the news that he had engaged a boat; but as two Muscovites lodged in the boat-man's house, and as many of the same nation were in the immediate vicinity, he advised the king to defer the passage awhile longer. It was accordingly decided that the latter should remain that night and the following day in the house of his kind-hearted host.

"The following day, Thursday, July 1., I assembled my people, to hear their opinion on this important passage of the Vistula, which lay so near my heart. We examined all the places where it might be attempted with any success. The counsels of my conductors were more or less bold, their views more or less feasible, according to the state of a brandy-bottle which lay before them: it was the bottle which presided, and regulated their deliberations. At first I heard nothing but timid proposals: there was no hope of passing over undis-covered; the promised recompence, great as it was, lost all its attraction; and prisons, tortures, gibbets, were the only things present to their imaginations. A new supply of the liquor insensibly raised their dejected courage, and I saw the moment would soon come when they would have faced the whole Russian camp, and led me, without fear, through a thousand batteries. I kept things in a sort of medium by the care which I took of the bottle, and by dealing out to each the dose of courage which each required."

But *spirits* thus raised, were not likely to remain long ex-cited: they were sure to sink with the stimulant which had

occasioned them. The little party set out; the host first, next
Stanislas, and the doughty conductors brought up the rear.
On both sides, appeared in the distance the fires of the enemy's
flying camps, which thus lighted the royal fugitive on his way.
The sight was by no means cheering to the peasants. Their
fright was increased on the host's riding back to say, that he
perceived troops of Cossacks before them, and that he was near
being intercepted by them. They now held a consultation
without the king's permission, and insisted in the end on returning. He strenuously opposed it, and so did the host; all
however would have been vain but for the threat, that if they
were so base as to abandon one whom they had so solemnly engaged to protect, he would himself call on the Cossacks to seize
both him and them, and would thereby have the satisfaction of
knowing that their situation would be no better than his own.
As the Cossacks moved away, the party proceeded onwards;
but the heroes of the preceding day kept a respectful distance in the rear, resolved, no doubt, to run away should they
behold their charge in jeopardy. At length they reached the
river, embarked, and made the long desired passage.

"We were about to land, when taking my host aside, and
affectionately thanking him for all he had done for me, I put
into his hand as many ducats, drawn from my pocket, as mine
could hold. This was an opportunity of relieving myself of
a weight of money which inconvenienced me. Besides, I was
discharging, as I thought, a debt, not conferring a favour.
The honest peasant, surprised and ashamed, drew back, and
endeavoured to escape me. 'No, no,' said I, 'it is in vain;
you must receive this present.' As I urged him more strongly,
and as he renewed his attempts to escape, the others supposed
that I was quarrelling with him, and advanced to appease me.
Perceiving this movement on their part, he hastily said, that
to satisfy me he would accept *two* ducats, which he would
always keep as a remembrance of the happiness he had had in
knowing me. This noble disinterestedness charmed me the
more, as I had no reason to expect it from a man in his condition. He took two ducats from my hand; but made such
faces that I cannot express them."

But the king's dangers were not yet ended. At a short dis-

x

tance from the other bank of the Vistula, the party (the host had returned) entered a considerable village, which they had the consolation of learning was often visited by advanced posts of the Russians. The three peasants, fancying that nothing was to be feared, threw themselves on a bed and were instantly asleep, while the poor fugitive kept watch. One of them he at length awakened, whom he despatched to hire or purchase a vehicle of some description. In about two hours the fellow returned, so drunk as to be unable to stand, with a man who had one to sell. The bargain was struck; when the sot, perceiving Stanislas return some ducats into a purse, began to extol his fidelity, the services he had performed, the risks he had run, and insisted on knowing on the spot what reward he was to have for all this. His vociferations soon assembled round him a considerable number of villagers, who listened in mute silence, or with marks of sympathy. All began to wonder how a peasant, as Stanislas seemed, could have collected twenty-five ducats (the price of the vehicle), and still more how he came to be attended by so many servants. Their suspicions were roused, and the result might have proved serious, had not the leader of the conductors exclaimed to the people —" Take no notice of this fellow. In his cups he always speaks as if he were in the company of kings and princes, instead of sinful peasants like me. If you listen to him, he will make me into some great personage or other." The fellow was ridiculed or hissed by most; by some he was supposed to have some " method in his madness;" but the party removed with all possible expedition, laying the bacchanalian at the bottom of the vehicle. They passed several villages occupied by Muscovite and Saxon soldiers; but luckily they escaped unobserved, until they arrived on the banks of the Nogat. How to cross it was the main point. There was no boat in sight, and none of the conductors were willing to run the risk of detection by enquiring for a boat at any of the scattered huts in sight. They insisted that the only point was to proceed to Marienburg — which would have been certain destruction — and cross the bridge of that fortress. Indignant at their opposition, the king resolved to approach a neighbouring house himself, for the purpose of giving information : —

" At the same time I prepared to alight from the vehicle
but with my people this was a day of contradictions: they opposed my design, apprehensive that my speech would betray
me. I ridiculed their fear, alighted, and went on. They
threw themselves before me, muttering that they would rather
die than suffer me to advance a step further. This impudence
I could not stand, and ran towards them as if resolved to leap
over them. A moment afterwards I smiled at my own vivacity; but how could I restrain it in the first heat of my resentment? My firmness made them open before me. ' Well,'
said they, ' since it is your wish to hang us, we leave you!'
' With all my heart!' was my reply: 'go as soon as you
please. A good journey!'

" I entered the house; and in tones as polished as my rustic
garb would permit (which I dared not contradict), I informed
the hostess that I wanted to pass the Nogat to purchase cattle,
and that I should be glad if she would point out the best place
for the passage. ' Oh!' she replied, ' you come at an excellent time: you need not be at the trouble of passing the
river — no pleasant or easy thing at any time. I have cattle
to sell you; and from your manner I see that we shall easily
agree as to the price.' I replied, that I could not purchase it
until my return, because I was compelled to pass the river to
receive a sum of money due to me, of which I would willingly
devote a portion to conclude the bargain with her. ' But
there is no boat in; — what will you do?' — ' Just as you
advise me,' was my answer, in an open, free tone: ' I prefer
receiving a favour from you rather than from any body else —
" I know the country," added I, " and that it is impossible for
you, who are obliged to maintain a constant intercourse with
the other bank, not to have some means of crossing in spite of
the Muscovites.' — ' I see you are a good fellow,' she replied.
' Stay! I will send my son with you: he will take you about
a quarter of a league from here. A friend of his, a fisherman,
who has a boat, lives on the opposite bank; and on a signal
being given, the man will cross over to take you in: you could
not have a safer or easier way of crossing !' I thanked the
woman in the most ardent terms, and left the house with her
son."

x 2

The king arrived at the place appointed, the signal was given, the fisherman appeared with the boat, and the illustrious fugitive was immediately landed in the Prussian dominions, where he was happily free from danger.   He found that orders had been given by the king to afford him every assistance, and show him every respect, in the towns through which he passed. At Konigsberg, he was royally entertained in the king's palace.   From thence he proceeded to France, to enjoy in his duchy of Lorraine, which his son-in-law the French king had conferred on him, a happiness which no throne could have sustained.

This Christian philosopher died in 1766.   His death was occasioned by fire accidentally catching his dressing gown, when no page was near to assist him.   The feeble old man (he was 89) was at length extricated from his immediate agony, but he did not long survive the accident: the wounds mortified and carried him off, to the regret of his subjects and of humanity.

APPENDIX C. Page 270.

STATISTICAL VIEW OF POLAND.

" THE kingdom of Poland is divided into *eight* palatinates ; *viz.* Masovia, Cracow, Sandomir, Kalisz, Lublin, Plotsk, and Augustowa. The population, according to the last census in 1829, was (exclusive of the army) 4,088,290, which may be thus classed * : —

By their several races :		*By their religion :*	
The real Poles - - 3,000,000		Roman Catholics - - 3,400,000
Rusini, or Rusniacks, from		Greek Church - - 100,000
the eastern parts of an-		Lutherans - - - 150,000
cient Poland - - 100,000		Calvinists - - 5,000
Lithuanians - - 200,000		Jews - - - 400,000
Germans - - - 300,000		Other Sects - - 5,000
Jews - - - 400,000			
	4,000,000		4,060,000

" The population of the towns is to that of the country as one to five.

Employed in agriculture, there are householders - - -	1,871,259
Their families and servants - -	2,221,188
Manufactures - - -	140,377
Their families - - -	358,035
Tradesmen - - - -	49,888
Their families - - - -	131,331
Landed proprietors - - -	4,205
Copyholders - - - -	1,886
Freeholders in towns - - -	41,654
Persons employed under government -	8,414
Patients in the 592 public hospitals -	5,376
Prisoners in the 76 prisons - -	7,926

" The proportion between the nobles and the plebeians is as one to thirteen.

" According to a verification made by the senate in 1824, there were in the kingdom 12 princes, 74 counts, and 20 barons, besides the inferior or untitled nobility.

* See No. XIV. of the Foreign Quarterly Review.

" The city of Warsaw reckoned, in 1815, only 80,000 in-habitants ; it now amounts to 140,000, besides the garrison. The provincial towns are Lublin, having 13,400; Kalisch, 12,100; Plotsk, 9,200, &c.   The population of the kingdom has been increasing since 1815, at the rate of 100,000 indivi-duals every year.

" It appears from Dr. Rodecki's statistical tables, published at Warsaw, in 1830, that there are Jews in almost every town of the kingdom of Poland ; that in 14 of these, their number is equal to that of the Christians, while in 114 it is greater : in three, the inhabitants are either all Jews, or almost entirely so.   In Warsaw alone they muster 30,000.   Their number is fast increasing.   They monopolise almost all trade, to the exclusion of the Christian population.   The government has endeavoured to check this evil, but with little success; and with this view Professor Chiarini has been employed in trans-lating the Thalmud, and in laying down a plan of reform for that singular people.

" The Catholic religion being that of the great majority of the kingdom, is under the *special protection of the government,* without infringing, however, on the public freedom of other forms of worship, and on the equality of individuals of every communion in the enjoyment of civil rights.   The Catholic hierarchy consists of the archbishop of Warsaw, primate of the kingdom, and eight bishops, one for each palatinate. There are 1638 parish churches, 117 auxiliary ones, 6 colleges, 11 seminaries, 151 male convents, and 29 female.   In 1819, Pope Pius VII. suppressed by a bull 31 male convents and 13 female.   The number of the clergy of the Latin Catholic Church is 2740.   The Greek Catholics have a bishop at Chelm, 287 parish churches, one seminary, and five male con-vents.   Their priests amount to 354.   There are, besides, six churches of the Russo-Greek communion under the jurisdic-tion of the bishop of Minsk, 29 Lutheran and 9 Calvinist churches, having their respective consistories, 2 of the sect of Philippines, 274 synagogues, and 2 Mahomedan mosques with their imams !

" The University of Warsaw was founded in 1816, in lieu of that of Cracow, and it consists of five faculties, having 48 professors, and about 750 students. There are besides at Warsaw four lyceums, besides other schools, Sunday schools for mechanics, and girls' school. In the provinces are 11 palatine schools and 14 district ones. In all the kingdom there are 1756 professors or teachers, nearly 30,000 students, and about 11,000 female pupils.

" In all chief towns of palatinates there are civil and criminal courts, besides commissions of peace in every district. The two courts of appeal and the supreme court assemble at Warsaw. The senate takes cognisance of offences against the state; there are also a court of commerce and a territorial court.

" The army consisted, in 1830, of 8 regiments of infantry of the line, besides the guards, 4 regiments of light infantry, 8 regiments of cavalry, besides the yagers of the guard, 2 brigades of foot artillery, and 2 ditto of horse, a corps of engineers, &c., in all 36,000 men. The arsenal and foundery are at Warsaw. There are two fortresses in the kingdom, Zamosk and Modlin. Every individual from 20 to 30 years of age is subject to military service, except in cases of exemption provided by the law. The two new military schools, formed in 1825, near Warsaw, have educated already 7000 pupils.

" The budget of 1827 consisted as follows : —

Receipt.	Florins.*
Direct taxes	17,646,652
Indirect ditto	40,685,630
Income of national lands and forests	7,048,265
Income from tolls and rates on bridges, roads, &c.	8,769,955
Receipt from mines, mint, prisoners' labour, &c.	2,837,600
Total	71,988,102

Expences.	Florins.
Civil list reduced in 1822, from 2,324,705 to	1,508,150
Viceroy, senate, council of state	924,609

* The Polish *florin* is about sixpence sterling. It is divided into 30 *groschet.*

x 4

Ministry of public instruction and religious worship - - -	3,831,821
Ditto of justice - - -	2,528,301
Ditto of interior or home department -	3,178,909
Ditto of war - - - -	30,927,795
Ditto of finances - - -	5,155,936
Secretaryship of state - - -	223,000
Superior central authorities - -	944,965
Commissions of administration in the palatinates - - - -	3,666,526
Pensions, repair of roads, public buildings -	11,422,007
Extraordinaries - -	1,866,410
Charges on separate administrations -	2,837,600
Total - -	69,016,030

" There are in the kingdom, especially about Kielce, mines of iron, zinc, coals, and also copper and lead.

" Of the 451 towns in the kingdom 353 consist more than half of wooden houses; 83 are entirely of wood; 6 have half their houses made of brick; and 9 consist of more brick than wooden houses. Warsaw contains 1540 brick and 1421 wooden houses.

" Besides the towns, of which 214 are national property, and 237 belong to private families, there are in the kingdom 22,365 villages, 5373 of which are national, and 16,992 private property.

" The communications have been extensively improved since 1815. Two fine substantial roads cross the whole kingdom, one from Kalisz to Brzesk Litewski, another from Cracow to the Niemen, both passing through Warsaw. Diligences have been established; inns and post-houses erected; 523 bridges have been constructed or repaired. Embankments, in great part of stone, have been raised to restrain the waters of the Vistula. The other rivers have been cleansed, and a canal has been cut to join the Narew to the Niemen.

" The city of Warsaw has wonderfully improved since the peace. New streets, squares, palaces, gardens, private and public buildings have been constructed either by government or by individuals, assisted, in many instances, by the public treasury. The streets are well lighted, several of them have been Macadamized. The management of prisons has been ameliorated; the convicts are employed in the public works; mendicity has been suppressed. A society of beneficence has been formed at Warsaw, as well as a society of the friends of science. A new exchange, a new theatre, the new church of St. Alexander, new barracks, and a monument to Copernicus by Thorwaldsen, have been raised.

" The exports of the kingdom consist chiefly in corn and cattle, besides honey, wax, timber, wool, hides, and tallow. The imports are wines, tobacco, colonial produce, and articles of luxury and fashion.

" The manufactures of woollen cloth, linen, carpets, and leather, have thriven since the peace. While in 1815 there were hardly 100 looms for coarse woollen cloths, there are now above 6000, which supply the whole kingdom, including the army. More than 10,000 families of foreign workmen, chiefly German and Swiss, have expatriated to Poland, where they have built new towns and peopled districts formerly deserted. There are numerous distilleries of spirits, and the brewing trade is also very extensive; they brew porter and ale equal to those of England, By the former laws of Poland commerce was depressed, and no noble, however poor, could, without degradation, resort to it, whilst he often served in a menial capacity a richer nobleman.

" The balance of trade between the kingdom of Poland and the neighbouring states in 1827 stood as follows: —

	Florins.
Imports from Russia -	- 11,079,683
Exports to ditto - -	- 14,548,522
Imports from Prussia -	- 20,318,433
Exports to ditto - -	- 15,544,730
Imports from Austria -	- 8,527,480
Exports to ditto - -	- 91,967
Imports from the republic of Cracow -	748,857
Exports to ditto - -	- 2,880,265

" Agriculture, which is still the principal occupation of the population, suffers under a depression of prices. In 1827, they reaped 4,439,399 *korzecs* * of rye, 3,183,023 of oats, 1,506,062 of barley, and 751,076 of wheat, besides 4,288,185 *korzecs* of potatoes, and hay, flax, hemp, and honey. The cattle are improving both in quantity and quality.

" In 1827, there were in the kingdom 694,728 cows; 475,946 oxen; 259,990 calves; 703,207 pigs; about 2,500,000 sheep; 192,841 horses; 8771 stallions; 167,901 mares. About one half of the extent of the territory of the kingdom may be reckoned to be cultivated, one fourth of the remainder is occupied by forests, and the rest by marshes and uncultivated lands.

" Since the establishment of the Grand Duchy of Warsaw, the peasantry of that part of Poland have been emancipated; they live on the estates of the great landlords, each family having a cabin and thirteen acres of ground, on condition of working for the owner three days in the week. They may remove themselves, by giving up their tenements. Several proprietors have adopted the system of free labour and wages."

* A *korzec* is nearly two hundred weight. It is divided into 32 *garniecs*, of four *kwarts* each.

INDEX.

A.

ACHMET SHAH, in pursuance of his treaty, advances on the confines of the Ukraine; receives no aid from the Polish king; assailed by the rival chief; flies for safety into the states of his allies, 126. After wandering through vast deserts, demands protection from his allies; seized by the palatin of Kiow, 128. Conducted to Wilna to wait the pleasure of the king; kept a prisoner for three years; appears before a diet at Radomski; reception of, by the king; his dignified complaints; detained at Troki, and obliged to promise that he would not escape; the khan of the Crimea urges his perpetual imprisonment; breaks his parole; flies from Troki; overtaken and brought back, and confined in the fortress of Kowno in Samogitia, 129.

Adelaide, a German princess, marriage of, with Casimir III.; her jealousy; banished to a fortress, 97.

Adolphus, Gustavus, successor to Charles, 177. Death of, 178.

Agnes, wife of Uladislas II., causes count Peter to be seized at an entertainment, thrown into prison, and deprived of his tongue and eyes, 61. Becomes the captive of the princes whose ruin she had all but effected; conducted to the frontier of the duchy, and desired to rejoin her kindred; excommunicated by the pope, 62.

Albert, emperor, wars of the, in Moravia, 83.

Albert, formerly Sigismund, established king of Bohemia and Hungary; death of, 113.

Albert, John, son of Casimir, at the head of the Poles, frees Lithuania from the Tatars, 120.

Albert, John, third son of Casimir IV., elected king of Hungary: taken prisoner; renounces all claim to the Hungarian crown: set at liberty, 121. Succeeds his father Casimir IV., 124. At the head of a considerable force o Poles, of Lithuanian and Teutonic auxiliaries, invades Wallachia; the sequel of this inglorious expedition; returns home; becomes more dear to the nation from his disasters, 125. Prevails on a Bulgarian khan to assist him in making head against the Muscovites and the other khan, 126. Makes peace with Ivan, and abandons his ally to his fate; his death and character, 127.

Albert of Brandenburg, grand master of the Teutonic knights, lays siege to some Pomeranian fortresses; opposed by Firley, palatine of Sandomir; sues for peace; his perfidy; again compelled to invoke the magnanimity of his uncle, 133. Embraces the doctrine of Luther; resigns his dignity; created prince of Eastern Prussia; marriage of, 134.

Albert, duke of Prussia, 144.

Alençon, the duke of, 156.

Alexander III., pope, at the entreaty of Casimir II. abolishes the law of Boleslas Wrymouth; declares the sovereignty of Poland hereditary in the descendants of the reigning grand dukes, 66.

Alexander, son of Casimir IV., elected grand duke of Lithuania, 124. Coronation of, by his brother, archbishop of Gnesna, 127. Death of, 129.

Alexander Koniecpolski, grand ensign of the crown, 183.

Alexander, emperor, interview of, with Napoleon, 253. His manœuvres with the Poles, 258. Popular in Poland, 262. Promises to unite Lithuania with Poland, 265.

Alexis, tsar, father of Peter the Great, 185; acquires vast territories at the expense of the republic, 191.

Ali, pacha, punished with death by the sultan, 181.

Amurath II., offers to raise the siege of Belgrade, on condition that Hungary would become tributary; it is indignantly rejected by Uladislas, 114. Exasperated at the perfidy of the Christians, returns with a mighty force to the theatre of war, 115.

Amurath IV., sultan, disavows the hostilities of his pachas, 181.

Andrew, brother of Zborowski, convicted of high treason, 166.

Anhalt, the margrave of, assassinates Prezemislas, king of Poland, 82.

Anne, princess, wife of Casimir the Great, death of, 97.

Anne, princess, niece of Casimir the Great, marriage of, with Uladislas IV., 111.

Anne, princess, sister of Sigismund, Augustus, 159.

Anne, grand duchess, her troops enter Courland, expel Maurice; soon after called to the imperial throne; invests Biron with the fief of Courland, 222.

Attila, 2.

. ustria, willing to restore Poland, 256.

B.

Bar, a little town of Podolia, a confederation formed at, for the avowed purpose of freeing the country from foreign influence, 238.

Barbarossa, Frederick, successor to Conrad, emperor of Germany, 62.

Batory, voivode of Transylvania, 158. 166.

Bautzen, the peace of, 22.

Bela, prince of Hungary, crowned king by Boleslas III., 35.

Benedict, pope, refuses to erect Poland into a kingdom, in consequence of its vices, 18.

Benedict IX., 31.

Bessarabia, 185.

Biron, banishment of, by Peter; recalled by Catherine II., 231.

Bogdan, a Wallachian chief, lays siege to Halitz, and next to Leopol; retreats at the approach of Sigismund; pursued by the castellan of Cracow, who vanquishes him in an action on the banks of the Dniester, 132

Bogdan Chmielnicki, a veteran Cossack, summoned before Alexander Koniecpolski, grand ensign of the crown; cast into prison, 183. Appeals to the diet at Warsaw for redress; his wife murdered; his habitation burned, in the flames of which his infant son perishes, 184. Seizes on the whole of the Ukraine; wreaks his vengeance on the Jesuits and Jews: joined by vast hordes of Tatars, 185. Advances into Red Russia; Leopol opens its gates to him; the whole palatinate acknowledges his power, 186. Indignant at the perfidy of the Poles, prepares for a new campaign; obtains a powerful ally, the Tatar khan Islaf, 188. Deserted by his ally the khan, is induced to accept the terms proposed by the king; scarcely reaches the Ukraine when he is obliged to prepare for another war; applies to the sultan for aid, but in vain; Greeks, Lutherans, Arians, and anabaptists flock to his standard, 189. His forces routed with great slaughter; retreats towards the Borysthenes, 189. Applies for aid to the tsar Alexis; offers to become his vassal, 190. Invests Kaminiec; his son killed, 190. Death of; stigmatised by the Polish writers as a traitor and rebel; a review of his life and actions, 194.

Bohemian garrisons, their victory over the combined Russians, Tatars, and Lithuanians, near Lublin, 83.

Bohemians, revolt of the, 26. Their chief assassinated in the tent of Henry V. of Germany; insist on returning to their homes, 55.

Boleslas, duke of Bohemia, 19.

Boleslas, son of Judith and Uladislas Herman I., birth of, 45. Reduces the Pomeranians in the fortress in Silesia, 48.

Boleslas, duke of Breslaw (son of Uladislas and Agnes), 66.

Boleslas, duke of Masovia, obtains the crown of Poland; deprived of it by Henry duke of Breslaw, 79.

Boleslas I., surnamed Chrobri, or Lion-hearted, son of Miecislas and Dombrowka, ascends the ducal throne; his immoderate ambition; his reception of Otho III., who elevates his duchy into a kingdom; is solemnly anointed by the archbishop of Gnesna; and the royal crown placed on his head by imperial hands, 20. His triumphs over the Bohemians; takes their duke, and his eldest son, prisoner; restores the ducal throne to Ulric, second son of the fallen chief; returns to Bohemia to espouse the interests of Ulric; driven from Bohemia, 21. Penetrates as far as Holstein; reduces the towns and fortresses in his way, filling all Germany with consternation; falls back on Silesia, to repair the disasters sustained by the arms of his son Miecislas, 22. Espouses the cause of Swiatopelk; marches against Yaroslaf, who had seized on the dominions of his fugitive brother; encounters him on the banks of the Bug; obtains the victory; pursues the fugitives to the walls of Kiow, which he invests and takes; gains another victory over the Russians on the banks of the Bug; defeats the Russians in a third battle on the Bug; returns to his capital, 23. The last six years of his reign he spent in endeavouring to repair the evils which his ambition had occasioned; convokes an assembly at Gnesna, in which his son is nominated his successor; his advice to his son; his death; the true founder of his country's greatness, 24.

Boleslas II., surnamed the Bold, succeeds his father Casimir, 34. Expedition of, in favour of Bela, prince of Hungary, who aspires to the throne of his brother Andrew, 35. Again invades Hungary, to espouse the interest of Geysa the son of Bela, 35. His expeditions into Russia, to espouse the cause of Isislaf; marches against Ucheslaf the son of Yaroslaf; subdues Volhynia; subdues Prezemysl; returns to Russia, 37. His generosity to the Kiovians, 38. His followers seven years absent from home (in Hungary and Russia); the consequence attending this absence, 39. His followers leave him, and return home; he also returns and inflicts vengeance on his soldiers and their guilty wives, 40. His cruelty; his character undergoes a complete change; Stanislas, bishop of Cracow, expostulates with him on his excesses; he is excommunicated,41. Assassinates Stanislas, bishop of Cracow; is deposed by pope Gregory VII.; his subjects absolved from their oath of allegiance, 42. An interdict placed on his kingdom; disdains submission to the church; endeavours to resist the execution of its mandates; is regarded with horror by the clergy and people; in daily fear of assassination by his own people; flies to Hungary, accompanied by his son Miecislas; his end is wrapt in great obscurity; various accounts as to what became of him; his character, 43.

Boleslas III., marriage of, to a Russian princess, 51. Hastens to humble the presumption of the Bohemians, who fly before him, 51 Raises the siege of Colberg, 52. His second expedition against the Pomeranians; makes a third expedition against them, and his rebellious brother Sbigniew; his expedition against the Bohemians, the cause of whose exiled duke he had espoused; marches into Pomerania, and furiously assails Belgard, 52. Intrepidity of, exhibited, 53. Requests the aid of his brother's troops, who refuses with expressions of insult and defiance; invades the territories of his brother; reduces his strongest places with rapidity, 53. Engages in a war against the Bohemians and with Henry V. emperor of Germany, who espouses their interest; is victorious; marches to reduce the town of Wollin, in Pomerania, that had revolted; invests the place; takes several prisoners, one of whom is his brother, 54. Exhorts the inhabitants of Glogaw to hold out; procures the assassination of the Bohemian chief, 55. Marriage of, with Adelaide, sister of Henry V. of Germany, 55. His ambition; recalls his exiled brother; yields to the incessant arguments of his courtiers, and agrees to the assassination of Sbigniew; his remorse; quells the insurrections in Pomerania; undertakes to convert it to the true faith, 56. Visits the shrines of several saints; imposes severe austerities on himself, 57. His defeat on the banks of the Niester by the Hungarians and Russians; divides his dominions among his sons; his death, 58.

Boleslas, prince, second son of Boleslas, 59.

Boleslas IV. confirms his brothers in their respective appanages, 62.

Summoned by Barbarossa to surrender his throne to Uladislas; aided by his brothers and his subjects, prepares to defend his own dignity and the national independence, 63. In one expedition reduces the Prussians; in a second expedition, his troops surprised and almost annihilated, 63.

Boleslas V., surnamed the Chaste, son of Lesko the White, a struggle for the guardianship of his person between his uncle Conrad, and his cousin Henry, duke of Breslaw, 72. Espouses Cunegund, daughter of Bela, king of Hungary, 74. Kept a close prisoner by his uncle and guardian, Conrad; his escape; claims the aid of Henry, duke of Breslaw, 74. Flees to Hungary; retreats to a monastery in the heart of Moravia; his pusillanimous desertion of his people draws on him the execration of those who survive, 75. Recal of; again flies into Hungary, 76. Subdues and nearly annihilates the Jadvingi; compels the few who survived to receive baptism; overthrows the Russians, 77.

Bonaparte deceives the Poles, 247. 252. 256.

Boris, marshal of the court of Moscow; his sister married to the tsar Feodor; ascends the imperial throne; makes an alliance with Sigismund, 172. Sudden death of, 173.

Brandenburg, marquis of, invests Dantzic, the chief city of Pomerania, 85.

Brandenburg, the elector of, besieges and takes the city of Elbing; assumes the title of king, 219. Recognised king of Prussia, 237.

Branicki, grand general of the crown, 230.

Breslaw, bishop of, son of Sigismund III., 186.

Bretislas, duke of Bohemia, invades Silesia, 48.

Bruhl, count, minister of Frederic Augustus, resembles his master in idle pomp and dissipation; his ascendancy over the king, 228.

Budchaz, the peace of, 203.

Bug, banks of the, a battle fought on the, between the Poles and Russians, in which the former were victorious; another battle fought between the Russians and Poles, in which the latter were vic-torious; a third battle fought on the, 23.

C.

Caplan Pacha, 203. Retreat of, beyond the Danube, 204.

Calvin dedicates a book to Sigismund II., 142.

Carlowitz, peace of, 219.

Casimir, prince, waited on by Polish deputies in the abbey of Clugni; is absolved from his monastic vows; his reception by his people, 31.

Casimir I. (the Restorer) conciliates Yaroslaf by marrying a Russian princess, 32. His success at home and abroad, 33, 34.

Casimir, prince, no portion left him by his father, 59. His honourable moderation 64. He at length accepts the ducal crown, 65.

Casimir II., procures the abolition of a great abuse, 65. Peculiar mildness of, 66. Triumphs over the Hungarians, Russians, and Prussians, 67. Clemency, death, and character of, 68.

Casimir, son of Uladislas III., made governor of Great Poland, 87. Marriage of, with a Lithuanian princess, 89.

Casimir III. (the Great), makes peace with the Teutonic knights; reforms abuses, makes laws, &c., 91, 92. The patron of industry, 95. His taste in building; procures the recognition of Lewis king of Hungary as his successor, 96. His great qualities sullied by excesses; he marries and repudiates the princess Adelaide, 97. Other excesses; age only tames him, 98. Death and character of, 98.

Casimir, prince, elected king of Bohemia; made grand duke of Lithuania, 113.

Casimir IV., refuses to swear to the pacta conventa; flees into Lithuania to escape his new subjects, 117. Transactions of, with the Russians, 118. Partiality of, towards the Lithuanians, 119. Death and character of, 123.

Castlereagh, lord, transaction of, at Vienna, 257.

Catherine (widow of Peter the Great), death of, 222.

Catherine II. orders her troops to take possession of Courland, 230. Seeks an alliance with Prussia, 231. Manœuvres of, 243.

Celestine III., pope, sends cardinal

Peter into Poland, 72. Approves the order of Teutonic knights, 73.
Cesarini, cardinal, 115.
Charles VII. of France, 115.
Charles IX., 152.
Charles Gustavus, accession of, 191. Proclaims himself the champion of protestantism, 192. Invades Poland; his success; invests John Casimir in Dantsig, 193. Recalled to the defence of his hereditary states; death of, 194.
Charles of Lorraine, 199.
Charles XII. of Sweden, 220. Invades Poland; procures the elevation of Stanislas, 221.
Charles, prince, elected duke of Courland; flies from thence, 229.
Chodkiewics, general, 170. Inflicts a terrible defeat on the Swedes, 172. Other exploits and death of, 179.
Christianity introduced into Poland, 16.
Christina, queen, abdication of, 191.
Clement V., pope, 85.
Colberg, 52.
Commendoni, the papal legate, 149.
Commerce flourishes, 55.
Condé, prince of, 199.
Conrad, emperor, 29. 62.
Conrad, brother of Lesko the White, 71. His exploits, 73. Aims at the life and throne of his nephew, 74. kindles the flame of civil war; death of, 75.
Constance, council of, condemns the doctrines of Huss, 109.
Constantine, grand duke, 266. His flight, 273.
Cossacks, their origin, religion, and habits, 162. Their fidelity, 164. Their first insurrection and failure, 183. Their harassing incursions, 184. Their second general insurrection, 184. Their successes, 191.
Courland, duchy of, 220. 222.
Cracow, city of, founded, 5. Fall of, 62. Throws off its allegiance to Miecislas III., 65. Battle fought near, 68. Council held at, 68. Besieged; its gallant defence, 78. Tribunal of, 164. Bishop of, his dissolute habits, and rebellion. Republic of, founded, 252. University of, suppressed, 251.
Cracus, the founder of Cracow, 5.
Crimea, 185.
Cujavia, bishop of, his condemnation of a married priest, 139.
Cunegund, princess of Hungary, 75.

Czarniecki, victory of, at Polouka, 155.
Czartorinskis, intrigues of the, 230.

D.

Dantzic, city of, its siege, 85. Refuses to acknowledge Stephen, 159. Among the first converts to the Christian faith, 143. War of, with Stephen, 160. Invested by Charles Gustavus, 193. Port of, closed, 262.
Daskiewits, Ostafi, disciplines the Cossacks, 163.
Decius, testimony of, 290.
Demetrius, a Russian prince, assassinated by Boris, 172.
Demetrius, the adventurer, appears in Poland, 172. Ascends the throne of the tsars, 173. Assassination of, 173.
Demetrius, another impostor, exploits of, 174.
De Thou, testimony of, 290.
Dissidents, the, 149. Persecution of, 223.
Dlugoss, testimony of, 289.
Dombrowska, princess of Hungary, marriage of, 16.
Dombrowki, general-in-chief of the Polish legions in Italy, 246. Advice of, to the Poles, 265.
Dulceans, heretics, 90. Quartered and burnt, 91.

E.

Elbing city, of, besieged and taken, 219.
Eleanor, Austrian princess, 201.
Elizabeth, regent of Poland, 100. Accepts the crown for her daughter Hedwig, 102.
Elizabeth, widow of Albert, her intrepidity, and transactions with Uladislas V., 111.
Ernest, archduke of Austria, 152.
Esther the Jewess, 97.
Eudoxia, a Russian princess, marriage of, 46.

F.

Fratricelli, a religious sect, 90.
Ferdinand, 222.
Firley, general of Sigismund, 133.
Firley, marshal, 148.
Flagellants, austerities of the, 99.
Franciscans labour to convert the Jadvingi, 77.
Frederic, cardinal, 127.
Frederic of Saxony, grand master, his death, 132.

Frederic Augustus, abjures the Lutheran religion; is crowned at Cracow, 218. Treaty of, with the tsar Peter, 220. Deposition of, by Charles XII.; restoration of, 221.

Frederic Augustus II., 227. Abandons himself to hunting and smoking; resides chiefly in Saxony, 228. Abandons Poland never to return, 231.

French revolution of 1830, sensation of, in Poland, 272.

G.

Galicia restored to Austria, 250.
Gedeon, archbishop of Cracow, 65.
Gedymin, duke of Lithuania, 89.
Gerilvius restored to Austria, 259.
Germany, passim.
George, son of Bogdan, recognised beyond the Borysthenes, 195.
Glinski, 129. 131.
Glogaw, city of, its heroic defence, 54.
Gnesna, once the capital of Poland, 4. Assembly at, recalls Casimir I., 31. Espouses the cause of the son of Boleslas Wrymouth, 61. Archbishop of, his dignity, 283.
Gnievomir, a powerful Pomeranian chief, 54.
Gottard, duke of Courland, 161.
Gratiani, voivode of Moldavia, 175.
Gregory VII., pope, 42.
Griffina, widow of Leako, will forged by her, 79.
Grodno, diet at, 222.
Guzaw, engagement at, 170.

H.

Halits, province of, rendered dependent on Poland by Casimir I., 71.
Hedwig, daughter of Lewis of Hungary, queen of Poland, 102. Her suitors, 103. Romantic attachment to duke William, but her wise marriage with Jagello, 104. Her unhappiness and death, 111.
Helen, princess, her credulity and disappointments, 59.
Henry of Bavaria, emperor, wars of, with Boleslas I., 24.
Henry V., emperor, attacks Glogaw, 54. Retreats, is defeated, and makes peace with Boleslas, 55. Approves the order of Teutonic knights, 73.
Henry, prince, 59. Expedition of, against the Russians, 63.
Henry, duke of Breslaw, 73. Invades Poland; his success and death, 74.

Henry (another of the name) invades Poland: the result, 79.
Henry of Waelfort, first grand master of the Teutonic knights, 73.
Henry de Valois, duke of Anjou, 150; proclaimed king of Poland, 152. Crowned, 154. Unpopularity of, 155. Becomes heir to the French throne, 156. Flight of, 157.
Herman of Salsa, fourth grand master of the Teutonic knights, 74.
Hirsowicz, Israel, founds a sect, 296.
Hungary erected into a kingdom, 18. Troops of, invade Poland, 6.
Huniades, general, his heroism against the Turks, 114, 115.
Huss, doctrines of, 109. Their progress in Pomerania, &c., 136.
Hussites, 113. And Calvinists, union of, 143.

I.

Ibrahim, pacha of Damascus, surnamed Shaitan, or the devil, 208. Contest of, with Sobieski, 209.
Isislaf, gratitude of, towards Boleslas, 38.
Islaf, khan, 188.
Ivan, tsar, invades Lithuania, 126.
Ivan, the Terrible, cruelties of, 145.

J.

Jablonowski, palatine, 206.
Jadvingi, inhabitants of Podlasia, their extraordinary strength and ferocity, 77.
Jagello, duke of Lithuania, united to Hedwig, 103. Baptism, coronation and marriage of, as Uladislas IV., 104.
Jeremy, prince, surprises the camp of Bogdan, 187. Is invested, 188.
Jews, 182. Condition and conduct of, in Poland, 292. 296.
John XIII., pope, 16.
John of Bohemia aspires to the Polish crown, 87; acquires the sovereignty of Silesia, 88.
John Casimir exchanges the dignity of cardinal for the title of king of Sweden, 186. Election and marriage of, 187. Intrigues of, with a Polish lady; the result, 189. Impolicy of, with respect to Sweden, 191. Flight of, into Silesia, 192. Transactions of, with Sweden, 194. Proposes a successor, 196. Grief of, for the death of his queen, 197. Abdication of, 198.
John Sobieski, castellan of Cracow, triumphs of, 201. As John III.,

proclaimed king of Poland, 206.
His splendid success, 207. Exploits of, at Zuranow, 208. Alliance of, eagerly sought, 210.
Exploits of, in the campaign of
Vienna, 212. Expedition of, into
Wallachia; pursues the aggrandisement of his family; uxorious-
ness of, 213. Last years and death
of, 215.
Joseph II., emperor, banishes Frank
the Jew, 296.
Judith, duchess of Poland; death
of, 45.
Julius, pope, complaints of, against
the Teutonic knights, 86. Hostility of, towards the Turks, 135.

K.

Kaminiec invested by Bogdan, 190.
By the Turks and Tatars; it falls,
195. Recovered by Frederic Augustus I., 219.
Kara Mustapha, vizier and generalissimo of the Turks, 212.
Kettler, grand master of the Livonian knights, 145. Resigns his
dignity, and is declared hereditary
duke of Courland and Semigallia,
146.
Kettler, duke of Courland (a de-
scendant of the former), marriage
of, to the archduchess Anne, 222.
Kiow, city of, invested and taken
by Boleslas I., 23. Again invested,
and subjected to the authority of
Isislaf, 57. Ceded finally to Russia by John III., 213.
Kiow, duke of, father-in-law to Boleslas III., 53.
Kosciuszko, generalissimo of the
Poles; his patriotic exploits, 244.
Is made prisoner by the Russians,
245. Name of, unwarrantably
used by Bonaparte, 252.
Kotzim, the fortress of, capitulates,
204. Is retaken by the Turks,
209.

L.

Ladislas, king of Bohemia and Hun-
gary, death of, 120.
Laws of Casimir the Great, com-
prised in two books, 92.
Lech I., 4.
Lech II., 5.
Lechia, a name sometimes given to
Poland, 4.
Lenszyca, legislative diet at, 66.
Leopol, school of, 179. Assembly
of, 221. College of, instituted by
Austria, 251.

Leopold, emperor, cowardice and
ingratitude of, 211, 212.
Lesko I., 6.
Lesko II., 9.
Lesko III., 9.
Lesko IV., 14.
Lesko, duke of Masovia, 66.
Lesko the White declared duke of
Poland, 68. Resigns the throne at
the instigation of his mother, 69.
Victory and second elevation of,
70. Wants vigour, 71. Assassination of, 72.
Lesko the Black, accession of; triumphs over the bishop of Cracow,
78. Conduct and death of, 79.
Lesczynski, Raphael, hostile to the
catholic hierarchy, 139. Speech
of, at the diet, 140.
Lesczynski, Stanislas, made king of
Poland by Charles XII.; fall of,
221. Re-election of; narrow escape of, from Dantzic, 227.
Lewis, king of Hungary, elected
successor to Casimir III., 96. Is
unpopular in Poland, 99. Confides
the regency to his mother Elizabeth; is recalled by the insubor-
dination of his Polish subjects;
moderate and prudent conduct of,
after his return, 100. Death and
character of, 101.
Lismanini, the Franciscan, 142.
Lithuania, 106. 187. 220, &c.
Lubomirski, grand marshal, an extraordinary man, 196.
Luther, the doctrines of, their progress in Poland, 136. Dedicates
a translation of the Bible to Sigismund II., 141.
Lutherans join Gustavus, 155. Severe law against the, 225.

M.

Mahomet IV., sultan, takes the
field, 202. Further exploits of,
207.
Malachowski, count, boldness of,
236.
Maria Louisa, queen, 185. 196. 197.
Margaret, lady, anecdote of, 39.
Marina, lady, elevation of, 173.
Transferred from a palace to a
dungeon, 174. Drowned, 175.
Martin V., pope, 120.
Masos, the unsuccessful rebel, 29.
Matthias, king of Hungary, 121.
Maurice of Saxe, 222.
Maximilian, emperor, 131. 159. 169
Melancthon, 142.
Michael, tsar, 175. 180.
Michael Koributh made king
against his will, 200. Transac-
tions and death of, 203, 204.

Miecislas I., accession and conversion of, 16. Causes every Polish pagan to be baptised, 17. Transactions with Germany, &c., 19. Death of, 20.
Miecislas II., indolence of, 25. engages in war with reluctance; forced to leave for a time his sensual pleasures, 26. Other acts of, 28.
Miecislas III., the Old, character of, 64. Distressed and expelled, 65. Invades Poland, 68. Stratagem and success of, 69. Deprived of his usurped powers,69.
Miecislas, prince, called from Hungary, 46.
Miecislas, prince, son of Boleslas III., 69.
Minucci, conversation of, 291.
Mofo, assembly held at, 36.
Mokranowski, 234.
Monluc, duplicity of, 151.
Moravia, a dependency of Bohemia, 48. Inhabitants of, revolt, 26.
Moscow, city of, burnt, 175.
Muscovites, *passim*.

N.

Napoleon. See *Bonaparte*.
Narva, battle of, 220.
Natolia overrun by Huniades, 114.
Neuberg, prince of, 199.
Nicholas, emperor, conspiracy at his accession, 271. Determination of, to put down the Poles in the present insurrection, 277. Disliked by the Jews, 298.
Notez, battle fought on the banks of, 47.
Novogorod, 161.

O.

Oginskis, the, 222.
Oliva, peace of, 194.
Oppelen, duke of, 101.
Orzechowski, canon, 141.
Osman, sultan, 177.
Otho I., emperor, 19.
Otho II., 19.
Otho III., 19, 20, 21.
Otho, bishop of Bamberg, 56.
Otho, duke of Posnania, 66.

P.

Pacta Conventa, 152. *et passim*.
Palatines, the twelve, unpopularity of, 6. Privileges of, 283.
Paz, the Lithuanian, 204.

Peter, count, fate of, 61.
Peter, cardinal, severity of, 72.
Peter I., tsar, treaty of, 219.
Peter III., 229.
Piast, celebrated as the founder of a great race of princes, 12.
Podlebraski, 120, 121.
Podolia, 129. *et passim*.
Poland, Pole, *passim*.
Polska, 2.
Polotsk, 37.
Pomerania, 26. 76. *et passim*.
Poniatowski, 229.
Popiel I., 9.
Popiel II., 9.
Posen, 82. 259. *et passim*.
Potocki, 193. 195. 230.
Philip of Burgundy, 115.
Prasmowski, primate, 201.
Predislas, 30.
Prezemislas, exploits of, rewarded by the sceptre, 8.
Prezemislas, duke of Great Poland, 76. Assumes the title of king, 81. Assassination of, 82.
Prussia, Prussians, 46, 47. 65. 71. 73. *et passim*.
Pultowa, 221.

R.

Radzechowski, chancellor, 191.
Radzivil, 205. 230.
Ragotski, duke of Transylvania, 185. 193.
Red Russia (now Galicia), 189. 202. *et passim*.
Reformation, progress of, 139.
Riga, archbishop of, 144.
Rixa, queen regent, abandons Poland with her son Casimir, 28.
Rixa, princess, 21. 82.
Rudiger, the lover of Wenda, 6.
Ruric, 172.
Russia, Russians, *passim*.

S.

Sabatayzavi, the Jew, 296.
Salomon, king of Hungary, 36.
Samatulski, 87.
Sapichas, the, 220.
Sbigniew, natural son of Uladislas I., neglected, 48. Drawn from his retirement by the Bohemian ruler, 49. Depravity and restlessness of, 53, 54. Recalled, and assassinated, 56.
Scanderbeg of Epirus, 115
Schonenberg, general, 133.
Sehin, general of the tsar, 180.
Sieciech, Polish general, 46. Victory of, 47. Influence of; tyranny

and unpopularity of, 48. Banishment of, 50.

Sigismund, emperor, 109.

Sigismund I., king, orders the trial of Glinski, 130. Victory of, over the Muscovites, 132. Legislative measures of, 135. Severity of, towards the Lutherans, 136. Death and character of, 137.

Sigismund II., disputes of, with his subjects concerning his clandestine marriage, 137. His queen crowned, 139. Weak policy of, with respect to religion, 142. Reception of, at Dantzic; ceases to interfere with the faith of his people, 143. Warlike actions of, 144. Death and character of, 146.

Sigismund III., coronation of, 168. Generosity of, towards his rival; prejudice, obstinacy, and bigotry of, 169. Transactions of, with Sweden, 172. With Russia, 174. Death and character of, 178.

Silesia, 20. 48. 51. 63. 88. &c.

Skirgeano, governor of Lithuania, 105. Rebellion of, 106.

Slavonian tribes, 2.

Smolensko, 180. et passim.

Sobieski, John, hetman, 195. 202, 203, 204. 206, &c. See John III.)

Sophia, empress, 213.

St. Adalbert, 17. Remains of, removed from Prussia to Gnesna, 20.

Stanislas, bishop of Cracow, murder of, 42.

Stanislas Leszcynski, 221. 227.

Stanislas Augustus, 237. Good intentions but weakness of, 243. &c. Deposition and death of, 245.

Starodubski, 108. 113.

Stephen Batory, marriage and coronation of, 159. Warlike deeds of, 161, 162. &c. Wise policy of, towards the Cossacks, 162. &c. Establishes a superior tribunal at Cracow, 164. Death and character of, 166.

Suwarrow, general, 245.

Swantopelk, governor of Pomerania, 71, 72. 76.

Swedes, 146. 193., et passim.

Swiatopelk, a Russian prince, 22, 23.

Swidrigal, governor of Lithuania. 107, 108.

T.

Talleyrand, prince, advocates the restoration of Poland, 257.

Targowitz, confederation of, 243.

Tarnowski, castellan of Cracow, 140.

Tatars, the, invade Poland, 75, . . Polish Russia, 119. Are defeated, 181.

Tenczyn, count, 155.

Teutonic knights, transactions of and with, 73, 74. 85, 86, 87, 88. 94. 118, 119. 134.

Thorn, affray at, between the Lutherans and Jesuits, 223. &c.

Trembowla, 207.

Trychtymirow, 164.

Turks, the, passim.

Tynieck, abbot of, 97.

U.

Uchanski, primate, 159.

Ucheslaf, 37.

Uladimir the Great, 19. 22.

Uladislas I., 44, 45, 46. 49. &c.

Uladislas II., 60—63.

Uladislas III. elected, 69. Resigns, 70.

Uladislas IV. the Short, 84. 90.

Uladislas V., Jagello, 105. 112.

Uladislas VI., 112. 116.

Uladislas (princes of that name), 50. 56. 59. 80. 83. 175.

Uladislas, king of Bohemia, son of Casimir IV., 121.

Ulric, a Bohemian prince, 21.

Uszebor, palatin of Sendomir, 61, 62.

V.

Vasil Shouiski, tsar, 174, 175.

Vasil, tsar, subjugates Livonia, 131.

Vasilevitch, Ivan, success of, 119.

Veto, the, 190. 237. &c.

Vienna invested by the Turks and Tatars, 211; celebrated treaty of, 259.

Volhynia, passim.

W.

Wallachia, invasion of, by John Albert; reprisals by the voivode of, 125. Invaded by John III., 213. et passim.

Wapowski, assassination of, 155.

Warsaw, diets held at, 230. et passim. Occupied by Suwaroff, 245. Grand duchy of, formed, 253. Destroyed, 257. University of, established, 262. Erection of state prisons at, 267. Emissaries of, in France, 272. Insurrection of, 273.

Wenceslas, king of Bohemia, claims the Polish crown, 79. Crowned at Cracow, 82. Subjects of, discontented; departure of, for Prague; called to the throne of Hungary, which he resigns to his son, 83. Death and character of, 84.

Wenda, his refusal of Rudiger, 5. Tragic end of, 6.

William, duke of Austria, attachment of, to Hedwig, 104.

William de Furstenberg, grand master of the Livonian knights, does homage to Sigismund, 144.

Wieliczka, mines of, 259. 262.

Wilna, diets held at, 145 et passim. Bishopric of, established, 106. University of, enlarged, 251. Students of, punished, 267.

Wisliza, code of, 92. 281.

Witold, intrigues of, in Lithuania, 106. War of, with the Tatars; death of, 107.

Wratislas, duke of Bohemia, 35.

Wyhowski, Cossack chief, 195.

Y.

Yaroslaf, duke of Kiow, 23. 25.

Z.

Zaluski, bishop, relation of, 214.

Zamosk, 186.

Zamoyski, starost of Beltz, 159. Obtains the chancellor's seal and marshal's staff, 161. Makes Maximilian prisoner, whom he treats nobly, 169. Exploits of, in Transylvania, Wallachia, &c., 170. Is enthusiastically cheered by the diet, 171. Defeats Charles, uncle of Sigismund, 172.

Zayonczek, lieutenant of Alexander, 262.

Zborowski, ambassador, 154.

Zborowski, Samuel, affray and banishment of, 155. Returns from exile without permission, and is arrested, 165. Implicates two brothers in a charge of high treason; is beheaded at Cracow 165.

Zemomysl succeeds Lesko IV., 14.

Ziemowit (Semovitus), disciplines the armies of Poland, 13.

Zolkiew, 217.

Zolkiewski, marshal, routs Shouiski, and joins Demetrius, 174. Return of, to Warsaw, 174. Cut off by the Turks, near the banks of the Dniester (Borysthenes); his head sent to Constantinople, 176.

THE END.

LONDON:

Printed by A. SPOTTISWOODE,
New-Street-Square.

THE

CABINET OF HISTORY.

CONDUCTED BY THE

REV. DIONYSIUS LARDNER, LL. D. F. R. S. L. & E.

M. R. I. A. F. R. A. S. F. L. S. F. Z. S. Hon. F. C. P. S. &c. &c.

ASSISTED BY

EMINENT LITERARY MEN.

THE

HISTORY OF POLAND.

A NEW EDITION.

LONDON:

PRINTED FOR

LONGMAN, ORME, BROWN, GREEN, & LONGMANS,

PATERNOSTER-ROW;

AND JOHN TAYLOR,

UPPER GOWER STREET.

1840.

LONDON :
Printed by A. SPOTTISWOODE,
New-Street-Square.

CPSIA information can be obtained
at www.ICGtesting.com
Printed in the USA
LVOW08*0450261217
560801LV00005B/24/P